The Early Years in Childhood Education

SECOND EDITION

The Early Years in Childhood Education

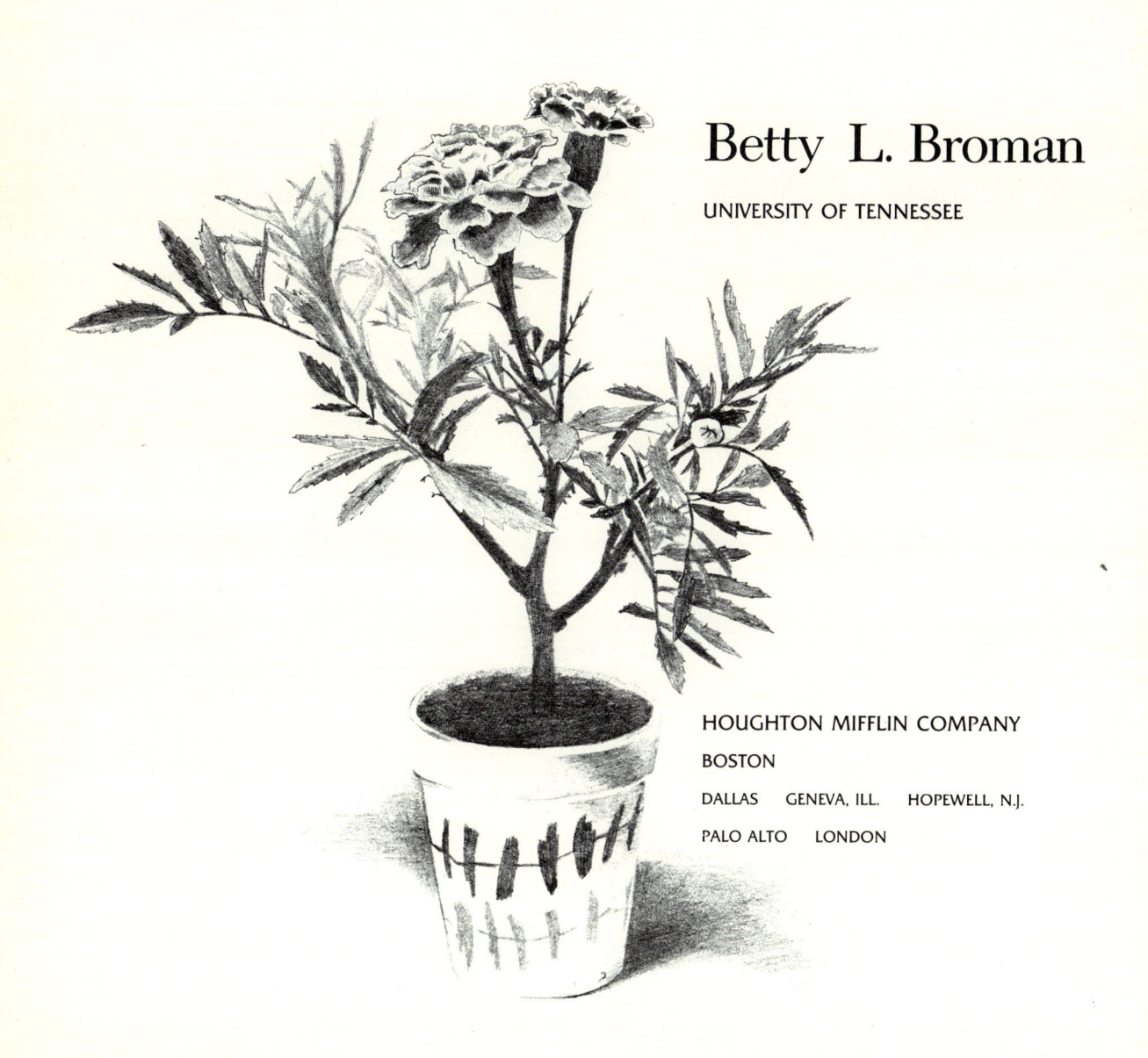

Betty L. Broman

UNIVERSITY OF TENNESSEE

HOUGHTON MIFFLIN COMPANY
BOSTON
DALLAS   GENEVA, ILL.   HOPEWELL, N.J.
PALO ALTO   LONDON

Creative illustrations by Nancy Hannans of *Bookmakers, Inc*.

Cover photograph by James Scherer.

Cup design by Elizabeth Granoff.

Copyright © 1982 by Houghton Mifflin Company. All rights reserved. No part of this work may be reproduced or transmitted in any form or by any means, electronic or mechanical, including photocopying and recording, or by any information storage or retrieval system, except as may be expressly permitted by the 1976 Copyright Act or in writing by the publisher. Requests for permission should be addressed in writing to Houghton Mifflin Company, One Beacon Street, Boston, Massachusetts 02108.

Printed in the U.S.A.

Library of Congress Catalog Card Number: 81-82557

ISBN: 0-395-31803-3

This book is dedicated to the memory of my mother and father for the delightful childhood they provided me, and to the members of my family and Isobel Griscom for their devotion, interest, and many kindnesses

Contents

Preface   xv

PART ONE   FOUNDATIONS

Chapter 1   An Overview of Early Childhood Education   4

Early Education Today   5
  Purposes   5
    Traditional goals, Early intervention, Day care
  Programs   7
    Settings, Experimental models, Current trends
Teachers   10
  Training   11
  Attitude   11
  Appearance   11
  Role   12
Career Opportunities   13
  Centers for Three and Four Year Olds   14
  Kindergarten Programs   17
  Elementary Schools   17
  Other Positions in Early Education   18
    Administrators, Aides
  Professional Organizations   21

Chapter 2   A Survey of Educational History and Philosophy   23

A Brief History of Education   24
  Development of Early Childhood Education   24
  Early American Education   30
Philosophies of Education   32
  Friedrich Froebel   32
  John Dewey   35
  Maria Montessori   36
    The Montessori method, Key terms, Criteria for materials, Influence
  Child Study Movement   41
  Ruggles Street Nursery School   42
  Other Influences   44
  The Present   45

Chapter 3 Learning and Development 48

The Learning Process 49
  Theories of Learning 49
    Acquisition of knowledge and skills (mechanism), Interactionism, Rationalism, Behaviorism, Humanistic psychology, Eclecticism, Newer approaches
  Piaget's Theory of Intellectual Development 53
    Basic concepts, Learning in the preoperational stage
  Factors Influencing Learning 57
    The teacher, Individual differences, Motivation, Retention, Transfer, Understanding, Reinforcement
  Research on Learning 59
Growth and Development 65
  Normative Data 65
    The three year old, The four year old, The five year old, The six year old
  Basic Psychological Needs 69
    The sense of trust, The sense of autonomy, The sense of initiative, The sense of duty and accomplishment, The sense of identity
The Exceptional Child 70
  Characteristics and Needs 71
    Learning disabilities, Intellectual giftedness, Mental retardation, Auditory and hearing disabilities, Speech and language disorders, Visual impairments, Orthopedic problems, Chronic physical illness, Behavior disorders
  Suggested Teaching Approaches 75
    Learning disabilities, Intellectual giftedness, Mental retardation, Auditory and hearing disabilities, Speech and language disorders, Visual impairments, Orthopedic problems, Chronic physical illness, Behavior disorders
  Support Systems 77

PART TWO SETTINGS

Chapter 4 Cultures, Values, and Goals: The Social Setting for the Curriculum 86

Cultures 87
  The Cultural Process 87
    The role of the family, The role of the school
  Cultural Differences 89
    Ethnic, Class, Language
Values 94
Goals and Observation 96
  Goals of Teachers and Children 96
  Observation 98
    Techniques, Observation and the assessment of goals, Observation forms

Chapter 5 Organization: The Physical Setting for the Curriculum 105

Factors Influencing Organization   106
Schedules and Plans   107
   Daily Schedules   107
   Lesson Plans   113
Individualization and Grouping   114
   Individualizing Activities   114
   Grouping   116
   A Child's Participation   116
Room Organization   117
   General Guidelines   117
   Activity Centers   118
     Reading center, Creative writing center, Listening center, Viewing center, Creative dramatics center, Mathematics center, Painting center, Clay center, Craft center, Sand table center, Garden center, Games and puzzles center, Biological science center, Physical science center, Construction center, Block center, Toy center, Cooking center, Sewing center, Weaving center, Current events center, Unit centers
Equipment and Materials   125
   Uses   125
   Permanent Equipment   125
     Tables and chairs, Storage and display, Resting equipment, Audio-visual equipment, Teacher's materials

PART THREE CURRICULUM

Chapter 6 The Language Arts 136

Theoretical Context   137
Oral Language   138
   Development of Speech   138
   Listening   139
   Factors Affecting Oral Language   140
     Environmental differences, Mental differences, Physical differences, Emotional and social differences
   Grammar   142
   Activities for Developing Oral Language   143
     Fingerplays, Dramatization, Puppetry, Flannelboards, Records and tapes, Pictures, Television
Reading   152
   Reading Readiness   153
   The Reading Process   153
   Reading Readiness Skills   155
     Vision development, Gross difference discrimination, Auditory discrimination, Finer differences in discrimination, Picture recognition and interpretation, Recognition of similarities among

objects, persons, and events, Cause-and-effect organization, Ideas in sequence, Meanings and ideas related to written symbols
    Books for Teaching Visual Discrimination   158
    Teaching the Alphabet   159
    Parents and Reading   160
    Dialect and Reading   161
    Picture Books for Beginning Readers   162
Literature   162
    The Teacher's Role   163
      Selecting books and stories, Becoming a good reader or teller of stories, Organizing your room and program, Selecting materials and equipment
    The Child's Part   167
    Storybooks for Young Children   168
Written Language   175
    The Teacher's Role   176
    The Child's Part   178
Spelling   179
Language Experience Charts   180

Chapter 7   Social Studies   202

Theoretical Context   203
Socialization   204
    The Teacher's Role   205
    Affective Education   205
    Affective Education Books for Children   209
    Affective Education Activities   212
      Listening to records and/or singing songs, Using a flannelboard, Using a mirror, Using photos, Using games appropriate for expressing feelings
Integration of Content Areas   215
    Dramatic Play   215
      Preparation, Goals, The child's participation
    Units of Work   219
    Field or Study Trips   223
    Resources: People, Objects, Animals   224
Materials, Equipment, and Books   225
    Replica Toys   225
    Commercial Materials and Equipment   227
    Materials and Equipment for Spontaneous Play   229
      A hat rack of careers, A treasure chest of role-playing equipment, The zoo at school, A plumber's box, Brick laying, Woodworking
    Books   234

Chapter 8   Science   251

Theoretical Context   252
The Teacher's Role   253
    Planning   253

Collecting and Ordering Supplies   254
Care of Living Things in the Classroom   256
Plants for the Classroom   259
The Child's Participation   259
Whole Group   260
Individualized Science   263
Incidental Science   263
Play Opportunities   264
Sand and Water Play   264
Play equipment, Water play, Environmental play
Cooking and Other Food Activities   266
The teacher's role, The child's participation, Noncooking suggestions, Cooking suggestions, Integration of cooking with other subject areas, Senses play
Science Books for Children   271

Chapter 9   Mathematics   285

Theoretical Context   286
Basic Concepts   287
Vocabulary of Comparison   287
Metric and English Standard Measure   289
Introduction of metric measure, Measurement activities
Numeration   292
Number Concepts   292
Sets   292
Conservation of Quantity   293
Plane Geometry   293
Mental Readiness for Mathematics   293
Books, Materials, and Equipment   296
Math Books for Children   296
Math Equipment and Materials   297

Chapter 10   Art   312

Theoretical Context   313
The Developmental Approach: How They Grow   313
The Cognitive Approach: What They Think   314
The Psychoanalytic Approach: What They Feel   314
The Cognitive-Developmental Approach: How They Think and Grow   316
Conclusions   316
Media   317
Forms   317
Classroom-Produced Media   318
Crafts for the Preschool Classroom   321
Dyes, Flower preservation
Art Materials   322
Instruction and Activities   324
Instruction   324

Creative Activities   327
    Arts and crafts for three year olds, Arts and crafts for four year olds, Arts and crafts for five year olds
Children's Books About Art   330

Chapter 11   Music   341

Theoretical Context   342
Motor-Rhythmic Activities   343
Listening   345
Singing   349
Materials and Equipment   351
   Musical Literature   351
   Records   351
   Instruments   353

Chapter 12   Play and Movement   363

Theoretical Context: Play   364
   Play at Different Ages   366
   Cultural Influences on Play   366
Physical Activities   368
Equipment Selection   370
   Criteria   370
   Basic Indoor Equipment   372
   Basic Outdoor Equipment   374
   Basic Equipment for Handicapped Children   375
Games for Young Children   375
Theoretical Context: Movement Education   377
   Developmental   378
   Cultural Representation   378
   Cognitive-Affective   379
   Children and Their Bodies   380
Movement Activities   381
   Curriculum Integration Through Pantomime   381
   Activities and Equipment for Movement in Space   382

PART FOUR   THE CHILD'S WELL-BEING

Chapter 13   Health, Nutrition, and Disease   394

Health   395
   Cleanliness   395
   Temperature and Air   397
   Common Happenings   397
   The Abused Child   399

Nutrition   399
   Nutrients   399
      The parent's role, The child's role, The teacher's role, Servings, Daily requirements, Snacks
   Recent Research on Balanced Diets   402
   Nutrition and the Disadvantaged Child   403
Disease   403
   Allergies   403
   Communicable Diseases   404

Chapter 14   Behavior and the Family   408

Behavior   409
   What to Do and When   410
   Research on Behavior   417
   Nonverbal Behavior   419
   Manners   419
   Praise   421
   Conclusions   421
Family Education   422
   Home Environment Research   422
   Problems in Family Education   423
   Home Visits   424
   School Visits   425
   Parent-Teacher Conferences   426
   Suggestions for Parents   428
   Other Ways of Communication with Parents   430

Acknowledgments   435

Index   437

Preface

Why does anyone ever write a book? This must be the most persistent thought of any author! Writing is hard work and time consuming, but for those of us who have had great teachers, colleagues, and students, the need to put on paper what we have learned seems to be overwhelming.

Purpose
The Early Years in Childhood Education is based on the assumption that effective teaching of young children is possible when the potential teacher is taught the foundations of early education, the content of the curriculum areas of early education, and the significant aspects of child growth and development.

Coverage and Organization
The second edition of *The Early Years in Childhood Education* is a thorough revision of a comprehensive text for the first course in early childhood education. Part One of the text provides an overview of the field of early childhood education, traces the historical basis for today's programs, and discusses the learning and developmental processes. Part Two describes the social and organizational factors that influence the teaching and learning of young children. Part Three offers a practical guide to the basic curriculum of early childhood education. Part Four provides useful suggestions about additional matters of concern to teachers of young children: health and nutrition, classroom behavior, and the role of a child's family in the educational process. Throughout the book, research studies are integrated into the text to present more than one point of view.

Writing Style and Level
The reading level of the text is appropriate for undergraduate college classes. The style is simple and direct, and every effort has been made to involve the reader personally in the topic under discussion. Interspersed throughout each chapter are projects that ask students to apply what they have learned to real-life situations and to their own experiences and beliefs.

Features

Practicality *The Early Years in Childhood Education* is filled with useful and concrete information, suggestions, and classroom activities. The topics covered in the text deal with a variety of practical concerns. For example, teachers are instructed on how to equip and organize a classroom, how to become a good reader or teller of stories, how to care for common classroom pets, how to relieve the pain of bee stings, and how to conduct a parent-teacher conference. To give readers a sense of what teaching the young is really like, the book presents detailed schedules of a typical day in a variety of early learning settings, as well as floor plans showing different types of classroom arrangements. In addition, the seven curriculum chapters in Part Three contain three unique and practical features: skills charts, which show the sequential development of skills within each subject area; lists of learning goals for children (by subject area); and mini unit charts (by age level and season), which help readers see the interrelationships among different subject areas and the spiral process through which children's skills and knowledge develop.

Emphasis on curriculum and methods An entire part of the book is devoted to these important topics and a separate chapter to each subject area: language arts, social studies, science, mathematics, art, music, and play-and-movement education. Within each chapter are numerous practical suggestions about teaching methods and techniques, as well as comprehensive and up-to-date lists of materials, equipment, and books for classroom use.

Teaching Aid

The Early Years in Childhood Education is accompanied by an *Instructor's Manual with Test Items*. This instructional aid contains for each chapter in the text: a chapter outline; a series of whole-class, small-group, team, and individual student projects; suggested teaching tools for students to construct; and a variety of evaluation materials, including short-answer, true-false, and multiple-choice items.

Acknowledgments

From my daily contact with teachers and students, questions of "How do you. . . ?" "How do you know. . . ?" "Where can I find. . . ?" "What if. . . ?" and "Help!" have inspired, pushed, and cajoled me into writing a book that describes the basic knowledge, skills, and materials important to teachers of young children.

Some answers I knew. Others required hours of research. The process of writing this book over the years has made me realize my indebtedness to the many individuals who have influenced my thinking and my learning:

John Anderson, for his many hours of discussion, explanation, and description of his research projects at the University of Minnesota; Helen Heffernan, formerly of the state of California Department of Education, for her sharing of ideas and materials and her challenging statements for me to think about and solve for myself; Mamie Heinz, an Atlanta nursery school director, for her practical, commonsense approach to teaching teachers and children; Gertrude Noor, for her many hours of discussion about human needs and cultural differences; Margaret Rasmussen, for her enjoyable creative approaches to teaching children and teachers; Alberta Lowe Wantling, for her influence as a teacher and interpreter of the writings of significant educators; and Isobel Griscom — a constant inspiration — for her demonstration of excellent teaching, concern, and caring for students and for her instruction and insistence on simplicity in the use of the English language.

I am grateful to my colleagues and friends at the University of Tennessee at Knoxville for their suggestions, discussions, books, and materials, and for reading the manuscript and writing some materials especially designed to fill a need in this book.

Many of the ideas and information included in this book were suggested and evaluated by a number of teachers, supervisors, consultants, directors, and principals of early childhood programs. I am expecially indebted to Hilda Avant, Marguerite Hullander, and Sara Shipley for suggestions for this edition. I wish particularly to thank the following reviewers, whose constructive advice helped so much in the development of this manuscript: Betty Beeson, Ball State University; Joseph Caruso, Wheelock College; George Etheridge, Memphis State University; and Ronald Padula, Delaware County Community College.

Books aren't written without excellent editors. A very special "thank you" to my editors at Houghton Mifflin for listening to my "mutterings."

Betty L. Broman

The Early Years in Childhood Education

PART ONE
Foundations

An introduction to early childhood education, a survey of the historical and philosophical basis for today's programs, and an examination of the processes of learning and development in children.

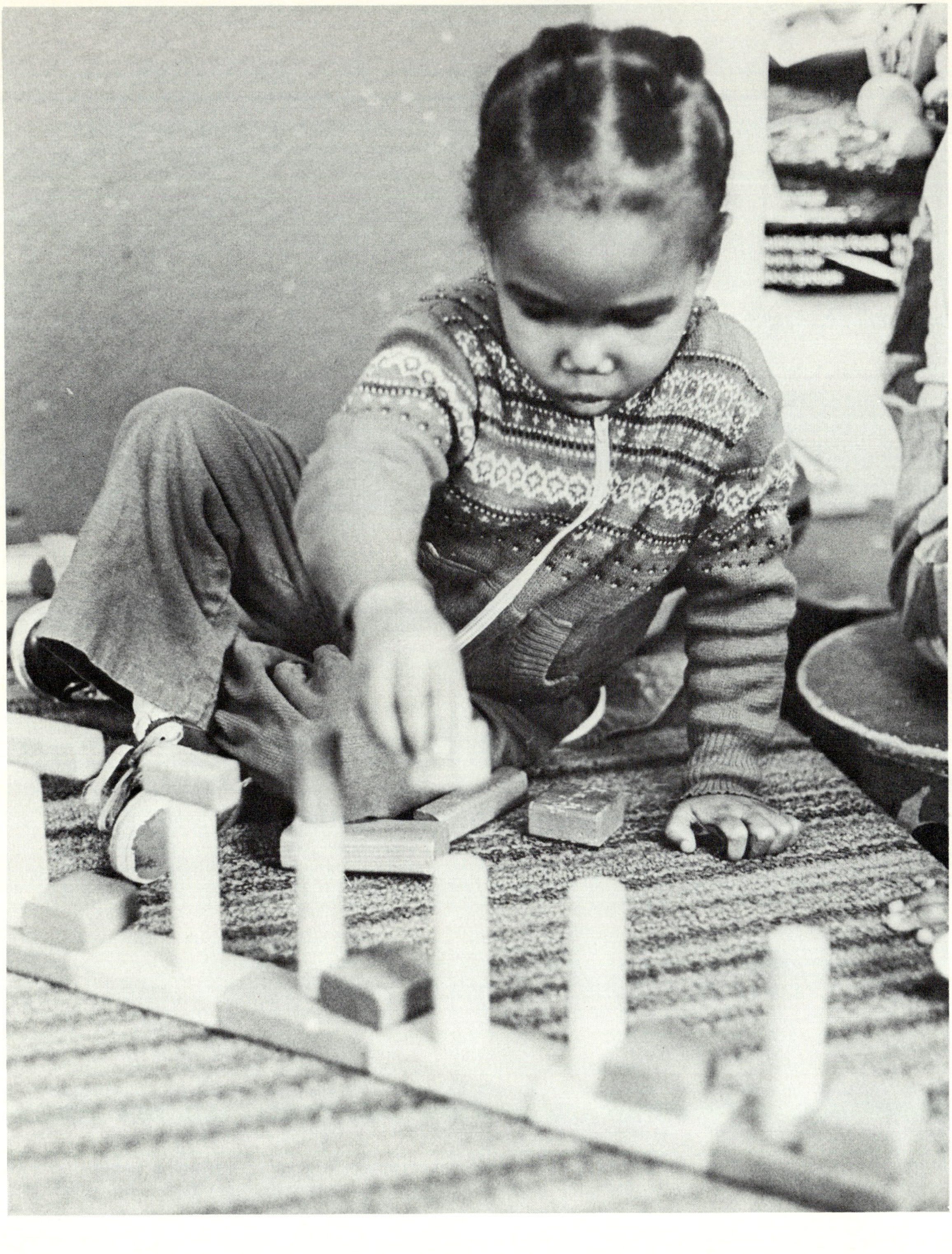

CHAPTER 1
An Overview of Early Childhood Education

Exploration Tasks

After studying this chapter, you should be able to complete these tasks:
- List the purposes of early childhood education.
- Describe research results on the effectiveness of programs for the young.
- Describe the various settings for early childhood education.
- List the roles of a teacher of young children.
- Identify the major career opportunities in the field of early childhood education.
- Describe a typical day for an early childhood supervisor or day-care director.

Children need to feel loved and wanted. Try to respond in ways which show that your pupils are cared about and prized.

Children need to feel that they belong. Try to respond in ways which are accepting and inviting.

Children need to feel successful. Try to provide many opportunities that insure genuinely successful achievements.

Children need to feel secure. Try to respond in ways which do not threaten or undermine their sense of well-being.

Children need to be free from intense feelings of guilt. Try to respond in ways which attend to the feelings and which do not shame or humiliate them.

Children need to be free from intense feelings of fear. Try to respond in calming and reassuring ways which do not ridicule children's fears.

Children need to be respected. Try to respond in ways which show genuine interest in who they are and in what they think.

Louis E. Raths

OVERVIEW

The giggle, the belly laugh, the look of wonder, and "I love you" all occur during the golden years of childhood. Who shall teach these children?

Did you ever laugh so hard that you cried? Have you ever beamed with such pride that your chest swelled? Have you ever been so satisfied and pleased with yourself that you couldn't stop smiling? Have you ever worked so hard that you could hardly speak? You have? You must be meant to be a teacher of young children!

Working with young children is a delight. The unexpected is the rule of the day. The simple joys of happy, active, talking children are spontaneous reactions to the most common events: a spider's web covered with dew, ice cream for lunch, the discovery of a ladybug on freshly picked wildflowers, the surprise of a new storybook, and the shining sun glimpsed through the dark winter clouds.

Background information concerning programs, teachers, and careers is important for a basic understanding of what educating young children is all about. These factors also determine the quality as well as the quantity of opportunities for children. Some individuals thrive on the verbal and physical interaction that takes place in any group of young children, while other individuals find the constant action too demanding — both physically and mentally.

Early education needs are expanding yearly and the possibilities of establishing a life-long pleasurable experience are many.

EARLY EDUCATION TODAY

Purposes

Today the majority of early education programs serve a wide variety of purposes. Parents wish for a variety of experiences for their children and, because of the great influx of parent-involvement activities into the school setting, the purposes of early education programs by necessity may vary greatly even within the same city.

Traditional Goals In traditional early childhood programs, opportunities for socialization and creative activities were emphasized. In some instances, beginning reading and math instruction was an important part of the day's program. These aspects of early childhood programs still dominate today's schools. Socialization, creativity, and an introduction to science, math, social studies, art, music, physical development, and reading are recognized as valid goals for all young children in early education programs.

Early Intervention A comparatively new concept in early childhood education was developed in the early 1960s. The concept of early intervention began with Project Head Start, a national comprehensive program for disadvantaged children that was created as a part of the War on Poverty. Head Start changed the direction of some of the previous early childhood programs in the United States. The studies of Bloom, Bruner, and Hunt, among others, seem to confirm the importance of environmental factors in facilitating the development of children.[1] Although many experimental programs still exist, research findings to date seem to reinforce the earlier studies regarding the effectiveness of early intervention prior to kindergarten.

A 1973 study reported that approximately 2.5 million children under the age of six come from poverty-level families where the mother does not work.[2] In addition to being economically disadvantaged, many of these children do not receive the environmental stimulation necessary for cognitive development.

A recent 1980 study reported more positive gains than other studies have reported. A Tennessee Department of Education study indicated that eighth-grade students who attended kindergarten scored nearly 6 percent higher on basic skills tests than did their counterparts who did not have kindergarten training.[3] The study also showed that students who attended kindergarten were less likely to repeat grades. Many other state departments of education are also reporting similar results.

Day Care In addition to traditional programs for young children in general and intervention programs for others, there is also a great need for programs and services for certain groups of children. Many mothers are now entering the work force, for economic reasons and to pursue career interests. The increase in the divorce rate has created many one-parent families that need adequate, full-day child-care services.

A 1979 study reported that 50.3 percent of all children ages three to five were in preschool programs. Of these children, 2,286,000 had mothers who were not working and 2,173,000 had mothers who were working. In addition, the study stated that 38 percent of day-care enrollment consisted of children with a single parent and 43 percent of all day-care families had incomes under $15,000 a year.[4]

---

[1] Benjamin Bloom, *Stability and Change in Human Characteristics* (New York: Wiley, 1964); Jerome Bruner, *The Process of Education* (Cambridge, Mass.: Harvard University Press, 1960); J. McV. Hunt, *Intelligence and Experience* (New York: Ronald Press, 1961).

[2] Linda A. Barker, *Preprimary Enrollment, October 1972* (Washington, D.C.: Department of Health, Education, and Welfare, 1973).

[3] *1980 Achievement Test Results* (Nashville, Tenn.: Tennessee Department of Education Division of Research and Planning, 1980). The High Scope Research Foundation of Ypsilanti, Michigan, has collected data similar to that of this study.

[4] U.S. Department of Health and Human Services, Pub. No. (OHDS) 80-30274 (August 1980), pp. 19, 69, and 72.

An overview of early childhood education / 7

Julie O'Neil/Stock, Boston

The 1980 Labor Force Report No. 130 stated that there are 987,000 married, working women with children under six years of age. If you add to this the 261,000 single parents of children under six, as reported by the 1979 U.S. Report of the Commerce Bureau of the Census, you have a grand total of 1,239,000 parents who need child care for their young children.

Others in need of quality care include children of mothers who are attending school or trying to upgrade their vocational skills, young children with handicaps who need specialized services, and children of mothers who are ill or handicapped.

A common goal of early education programs is to create an environment that encourages the interests and involvement of young children.

Programs

Settings Early childhood programs function in a variety of settings.[5] Teachers need to be aware of the many variations that exist in these settings.

[5] For more information, see: Richard H. deLone, *Small Futures: Children, Inequality and the Limits of Liberal Reform* (New York: Harcourt Brace Jovanovich, 1979); Joanne Hendrick, *The Whole Child New Trends in Early Education*, 2nd ed. (St. Louis, Mo.: Mosby, 1980); Lillian G. Katz, ed., *Current Topics in Early Childhood Education*, Volume II (Norwood, N.J.: Ablex Publishing Corp., 1979).

Children may attend from two and one-half to eleven hours daily. The class may be housed in a separate building, an elementary school, a neighborhood agency, or an industrial complex. The children served may be from low-income families, middle- to high-income families, or a mixture of each. Licensing requirements, particularly for day-care programs, are influenced by federal, state, and local regulations. Because of this, great variations exist in the number of children served, in the adult-child ratio, and in the types of ancillary services provided as part of the program.

Many programs are private, profit-making businesses, usually owned by an individual or a chain and serving middle-class clientele. Typically they offer a half-day program with emphasis on social and emotional development as well as academic readiness. Many churches and temples also sponsor private programs, but usually they are nonprofit. The children tend to be middle class, although often some children from low socioeconomic groups are also enrolled. Most of these programs tend to offer half-day sessions with heavy stress on social and emotional development.

Some private, nonprofit organizations also sponsor early education programs. These include settlement houses, neighborhood agencies, and family-service agencies that cater mainly to children from low socioeconomic backgrounds. These organizations generally provide full-day programs, but many of the programs are flexible to meet parental needs as well as the children's needs.

Full-day programs are usually called *day-care centers*. These programs differ from half-day programs in that they provide two to three meals a day, a full rest time in contrast to a nap, and many more free-play activities. These day-care centers are of three basic types. One type offers custodial care only. Major concerns are the safety of the child, age-appropriate food, and the physical care necessary while a child's parents are at work. A second type, the cooperative day-care center, offers health, educational, and social services in addition to custodial care. These ancillary services are arranged through cooperation with other agencies. The third type, omnibus day-care centers, offers the services described above along with a variety of health, educational, and social services provided through the efforts of their own staffs. Many of these programs emphasize the child's social, emotional, and intellectual development. Day-care centers may be private, profit-making organizations; private, nonprofit organizations; public, nonprofit centers supported through state and/or federal funding; and public, profit-making centers.

Head Start provides both half-day and full-day programs. These federally funded programs are administered by a variety of agencies including public schools, community agencies, or Model Cities programs. The majority of the children served are from low socioeconomic backgrounds.

Some early education programs are operated under the auspices of universities, colleges, and public schools. These centers are usually demonstration schools that serve primarily as observation and participation facilities for high school and college students.

Experimental Models To understand today's early childhood programs, an overview of early experimental models is necessary. The British Infant School concept and the Montessori method of teaching young children are not new, but they were not widely accepted in the United States until after the introduction of Head Start.

The Bloom work cited earlier showed that a child's intelligence grows as much during the first four years of his or her life as it does during the next thirteen years.[6] This knowledge has accelerated the demand for programs that will develop potential in a positive, creative manner. The programs or *models* (a term used for experimental approaches) vary from a highly structured organization (academically oriented) to a very flexible, nondirected organization ("free school" plan that developed out of the British Infant Schools). Some of the programs are designed for disadvantaged children; others claim success with all children; a few are designed for academically gifted children; many are developmentally oriented, with emphasis on individualization for ability, interests, and rates of development.

The British Infant School concept was imported from Europe where it is used with reported success. Though the British Infant Schools do not have prepared class lessons, the teacher observes, assists, stimulates an experience when necessary, and keeps detailed records of each child's progress. Each room or area has a wide array of materials and several activities going on simultaneously. According to the Institute for the Development of Educational Activities (I/D/E/A), the children teach each other or are taught by older children.

A program also based on materials, the Montessori plan is built around a prepared environment and materials specifically designed for stages of growth. The materials are cognitive; that is, they are geared to helping a child think through a concept to identify it. Teachers prepare the environment and each child works in a nongraded group using materials that are self-educative. The teachers introduce new materials and experiences when they believe the child is ready for them.

In the United States during the 1960s and 1970s, ten basically different programs or models were introduced and studied. These include the academically oriented preschool model, the Bank Street College model, the behavior and analysis model, the cognitive model, the enabler model, the Florida parent-educator model, the Institute for Developmental Studies model, the responsible model, the Responsive Environment Corporation model, and the Tucson early education model. These and twenty-four other programs or models that are modified versions of the preceding ten programs

---

[6] Bloom, *Stability and Change*.

or models are described in *Preschool Breakthrough: What Works in Early Childhood Education*, a 1970 publication of the National School Public Relations Association.

Current Trends Early childhood programs in the early 1980s continue to explore new approaches. Our knowledge of how children learn and the factors that influence learning has increased greatly. While some early programs concentrated on "catch-up" techniques, today's programs emphasize socialization and cultural diversity as well as learning activities. The current concern for teaching the basics is making the academically oriented programs quite popular as well. The tradition of middle-class uniformity is being challenged by many young parents who themselves grew up in a middle-class environment. Individual abilities, needs, and wants are more acceptable to parents and teachers. Teachers have become more knowledgeable and more expert in management and assessment.

Today's schools actively involve parents in the education of their children, thus providing each child with more opportunities for adequate physical, social, emotional, and intellectual development. University centers, day-care centers, public school programs, and private school programs are working together to provide quality care and programs for young children. As the segmentation of factors influencing the development of children lessens, more children are being equally served and new types of services — including infant day care, extended day care, school-age day care, respite care, and occasional care — are becoming more common. Yet many problems still exist, and variances in quality and availability of services are great. Three sources that will provide in-depth descriptions of current programs are: S. Kilmer, ed., *Advances in Early Education and Day Care: A Research Annual* (Greenwich, Conn.: Jai Press, 1980); D. G. Ronge, J. R. Layton, and D. L. Roubinek, eds., *Aspects of Early Childhood Education: Theory to Research to Practice* (New York: Academic Press, 1980); and M. E. Ramsey and K. M. Boylers, *Kindergarten: Programs and Practices* (St. Louis: C. V. Mosby, 1980).

TEACHERS

The most important factor in helping young children adjust to a school setting is the teacher.[7] Young children need well-adjusted, intelligent, en-

---

[7] See the following sources: Ann Cook and Herb Mack, *The Teacher's Role* (New York: Citation, 1971); David L. Elliott, "Needed: A New Early Childhood Educator," *Educational Leadership*, 28.8 (May 1971): 837; Sylvia Famham-Diggory, *Cognitive Processes in Education* (New York: Wiley, 1973); Dorothy E. M. Gardener and Joan E. Cass, *The Role of the Teacher*

ergetic, and creative teachers. To such individuals, each day will be challenging and satisfying and yet at times very frustrating. Those who like talkative, inquisitive children will find teaching the young exciting, demanding, and rewarding.

Training

Teaching the young should not be regarded as simply a part-time job; nor is it an unguided "play" situation. Early childhood teaching is a highly professional occupation and should be staffed by well-trained and committed persons. Professional preparation does not end with a college or university degree; there is a constant need for continuous re-education. Each year research, materials, and experiences will be added to the teacher's knowledge about children and about how to develop their optimum growth. The professional teacher will be involved in formal study through colleges and universities and in informal study through in-service programs, conferences, and professional reading.

Living with children as they learn will increase the teacher's insight. These experiences, plus the experiences with other adults, will aid the teacher in looking forward to a continually challenging professional life. No person should contemplate teaching without realizing that professional growth will never end.

Attitude

If talking, wriggling, "why" questions, tall tales, occasional accidents, forgetfulness, slowness, and reluctance bother you, or if subject matter, such as math, science, or history is your love, teaching the young is not for you. To be with young children daily, week after week, you must be interested in things that crawl and a few that don't; find satisfaction in teaching children to hang up their coats, tie their shoes, and eat with all utensils; and have patience while they paint themselves as well as their paper. Through all this the teacher of the young must be gentle but firm, patient and encouraging, comforting yet demanding.

"You wanta see something?"
"What is it?"
"My worm." (Pulls worm out of pocket.)

Appearance

The satisfactory teacher is always beautiful to his or her children. Beauty to young children is a pleasant personality, a comforting nature, and bright cheerful clothing. Clothing that is washable will make unavoidable accidents just another happening and not a major disaster. An interested teacher will

---

in the Infant and Nursery School (Oxford, England: Pergamon Press, 1965); Lillian G. Katz, "Teacher-Child Relationships in Day Care Centers," (1972), ERIC document no. 046-494; and Patrick C. Lee, "Male and Female Teachers in Elementary Schools and Ecological Analysis," *Teachers College Record*, 75.1 (September 1973).

be conscious of the types of messy activities and occurrences that are normal in an early childhood classroom and will dress accordingly.

Since teaching is an active rather than a passive activity, clothing must be suitable for bending, crawling, sitting, and getting into things. The teacher is an active participant in all of the children's activities.

Role

The major role of the classroom teacher is to establish a physical, social, emotional, and intellectual environment where children can learn to function in a group setting. Most of the child's time in the classroom will be spent in interacting with other children and in some interacting with adults (teacher's aides, students, teachers, parents, and other school personnel). The success of this major role is mostly determined by the teacher's duties as a program planner.

A second role of the teacher is selecting and developing the goals and objectives of the program and converting them to activities that are appropriate for the needs of the children. After these activities are completed, the teacher must evaluate the progress made by the children in obtaining the original objectives or goals. At this point, the teacher becomes a diagnostician and starts the individualization of the program. After diagnosing each child's needs in light of what is important for that child to learn, the teacher varies materials, content, skills, and activities. Each teacher must develop a systematic method of evaluating and recording each child's acquisition of the objectives or goals established.

A third role is classroom manager. Duties include making daily and weekly schedules, grouping, individualizing, purchasing materials, directing the aides' responsibilities, sharing with and teaching student teachers, communicating with parents as they visit the classroom, and maintaining a controlled classroom according to policies established by the school.

Another role taken frequently is that of a liaison between the school and the parents. This role requires the arrangement of home visits, special programs, teas, conferences, parent observation visits, and early introductory sessions for parents and children. Both parents and children should visit with the teacher and the aide as well as tour the school. The first introductory visit occurs the spring before the children are to enter school in the fall. The teacher is also a liaison between the child and the next teacher and grade. Usually the child visits the children and teachers at the next level late in spring.

The fifth role of a teacher of young children is that of a member of the entire faculty. The teacher is a representative for the children and parents as well as a representative of the program. Total involvement in all school functions by the teacher will provide a basis for understanding the program and acceptance and inclusion in the total activities of the school.

> Mother, picking up child after school:
> "Jack, did you tell your teacher you had a good time today?"
> "No."
> "Well, go back and tell her."
> "Hello, teacher, my mamma said I had a good time today!"

CAREER OPPORTUNITIES

As a person who is considering becoming a teacher of young children, you will be interested in the many career opportunities that exist for you in the field of early education.

People choose to become teachers for a variety of reasons. Research tells us that individuals become interested in teaching because they enjoyed school; the most influential person in their lives was a teacher; several of their family members are or were teachers; they wish to serve others; or they wish to improve teaching because as individuals they enjoyed learning but the teachers they had were inadequate in some way. The following descriptions will help you decide which age child you would enjoy; what type of activities you would enjoy; and whether you want to help young children by working with adults involved in teaching children. Many occupations in early childhood education give supportive services to teachers and help them become better teachers.

Centers for Three and Four Year Olds

If you are a person who likes very young children, teaching at this level could be very satisfying for you. Programs for these ages are often called *nursery schools*. In other situations, programs for three and four year olds may be called *preschools* or *prekindergartens*. Full-day programs for this age group are most often found in day-care centers. Generally these settings provide a well-planned program of creative play, socialization, beginning subject area skills (such as oral language, math, science, art, and music), and participation by parents in the education of their children. The schedules that follow will give you an idea of what a typical day might be like for a teacher of this age group.

A typical day of a nursery school teacher and aide of four year olds

8:15   Teacher and aide review plans for day.

Teacher and aide check availability of materials and supplies to be used.

8:30   Teacher and aide greet children, help with clothing, and talk to children.

8:45   Teacher and aide listen to, encourage, and observe children.

Children engage in free play in family living center, truck and block area, art center, and puzzle and manipulative area.

Teacher helps children use listening station and reads a story to those who wish to listen.

Aide helps children in manipulative area and in art center.

Teacher leads or helps children lead group singing. Aide prepares snack.

10:00   Snack. Children help serve, teacher and aide converse with children and establish table manners.

10:10   Outdoor play. Teacher and aide supervise and play with children.

10:30   Toilet.

10:45   Round robin of activities: puzzles, peg boards, sewing cards, stringing beads, picture books on children's activities, string pictures, Tinkertoys® and building logs in block center.

Teacher helps children with string pictures.

Aide listens to, discusses, and looks at picture books with children.

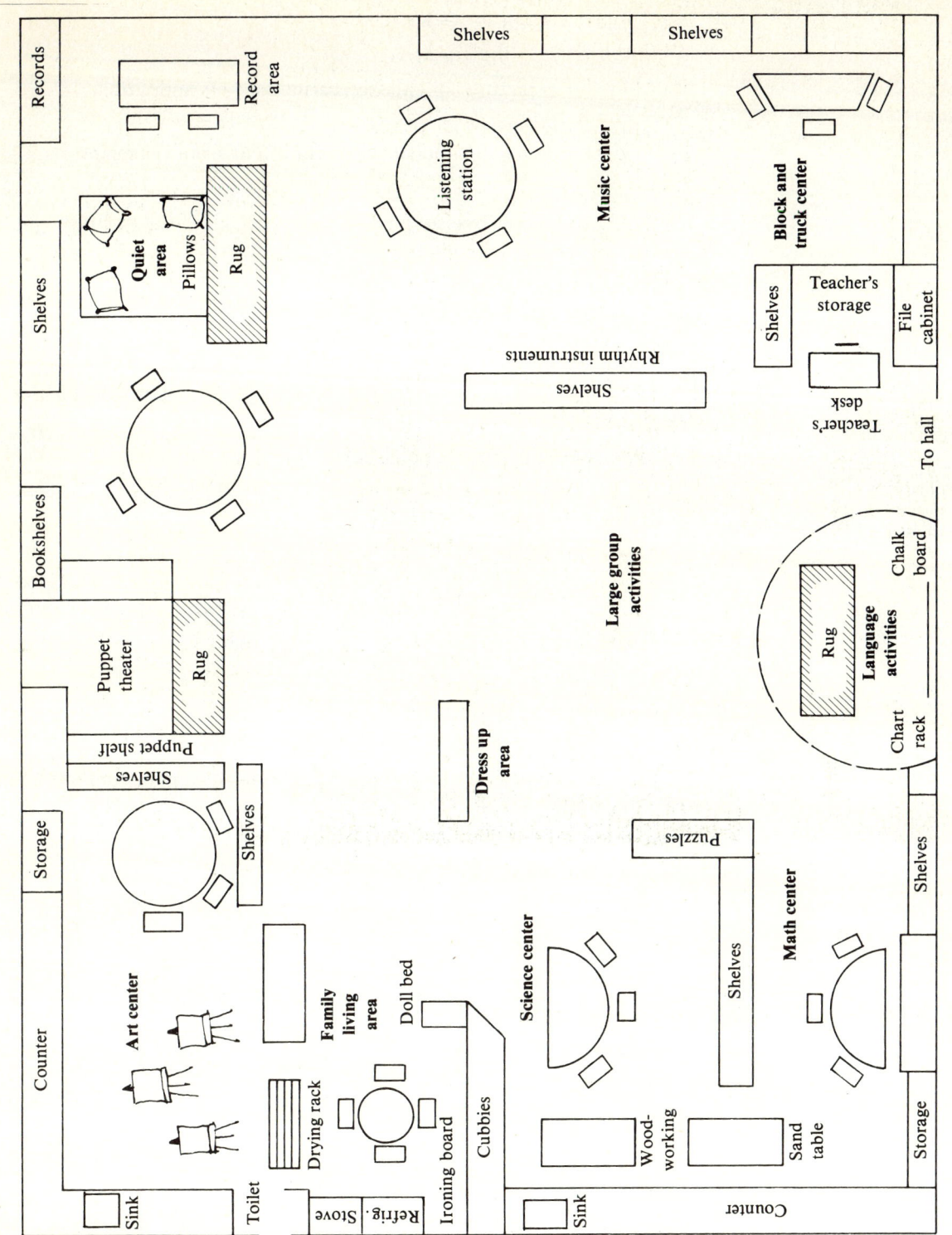

Figure 1.1 A Typical Classroom Design for Four and Five Year Olds

11:30 Unit topic: Caring for pets.

Children discuss their pets.

Teacher shows pictures of children caring for pets and writes a chart: Pets in our room.

Aide gives picture of a pet to each child (cut from magazine).

11:45 Toilet.

11:55 Children sing good-bye song or "I had a good day" song as they get wraps and other belongings.

12:00 Children leave.

12:15 Teacher and aide have lunch.

12:45 Teacher and aide straighten room.

1:15 Teacher and aide evaluate the day's program and make plans for the next day.

Teacher and aide make "peek boxes" of pets.

Teacher writes three notes to parents telling them about improved behavior.

Aide goes to library to return books and get new ones.

3:15 Teacher and aide leave.

A typical day of a day-care teacher of four year olds

(One cook already at center.)

6:15 Morning teacher arrives and opens one entrance door and turns on lights in playrooms and nap rooms.

6:25 Children begin arriving. Some curl up on cots and sleep while others eat breakfast.

7:20 Three more teachers arrive.

7:30 Toileting for all children.

7:45 Free play and TV watching as children finish eating and toileting.

8:15 Four more teachers arrive.

8:30 All children go to individual classrooms.

8:35 In large group setting children sing a good morning song.

8:40 Teacher takes roll; discusses day, month, year, type of weather with children.

8:50 Children share orally the happenings of the night before.

9:00 Children have free play activities under the guidance of the teacher.

9:45 Teacher reads a story to children in a large group setting.

10:00 Toileting for all children.

10:10 Snack time and discussion time with teacher.

10:30 Work time at centers. Teacher gives instructions at the manipulative center.

11:00 A movement activity to music. Children sing songs as they move to the music.

11:10 Teacher presents a science lesson on the shape and color of fall leaves.

11:30 Toileting for all children before lunch.

11:40 Lunch with children.

12:10 Teacher takes children to nap room and stays with children.

12:10 Children listen to music for fifteen minutes as they rest and become sleepy.

1:00 Teacher leaves nap room. (Place taken by afternoon teacher.)

1:00 Teacher calls parents of absent children.

1:20 Teacher plans and sets up activities for next day.

2:00 Teacher leaves plans in director's office.

2:15 Morning teacher leaves. Children cared for by afternoon teacher, aides, and director. Center remains open to 6:00 p.m.

Kindergarten Programs

The kindergarten teacher's position is the most widely known early education position. A kindergarten program is designed for five-year-old children. It provides for active and quiet pursuits; for individuals, small groups, and large groups; for unit studies in social studies and science; for a concentration on developing oral language skills; and for beginning instruction in math, art, music, health, and physical activities. It provides opportunities for children to become interested in all school-related activities. Its purpose is to further the growth of the children through events that are active, planned, interesting, and useful. Kindergarten, in contrast to programs for younger children, becomes more structured as to activity and accomplishment as the year progresses. Usually teachers and aides begin diagnosing instructional gains as well as physical, social, and emotional gains. Math and certain aspects of language arts (printing and the alphabet, for example) are introduced in formal small groups.

Elementary Schools

The teacher of young children generally possesses a document certifying him or her to teach kindergarten through grade three or sometimes even kindergarten through grades six or nine. In some instances an endorsement is added to an elementary certificate — an endorsement for grades one through six or nine. The endorsement is an add-on area to a certificate already received for other area(s) of instruction that the individual is qualified to teach. Because of these certification requirements, an understanding of the primary years in an elementary school setting is necessary.

The primary years in an elementary school are usually designated as first grade, second grade, and third grade for children ages six to nine. Programs generally constitute a sequential series of steps in each instructional area, providing opportunities for introduction, repetition, review, and evaluation of the content and skills taught. Generally during these first three years, all the foundation skills of the seven instructional areas (language arts, social studies, science, mathematics, art, music, and physical education) are introduced and developed to the extent that children master the basics and can recall them whenever needed. The later years in the elementary or middle school are usually devoted to the extension and enrichment of these basic, foundation skills. The content of the seven instructional areas is developmental in nature; facts or knowledge can be expanded with experience and maturity.

This book is designed to aid teachers in identifying the needs of the children they teach, in light of what they have been taught and of what they will be taught. It offers examples of primary-level methods, activities, and experiences to help teachers make better decisions concerning the children in their classes. It is hoped that these suggestions will be integrated with the content of other methods courses required for certification.

Other Positions in Early Education

Administrators Besides classroom teaching positions for college-degreed individuals, administrative positions are also available. The number and type of positions depend upon the number of children served and the financial basis for the program.

Most public schools have at least one supervisory position. Special resource teachers or other subject matter supervisors may act as consultants for the classroom teachers. In large school systems, directors of parent activities, nutritional experts, and social workers are hired to assist classroom teachers. Private schools (day-care centers, church-related schools, or other agencies) usually have a director of programs in addition to teachers and aides. Because of adequate financing, Head Start centers serving many children may have head teachers in addition to a director, regular teachers, aides, and the other supplementary positions found in the public school setting.

The schedules that follow may give you an idea of the various types of functions performed by administrators.

An overview of early childhood education / 19

A typical day of an early childhood supervisor

8:00   Check daily schedule with secretary.

8:10   Call two principals for visitation next week.

8:25   Drive to a school to observe a new teacher.

Confer with principal.

Observation of and conference with teacher.

Greet other teachers.

Confer with principal.

11:30   Drive to another school.

Confer with principal.

Have lunch with teachers to plan parents' meeting for next month.

12:45   Drive to another school.

Confer with principal and teacher concerning a program and material for a deaf child.

2:30   Return to office.

Answer phone calls. Write three letters: (1) requesting speaker for in-service program, (2) ordering new materials, and (3) requesting copy of a curriculum guide.

3:45   Attend budget hearings for next year based on projected enrollment.

5:15   Leave.

A typical day of a day-care director

Day-care centers serve working parents and therefore must open early and close late. The day-care center below opens at 6:00 when the cook and maintenance person arrive. At 6:15 one teacher is on duty, at 7:30 the second teacher arrives, and at 8:00 four additional teachers and two student teachers arrive. Day-care directors arrive for duty at varying times and do not always arrive at the same time every day.

10:00   Visit each room and talk to each teacher about needs and problems.

10:30   Check menu and discuss rest of the week's meals: breakfasts, snacks, lunches, and midafternoon snack.

10:45   Tour indoor and outdoor play areas, checking equipment and conditions.

10:55   Collect supplies needed by teachers and deliver them. Check nap areas for cleanliness.

11:10   Hold conference with student teachers and plan new responsibilities for them.

PROJECT
Planning Your Future

There are many different kinds of career opportunities within the field of early childhood education. As you prepare for your professional life, it is important for you to try to analyze your abilities, recall your past educational experiences, and think about your own wants and desires, so as to plan the type of career that will give you the greatest satisfaction and sense of accomplishment.

1. Write a paragraph describing the difference in teaching style and methods between a teacher you had who was merely "all right" and one who was truly excellent.
2. List the most important attributes that you believe a teacher should have.
3. Make a checklist of these attributes. Analyze your own abilities. Do you have most of these attributes? If you think you are weak or lacking in some areas, talk to your advisor or instructor about how to go about developing these abilities.
4. Using the material in Chapter 1 as a guide, write a chronological outline of how you would like your career to develop.

11:30 Review teacher plan books with state licensing worker.

Escort licensing worker to the three year olds' room for observation.

11:50 Call food distributor and supply company for goods and materials for next week.

12:00 Call two parents concerning absent children.

Write a note to a parent to be pinned on child while child is waiting to be picked up (4:30).

12:45 Eat lunch with state licensing worker and cook.

1:15 Leave center to deposit money, pick up films and books from public library, and buy one pound of ten-penny nails.

2:15 (First teacher on duty leaves.)

Deliver books to various rooms.

Set up projector for film to be shown at 4:00.

2:45 Meet and discuss afternoon activities with two college students who are to be on duty until 5:00.

3:00 Meet with two teachers to discuss their plans for the next week.

3:30 Second teacher on duty leaves.

4:00 All regular teachers have left. Two college students and director on duty.

Run projector for movie.

4:30 Hold conference with parent and make out receipt for payment of weekly fee.

   Greet parents as they arrive to pick up their children.

   Help children with wraps and talk to them as they play.

5:30 College students leave.

5:45 Last child is picked up.

   Tour building to check windows and lights.

6:10 Leave for day.

Aides Another position in early education is that of an aide. The early childhood classroom aide is very important — not only as an aide to the teacher but as a helper, guide, and friend to the children. The adults in the classroom are really a team, but each has his or her own responsibilities. An aide is not usually responsible for the initial instruction of skills or content but assists in the follow-up activities or experiences that occur after the teacher has taught or presented the lesson. Because of this, it is important that the aide be included in the daily planning session so that the goals of the lesson are known by both teacher and aide. The aide also assists the teacher and children prepare for a lesson and clean up after an activity or at the close of the day. In addition, aides may be in charge of any activities that do not require new instruction — such as lunchroom guidance, playground supervision, bathroom visits, and bus duty.

Some aides receive training from their local school systems on how to teach the use of materials or activities and become involved in limited teaching. In addition, junior colleges and community colleges offer two-year programs for teacher aides and these individuals also teach children under the guidance of the regular teacher. These graduates in many cases receive a Child Development Associate (CDA) degree.

Qualifications for aides vary. In some schools aides must be high school graduates, in other schools they must have two years of college, and in some situations they must be parents of young children. Because of the current oversupply of public school teachers in some areas of the country, some aides in public kindergartens are college graduates.

Professional Organizations

As a teacher of young children, you will want to belong to one or more professional organizations to update your skills, improve your knowledge of research data, and participate in activities with others who have similar interests. The following organizations have national meetings, publish materials, and provide leadership for the causes of young children.

Early childhood professional organizations and journals

American Association of Elementary-Kindergarten-Nursery Educators. 1201 Sixteenth Street, N.W., Washington, D.C. 20036. *Educating Children*.

American Home Economics Association. 2010 Massachusetts Avenue, Washington, D.C. 20036. *Journal of Home Economics*.

Association for Childhood Education International. 3615 Wisconsin Avenue, N.W., Washington, D.C. 20016. *Childhood Education*.

National Association for the Education of Young Children. 1834 Connecticut Avenue, N.W., Washington, D.C. 20009. *Young Children*.

Organisation Mondiale Pour l'Éducation Prescolaire and the United States National Committee for Early Childhood Education. 81 Irving Place, New York, N.Y. 10003. *International Journal of Early Childhood*.

The Day Care and Child Development Council of America. 1012 14th Street, N.W., Washington, D.C. 20005. *Voice for Children*.

SUMMARY

Knowing the present status of early childhood education today is important to you as you prepare to teach. Knowledge of current purposes, programs, and teaching opportunities give you a basis for comparison and contrast with what occurred in the past, with what is happening in your area of the country now, and with future developments in the field.

For many persons the exciting involvement in early childhood education is the most important aspect of their lives. Because of the diversity of types of programs, the kinds of children, the many different positions available, and the possibility of change and growth in the field, many persons find in early childhood education a lifetime of pleasure as well as a profession.

ADDITIONAL READINGS

Cohen, Dorothy J., and Edward Zigler. "Federal Day Care Standards: Rationale and Recommendation." *Young Children*, 33 (1978): 24–32.

Decker, Celia, and John Decker. *Planning and Administrating Early Childhood Programs*. 2nd ed. Columbus, Ohio: Charles E. Merrill, 1980.

Katz, Lillian G., ed. *Current Topics in Early Childhood Education; Volume II*. Norwood, N.J.: Ablex Publishing Corp., 1979.

Morrison, G. S. *Early Childhood Education Today*. Columbus, Ohio: Charles E. Merrill, 1980.

Sciarra, Dorothy Jane, and Anne G. Dorsey. *Developing and Administering a Child Care Center*. Boston: Houghton Mifflin, 1979.

CHAPTER 2
A Survey of Educational History and Philosophy

Exploration Tasks

After studying this chapter, you should be able to complete these tasks:
- Describe three significant events in the history of education that changed the approach to teaching young children.
- List the names of some of the early educators and describe their contributions.
- Describe early American education.
- Explain a few of John Dewey's ideas on education.
- Discuss Montessori's idea of self-correcting materials.
- State the main ideas of the child study movement.

Rules for Teachers, 1872

Teachers each day will fill lamps, clean chimneys.

Each teacher will bring a bucket of water and a scuttle of coal for the day's sessions.

Make your pens carefully. You may whittle nibs to the individual taste of the pupils.

Men teachers may take one evening each week for courting purposes, or two evenings a week if they go to church regularly.

After ten hours in school, teachers may spend the remaining time reading the Bible or other good books.

Women teachers who marry or engage in unseemly conduct will be dismissed.

Every teacher should lay aside from each pay a goodly sum of his earnings for his benefit during his declining years so that he will not become a burden on society.

Any teacher who smokes, uses liquor in any form, frequents pool or public halls, or gets shaved in a barber shop will give good reason to suspect his worth, intentions, integrity and honesty. The teacher who performs his labor faithfully and without fault for five years will be given an increase of twenty-five cents per week in his pay, providing the Board of Education approves.

Source unknown

OVERVIEW

Times have changed! Today teachers no longer need concern themselves with rules about sharpening quill pens, carrying buckets of water or scuttles of coal, and remaining unmarried.

Times change, but why? Many forces combine to change the traditions of any phase of life. In education this is also true. The need for change is generally felt for practical reasons; the needs are met by new philosophies and developed by the perceptive minds of one or two individuals.

In a review as brief as the one we present in this chapter, descriptions of economic and social events, educational changes, and individual philosophies of education cannot be discussed in depth. A detailed study of the history of education probably was developed in one of your foundation courses. What this chapter seeks to do is place the development of early childhood education within a broad historical frame. In addition, the section on philosophies of education will help you become more aware of various approaches to teaching young children. The references at the end of this chapter will provide you with opportunities for additional reading on these subjects. You are encouraged to enroll soon in a course devoted to the history of early education and to read further on your own.

A BRIEF HISTORY OF EDUCATION

We study the history of education for several reasons. First, to avoid making the same mistakes others have made. Second, to understand the reasons for the major changes in education. Third, to learn how philosophies of teaching have developed and changed through the years. Fourth, to encourage us to use our own "perceptive minds" to develop new educational materials and activities and our own personal philosophies of education.

History can be fun and informative. If you think through the changes of the past in relation to their historical importance, you will be able to analyze current everyday changes and adapt them appropriately for your own students. Knowing your history will help you prevent serious, time-consuming errors of instruction.

To provide your study of early childhood education with a historical perspective, this section contains a summary of significant historical events in the field of education and a brief review of American education from the colonial period through the nineteenth century.

Development of Early Childhood Education

Table 2.1 traces the history of early childhood education from ancient Greece to present-day America. It has been constructed to help you connect the outstanding events in the development of this field with both the general history of education and specific significant world events. Before reading this table, turn to the project on page 30.

Table 2.1 Significant Events in the History of Early Childhood Education

Political, economic, and social events	Educational changes and persons initiating them
431 B.C. The Peloponnesian War.	Socrates (470–399 B.C.). Athens, Greece: Taught Plato (428–348 B.C.). Athens: Spoke of educating children under six.
	Aristotle (384–322 B.C.). Athens: Believed in educating the young and recognized individual differences.
	1442. Hornbook: A single sheet of paper attached to a board that had a handle (3″ × 4″). The paper was covered with a thin sheet of horn to protect the paper. The material on the paper was usually the alphabet, vowels and consonants, the Lord's Prayer, or Bible verses. Some of these books were still in use in the early 1800s.
1492. Christopher Columbus reached America.	Erasmus (1466–1536). Rotterdam, Holland: A humanist interested in the nature of good schooling.
1520–1648. Reformation. Arose from objections to doctrines and practices in the medieval church and ultimately led to the freedom of dissent.	Martin Luther (1483–1546). Germany: Believed that girls as well as boys should be taught and that schools should include a range of courses. He was the first educator to include the teaching of music as a basic skill.
1533. Photography. In the book *Natural Magic*, Giovanni Battista della Porta described how an invented image of an outdoor scene could be projected on the opposite wall of a room with a single small opening. John W. Draper is thought to have made the first daguerreotype portrait in 1839.	John Comenius (1592–1670). Czechoslovakia: Designed first illustrated children's textbook, *Visible World*, in 1658. In 1628 he wrote *School of Infancy*. His ideas included the "school of the mother's knee" — by the age of six children were to know the foundations of all knowledge.
	John Locke (1632–1704). England: In 1693 wrote *Some Thoughts Concerning Education*, which emphasized "natural" methods of education in contrast to harsh discipline.
1647. "Old Deluder Satan" law in Massachusetts instituted local control in the American school system; supposedly the "chief project" of Satan was to keep people from knowing the Scriptures.	1690. *The New England Primer* printed in London; was still widely used in the United States in 1850.
	1697. *Mother Goose Tales* collected by Charles Perrault in France. ("Little Red Riding Hood," "Sleeping Beauty," "Cinderella," and others). Translated into English in 1729.
1750–1850. Industrial Revolution. Phenomenal changes in society and in economic structure took place as technological innovations created factories and mass production.	Jean Jacques Rousseau (1712–1778). France: Wrote *Émile* in 1762. This story of a child reared apart from other children by methods of experimentation is generally accepted as the basis for modern elementary education. Stated that children have within them the power to be agents of their own learning.
	Johann Pestalozzi (1746–1827). Rural Switzerland: A teacher of young children who held that public

Table 2.1 *(cont.)*

Political, economic, and social events	*Educational changes and persons initiating them*
	education must consider the circumstances of family and environment or education will "lead to an artificial and methodical dwarfing of humanity." He developed no definite plan or organization of learning.
1775–1783. American Revolution. A struggle by which the thirteen British colonies on the Atlantic seaboard of North America won independence from Great Britain.	1783. Noah Webster published his *Blue-backed Speller*, which helped to standardize spelling in the United States.
1789–1802. French Revolutionary Wars. One cause of the war was that France's rapid economic and intellectual development was not matched by social and political change. Another cause was the chaotic state of the government's finances, which the privileged few refused to help.	Friedrich Wilhelm Froebel (1782–1852). Central east Germany: Known as the Father of the Kindergarten. Believed that kindergarten was an essential step in the process of education because progress was hampered in later years due to lack of attention, training, and occasionally, physical abuse. Maintained that the aim of education was to produce a pure, faithful, complete, and therefore holy life. Saw play as the "germinal leaves of all later life."
1803–1815. Napoleonic Wars. Wars against Napoleon I.	
1861–1865. Civil War. A conflict between the northern United States and the eleven southern states that had seceded from the Union and formed the Confederacy.	Margorethe Schurz (1832–1876). Watertown, Wisconsin: A student of Froebel. Opened the first U.S. kindergarten in 1856. Six students were taught in German.
1865–1870. Amendments to the Constitution (13th, 14th, 15th) abolished slavery; guaranteed civil rights; and ensured voting rights for all, except women.	Elizabeth Palmer Peabody (1804–1894). Massachusetts: Met Margorethe Schurz in 1859 and became interested in kindergartens and Froebel. Started the first English-speaking U.S. kindergarten in 1860 in Boston with thirty children. By 1873 four kindergartens had been started in Milwaukee. In 1871 Peabody began a letter-writing campaign to William T. Harris of St. Louis, a leading educator. Harris and Susan Blow opened first public kindergarten in St. Louis in 1873.
	John Dewey (1859–1952). Chicago: An American philosopher and educator known for his educational ideas of learning through experimentation and practice.
1876–1877. Alexander Graham Bell patented the first device for a telephone.	Philadelphia: Exposition of 1876 featured exhibit of a model kindergarten taught by Ruth Burritt in the Woman's Pavilion (started by Elizabeth Peabody).
	1878. Kate Douglas Wiggin, a student of Peabody, became director of the Silver Kindergarten in San Francisco, the first free kindergarten west of the Rockies.
	1878. Peabody formed the American Froebel Union.
	1880. The first teacher-training program for kindergarten

Table 2.1 (*cont.*)

Political, economic, and social events	Educational changes and persons initiating them
	teachers was started in the Oshkosh Normal School. Four black women became kindergarten teachers in 1881 in Philadelphia.
	1884. Elementary-Kindergarten-Nursery Education (E/K/N/E) founded to help unite elementary educators. The International Kindergarten Union (IKU) was organized in 1892 at Saratoga Springs, New York.
	Margaret McMillan (1860–1931). Great Britain: started the open-air nursery school with several children ages one to six. The main emphasis was outdoor play, baths, clean clothes, meals, and some learning experiences. She also emphasized medical and dental care as well as working with parents.
	Maria Montessori (1870–1952). Italy: Became director of tax-supported school for defective children in 1898. In 1907, organized a school for small children who were otherwise left unsupervised in a Rome tenement.
	1896. Susan Blow went to Teachers College to represent the Froebelian point of view and Patty Smith Hill was appointed to represent the "new" developmental approach. The differences in the two approaches were (1) opposing interpretations of "work" and "play"; (2) Herbartian theories of interest and apperception; and (3) the relative merits of free and directed play. Working as a team they taught one course of fourteen meetings from 1905 to 1909.
1903. The first controlled, sustained flight in a power-driven airplane.	By 1903, conflict within IKU became so disruptive that Committee of Nineteen was established to "formulate contemporary kindergarten thought."
1912. Children's Bureau established as part of the U.S. Department of Commerce and Labor (now under the Department of Health and Human Services).	1913. The Committe of Nineteen's report showed such diverse thought that three separate reports were given (conservative, liberal, and liberal-conservative).
1914–1918. World War I: Largest conflict in the world up to that time. Major causes were imperialistic, territorial, and economic rivalries between Germany, France, and Great Britain and between Russia and Austria-Hungary.	1915. Child Education Foundation in New York City organized its first nursery school, which was Montessori-oriented.
	1916. First cooperative nursery school established by faculty wives of the University of Chicago.
	1919. New York: Harriet Johnson (a nurse) established laboratory nursery school, now called Bank Street.
	1921. Laboratory preschool begun at the University of Iowa; Columbia University Nursery School started by Patty Smith Hill.

Table 2.1 (*cont.*)

Political, economic, and social events	*Educational changes and persons initiating them*
	1922. Abigail Eliot, a social worker, began the Ruggles Street Nursery School in Boston. In Detroit, the Merrill-Palmer School (now Institute), started in 1922 by Edna Noble White, a home economist, had one of the first nursery schools.
	1923. *The Preschool Child* written by Arnold Gesell.
	1924. The professional journal *Childhood Education* published by IKU.
	1924. Twenty-eight nursery schools established in eleven states.
	1926. National Committee on Nursery Schools formed. Jean Piaget published *The Language and Thought of the Child*; saw intelligence development as a continuous process with four main periods of growth: sensorimotor (0–2 years), preoperational (2–7), concrete operational (7–11 years) and formal operational (11–15).
	1928. *Psychological Care of Infant and Child* written by John B. Watson. Influenced child rearing from 1920 to 1940 with advice: "Treat [children] as adults . . .; never hug and kiss them, never let them sit in your lap. If you must, kiss them on the forehead when they say 'goodnight,' shake hands with them in the morning."
	1930. National Association for Nursery Education formed. IKU enlarged its membership and changed its name to Association for Childhood Education (ACE).
1935. Social Security Act: Federal government makes grants to states with approved plans of assistance to dependent children.	1932. The project method, developed by Kilpatrick, was common curriculum procedure; article, "The Effect of Preschool Attendance upon the IQ" written by Beth Wellman. In lab studies at Iowa Child Welfare Station, she discovered an average gain of about seven points between the fall and spring tests.
1938. The Fair Labor Standards Act: Set sixteen as minimum age for employment of children producing goods for interstate or foreign commerce.	1933–1942. WPA nurseries established to combat the Depression. Their main purpose was to provide jobs for teachers and other workers.
1940. The Lanham Act passed by Congress to provide funds to help war-impacted areas.	1941–1946. The Lanham Act War Nurseries. About one-third of American women, working in defense plants during World War II, needed care facilities for their children.
	1943. New York City established comprehensive day-care centers, designed for health care, to meet social and emotional needs and to provide educational experiences.

Table 2.1 (*cont.*)

Political, economic, and social events	Educational changes and persons initiating them
	1944. *Young Children*, a journal, established by NANE; originally called the *NANE Bulletin* (NANE later became NAEYC).
1945. First marketing of television sets.	1948. World Organization for Preschool Children (OMEP) founded. It meets every third year in cities around the world; National Committee for Early Childhood Education is the U.S.-member organization.
1954. Supreme Court decision on civil rights, state decision.	1964. NANE reorganized to become National Association for the Education of Young Children. *Stability and Change in Human Characteristics* written by Benjamin Bloom; illustrated the importance of the early years of life and the difficulty of effecting change later.
	1965. Elementary-Secondary Education Act; Project Head Start established to provide comprehensive health and nutritional program and educational experience for four-and five-year-old children of poverty. By 1972, Head Start involved younger children because most states had public kindergarten programs for five year olds.
	1968. National Laboratory on Early Childhood Education established at the University of Illinois; initiated ERIC clearinghouse on early childhood education at the University. Federal Panel on Early Childhood established by the White House.
	1975. Public Law (PL) 94–142 passed by Congress. Between 1975 and 1980, federal and state legislation and court rulings established laws requiring some form of public education for all handicapped children. Federal goals called for adequate educational opportunities for all handicapped children by 1980.
1978–1980. Immigrants to the United States from Asia, Cuba, and other South American countries.	1980. Federal funds guidelines: A "bilingual/bicultural" program is mandatory if there are twenty or more students of similar linguistic background in a district. Based on 1974 ruling by the Supreme Court (*Lau* v. *Nichols*).

Source: Samuel J. Brun and Esther P. Edwards, *History and Theory of Early Childhood Education* (Worthington, Ohio: Charles A. Jones, 1972); Ellis D. Evans, *Contemporary Influences in Early Childhood Education*, 2nd ed. (New York: Holt, Rinehart and Winston, 1975); Marvin Lazerson, "The Historical Antecedents of Early Childhood Education," in Ira J. Gordon, ed., *Early Childhood Education, Seventy-first Yearbook of the National Society for the Study of Education* (Chicago: University of Chicago Press, 1972); D. Keith Osborn, *Early Childhood Education in Historical Perspective* (Athens, Ga.: Education Associates, 1975); Evelyn Weber, *The Kindergarten: Its Encounter with Educational Thought in America* (New York: Teachers College Press, 1969); Agnes Snyder, *Dauntless Women in Childhood Education* (Washington, D.C.: ACEI, 1972); and *World Book Encyclopedia* (Chicago: Field Enterprises, 1973).

PROJECT
Thoughts to Ponder

Before you read and discuss Table 2.1, try to answer some of these questions.

1. Do national or international events affect programs for early childhood education? If no, why not? If yes, what events do you think have affected programs for the young child?
2. What is the earliest event in education you can remember? Why do you remember it?
3. Name three persons who made a significant change in the education of young children. What changes did these persons make and why are the changes important?
4. Of the aspects of an early childhood program now in general use — equipment, techniques, content, philosophy — which do you think has been in use the longest? Explain why you chose your answer.

Early American Education

The early settlers of America came basically for two reasons: religious and economic. Those who came for religious reasons sought the opportunity to practice their religion according to their own interpretation of the Bible. For people to interpret the Bible, they had to be able to read. Therefore, the main purpose of the early schools was to teach children how to read the Bible. Those who came for economic reasons might also have come for religious reasons but their main motivation was to seek the prosperity to be had in trade, furs, and land ownership. Those who came for economic reasons needed to be educated for recordkeeping and monetary reasoning. They needed to be skilled in "reading, writing, and arithmetic." A third purpose of colonial education was to enable the wealthy to appreciate the arts, history, and science. Sons of well-to-do families were educated to be the leaders and the connoisseurs of the nation; daughters of well-to-do families were educated to be good wives, mothers, companions, and "culture bearers" for the next generation.

Early American schooling took place in several settings. It took place at home either as a family project or under the supervision of a hired tutor or a local spinster or bachelor met with a small group of children in the "parlor." In other communities, the "preacher" taught the children.

This may help you understand why the first schools as we understand them today — with buildings, scheduled classes, majors and minors, and so on — were started at the private college level. Harvard, founded in

A kindergarten class in the North End of Boston, 1881. In what ways does it resemble or differ from present-day kindergartens?

1636, was soon followed by William and Mary, Yale, Princeton, Pennsylvania, Brown, Rice, Dartmouth, and Kings College (Columbia University). The graduates of these colleges were important to early childhood education because many of them became teachers of young children.

Public secondary schools didn't begin until 1821 in Boston, 1838 in Philadelphia, and 1856 in Chicago. But by 1860 there were over three hundred public high schools in the United States.

Public elementary school had a very slow beginning. In 1642 Massachusetts passed legislation to establish public elementary schools; but the law was not implemented. This was also the pattern in a few other states.

Finally, in 1806 in New York City, mass public elementary education started in earnest. The Lancaster, or monitorial, system from England was adopted. The keys to the practical success of this program were large groups of children meeting at one time with one teacher, slates instead of paper, blackboards instead of many different books, and oral recitation and memorization in place of written papers and workbooks. One of the greatest selling points of this system was that five hundred children could be taught at an annual cost of two dollars per child.

Probably one of the reasons that free public kindergartens did not become a reality in the United States until 1873 was that you couldn't teach large groups of five year olds at an annual cost of two dollars each! As was true of most educational developments, kindergartens were thriving in Europe long before they were adopted in the United States. Elizabeth Peabody (see Table 2.1) became captivated with European early childhood programs and besieged William T. Harris, Superintendent of Schools for the City of St. Louis, with letters about the "wonders" of these programs. As a result, in 1873 Mr. Harris hired Susan Blow as a teacher for kindergarten children.

As time went on, economic and social changes eventually led to public education for all children. Not only did the time come when it was made available to all children, but in the late 1930s laws were passed making it mandatory for children to attend school. Some states required children to stay in school until they had completed a specific grade level while others required them to attend until they had attained a certain age.

What were some of the reasons for the growth in public education in the United States? The most important reason was the belief by many Americans in the importance of universal mass education. The idea that an education can be a "steppingstone" to success is still present in our society. Another reason was the desirability of having a literate electorate in a democracy. A third important reason was the need to transmit the common American culture to a great variety of immigrant cultural groups. There are of course other reasons, but these are the main ones.

PHILOSOPHIES OF EDUCATION

Knowing the philosophies that have influenced early childhood education's development should help you understand how and why early childhood programs differ. Our survey of educational approaches begins with Friedrich Froebel rather than with Johann Pestalozzi. Although Pestalozzi was the earliest great teacher of the young, his teaching was generally done by intuition. He had no established method and could give no direct explanation of his ideas, plans, or intentions. In contrast, Froebel, his student, developed a valid and useful approach, which he applied to the first kindergarten. The main tie between the two men was their affectionate concern for and their interest in the protection of young children. The first published philosophy for teaching young children that was readily avaliable for use by teachers was developed by Froebel.

Friedrich Froebel (1782–1852)

As the "father" of the kindergarten concept, Froebel dominated education of young children for generations.[1] Froebel, a German educator who orig-

---

[1] Friedrich Froebel, *Pedagogics of the Kindergarten*, trans. Josephine Jarvis (New York: D. Appleton and Co., 1895); and *The Education of Man*, trans. William N. Helmann (New York: D. Appleton and Co., 1889).

inally studied architecture, felt that children needed enrichment in their early years to reach their potential later. To extend this idea he organized each step of his program in very specific ways to aid children in their intellectual, physical, and moral development.

Froebel believed in a balance between an individual's freedom and society's responsibility to develop the skills, knowledge, and values that allow each individual to live in society. Play was the most natural and effective way for children to learn and to develop their abilities. One of Froebel's basic tenets was that productive self-activity was needed in children's play. He believed the value of play depended on the amount of freedom children had to express their own aims and on their ability to carry out their own decisions. In the kindergarten Froebel attempted to systematize play under the leadership of adults without robbing play of its freedom or taking spontaneity and independence of action away from the children.

Stressing the influence of the environment on development, Froebel believed that children could not develop true self-active interest unless they were placed in interesting conditions appropriate to their age and experience. He felt that the teacher's responsibility lay in providing these conditions of interest; the environment should be organized with materials that would stimulate creative self-activity. The teacher of the kindergarten, moreover, should be responsible for selecting the appropriate environment and materials to suit different ages and degrees of development. Froebelian classes always provided conditions in which children could define their sensations and emotions. Froebel's book describes activities specifically designed to foster and stimulate the emotions. He constructed many "gifts" — toys and activities geared to aid child development during kindergarten. Gifts and occupations made up the kindergarten system. Several of these activities are still used in a modified form in today's preschool programs.

The "gifts" of Froebel's kindergarten included balls, cubes, cylinders, and blocks of several different sizes and dimensions. They were not used freely in class but were presented and utilized in prescribed ways. By handling the different geometric shapes, children were to learn to observe and compare. Emphasis was put on the relationships of the physical properties of the objects (such as angles to faces of a cube). The children exercised the small muscles when handling the ball as they learned to distinguish form, color, size, weight, and so forth. The blocks used were small table blocks (larger blocks were not included in Froebel's system), which when put together formed a large cube. Lessons began with only eight blocks at a time. The children were instructed by the teacher to make a form of life, such as a chair; a form of knowledge, for example, four equal piles of the blocks; or a form of beauty, that is, any shape that appealed to them.

Other activities involved arranging other objects: tablets (small flat wooden squares and triangles), sticks, and beans and rings. Occupations included drawing, coloring, using water colors, modeling clay, folding paper, weaving

PROJECT
What Do You Remember About Your Schooling?

Before you read the section on Dewey, answer the following questions:

1. Was your teacher's desk in the middle or the front of the room?
2. Were the desks screwed to the floor in rows?
3. Were you taught reading, writing, science, math, geography, history, and so on, as isolated subjects or as related subjects? How did the teacher organize the curriculum to accomplish his or her method of teaching?
4. Did you learn to cook or sew or have manual training?
5. Did you read about science or did you do "experiments"?
6. Did you go on field trips? Where did you go and why?
7. How does today's education differ from your experiences?

As you may realize from your answers to the questions, the first three questions concern the traditional educational practices against which John Dewey was reacting. The next three questions reflect Dewey's ideas.

---

mats, and working with peas and corks (small peas connected to each other by sticks, similar to Tinkertoys®).

Perforating paper with a needle and performing intricate sewing were thought to be less desirable tasks in American Froebelian schools because of eye strain and small children's inability to control finger muscles.

It is evident that Froebel placed a major emphasis on fine motor control. Today we know that these finer muscle coordinations are the last to be developed in the young child. While we provide children with exercise in manipulative play, we also provide experiences that will help them coordinate gross motor movements. Froebel offered movement plays, similar to our fingerplays, which gave the child some gross motor experiences. He also incorporated gardening in his curriculum for large muscle movement and coordination.

Froebel emphasized and developed many of today's issues and trends. He considered parent education important for ensuring the child's early development. In his book *Mother Plays*, he supplied activities for mothers to use to stimulate their children's intellectual and physical growth.[2] He believed in educating the young child through the senses by supplying concrete objects for learning through play. This is compatible with Piaget's theory that the young child's primary mode of learning is through senso-

---

[2] Friedrich Froebel, *Mutter-und Kose-Lieder* (Leipzig: Witive und Sohns, 1911).

Table 2.2 Differences Between Approaches of Froebel and Dewey

	Froebel	*Dewey*
Philosophical base	Idealism	Pragmatism
	Symbolism	Objective (scientific)
Process	Unfolding	Potential developed through social interaction
Play	Symbolic: highly structured (gifts and occupations)	Based on realities: free play according to interests of the child
Teacher role	Teacher directed	Child centered: teacher is stage setter and guide
Contents of materials	Structured	Everyday common materials

Adapted from Lynn Cagle, Unpublished paper, University of Tennessee, Knoxville, Tenn.

rimotor and concrete experiences. As do today's educators, Froebel felt that the total developmental needs of the child should be considered. One of the first and most ardent proponents of play as a mode of learning in the kindergarten, Froebel taught that parents and teachers should always accompany actions with words (later used by Ira Gordon) as an infant stimulation technique. Froebel's philosophy also stressed individualization in the classroom. The basis of open education is provided in Froebel's idea of teachers designing environments that are stimulating to the child.

John Dewey (1859–1952)

Progressive education did not actually start with John Dewey, but came about because of Joseph Mayer Rice's survey of public education in 1892 and comparison of the "old" and "new" educational systems.[3] However, John Dewey, like Froebel, gave direction to the basic ideas developing at that time in the schools — a unified curriculum, work activities, self-directed activities, an emphasis on science, and a changed attitude toward children. The term *progressive education* has become associated with the idea of permissiveness and unbridled behavior. The educational system Dewey espoused did not conform to this idea.

In 1896 Dewey formed a laboratory school at the University of Chicago. At the lab school a group of four- and five-year-old children were designated as subprimary. Since there were already many kindergartens in the United States, Dewey's use of another term for the same group was probably a reaction against the Froebelian influence. Several basic differences between Froebel and Dewey are outlined in Table 2.2.

[3] Joseph Mayer Rice, *The Public-School System of the United States* (New York: The Century Co., 1893).

Although much of Dewey's writings is long and involved, his "My Pedagogic Creed" is simple, direct, and readable. Many of the ideas expressed in his creed are the basis for today's philosophy of education. To help you understand Dewey's influence on today's early childhood education programs, see Table 2.3, which presents a synopsis of Dewey's creed along with current-day expressions of these concepts.

If you haven't read John Dewey's creed, you might enjoy analyzing all its aspects in light of what you know about today's educational process.

Maria Montessori (1870–1952)

In 1907 in Rome, Maria Montessori was making innovative changes in instruction and ideology for Italian slum children. She was the first to design materials to teach her selected concepts. She included many everyday aspects of life in her curriculum such as exercise, diet, muscle development, nature study, work, development of the senses, language, reading, writing, mathematics, and discipline.

The Montessori Method Montessori developed several general methods for teachers to use while they were teaching young children. She believed that life must be arranged to provide abstract experiences that start the mind on paths leading to knowledge. To do this she developed materials that always taught something. To succeed, the material had to be interesting, although teachers could not know what would interest a particular child until the child tried the material.

To understand Montessori's approach to teaching young children, you need to understand the terms she used in her writings as well as the criteria she developed for selecting materials and methods.

Key Terms The following list of terms provides a brief definition of each term to help you grasp the full meaning of her philosophy of educating the young.

Montessori terms

Absorbent mind The ability and ease with which the young child learns unconsciously from his or her environment.

Control of error The self-correcting aspect inherent in the Montessori materials of making the mistakes made by the child apparent, thereby allowing for identification of the errors after completing the exercises and for correction of them.

Cycles of activity Those periods of concentration on a particular task that should be worked to completion.

Deviated child A child who has not yet found herself or himself and thus is restless and difficult to control.

Table 2.3 Key Concepts of Dewey's "My Pedagogic Creed"

Concepts	Current terms
Article I: What education is	
Cultural influences mold the individual.	Cultural education.
Socialization stimulates the inner being.	Children develop feelings through interaction with others.
Education is an internal process.	Children must react to stimuli on an individual basis.
Mental growth occurs both psychologically and sociologically.	A child's intellect develops from within as well as from a social setting.
It is impossible to prepare a child for a precise future.	As individuals grow and mature, their special abilities change.
An individual's interests and abilities are the basis for education.	Individualize instruction to meet a child's needs.
Article II: What the school is	
Schooling interprets a child's environment in the simplest terms and concepts.	The analysis of a child's environment is a school's responsibility.
School life should develop out of home life.	Schools and parents must work together.
School life builds and extends home life.	Start where the child is.
Schooling is not for the future but for the present.	Assess current needs and build in a special fashion.
Moral education occurs when an individual enters into a social unity of work and thought.	Provide many opportunities for children to think about why they do things.
The teacher selects the influences in the community that affect the individual and helps the individual respond to these influences.	The teacher is the selector of the goals to be attained by the child.
Discipline is a natural part of group living.	Provide many opportunities for children to interact in large and small groups.
Tests should be diagnostic and not for grading or promotion.	Evaluate progress to determine needs of children.
Article III: The subject-matter of education	
Social studies activities are the basis for the correlation of school subjects.	Social studies provide the setting for learning basic skills.
The arts are the center of the subject matter correlation.	Through the arts children express their creative responses to the learned subject matter.
Science is of value because it provides for interpretation and control of experience.	Observation and inquiry are essential to learning.
The language arts are social tools and devices for individual expression.	Oral and written expertise develops from social experiences and individual performance.

Table 2.3 (*cont.*)

Concepts	Current terms
Education is a continuing reconstruction of experience.	You only know what you have experienced.
Article IV: The nature of method	
Active experiences are better than passive experiences.	Children learn by doing.
Movement increases consciousness.	Children have to think when they move by design.
Observation of children's interests provides teachers with a basis for beginning teaching.	Observation of physical reactions of children is a valuable guide for assessing growth.
Emotions are an appropriate and desirable outcome of experiences.	The expression of feelings should be encouraged.
Article V: The school and social progress	
The ideal school provides for the needs of the individual and for the needs of society.	Individualized instruction develops creative, intelligent, and stable individuals.
The teacher not only provides for learning to occur but also participates in establishing social behavior.	A teacher is not only the guide but a participant in a child's education.

Source: John Dewey, "My Pedagogic Creed," *The School Journal*, 54.3 (January 1887), 77–80.

Didactic materials   The instructive materials used in teaching.

Discovery of the child   The young child's awareness and realization of his or her abilities and spontaneous love of work and learning.

Freedom   The child's free movements and experiences in an environment that provides discipline through liberty and respect for the child's rights.

Normalized child   A child who adapts easily and has acquired the self-discipline and control necessary to a healthy life.

Practical life exercises   Those exercises through which the child learns to care for himself or herself and for his or her environment.

Prepared environment   An atmosphere created to enable the child to learn through activity in orderly surroundings adapted to the child's size and interests.

Sensitive periods   Those periods of learning (to walk, to talk, to write, and so on) during which a child is particularly sensitive to a specific stimulus.

Sensorial exercises   Those exercises that center on the development of the five senses and that provide a foundation for speech, writing, and arithmetic using the sensorial materials.

Sensorial materials   The equipment designed to teach the child by focusing the mind on specific sensory responses.

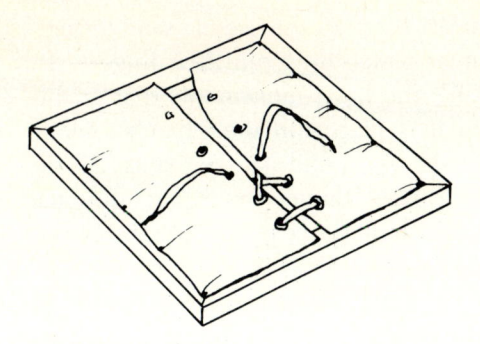

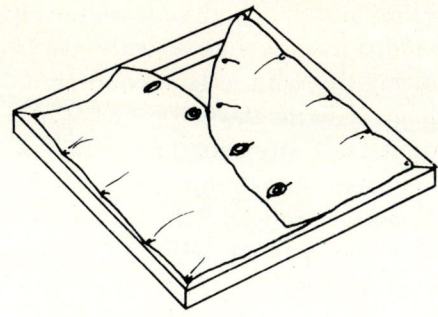

*Figure 2.1
Montessori Frames for
Buttoning Clothes and
Tying Shoelaces*

Criteria for Materials   Since Montessori believed that abstract experiences start the mind on paths to knowledge, she developed what she called *didactic materials*. The materials were to be simple but not easy to use. Didactic materials were also to be inherently interesting. Montessori emphasized that children should have repetitive games that include arranging and rearranging sets of the materials. Generally her rule was that teachers do not know what materials will interest a child until the *child* tries them. This is easy to accomplish if materials are available; the child will find something that interests him or her. Active play is work; boredom may occur, she said, if the teacher forces the situation, insisting that everyone be interested in the same story, demonstration, or lesson.

If the children work on their own, however, the materials must be self-correcting. Montessori stressed the idea that the teacher must not tell children they are wrong but should put the materials away to be tried again later. Unless the child can see whether an answer is right or wrong, didactic materials may be ineffective. This self-correcting quality was termed *objectivity* and is achieved when there are literal objects the child has arranged either correctly or incorrectly and which can then be examined.

If self-correcting materials are used well in a classroom, they must first be thoroughly comprehensible to the teacher. However self-checking the material may be, the teacher must know when to present or withhold it, how to verify what was learned, and how to improve or eliminate elements of error. The teacher is so important in the child's life that the teacher cannot avoid influencing what the child perceives. Apart from certain physical limitations, most materials are self-correcting only when a teacher makes them so.

Another aspect of Montessori materials, desirable for different reasons, is the involvement of muscles and the tactile sense in fundamental learning operations. The Montessori frames for buttoning clothes and tying shoelaces, excellent examples of this operation, have become standard equipment in early childhood programs (see Figure 2.1).

The most famous example of Montessori's use of muscles and the sense of touch is her prescription for teaching reading and writing. In the Montessori system, children learn the alphabet through the use of "sand letters" (sandpaper insets on smooth boards) over which they run their fingers. By tracing the sand letters, children acquire the basic movements that enable them to write the letters when a pencil is placed in their hands. Again, Montessori stressed the control of error: the child's finger runs off the sandpaper onto the smooth wood. One problem that occurs is "the muscular memory." "Indeed," she added, the child "sometimes recognizes the letters by touching them, when he cannot do so by looking at them."[4]

After learning the alphabet in this way, the child constructs words by using alphabet cards. The child takes the cards from a box and spells dictated words. The self-checking feature is that the child "will have the proof of the exact solution of his problem when he rereads the word." Having learned to trace and write the letters and to put words together with preprinted letter cards, the child discovers he or she can write whole words.

In mathematics, some of the Montessori materials have been outdated by Cuisenaire® rods. In the Montessori materials, the unit of length is greater than the unit of the cross section of the rod, which means that only addition and subtraction problems can be done. The Cuisenaire® rods, with a one-centimeter cube as the unit, provide opportunities for doing all four arithmetic processes: addition, subtraction, multiplication, and division.

Montessori's views of art and music were generally those of the nineteenth century; but she did feel that musical instruments should be invented for young children. She was careful to separate musical sounds from "disordered and ugly noises." In art, Montessori's definition of art was confined to the literal portrayal of reality. The child who painted a tree trunk red, for example, was not ready to advance in abstract education.

Influence Montessori's work still influences present instruction and methods. Not only are there many Montessori schools that deviate little from her original plan, but many of her materials are used in all early childhood programs. Dressing frames, sandpaper numbers and letters, movable alphabet letters, pictures and sounds, colored circles, scent bottles, sound bottles, command cards, rough and smooth boards, finger paint, and clay are all materials developed by Montessori. (However, as a teacher in the eighties, you would be mistaken to assume that only the materials developed by Montessori can accomplish her purposes.) In addition, as was true with Froebel and Dewey, many of Montessori's ideas have crept into our philosophy for teaching young children and have almost lost their identity.

[4] Maria Montessori, *The Montessori Method*, trans. Anne E. George (New York: Schocken Books, 1964), p. 277.

Child Study Movement

During the early 1920s there were very few experienced educators in the United States. Three who were experienced in working with young children — Bird Baldwin, Arnold Gesell, and G. Stanley Hall — began collecting what we now call *normative data information*. Bird Baldwin and his students kept "logs" on observations of children that included reactions to stimuli and the conditions of the settings where the observations took place. Gesell's writings and research began the concentration on the child rather than on abstract theory. Through timed visual observations and filmed observations, Gesell and his assistants began collecting data on young children in controlled settings. Using one-way viewing glass, soundproof rooms, and hidden cameras, data was collected with an exactness not tried by others. This emphasis began the child study movement. For more information on normative data, see Chapter 3.

The child study movement not only encouraged collection of normative data but also set the stage for research into the "why" of learning, behavior, and physical growth. From the child study data and the ensuing research, conflicting philosophies of education for young children developed.

One issue was the conflict between attitudes toward education. One faction (Frank, Dewey, and Erikson) believed that early education should be developmental and that as the child developed at his or her own rate the immediate environment, both physical and academic, should be enriched. The prime goal of these theorists was to develop social skills, foster self-expression, and provide for creativity. They also believed that the child's potential naturally occurred from within.

The other faction (Gesell, Stolz, Eliot, and McMillan) believed that education is enforcement from without. These individuals believed that structured environments, behavioral objectives, and competence-based instruction should be the goals of programs developed for young children.

There are varying degrees of acceptance of these two schools of thought and there are probably few pure examples of either. The author's position is a moderation of both sides of the issue. Enrichment experience should be available for all youngsters. Social skills, self-expression, and creativity are important aspects of human development. At the same time, however, a teacher must be competent in instruction, planning environments, and planning for accomplishment of behavioral objectives. A teacher certainly should be competent in human relationships, instructional techniques, and knowledge.[5]

---

[5] Two extremely interesting articles on this subject may provide more insights into the basic problems: David Elkind, "Preschool Education: Enrichment or Instruction?" *Childhood Education*, 45 (February 1969): 321–328; and Edyth Margolin, "Crucial Issues in Contemporary Early Childhood Education," *Childhood Education*, 45 (May 1969): 500–504.

From the beginning of the child study movement in the 1920s until World War II and the passage of the Lanham Act (1940), which provided federal funds for child care, little emphasis was placed on early education by educators or lay persons. In 1946, after the war had ended, the money stopped and programs ceased to exist. But interest in programs for young children still remained high with educators such as Hymes, Frank, and Hunt, who knew it made a difference.

In the late fifties and early sixties, persons interested in young children began to realize the great importance of the young child's environment on his or her potential development. At about the same time, poverty and the civil rights movement became important issues in the United States. In 1965, large federal grants were provided for programs for young children. The Head Start program was the first nationwide emphasis on programs for the young since the Lanham Act.

All of these developments had their beginning in the child study movement, which was the impetus for the search for the most appropriate means of educating young children.

Ruggles Street Nursery School

At about the same time the child study movement started, Abigail Eliot designed a program for the Ruggles Street Nursery School and Training Center. Part of the report she prepared in 1924 is of interest not only because of the theory of education it imparts but also because of its detailed descriptions of the activities.

[The main playroom contained low tables and chairs, blackboards, blossoming plants on low window sills, an aquarium containing goldfish, a sandbox, packing box, boxes of "mighty blocks," piano and low shelves.] In the toilet rooms beyond low sinks containing basins with low faucets and low soap containers: the mirrors are low, and so are the hooks for towels, combs, cups, tooth brushes, each marked with a child's name and a small distinguishing picture. Upstairs two large sleeping rooms are full of little beds, mostly of the folding variety for use out-of-doors in good weather; each child has his own bed and blanket sleeping bag. [The yard is complete with flower garden, pool and sandbox.] What do they do all day? During the hour when they are arriving, there is in attendance every day a nurse from the Community Health Association who inspects each child for symptoms of contagious disease. She also talks with the mothers about health problems, and the mothers in turn consult her; she helps teach the children health habits. The steadily growing group of children plays about, each as he chooses, until the nurse is ready to wind up with a unanimous gargle of salt and water — a fascinating noise truly! The next half hour is spent partly in the kindergarten "circle," but chiefly in music, rhythm work, songs, dramatic games, and "the band." Preparations follow for the mid-morning lunch — preparations all quite in the children's charge, from handwashing to placing of tables and chairs, passing the cups and napkins, pouring milk and handing out round crackers. Clearing up afterwards is also done by the children, in turn day by day; they wash and wipe the cups, clear the tables, sweep the floor.

Next follows a period of "quiet" occupations at tables or on the floor. With a little wise guidance perhaps, each child selects what he wants from a special closet containing a variety of material — certain of the kindergarten gifts, some of the Montessori apparatus, and some of Miss McMillan's; also chalk, scissors, paste, plasticine, hammers and nails, and several kinds of blocks.

In this work he is guided as little as possible and is limited only in two ways; he must make a genuine attempt to use what he has taken, and he must put away one thing before taking another. Sometimes a child will remain busily engaged with one occupation for as much as three-quarters of an hour; another may in the same length of time try his hand at three different things. Often the older children like to be gathered in a group to work out some simple "project." In due season, everyone is seen putting away his occupation and, if it is an out-of-doors day, lugging his chair within and perhaps replacing it by some of the big playthings . . . for this is the period of active play. . . .

Dinner hour is approaching. The company swarms again into the toilet rooms and with immense pride and zest prepares itself with an elaborate washing of faces and hands, combing of hair, drinking of water, and tying on of bibs. Even more than the luncheon, dinner gives scope for amazing baby achievements — patience in waiting, skill in passing, courtesy in giving and receiving — and all with perfect decorum yet perfect conduct.

Dinner over, they brush their teeth and clamber gaily upstairs, or trot out under the trees, take off their shoes, crawl into the bags, and sleep. After nearly two hours of sleep or quiet resting, they get up happy and fresh and are ready for a drink of orange juice and a romp or stories or games before going home.

Educational aspects

Education begins at birth. Much that many people think of as inherited is learned in the earliest years. These years are the most fruitful time for teaching, since a little child learns at a greater speed than he ever will again, and the early associations have a permanence which none formed in later life can rival. Psychologists say that the fundamental bases of character and personality are established during this period when the brain is growing. Mental hygienists are finding that the roots of mental and nervous disorders lie in maladjustments formed at the beginning of life.

Educationally all this may be called "habit." In the early years habits are easily formed, and these habits may be kept all through life. Habits of manner, behavior, interest, attitude have their foundation in the response of the little child to his environment. So the education of the nursery school children is guidance into good habits. Such education can be accomplished only by studying the children individually, by discovering what habits should be changed or developed. The schools herein described aim to create an environment in which self-control, self-development, and self-expression are encouraged, and to let the children live in it. Freedom within law, self-dependence, orderliness, love of beauty is the standard set.[6]

The philosophy for Miss Eliot's program developed over many years. Its fundamental principles, as listed in a 1944 report, indicate in a brief way how theory had changed from Froebelian influences.

Children are persons.
Education should always be thought of as guidance [teaching] that influences the development of persons [personalities].
Maturing and learning must go hand in hand in the process of development.
It is important that personalities be well balanced. Therefore in guiding children, we should aim to help them develop balancing traits at the same time that we try to supply what they need for self-realization. Some of the balancing traits are:
Security and growing independence
Self-expression and self-control
Awareness of self and social awareness
Growth in freedom and growth in responsibility
Opportunity to create and ability to conform.[7]

As is apparent from the quoted publication, the Ruggles Street Nursery School was fully operational in 1924. It is interesting to note that, if the language was updated and the name left off, the publication would be a rather accurate description of many of today's day-care facilities and programs.

Other Influences

Several individuals influenced the changes in early childhood education although they did not personally write or develop philosophies of education.

Patty Smith Hill, a great organizer and a strong advocate of John Dewey's ideas, was an early pioneer in establishing national organizations for the education of the young child. At Columbia Teachers College she influenced the thinking of many students and initiated a laboratory nursery school.

Another individual, Lawrence Frank, brought about considerable changes in early childhood education. In 1923 the Laura Spelman Rockefeller Memorial made five-year grants for research in child study and parent education. Lawrence Frank was the administrator of these grants. Under his guidance child development as we now know it became a reality.

An event also influenced the early childhood movement. In 1933 the Work Projects Administration (WPA) developed a plan whereby out-of-work school teachers taught young children who had been deprived because of

---

[6] Adapted from the Ruggles Street Nursery School and Nursery Training Center of Boston, May 1924.
[7] Nursery Training School of Boston, "Fundamental Principles" (mimeo), 1944.

the Depression. Two trends were initiated because of this government-financed program: education for the young became popular and professional educators became acquainted with programs and theories for teaching the young.

The increased influence of psychology and cultural anthropology have also added new dimensions to early childhood education. The broadening of our knowledge of the intellectual, social, and emotional development of children has increased teacher awareness of providing children with experiences and environments that enrich individuals rather than whole groups. Cultural anthropology has provided more accurate descriptions of the many diverse cultures in the United States and has added to our understanding of the relationships among these cultures and the general culture of the United States. Anthropology has made it easier for teachers to understand a child's cultural environment. The old adage "Take the child where you find him" has more meaning and becomes possible when you have information gathered from the area of cultural anthropology.

The Present

If we have learned anything over the last twenty years it is probably that there is no one way to teach children and that no one theory is best for all children. The studies of early childhood have expanded our knowledge of this field. New ideas, materials, equipment, and theories, based on reliable data, have been researched over a long period of time. We are now in an era of research and modification of practices. In the decade of the eighties, educators will solve some old problems and encounter new ones.

Changing roles and characteristics of the American family have led social scientists, educators, and parents to question what families need to support the development of their children. Recent social and economic trends have helped to shift a portion of the traditional family responsibilities for the care of children to specialists and institutions outside the family. Grants by the Administration for Children, Youth, and Families have provided funds for several in-depth research studies that have provided valuable new information about caring for children.

Because of the changing roles and characteristics of families, programs for young children now include infant day care, extended day care, school-age day care, respite care, occasional care, mother's-day-out programs, and home learning activities designed as packets or units by school systems. Early childhood programs are beginning to be developed as care extenders and as well as learning centers.

In the 1980s new emphasis on and study of how children learn to read and how reading should be taught form an important aspect of each early childhood program. Not only is the teaching of reading being scrutinized, but the teaching of each of the major subject areas (social studies, science,

PROJECT

An Inventory of What You Know

1. After studying this chapter, identify materials and equipment found in a classroom that you have observed as being products of Froebel, Montessori, Dewey, or a later philosopher.
2. Which philosophies of education do you think would work best to meet the special needs of the following groups of children? Justify your answers.

    Urban children
    Rural children
    Slum children
    Minority children
    Gifted children
    Slow learners
    Children with learning disabilities
    Children with other handicaps

3. Develop a social study unit integrating the skills and subjects recommended by John Dewey.
4. Select one of the political or economic events that affected education and explain the reasons for the event.

math, art, music, and so on) are also being analyzed and researched in regard to theory, content, and skill development as the basis for teaching the subject.

The 1980s will be an exciting period to be involved in the teaching of young children because of the possibilities to serve children and their families in a variety of innovative programs and curriculum approaches.

SUMMARY

A study of the history and the philosophies of early childhood education is important to today's educators in many ways. As a teacher you ought to be able to explain what you are doing and why you are doing it. A study of the past can help you understand how certain aspects of today's programs developed and how they are changing. A study of educational philosophy offers a basis for explaining the reasoning underlying the activities, planning, and materials selected for today's classrooms. Knowledge of educational history and philosophy will enable you to make judgments on whether or not "new" ideas are really new. It will also enable you to base your teaching methods on a philosophy and should provide a consistency in the type of activities you plan and the goals you set. As you teach young children, your planning and your goal setting should be structured around what you know about past developments and should be established before your school year begins.

ADDITIONAL READINGS

Archambault, Reginald D., ed. *John Dewey on Education — Selected Writings*. New York: Random House, 1964.

Auleta, Michael. *Foundations of Early Childhood: Readings*. New York: Random House, 1969.

Braun, Samuel J., and Esther P. Edwards. *History and Theory of Early Childhood Education*. 2nd ed. Belmont, Calif.: Wadsworth, 1977.

Cole, Luella. *A History of Education: Socrates to Montessori*. New York: Rinehart and Co., 1950.

Matthews, G. B. *Philosophy and the Young Child*. Cambridge, Mass.: Harvard University Press, 1980.

CHAPTER 3
Learning and Development

Exploration Tasks

After studying this chapter, you should be able to complete these tasks:
- Describe some of the various theories of learning.
- List Piaget's four stages of intellectual development.
- Describe how children learn in the preoperational stage.
- List and explain the factors that affect how children learn.
- Identify several research findings on how children learn.
- Describe the normative data information for three, four, and five year olds.
- Identify and describe the basic needs of children.
- List the characteristics of exceptional children.

You cannot hurry human growth.
It is slow and quiet.
Quiet and slow
As the growth of the tree.

Agnes Snyder

OVERVIEW

Foundation courses in psychology are usually required of persons planning to be teachers. These courses are the basis for understanding how children acquire knowledge and for comprehending children's intellectual and social growth and development. From learning theories and from the normative-descriptive data collected by researchers who have observed large numbers of children, teachers can gain insight into the general characteristics of young children.

This chapter discusses the basic theories of learning and child development that teachers of young children should understand. For those of you who have not yet studied these topics it will serve as a concise introduction. For those of you who have explored these topics in a previous course, this chapter will help you review and recall the information that you learned. The chapter concludes with an examination of the special needs and characteristics of exceptional children.

THE LEARNING PROCESS

Why does one child want to learn, while another does not? Why does one child remember the events of a story while another forgets? How can more children be stimulated and helped to want to learn, to learn well, and to remember what they learn? The answers to all of these questions are determined to a large extent by what you, the teacher, understand about the learning process.

The experiences children have in school are influenced by what the teacher regards as learning. The responsibility of the teacher, therefore, is to provide a classroom environment that stimulates and guides learning, for it is through interaction with the environment that children learn.

Theories of Learning

What is a theory? A *theory* is an organized system of knowledge related to procedures, principles, or assumptions that is designed to explain how something works. In education, a theory is an idea, plan, or scheme developed to explain how children learn, how they should be taught, and/or what they should be taught. The complexity of the analysis of facts and the original thought required to develop a theory of education explain why there are not many theories and why the application of existing theories is slow to be changed or modified.

Learning theories (sometimes called *systems*) are related to the philosophical and psychological foundations from which they were developed. An *open theory* is one that states that the internal process in a human is what determines learning; a *closed theory* is one that emphasizes external forces that determine learning; and a *transitional theory* is one that uses

Table 3.1 Influences upon Educational Thinking

Open systems	Transitional systems	Closed systems
Phenomenology	Progressivism	Behaviorism
		Cultural transmission
		Mechanism
Child-centered	Interactionism	Society-centered
	Transactional psychology	
Subjective psychology	Humanistic psychology	Objective psychology
Rationalism	Transcendentalism	Analytic philosophy
Humans mold the environment	Humans mold the environment — humans are molded by the environment	Humans are molded by the environment
Emphasis on internal states		Emphasis on internal states
Rousseau	Plato	Watson
Freud	Hegel	Skinner
A. S. Neill	Kant	
Rogers	Dewey	
Combs	Piaget	

Reprinted from I. V. Ahnell, "Implementing an Open Model for Inservice Competency Development," in *Inservice Education Programs to Improve Teaching Competence*, ATE Bulletin No. 39 (Washington, D.C.: Association of Teacher Educators, 1975), p. 13.

aspects of both open and closed theories. (In some texts and in Table 3.1 the word *system* is used instead of *theory*).

Table 3.1 lists the concepts and people who have influenced learning theories from a philosophical and psychological viewpoint and categorizes them by the type of learning system they represent. Let us examine more closely some of these important theories.

Acquisition of Knowledge and Skills (Mechanism) For many years learning was regarded as identical to knowing. The proof of learning, according to this theory, lay in the child's ability to repeat to the teacher material the child had memorized. This concept of learning influenced every part of the traditional school program. Seats were fastened to the floor in rows. Whole-group recitations and responses were required, and children were expected to memorize their textbooks or information given to them orally by their teacher. There was no problem solving or development of children's interests; motivation was based on rewards and punishment; evaluation of learning was by formal tests of memory; and movement up through the grades usually resulted from the achievement of minimal marks. This type of learning theory is an example of a closed system.

Interactionism Recent years have seen acceptance of the view that learning involves the modification of behavior and comes about through interaction with the environment.[1] According to this theory, the acquisition of knowledge and skills represents only a part of the learning process. Learning takes place only when an individual has an experience that influences behavior and makes him or her a different person.

This concept considers the influence of more factors in the learning environment than does the learning-is-knowledge concept. While it is true that a child may learn from a textbook, a child may also learn from another child, from something seen on a trip, or from something that happens on the bus. Learning is a function of the child's total environment. This concept also describes the effects of the learning experience upon personality or character. The child who has really learned will behave differently in the future. This theory is an example of transitional system.

Rationalism In the rationalistic point of view, individuals mold their environment. Emphasis is placed on the internal process of thinking through problems. Learning takes place when teachers or other individuals pose situations that require children to rationalize what is required to be done. This theory is an example of an open system.

Behaviorism The behavioristic view of learning, whether called stimulus-response, conditioning, trial-and-error learning, or bond psychology, is based on common assumptions. It assumes that wholes are built from parts and that learning is an additive process. The learner reacts as a collection of parts rather than as a unified whole; repetition and drill precede learning. The many experiments with animals are the basis of the behavioristic concept of the learning process. This theory is an example of a closed system.

Humanistic Psychology According to humanistic theorists, learning is a growth process and is the result of inheritance, insight, maturation, and differentiation rather than repetition. In the mental growth of the child, whole concepts come first; parts have meaning because of their relationship

---

[1] Burton L. White, B. T. Kaban, and J. S. Attonucci, *The Origins of Human Competence: The Final Report of the Harvard Preschool Project* (Lexington, Mass.: D.C. Heath & Co., 1979).

to the whole. The child's first concepts are class concepts. Any animal may be called "dog." Later the concepts become specific and the child differentiates between "dog" and "cat." Social studies unit experiences, learning to read through experience charts, and the teaching of whole concepts in math, music, art, and language first are examples of the humanistic concept. This theory is an example of a transitional system.

Eclecticism Approaches to learning that combine aspects from each of the learning theories are receiving support from some psychologists. Ernest R. Hilgard believes that each theory of learning has something to offer. A. T. Jersild feels that the child-centered approach should use all approaches to learning as an aid in teaching. J. W. Tilton recommends that educators should be eclectic and that it is impossible to avoid eclecticism.

Newer Approaches Many advances in learning theories have resulted from direct observation of children's behavior. As a result of such studies, John Dollard and Neal Miller have identified four elements that must be present for a child to learn: The child must *want* something, *notice* something, *do* something, and *get* something.[2]

Other studies have led Marylou Ebersole et al. to develop a list of six stages of learning.[3] Each stage builds on the previous stage although there is some overlapping at each stage. In contrast to Piaget's theory of learning (which we will discuss shortly), ages are not emphasized. According to these researchers, if any stage is omitted or insufficiently experienced, learning problems will develop. The six stages are:

1. *Gross motor stage* Children acquire information about their environment as they move. They learn how to coordinate motor behavior and adapt it to specific situations. The gross motor stage has four components: locomotion (the body moving through space), balance and posture, contact with objects, and contact with moving objects.
2. *Motor-perceptual stage* Children relate data they have acquired during motor explorations to data gained through their senses.
3. *Perceptual-motor stage* Children acquire the ability to match their perceptual information with motor information. They go toward or move away from what they see or hear.
4. *Perceptual stage* Children are able to differentiate one perception from another without the intervening motor activity. For example, they can look at fruit and discriminate between oranges, apples, and bananas without having to feel each one.

[2] John Dollard and Neal E. Miller, *Personality and Psychotherapy* (New York: McGraw-Hill, 1950).

[3] Marylou Ebersole et al., *Steps to Achievement for the Slow Learner* (Columbus, Ohio: Charles E. Merrill, 1968).

5. *Perceptual-conceptual stage* Children can deal with perceptual similarities and form concepts (that is, form ideas that include many different aspects of information already known).
6. *Conceptual stage* Children learn to group perceptual information into meaningful generalizations. An element of abstract thinking is involved in this stage, although it is still based on concrete perceptual motor information. Relating perceptions by space, time, and use teaches the development of a concept.

Piaget's Theory of Intellectual Development

A discussion of learning and young children is not complete without a description of Jean Piaget's theory of how children learn and grow intellectually. Jean Piaget (1896–1980), a Swiss psychologist, received his first training in biology; at the age of 24 he began his study of psychology. At 25 he joined the Jean Jacques Rousseau Institute in Geneva, where he initiated his studies into the thought processes of children. Piaget published his findings and conclusions in many articles and books. During the 1930s his ideas received much attention and were widely discussed in the United States. This interest was revived in the late 1960s and early 1970s. Today Piaget is considered by many educators to be the foremost theorist in intellectual development.

Basic Concepts The following general summary of Piaget's main ideas will help you understand his theory that children, moving through stages of mental development, have different abilities at different stages.

Intellectual development occurs, according to Piaget, because of two inborn attributes, which he called organization and adaptation. *Organization* is the building of simpler processes, such as seeing, touching, naming, and hearing, into higher-order mental structures. Through these processes, an individual composes his or her own systems of understanding the environment. *Adaptation* is the continuing change that occurs in an individual as a result of interactions with the environment. Adaptation occurs as the individual (1) assimilates experiences, (2) fits them into existing mental structures, and (3) modifies the mental structures that do not fit so that they are ready for inclusion of the experience. Mental development is influenced by four interrelated factors: maturation, experience, and social interaction, along with a factor called *equilibration* — the joining of the previous three factors to build and rebuild mental structures.

Children have mental structures that differ from those of adults. Because of this, they have their own way of determining reality and viewing their environment. Children's mental development progresses through four definite stages that occur in a fixed sequence that is the same for all children. Although these stages occur in a fixed order, different children move from one stage to another stage at different ages. A child may simultaneously function in one stage for some topics and in a different stage for other topics.

The four stages of mental development are as follows:

1. *Sensorimotor (ages 0–2)*   In this stage children learn from sensory experiences, such as smelling and touching, and from motor activities or body movements.
2. *Preoperational (ages 2–7)*   During this stage children reason and explain through intuition rather than logic. They have difficulty expressing the order of events, explaining relationships, understanding numbers and their relations, understanding what others say accurately, and understanding and remembering rules.
3. *Concrete operational (ages 7–11)*   In this stage children develop concepts of numbers, relationships, and processes. They attack problems mentally but still think in terms of concrete objects, not abstractions.
4. *Formal operational (ages 11–15)*   In this stage children use abstractions and form theories about everything.

Operations, actions carried out mentally, are necessary components of rational thought. The two types of operations are conservation and reversibility. *Conservation* is the recognition that properties such as number, length, or quantity (volume) remain the same regardless of changes in grouping, order, position, or shape. *Reversibiity* is the recognition that any change in order, position, or shape can be reversed to return to the original order, position, or shape.

Teachers can derive many useful pronciples from Piaget's theory of learning, including the following:

- Children's mental development imposes limits and conditions on what and on how they learn.
- Children's thoughts develop from actions and not from oral or written words.
- Knowledge cannot be given to children but must be discovered and constructed through the children's own activities.
- Children learn best from concrete [real] experiences.
- By nature children are active, continuously seeking to find out about and make sense of their environment. As a result they remake their mental structures, which allows for more complex thought. The remaking of mental structures makes possible learning that is stable and lasting. When the necessary mental structures are not present, learning is not usable and will not last.

Learning in the Preoperational Stage   The preoperational stage of intuitive thought, which Piaget said occurs between ages two and seven, covers the period of intellectual growth of children studied in this book. Therefore,

Children learn best from concrete, hands-on experiences.

we will take a closer look at this stage, especially in regard to ten specific areas: language, thinking and reasoning, classification and relationships, numbers, honesty, acceptance and obedience, guilt and punishment, rules and games, competition, and social behavior.

Verbal language is of two types — communicative and egocentric. *Communicative speech* transmits information or asks questions. *Egocentric speech* consists of a monologue or mimicking sounds and words. According to Piaget, 40 percent of the total talk of children in this stage is egocentric speech. Teachers of young children should be aware of the fact that it is perfectly normal for children aged two to seven to talk to themselves. The children do not have the ability to listen accurately, and they have difficulty understanding each other or remembering directions more than one step at a time. They have begun to use verbal mental images and more sophisticated words and expressions (which they may not understand). Arguments are also normal. Their vigorous verbal squabbles can have a devastating effect on feelings. Name-calling is particularly harmful, according to Piaget, and should be strongly discouraged.

The lack of *logical thinking and reasoning* in young children is probably the most troublesome for adults. At this stage young children do not think through operations. They cannot add and subtract, follow steps in problem solving, group and regroup, put events in order, name steps in a process, or describe how to get from one place to another.

Classification and relationship skills develop rapidly in the preoperational stage. Children become capable of making collections and can group and regroup within the collection. Most children aged two to five cannot arrange objects in order (smallest to largest, shortest to longest). By the age of six, though, they can do this very accurately, although they may do so through trial and error. Six year olds can usually pair objects on a one-to-one relationship, but this may also be done by trial-and-error.

Piaget's explanation of *number conceptualization* surprised most teachers of young children because most teachers believed that as soon as children can count they can begin learning basic number facts. Piaget's studies showed that counting and conservation of numbers do not follow each other. Regular classroom teachers have found that children aged six or even younger can add and subtract, but Piaget insisted that children cannot do and understand number operations until they are able to establish one-to-one correspondence in sets and to conserve that correspondence (to realize that the number doesn't change when the objects are rearranged).

Honesty, or knowledge of the difference between fact and fiction, is not a common trait of children in the preoperational stage. Fiction or tall tales are generally not tolerated by teachers. Children at this age do not actually lie, intending to deceive; they get facts mixed up. An event may just sound better the way they tell it; or if one child tells an experience, another child may just claim to have done the same thing.

Acceptance and obedience are slow to develop and sometimes nonexistent in children aged two and three (the "terrible twos" is a phrase often used to characterize this age group). For children aged four and five, acceptance and obedience are normal reactions to adult authority. Obedience is an individual matter; the children have no conception of whole-class responsibility nor do they expect to be punished for the misbehavior of others. By ages six and seven, this total acceptance of adult authority begins to weaken, although generally children in this age group obey adults.

Guilt and punishment, according to Piaget's studies, are a normal happening in the minds of young children. Guilt is being caught misbehaving and misbehaving is just disobeying adult rules. Therefore, punishment is natural, expected, and necessary.

Rules and games become necessary as the child becomes more social. Favorite games such as tag and hide-and-seek require rules on how the game is played, not on who wins. Young children will follow only the simplest rules and probably will break them because they can't remember two things at once — what they want to do and how to do it.

Competition in work or play means nothing or little to children aged two to seven. Each child plays or works for the fun of it. Winning, losing, or playing against others has no meaning.

Social behavior changes at ages six and seven from self-centered play to more participation in games. Others are wanted in play, not merely tolerated. Children at this stage are highly imitative; a weird noise, a funny face, or a funny walk will cause laughing and imitation of the noise or gesture.

The extent of Piaget's research cannot be summarized completely in such a short overview. As more individuals become aware of Piaget's findings and of how they pertain to the teaching of young children, more exact and purposeful teaching will result.

FACTORS INFLUENCING LEARNING

There are many factors that influence each child's learning. Some of these factors are briefly described on the following pages. An awareness of these factors will help you achieve your basic teaching objective: to ensure that the individuals you teach learn.[4]

The Teacher The teacher is the organizer, the preparer of materials, the selector of subject matter, the presenter, the guide, the helper; the child is the learner. Before, during, and after teaching, the teacher should analyze instruction using the following guidelines:

1. Every lesson should begin with easily related materials.
2. Every task must be broken down into specific components.
3. In some learning situations, the task to be learned is the last thing to be done. Because of this, the sequence must sometimes be taught backwards.
4. Some tasks are "drill" tasks and therefore must be taught by repetition.
5. Desired responses should be analyzed into sequential steps, always allowing for individual differences in scope and depth of understanding.
6. Seeing or hearing someone else being rewarded has a positive effect on group learning.

---

[4] The factors discussed here are listed in Norman Tallent and Charlotte Spungin, *Psychology: Understanding Ourselves and Others* (New York: American Book Company, 1972) and in Ernest R. Hiligard and Richard C. Alkinson, *Introduction to Psychology*, 4th ed. (New York: Harcourt, 1967). The ideas for the discussion of each factor were found in Muriel Beadle, *A Child's Mind*, 2nd ed. (New York: Doubleday, 1975) and in *Annual Editions Readings in Human Development 1973–74* (Guilford, Conn.: Dushkin, 1973).

58 / Foundations

Motivated and interested children are important to the success of any learning activity.

7. Every new task should include active involvement (manipulation of materials, physical action, or verbal response), knowledge on the part of the child of the desired result (goal setting), feedback for the child regarding progress, and some type of reward (praise, grades, a smile, a pat on the back, or special privileges).

Individual Differences Children differ in intelligence, temperament, personality, environmental influences, and learning patterns.

Motivation Interest and attention to tasks can be developed from past success in accomplishing similar tasks. Attention and curiosity can be promoted by creating a reasonable amount of excitement. Attention is a learned response and should be rewarded.

Retention The time that elapses between the learning experience and its use does not directly influence the process of forgetting. During this time lapse, however, interjection of new experiences may interfere with or change what was learned. The interference of new experiences can be reduced by planning lessons for review and maintenance. Teachers should make a point of teaching the similarities and differences between old and new experiences and the children's responses to such experiences. Children should have numerous opportunities for transference and reinforcement — learning the given task by practicing it in varying situations.

Transfer When a child is having difficulty with a task, prior learning may be interfering or the child may not be identifying the similarities and differences between the new lesson and previous lessons. Teachers can expect identical stimuli to transfer. When there is no transfer, the teacher should attempt to identify some differences in the new situation.

Understanding Understanding occurs when the child has had prior appropriate learning experiences. Understanding is best developed when a child has a *spiral continuity* of learning tasks; that is, when learning proceeds from the simple and concrete illustrations to the more complex and abstract concepts. Do not teach isolated tasks or a high-level task before establishing a background for the tasks. This concept is developed more fully in later chapters.

Reinforcement Children should always be aware of their progress in learning a given task. Rewards for positive results should be immediate. Children should not be punished to weaken responses. Punishment may be used to inhibit and to control physical behavior, but when used as reinforcement, it should be immediate. The child must relate the punishment to unacceptable responses, not to interfering stimuli. Never let a child end a lesson with an error as a last response.

Research on Learning

Research on learning and attention to those environmental factors that influence learning will help teachers understand why children differ in physical, social, emotional, and intellectual abilities. The following brief comments on various findings of researchers may help you recall the detailed information given in psychology courses. Note, however, that some findings are conflicting.

Because brain growth is rapid during the child's first year, a child who does not have an adequate, balanced diet during that year may be permanently stunted. Malnutrition after age two will probably not produce lasting physical effects (Eichenwald and Fry, 1969).[5] After birth, the tissue for motor maturity appears to develop first, with sensory, visual, and au-

Tiger Lil had been a nursery school cat all her life, so it was perfectly natural that she should be nurturing her four babies in a box especially decorated by the children and placed in a sheltered spot in the room. One day, while the children were resting on their mats, Tiger Lil decided to move her family to the doll bed in the housekeeping corner. The resting children watched as she carried each kitten one by one to the doll bed. After the fourth kitten had been placed in the bed, she didn't return to the box. The teacher said, "She knows she has each of her kittens." Whereupon Doug piped up, "She knows how to subtract. You know one by one until they are all gone."

---

[5] H. Eichenwald and P. Fry, "Nutrition and Learning," *Science*, 163 (1969): 644–648.

PROJECT
Identifying Learning Processes

As a teacher you will have opportunities to observe children as they learn. These observational experiences can be an excellent time to reinforce your own knowledge of how children learn and how teachers prepare for optional learning performances. The following are examples of observations of classroom teachers observing other teachers teach. Can you identify the learning process that occurred in each situation? Write a brief summary of the teaching techniques used in the space provided. (The first three have been done for you as examples.)

Observation of three year olds: Recess

What was taught	*Learning process*
1. To form a line	Following oral directions
2. To walk and stay in line	
3. To do things for themselves	Following oral directions and learning from example
4. Safety on the playground	Problem solving

What did the children learn?

1. To form a line before walking out of the classroom
2. To walk and stay in line while walking to the playground
3. To wait while one child tied shoelaces
4. To sit down on the swings while swinging and to sit down on the merry-go-round instead of hanging over the bars

Evaluation

1. Each child stood behind another child before walking outside.
2. Almost all stayed behind those they were walking behind while on the way to the playground.
3. Mary said to Marilyn, "Fix it, Marilyn, we'll wait for you," thereby encouraging self-reliance. Everyone else waited in line while she tied her shoelaces.

4. All went as a group to the swings. Before swinging they were asked what to do on the swings and they responded in unison, "Sit down."

Observation of four year olds: Science

What was taught   *Learning process*
1. Where squirrels build nests (in trees)
2. What you might find in a book with a picture of a squirrel on the front
3. Practice in recognizing pictures of animals in a book
4. Concept of "animal" ("a squirrel is an animal; a dog is an animal")
5. Remembering (naming animals that were in a book after the book was closed)
6. How mother cats carry kittens (When one child told of her mother cat carrying her kittens, the teacher quieted the other children to listen.)

What did the children learn
1. Where and how squirrels live
2. To pronounce animal names
3. To recall names of animals when pictures are out of sight

Evaluation
1. Children discussed twigs dropped by squirrel in trying to build a nest.
2. Children called out (individually) names of animals found in book.

Observation of five year olds: Art

What was taught   *Learning process*
1. Art: cutting, staying on orange line, designing, or drawing
2. Eye-hand coordination
3. Colors
4. Uses of chalk (different)
5. Taking turns

61

What did the children learn   *Learning process*

1. To use chalk on construction paper
2. To blend and use different colors together
3. To create their own design or picture
4. To use and handle scissors correctly
5. To follow the line drawn by the teacher and stay on it to form a certain thing
6. To wait their turn before going to one of the easels

Evaluation

1. Each child in the group selected one or more colors of chalk and used it to draw or blend with another color. Each turned in a chalk picture for his or her folder.
2. Some children turned in tempera paintings; others waited their turn at the easel.
3. Some children cut and stayed on the line and told the teacher what their cut-out form was (worm, snake, or other).
4. No trouble was evidenced while handling the scissors.

ditory maturity developing later (Tanner, 1964).[6] Most brain growth after birth occurs in building pathways that connect and coordinate the primary areas — motor, sensory, auditory, and visual (Diggory, 1972).[7]

Institutionalized infants under one year of age showed a drastic reduction in development; the impairment was irreversible (Spitz, 1945).[8] Data suggest that extreme social deprivation can be overcome to some extent by remediation efforts initiated when children are a year old (Skeels et al., 1938,

---

[6] J. M. Tanner, "Human Growth and Constitution," in *Human Biology: An Introduction to Human Evolution, Variation, and Growth*, eds. G. Harrison et al., (New York: Oxford University, 1964).

[7] Sylvia Farnham-Diggory, *Cognitive Process in Education: A Psychological Preparation for Teaching and Curriculum Development* (New York: Harper & Row, 1972).

[8] R. Spitz, "Hospitalism: An Inquiry into the Genesis of Psychiatric Conditions in Early Childhood," in *Influences on Human De-Development*, ed. Urie Bronfenbrenner (Hinsdale, Ill.: Dryden, 1972).

1948, 1966).[9] Disadvantaged children often have no stable representation of the real world and no intrinsic motivation to construct and differentiate activities.[10] Children from disadvantaged homes do not play with words or materials as advantaged children do (Murphy, 1972).[11]

Disdvantaged adults use language primarily for social reasons, not for logical reasoning and problem solving (Bernstein, 1958, 1961).[12] Homes of disadvantaged children have high noise levels; children do not receive the repetition, explanations, and general patterning of sounds needed to develop fine auditory discriminations (Hunt, 1961; Bloom, Davis, and Hess, 1965; Deutsch and others, 1967).[13] Children can learn by listening and looking without manipulating, touching, or "experiencing" objects (Bandura, 1963, 1968).[14] Environment plays a regulatory role; a biologically mature human does not develop complete symbolic representative systems without adults or experiences to help stucture the world in complex and highly different ways (Bruner, 1966, and Anglin, 1973).[15] If a child is to organize his or her world, consistency is a requirement. Designated activity areas in a classroom help the child accomplish this (Diggory, 1972).[16]

During the preoperational (intuitive) stage (ages 2–7), the child represents the world in actions, in images, or in words (Bruner, 1966).[17] Although five

---

[9] H. Skeels, R. Updegraff, B. Wellman, and H. Williams, "A Study of Environmental Stimulation: An Orphanage Preschool Project," *University of Iowa Studies in Child Welfare*, 15.4 (1938); H. Skeels and I. Harms, "Children with Inferior Social Histories: Their Mental Development in Adoptive Homes," *Journal of Genetic Psychology*, 72 (1948): 264–294; H. Skeels, "Adult Status of Children with Contrasting Early Life Experiences: A Follow-up Study," *Monographs of the Society for Research in Child Development*, 31.3 (1966).

[10] P. Wolff, "Operational Thought and Social Adaptation," in *Play and Development: A Symposium*, ed. Maria W. Piers (New York: Norton, 1972).

[11] L. Murphy, "Infants' Play and Cognitive Development," in *Play and Development: A Symposium*, ed. Maria W. Piers (New York: Norton, 1972).

[12] B. Bernstein, "Some Sociological Determinants of Perception," *British Journal of Sociology*, 9 (1958): 159–174; B. Bernstein, "Social Structure, Language, and Learning," *Educational Research*, 3 (1961): 163–194.

[13] Benjamin Bloom, A. Davis, and R. Hess, *Compensatory Education for Cultural Deprivation* (New York: Holt, Rinehart & Winston, 1965); J. M. Hunt, *Intelligence and Experience* (New York: Ronald, 1961); Martin Deutsch, A. Levinson, B. Brown, and E. Peisach, "Communication of Information in the Elementary School Classroom," in *The Disadvantaged Child: Studies of the Social Environment and the Learning Process*, eds. Martin Deutsch et al. (New York: Basic Books, 1967).

[14] A. Bandura, "Social-Learning Theory of Identificatory Processes," in *Handbook of Socialization Theory and Research*, ed. David A. Goslin (Chicago: Rand McNally, 1969).

[15] Jerome Bruner and Jeremy M. Anglin, eds., *Beyond the Information Given: Studies in the Psychology of Knowing* (New York: Norton, 1973); Jerome Bruner, *Toward a Theory of Instruction* (Cambridge, Mass.: Harvard University Press, 1966).

[16] Sylvia Farham-Diggory, *Cognitive Process in Education*.

[17] Jerome Bruner, "Toward a Theory of Instruction, Poverty and Childhood," in *The Preschool in Action*, ed. R. Parker (Boston: Allyn and Bacon, 1972).

year olds did not spontaneously use paper visual models as memory aids, they were easily taught to do so (Corsini, Pick, and Flavell, 1968).[18] Three to five year olds were taught to use pictures as cues for remembering the spatial locations of toys; they learned to use a picture as a guide for placing zoo animals in a cage (Ryan, Heglon, and Flavell, 1969).[19] Lists of paired words were best taught to younger children by action sentences. The types of sentences used in the study were conjunctive (the cat *and* the table), prepositional (the cat is *under* the table), and verb action (the cat *bites* the table) (Rohwer, 1970).[20]

A comparison of many experimental studies of learning concluded that no learning theory accounts for all of the data concerning how children learn. The two most common sources of learning difficulty were failure to pay attention to stimuli and inability to determine the critical features by which the stimuli differ (Stevenson, 1970).[21]

During the 1970s many research studies were undertaken in the field of helping young children learn to read. Goetz (1979), Nurss (1980), and Spodek (1979) conducted review research to find out what methods were used to teach reading to young children.[22] The most commonly used approach is called ideational orientation (language approach) by most researchers (Feldman, 1977; Halliday, 1970).[23] Other research studies were conducted in the area of decoding instruction as a means of intitial reading instruction for young children. This is called skill orientation by most researchers (Smith, Otto, and Hansen, 1978).[24] Loban (1978) researched both methods and found similar behaviors in both means of instruction.[25]

---

[18] D. Corsini, A. Pick, and John H. Flavell, "Production Deficiency of Nonverbal Mediators in Young Children," *Child Development*, 39 (1968): 53–58.

[19] S. Ryan, A. Heglon, and John H. Flavell, "Nonverbal Mediation in Preschool Children" (mimeo, Minneapolis: University of Minnesota, 1969).

[20] W. Rohwer, "Images and Pictures in Children's Learning: Research Results and Educational Implications," *Psychological Bulletin*, 73 (1970): 393–403; W. Rohwer, "Implications of Cognitive Development for Education," in *Carmichael's Manual of Child Development*, 3rd ed., Vol. 1, ed. Paul H. Mussen (New York: Wiley, 1970).

[21] H. Stevenson, "Learning in Children," in *Carmichael's Manual of Child Psychology*, 3rd ed., Vol 1, ed. Paul H. Mussen (New York: Wiley, 1970).

[22] E. M. Goetz, "Early Reading: A Developmental Approach," *Young Children*, 34, no. 5 (1979): 4–11; J. R. Nurss, "Research in Review. Linguistic Awareness and Learning to Read," *Young Children*, 35, no. 3 (1980): 57–66; B. Spodek, "Early Reading and Preprimary Education," (paper presented at the annual meeting of the American Educational Research Association, San Francisco, April 1979).

[23] C. F. Feldman, "Two Functions of Language," *Harvard Educational Review*, 47 (August 1977): 282–293; M. A. K. Halliday, "Language Structure and Language Function," in *New Horizons in Linguistics*, ed. J. Lyons (Baltimore: Penguin, 1970).

[24] R. J. Smith, W. Otto, and L. Hansen, *The School Reading Program* (Boston: Houghton Mifflin, 1978).

[25] W. Loban, "Our Expanding Vision of Reading," *Claremont Reading Conference 42nd Yearbook* (Claremont, Calif.: The Claremont Reading Conference, 1978).

Research studies on the learning styles of black children were also undertaken in the 1970s. Guttentag (1972) found that black children may learn faster with techniques that involve movement in the learning process.[26] Boykin (1977)[27] found that varying the format in problem-solving tasks increased performance for black children.

A new phase of research on learning (1980), brain functioning research, has brought new insights to child development and education. Educators are delving into the scientific research in hemispheric lateralization, neurological development, recognitive processes, and neurochemistry. Recent educational literature documents the importance of the study of the brain and learning.

GROWTH AND DEVELOPMENT

In reviewing growth and development, descriptive data are important because the characteristics of real children — physical, emotional, intellectual, and interpersonal — prescribe the program, activities, methods, and materials to be used in the classroom.[28]

Normative Data

Although individual children may not always fit these general normative patterns exactly, teachers can use these data to gain insight into the general characteristics of young children at specific age levels. By comparing their classroom observations with research data on growth and development, teachers will be better able to identify severe deficiencies in particular students. These comparisons can also aid teachers in individualizing curriculum content, methods, and activities to the needs of their students.

The classic studies done by Arnold Gesell and Frances L. Ilg and by Jean Piaget are the bases of the many, more recent studies. The following general characteristics of three, four, five, and six year olds common to these studies will aid teachers in establishing goals for their curriculum.

The Three Year Old

Physical Gaining greater motor activity and improved coordination, three year olds maintain a better balance and equilibrium than two year olds when running. Three year olds are more vigorous and boisterous than two

---

[26] M. Guttentag, "Negro-White Differences in Children's Movement," *Perceptual and Motor Skills*, 35 (1972): 435–436.

[27] A. W. Boykin, "Psychological/Behavioral Verve in Academic/Task Performance: Three Theoretical Considerations," *Negro Education* (1978): 343–354.

[28] For more information, read Doria Pilling and Mia Kellmer Pringle, *Controversial Issues in Child Development*. (New York: Schocken Books, 1978).

year olds and like to play with large blocks, wagons, slides, and other equipment. This play develops large muscles.

Three year olds become more skillful with their hands. They can draw a crude circle, can pour a half-pint of milk into a glass, and enjoy using clay and crayons.

Emotional A two year old's favorite word is "no." But at three, children like to give and share. They are more cooperative and like to conform. They still have difficulty handling emotional energy and still have temper tantrums; however, the outbursts happen less frequently and do not last as long. The three year old can be jealous of a younger brother or sister.

Because they are curious, they can become unintentionally destructive, pulling up flowers or pulling an arm off a doll.

Intellectual Three year olds understand simple questions, statements, and directions. They ask many questions and understand more words than they use. Abstract words are beyond their understanding.

They like stories rich in sense impressions and actions and are most responsive to things that move: boats, animals, other children. Rhythm, repetition, and humor please them.

Interpersonal Three year olds have a great desire to please. They still like parallel play but are beginning to share and take turns. Mother is the favorite companion. They look to her for security, recognition, and encouragement.

The Four Year Old

Physical Four year olds become noisier, speedier, and stormier as the days pass. They hit, kick, jump up and down, and love to dash off in the opposite direction. Destructive action, such as throwing stones or breaking something, is fully intentional now.

At the same time they are becoming more skilled in motor activities such as skipping, running, or jumping — all at breakneck speed. Boys and girls like to throw balls, cut, saw, lace, color, and build with small blocks.

Emotional Four year olds are not too concerned about the feelings of others and are not very sensitive to praise or blame. Sometimes they praise themselves by bragging. They like to pursue their own course, and occasional frustrations generally do not bother them much.

Intellectual They constantly ask questions. Their imagination is limitless and what they tell is a mixture of truth and fiction. They have fun with their imaginary friends. They go from one activity to another and dislike repetition. Dramatization of simple stories, group singing about everyday experiences, and informational material delights them.

Interpersonal "No, I won't!" is the order of the day for four year olds. They are defiant but they do want to be like others in their group. They like to talk on the phone and take short trips. They may become very silly and call people silly names or they may become very bossy.

The Five Year Old

Physical Five year olds are poised and controlled. They swing, climb, jump, and skip with dexterity. They busily engage in purposeful activity. Painting, drawing, coloring, cutting, and pasting are great fun. Riding or pushing wheeled toys is satisfying. They like to copy designs, letters, numbers; some five year olds can print their names. They are fascinated by puzzles and tools. They are able to dress, wash, and feed themselves.

Emotional The five year old is more conservative in action than a four year old. They are extremely interested in home activities and like to help. Both boys and girls like to play house. Babies are of great interest. Boys also enjoy playing with dolls. Five year olds can become anxious about whether Mother will be home when they leave school.

Intellectual Five year olds are still factual and literal. They do not ask as many questions as four year olds. Stories that are short, full of action, and here-and-now interest them. They are not interested in the unreal or in impossible stories. They may be slow in action but they are persistent. They usually have an idea of what they are going to build or draw.

Interpersonal The five year old is friendly, but shy with strangers. Five year olds like best to play with other five year olds. They want to be good but can't always differentiate right from wrong. When something goes wrong, they may blame the nearest person.

The Six Year Old

Physical About the time of the sixth birthday, there is marked physical growth. The size of the body is out of proportion to muscular control, which may cause awkward and clumsy behavior. Large muscles are better developed than small muscles, but eye-hand coordination is not well established. Constantly moving whether sitting or standing, the six year olds wiggle and squirm.

Emotional Their feeling patterns go from one extreme to another; from smiles to tears, from love to hate. But regardless of the feeling, five year olds express it with vim and vigor. Emotionally, they are still anchored at home and are full of inconsistencies; they want to be big and small at the same time. They want to be independent and yet dependent. They can't make decisions as easily as they did at five. They like new things and they are usually enthusiastic and eager.

Intellectual Their favorite question is "Why?" They ask questions and often may try to answer them without seeking help. Their listening vocabulary is large but their own use of the vocabulary is limited. They are beginning to see a connection between the spoken and printed word. Their vocabulary is concrete. They have little concept of time and space. Their interest span is lengthening and they like using crayons and pencils. They prefer stories that are real and enjoy having them told over and over again.

Interpersonal Six year olds are beginning to be concerned about social approval. They may be in the early stages of gang formation. The children may hit one another to attract attention. They like to tease. They want to be "it" and want to be in a group. They seldom want to give up their place. Usually their best friends are of their own sex.

Basic Psychological Needs

All children have basic psychological needs and strive to meet them. The needs are the same for all but vary in emphasis according to each child's age and environment. The needs of a sense of trust, autonomy, initiative, accomplishment, and identity, as described in Erik H. Erikson's *Childhood and Society*, are generally conceded by psychologists as elements that motivate the behavior of children.[29]

Since these factors motivate the behavior of children, teachers must be aware of these needs and take them into account in planning programs and activities, selecting materials and equipment, and understanding and accepting normal behavior.

The following statements describe the development and stages of needs in children and are adapted from Erikson's work. If you have not already read this classic in your psychology or child development classes, you would profit from reading it now.

The Sense of Trust A sense of trust in having basic needs taken care of appropriately and consistently emerges during the most vulnerable time in a child's life — the first year. And because nature and culture make the mother more maternal at this stage, the sense of trust is unlikely to be harmed by external environmental influences.

The Sense of Autonomy After the sense of trust is established, children spend much of their energy for the next two years asserting that they have minds and wills of their own.

The Sense of Initiative Establishing that they are persons in their own right (for the time being), children of four or five want to discover what they can do. This is a time of enterprise and imagination, when play and fantasy substitute for literal execution of desires. This is also a time of vigorous learning, when they move away from their own limitations into future possibilities. Vigorous locomotion and intrusion into the unknown are common because of a consuming curiosity. Children at this age may physically attack others for their interference, and they are loud and persistent in their questioning.

The Sense of Duty and Accomplishment This fourth stage of the basic needs starts somewhere around six years of age. Children want to be involved in real tasks that they can complete. After a period of fantasy and

---

[29] Erik H. Erikson, *Childhood and Society* (New York: W. W. Norton and Company, Inc., 1950). Two additional needs are stated by Erikson, — integrity and parental sense, but they are developed in the late teens and twenties.

imagination, they want to learn exactly how to do things and how to do them well.

The Sense of Identity This stage usually is reached during adolescence when children are seeking to clarify who they are and what their future roles in society are to be.

THE EXCEPTIONAL CHILD

Patti was deaf. After three years in a special class for deaf children, she was enrolled in a regular kindergarten room. Patti had learned to speak a little and she was very alert and learned quickly from watching the other children. Her greatest joy was working at the woodworking bench and she soon became an expert in turning out bird feeders and houses for admiring relatives. One day the classroom guinea pig, Zipp, must have decided he needed a little peace and quiet — he disappeared. Patti, working on her birdhouses, found him snuggled up inside a freshly painted birdhouse. As she cuddled him to her chest near the receiver of her hearing aid, her face lit up with joy and she exclaimed, "He's saying Patti, Patti, Patti!"

Up to this point, our discussion of learning and development has centered on generally applicable theories and normative data. But teachers must also be aware of the great variety of needs and abilities that children possess. Thus, it is important to understand the characteristics and special needs of exceptional children.

The term *exceptional child* is used in many ways. Some educators use the term to refer to particularly bright children or to children who have unusual talent. Others use the term to refer to any atypical or deviant child. Generally, however, the term refers to physically and/or mentally handicapped children and to gifted children.

After the passage of Public Law (PL) 94-142 (also known as the Education for All Handicapped Children Act) by Congress in 1975, and other related federal rulings, all state governments passed laws requiring that handicapped youngsters between the ages of three and twenty-one be given the opportunity to spend at least part of their school day in a regular, appropriate, and public classroom setting. In many cases the child spends most of the day in the regular classroom and a short period each day with a resource teacher in a special room. This procedure is called *mainstreaming* and involves including all children who are capable of learning in a regular classroom setting. The idea behind mainstreaming is to place the children in the least restrictive environment possible. This aids both the exceptional child and the average child by creating an atmosphere where all characteristics are accepted and become the "norm."

Because the legislation is recent, many colleges and universities have no required general courses in teaching the exceptional child. The courses that are offered usususally come under the category of "special education" and are not always taken by elementary education majors. If you have not taken a course in teaching the exceptional child, including the handicapped child, you are strongly advised to do so. You should remember, however, that being identified as handicapped does not imply mental dullness.

There are nine general categories of exceptional children. These are: the learning-disabled; the intellectually gifted; the mentally retarded; and children with auditory and hearing loss, speech or language disorders, visual impairments, orthopedic impairments, chronic physical illness, and behavior disorders. Each category will be discussed in terms of characteristics, school needs, and appropriate teaching methods. Following the discussion is a list of organizations that support the needs of exceptional children.

Characteristics and Needs

Learning Disabilities   Learning disabilities has been used as a category for exceptional children for approximately twenty-five years. Some children are not deaf but they cannot understand language; some children are not blind but they cannot perceive visually; and some children are not mentally retarded but they cannot learn by conventional instruction methods. These children have specific learning disabilities.

The symptoms or characteristics of learning-disabled (LD) children may include motor disinhibition (not being able to refrain from responding), disassociation (responding to the elements of a stimulus rather than the whole stimulus), figure-ground disturbance (confusing a figure with its background), perseveration (not changing from one task to another), and absence of a well-developed self-concept and body image.

The needs of these children are met in school and in society by reducing the environmental stimuli; by reducing the physical space in which the child works, plays, and lives; by simplifying the physical environment to reduce the number of choices; and by maximizing the stimulus of the task or material.

Intellectual Giftedness   There are many kinds of talented or gifted children. There are also great differences among the experts on who is and who isn't gifted. Generally the intellectually gifted represent the upper group of children on the intelligence scale. These children have potential IQs above 140 and represent about 1.33 percent of the population.

Other authorities define giftedness in more general terms and refer to children with special abilities and aptitudes as "talented." These talents may be in social, mechanical, artistic, musical, physical, linguistic, and academic areas. There is much overlapping in aptitudes and abilities. The talented or gifted child may

- Learn quickly and easily
- Reason, recognize relationships, and comprehend meanings
- Retain what was learned
- Have a large vocabulary and use it accurately
- Ask many questions on many topics
- Be original in thought and methods
- Be keenly observant and respond quickly

The needs of these children are met in various ways, including early school admission, skipping grades, telescoping grades (as in ungraded primary programs), enrichment, or special schools and classes.

Enrichment is widely used in the elementary years. *Enrichment* is the provision or presentation of additional or more in-depth activities, materials, and skills related to the topic being taught. Administrative procedures include additional readings, extra assignments, grouping of children, additional subjects, special enrichment teachers, and establishing higher standards of performance.

Mental Retardation Mentally retarded children are divided into four groups: the mildly retarded (IQ 55 to 69), the moderately retarded (IQ 40 to 54), the severely retarded (IQ 25 to 39), and the profoundly retarded (IQ below 25). The definition and classification of these groups are based on the concept of interindividual differences when compared to other children on a continuum. However, classification of children on the basis of intelligence scores leaves much to be desired. Intelligence scores should be used carefully and should never be the sole basis for the instruction or placement of a child.

Children with *mild retardation* do not grasp ideas, facts, or skills rapidly. They need repetition of the material taught, but they do learn and can use the content and skills taught in a regular school program.

Because of subnormal mental development, the *moderately retarded* child is unable to profit from regular methods of instruction but does have potential ability in three areas: academic subjects at a minimal level, social adjustment to the extent that the child can get along independently in the community, and occupational abilities to a degree the child can support himself or herself financially (partially or totally) as an adult.

Until recently most moderately retarded children were not identified until the primary years. Now, through early screening, the problem is being identified at the preschool or entry level.

The needs of these children are met through individual instruction in the academic areas; whole-group participation in social, fine arts, or physical education activities; and special occupational training in junior high and high school.

The *severely retarded* child only has the potential for learning self-help skills; for social adjustment; and for economic usefulness in the home, in a residential school, or in a sheltered workshop. In most instances, such children are known to be retarded from infancy or early childhood.

The *profoundly retarded* child is totally dependent on others for physical care, for socialization, and for economic support. These individuals require complete care throughout their lives. Severely and profoundly retarded children are not usually placed in regular school settings.

Levels of retardation may also be recorded by the adaptive behavior method. The same classifications are used — mild, moderate, severe, and profound. However, the adaptive behavior scale for young children does not have definite limits as does the intelligence quotient (IQ) system. The scale consists of items such as self-sufficiency (dressing, eating, sleeping, walking, and so on), sensory ability, motor development, language development, and social adaptability. Instead of a formal test, a person observes and records the levels of retardation on the scale.

Auditory and Hearing Disabilities The age at which a child becomes deaf or develops a hearing loss has a significant influence on learning and schooling. A child with a hearing loss of 40 to 50 decibels hears conversational speech and therefore has probably learned to speak at the appropriate age. A child who is born deaf or loses hearing before he or she learns to talk progresses much more slowly in speech and in understanding language.

For many years, hard-of-hearing children were taught in special classes. But because of improvements in hearing aids, they are now placed in regular classrooms where, research has shown, they are capable of performing normally. A few children with extreme deficiencies in academic areas receive specific tutoring for short periods during the day. Children with severe (70 to 90 decibels) and extreme (90 or more decibels) deafness levels are enrolled in special education programs at day or residential schools, where they are taught speech reading (lip-reading), use of residual hearing, reading, writing, finger-spelling, or sign language.

Speech and Language Disorders There are many forms of speech disorders: articulation; voice production; stuttering; retarded speech; and speech disorders associated with cleft palate, cerebral palsy, impaired hearing, and aphasia.

Speech correction is done in hospital clinics, speech and hearing centers, university training programs, and in public school classes. The place or persons conducting the corrections depend upon the severity of the problem and the availability of help. In public schools, speech therapists may teach children once or twice a week. They also prepare assignments for teachers and parents to use to reinforce the skills taught by the therapist.

Visual Impairments Total blindness is usually detected in a child before one year of age, but visual defects may remain undetected until the child enters school. Early childhood programs, therefore, provide excellent opportunities for screening for visual handicaps or potential visual handicaps such as amblyopia.

The characteristics of a child with a visual impairment include tilting the head, holding objects close to the eyes, rubbing the eyes, squinting, sensitivity to light, rolling eyes, inattention to visual tasks (pictures, puzzles, reading), awkwardness in games, avoidance of work requiring use of the eyes, and complaints about not being able to see or about tired eyes.

At the early levels of education totally blind children are still being taught in day or residential schools. However, the current trend in teaching visually handicapped youngsters is to place them in a regular school setting with sighted youngsters and provide services through itinerant teachers or resource rooms.

Orthopedic Problems The exceptional child who is crippled or deformed or who has other physical handicaps has a unique problem, which limits his or her ability to cope with the academic and social experiences in a school setting. Not all children with physical handicaps have the same degree of impairment; those who are mildly incapacitated can attend regular classes.

In the past, physically impaired children with mobility problems or manual dexterity problems were placed in special classes. Because the architectural designs of schools have been changed, these children can now attend regular classes. Children who are placed in special classes have problems of coordination, perception, and cognition as well as mobility problems.

Currently, physically handicapped children are placed in a combination setting. They are placed in special classes with other handicapped children for games and activities that require little mobility and in regular classes with nonhandicapped children so that they learn about the activities of normal children.

To accommodate orthopedically handicapped children, a school setting must include ramps, elevators, sturdy and steady equipment, hand rails, wide halls, large classrooms, and bathrooms equipped with self-help aids.

Chronic Physical Illness Cardiac disorders, diabetes, respiratory disorders, and undernourishment are examples of chronic illnesses. Each of these disorders requires special consideration when teachers plan activities for the children. The two main factors to be considered are (1) the disorder is always present and (2) physical activity has to be limited.

Children with these handicaps may be taught by home-bound teachers, in the regular classroom, in special classes, or in a hospital. With such a wide range of chronic disorders, no one solution is possible.

Behavior Disorders Behavior disorders are described or defined as responses that deviate from the normative data characteristics (described earlier in this chapter) and that interfere with the child's own development and/or the lives of those around the child.

Children with behavior disorders may be classified as unsocially aggressive (they defy authority and are cruel and assaultive), socially aggressive (the gang or group to which they belong gets into trouble), or overinhibited (withdrawn, timid, and sensitive).

The majority of children with behavior disorders are enrolled in regular classrooms where they may receive help from a guidance teacher or a social worker. More severe cases may be placed part time or full time in special resource rooms. Very severe cases are usually placed in a special day or residential school. Abnormally severe cases are placed in hospitals with schools especially adapted for such cases.

Suggested Teaching Approaches

The following suggestions will help you deal with exceptional children in your early childhood classroom. Also, the organizations listed at the conclusion of this chapter will be able to provide you with materials and additional ideas.

Learning Disabilities Establish a quiet station with partitions four feet high. Lay out the tasks to be completed so that the child does not have many choices to make. Organize some space in the room where the child may play where all the stimuli are devoted to a single task.

Intellectual Giftedness Provide many extra tasks, activities, and materials so there is never a dull moment. Establish a helper's station where one child can help another child. Provide problem-solving experiences.

Mental Retardation Stress personal cleanliness; good toileting, eating, and safety habits; and care of materials and equipment. Help the child identify persons by the roles they play (parents, siblings, police, firefighters, and so on). Develop the senses: names; shapes; colors; sizes; positions; natural phenomena (rain, clouds, sun, moon, hail, trees, grass, birds, and so on); recognition of objects by sound, smell, and touch; and recognition of food by taste. Emphasize clear enunciation, correct baby talk, and identify speech deficiencies. Provide rhythm exercises (marching, dancing, and running games) and materials such as walking boards, up-and-down steps, and a trampoline. Have a woodworking area for hammering nails, sawing wood, and painting. Make a sewing box for strings, yarn, cloth, spools, beads, and buttons.

Auditory and Hearing Disabilities Stand or sit where the children can observe your facial expressions and lip movements. Provide seating that is close to you and that has the child's back to the light. Speak in complete sentences. If you make a mistake in giving instructions, repeat the entire sentence. If the child has a hearing aid, encourage the child to use it.

Speech and Language Disorders Use clear enunciation and pronunciation. Provide many opportunities for the child to speak. Establish a listening station using a Language Master. Praise and encourage a child who shows some improvement. Practice identifying the likenesses and differences in sounds to help the child gain an accurate knowledge of what the sound is supposed to be. Use lip, tongue, and jaw exercises that strengthen muscles and control the movement of the tongue. Group participation in choral speaking, puppetry, and dramatic play will help the child practice correct speech.

Visual Impairments Children with visual handicaps differ widely in ability to see; therefore, education programs must be individualized. Experiences are needed using the other senses (hearing, smelling, touching, and tasting). Finger painting, clay modeling, and collecting various items provide tactile experiences. An encouraging environment results when one person orally describes experiences and, at the same time, listens to the child's questions and comments.

Visually impaired children may need picture books with large illustrations, large print letters, or large print name labels. They may need to hold objects very close to their faces (or eyes). They may need another child to act as a buddy (guide) when moving about the room or building. Often they will need to feel things and to have things repeated to them orally. Usually a combination of these activities are needed.

Orthopedic Problems   Regardless of their needs for equipment, space, and buildings designed for easy mobility, children with physical limitations learn the same way normal children do and, therefore, need the same experiences. Many of the centers for young children are designed for varying degrees of physical activity and provide normal settings for participation.

Chronic Physical Illness   Chronic physical illness is extremely serious and often does not have outwardly visible symptoms. Because of this, consult the child's physician for any limitations on physical and mental activities. Remember, however, that you are still the selector of the content and skills that are basic for the child's education.

In general chronically ill children need to be kept quiet, need a variety of different types of activities to keep their interest, need to have contact with children their own age, need to have classroom responsibilities according to their ability, and need to help others.

Behavior Disorders   Establishing reasonable limitations for behavior and consequences for misbehavior will help both you and the child reach an understanding of what is permissible and what is not. As a teacher you must be consistent in your expectations and firm in your insistence that behavior be socially, emotionally, and physically acceptable. A quiet corner, a rocking chair, a "cooling off" area, equipment and material that can be handled roughly (children of three, four, and five do not have excellent control of small muscles), and an understanding on your part of what is "normal" behavior for the age child you teach will enable you to select appropriate techniques for each child.

These children like all children need to have a setting that is conducive to free movement as well as an area where they can be alone. They need to have an opportunity to express themselves through language, music, and the arts. They need a regular daily routine and a firm, consistent set of rules for behavior. While they need a listener and a friend, they also need a mature, adult teacher.

Support Systems

The following organizations distribute information, activities, materials, and data that will help you teach exceptional children.

Alexander Graham Bell Association for the Deaf, Inc., 1537 35th Street N.W., Washington, DC 20007

PROJECT
A Think Sheet

Selecting a position and a group of children who you will enjoy teaching based on what you already know about children will help you develop materials, experiences, activities, and programs in each of the subject areas. Now that you have the facts on career opportunities and have reviewed the data on how children learn and develop, the following "think sheet" will help you select the children and room for your first observations and teaching.

The children
1. What age child do I like best? Why? What do I know about handicapped children? Describe one child.
2. What type of child do I like best? Why? What do I know about understanding and improving behavior? Describe one way.

Teaching
3. What are the characteristics that I like most in a teacher?
4. What philosophy of education do I like best?
5. What theories of learning do I know? Name them.
6. Can I analyze my teaching methods? Analyze one lesson.
7. Can I discuss a learning process the children used? Describe one activity.

American Academy for Cerebral Palsy, University Hospital School, Iowa City, IA 52240

American Association for Health, Physical Education, and Recreation, 1201 16th Street N.W., Washington, DC 20036

American Association on Mental Deficiency, 5201 Connecticut Avenue N.W., Washington, DC 20015

American Association of Workers for the Blind, Inc., Suite 637, 1151th Street N.W., Washington, DC 20005

American Foundation for the Blind, 15 West 16th Street, New York, NY 10011

American Orthopsychiatric Association, Inc., 1790 Broadway, New York, NY 10019

American Printing House for the Blind, 1839 Frankfort Avenue, Louisville, KY 40206

American Public Health Association, Inc., 1740 Broadway, New York, NY 10019

The American Speech and Hearing Association, 9030 Old Georgetown Road, Washington, DC 20014

Association for Children with Learning Disabilities, 2200 Brownsville Road, Pittsburgh, PA 15210

Association for Education of the Visually Handicapped, 711 14th Street N.W., Washington, DC 20005

Child Study Association of America, 9 East 89th Street, New York, NY 10028

The Council for Exceptional Children, 1920 Association Drive, Reston, VA 22091

Joseph P. Kennedy, Jr. Foundation, Suite 510, 719 31th Street N.W., Washington, DC 20005

Muscular Dystrophy Association of America, Inc., 1790 Broadway, New York, NY 10019

National Association of the Deaf, Suite 321, 2025 Eye Street N.W., Washington, DC 20006

The National Association for Gifted Children, 8080 Springnally Drive, Cincinnati, OH 45236

The National Association for Mental Health, Inc., Suite 1300, 10 Columbus Circle, New York, NY 10019

National Association for Retarded Children, 420 Lexington Avenue, New York, NY 10017

National Committee for Multi-Handicapped Children, 239 14th Street, Niagara Falls, NY 14303

National Council for the Gifted, 700 Prospect Avenue, West Orange, NJ 07052

The National Easter Seal Society for Crippled Children and Adults, 2023 West Ogden Avenue, Chicago, IL 60612

National Epilepsy League, Inc., Room 2200, 203 North Wabash Avenue, Chicago, IL 60601

National Society for Low Vision People, Inc., 2346 Clermont, Denver, CO 80207

Social and Rehabilitation Service, Children's Bureau, 330 C Street S.W., Washington, DC 20201

United Cerebral Palsy Association, Inc., 66 East 34th Street, New York, NY 10016

U.S. Office of Education, Bureau of Education for the Handicapped, 7th and D Street S.W., Washington, DC 20202

SUMMARY

In this chapter we have presented a review of the learning process through a discussion of theories of learning, a review of Piaget's theory of intellectual development, a summary of factors influencing learning, and a brief review of research on learning and young children. We have also reviewed the growth and development factors of normative data information and basic psychological needs. These aspects were also discussed with regard to teaching the exceptional child, the characteristics and needs of exceptional children, teaching approaches, and support systems.

ADDITIONAL READINGS

The Learning Process

Beadle, Muriel. *A Child's Mind*. 2nd ed. New York: Doubleday, 1975.

Bigge, Morris L. *Learning Theories for Teachers*. 3rd ed. New York: Harper & Row, 1976.

Landreth, Catherine. *Preschool Learning and Teaching*. New York: Harper & Row, 1972.

Piaget, Jean. "The Child and Modern Physics." *Scientific American*, 196, 3 (1957): 46–57.

———. *The Child's Conception of Physical Causality*. London: Routledge & Kegan Paul, 1930. Reprint. Totowa, N.J.: Littlefield, Adams, 1955.

———. "The Definition of States of Development." In *Discussions on Child Development*, ed. J. Tanner and B. Inhelder, pp. 116–135. New York: International Universities Press, 1960.

———. "The Development of Time Concepts in the Child." In *Psychopathology of Childhood*, ed. P. Hoch and J. Fubin, pp. 34–44. New York: Grune and Stratton, 1955.

———. *The Early Growth of Logic in the Child*. New York: Harper and Row, 1964.

———. "Equilibration and the Development of Structures." In *Discussions of Child Development*, ed. J. Tanner and B. Inhelder, pp. 98–115. New York: International Universities Press, 1960.

———. "How Children Form Mathematical Concepts." *Scientific American*, 189, 20 (1953): 74–79.

———. *The Psychology of Intelligence*. London: Routledge & Kegan Paul, 1950. Reprint. Totowa, N.J.: Littlefield, Adams, 1968.

——— and B. Inhelder. *The Growth of Logical Thinking from Childhood to Adolescence*. New York: Basic Books, 1958.

Pitcher, Evelyn Goodenough, et al. *Helping Young Children Learn*. 3rd ed. Columbus, Ohio: Charles E. Merrill, 1979.

Growth and Development

Almy, Millie. *Child Development*. New York: Holt, 1950.

Ames, L. B., and F. L. Ilg. *Your Five Year Old*. New York: Delacorte Press, 1979.

Breckenridge, Marian E., and Margaret N. Murphy. *Growth and Development in the Young Child*. Philadelphia: Saunders, 1969.

Bruner, Jerome, and Alison Garton. *Human Growth and Development*. Wolfston College Lectures 1976. New York: Oxford University Press, 1978.

Cohen, Dorothy, and Virginia Stern. *Observing and Recording the Behavior of Young Children*. New York: Teachers College Press, 1965.

Donaldson, Margaret. *Children's Minds*. New York: Norton, 1979.

Erikson, Erik H. *Childhood and Society*. New York: W. W. Norton, 1950.

Gardner, Bruce D. *Development in Early Childhood*. New York: Harper & Row, 1963.

Gesell, Arnold, and Frances L. Ilg. *Child Development*. New York: Harper & Row, 1963.

Havighurst, Robert J. *Developmental Tasks and Education*. New York: David McKay, 1952.

Jersild, A. T., et al. *Children's Interests and What They Suggest for Education*. New York: Bureau of Publications, Teachers College, Columbia University, 1949.

Landreth, Catherine. *Early Childhood Behavior and Learning*. New York: Knopf, 1967.

Maier, Henry W. *Three Theories of Child Development*. New York: Harper & Row, 1965.

Smart, Russell, and Mollie Smart. *Children: Development and Relationships*. New York: Macmillan, 1967.

The Exceptional Child

Clark, Louise. *Can't Read, Can't Write, Can't Talk Too Good Either* (dyslexia). New York: Penguin, 1974.

Crow, Gary A. *Children at Risk: A Handbook of the Signs and Symptoms of Early Childhood Difficulties*. New York: Schocken Books, 1978.

DeVries-Kryut, T.A. *A Special Gift: The Story of Jan* (mongolism). New York: Peter M. Wyden, 1971.

Feingold, Ben F. *Why Your Child Is Hyperactive*. New York: Random House, 1975.

Gliedman, John, and William Roth. *The Unexpected Minority: Handicapped Children in America*. New York: Harcourt Brace Jovanovich, 1980.

Guarlnick, Michael J., ed. *Early Intervention and the Integration of Handicapped and Non-Handicapped Children*. Baltimore: University Park Press, 1978.

Hendrick, Joanne. *The Whole Child, New Trends in Early Education*. Chapter 18 (extended reference list). St. Louis, Mo.: Mosby, 1980.

Moores, D. F., et al. "Early Education Programs for Hearing Impaired Children: Major Findings." *American Annals of the Deaf,* 123 (1978): 925–936.

Nichtern, Sol. *Helping the Retarded Child.* New York: Grossett & Dunlap, 1974.

Safford, Phillip L. *Teaching Young Children with Special Needs.* St. Louis, Mo.: C. V. Mosby Co., 1978.

Thomas, Linda. *Cooking and Caring for the Allergic Child.* New York: Drake, 1974.

PART TWO
Settings

A study of the social and classroom organizational factors that influence curriculum decisions.

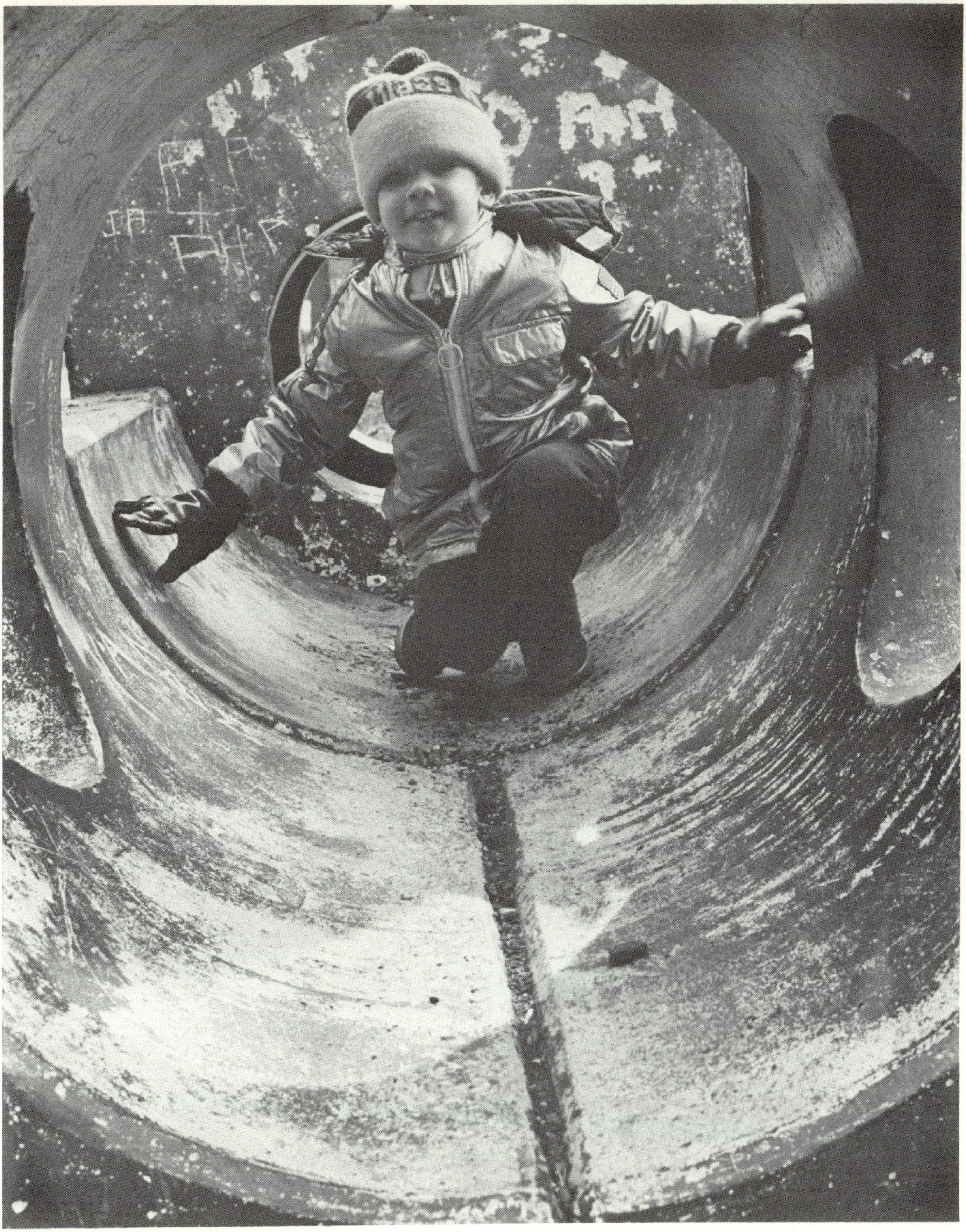

CHAPTER 4
Cultures, Values, and Goals: The Social Setting for the Curriculum

Exploration Tasks

After studying this chapter, you should be able to complete these tasks:
- Describe the roles of the family and the school in the cultural process.
- Discuss the characteristics of some of the major cultures of the United States.
- Define values.
- List some of children's lifetime goals.
- Discuss the importance of assessing goals.
- Describe several observational methods.

What confronts a child in school is not a curriculum, but a specific material and social environment. Children cannot directly experience something called curriculum; that is an adult abstraction. . . .

David Hawkins

OVERVIEW

Before you can actually start teaching the curriculum subjects appropriate for young children, you need to think about the social setting of the child at home and at school. An understanding is necessary of the various cultures of the children; the values of the children and their families; and the goals of the teachers and the children and the role of observation in assessing these goals. All these factors make up the social setting for the curriculum.

Teaching is a complicated process and there is much to learn besides the content of each of the subject areas. This chapter should help you in your first experiences in the classroom and should also provide you with a basic background so that you can perceive each of the curriculum subjects discussed in Part Three as a part of a whole. Teaching isolated subjects will not prove valuable for successful teaching or for successful learning. To be an effective teacher, you need to understand the social factors influencing children's learning before you decide what specific information and skills in the different subject areas are important for the children in your classroom to know.

CULTURES

Children are unique in many ways — physically, socially, emotionally, and intellectually — but cultural differences are probably the most misunderstood differences that teachers must know and understand.

The Cultural Process

The term *culture* can be defined as all activities and achievements in a society that individuals pass on from one generation to the next. Generally, a culture is divided into five categories[1]:

1. *Technology*   The way people provide themselves and others with the necessities of life.
2. *Institutions*   Homes, schools, governments, religious groups, and other organizations.
3. *Language*   Types of speech suitable for special situations that convey meaning to the listener.
4. *Customs*   Special use of art, music, and the dance.
5. *Ideology*   A guiding set of beliefs.

The Role of the Family   The process of socialization (cultural transmission) ideally begins at home. Allison Davis and Robert J. Havighurst, in their

---

[1] Peter B. Hammond, *An Introduction to Cultural and Social Anthropology* (New York: Macmillan, 1971), pp. 13–22.

book *Father of the Man*, describe the process by which culture may be transmitted from one generation to the next.

The human being starts to learn his culture at his mother's knee. . . . It gives him his concepts of right and wrong and underlies a great part of his personality. The average mother has learned from her own parents a very deeply fixed culture which in turn largely determines her methods and goals in training her own children. . . . A mother needs to know how this early social training of her children influences their personalities. . . . The way in which the cultural training of the child is administered also helps determine his individual disposition. The history of this training will influence whether the child is cooperative or sullen, lively or apathetic, brave or timid. These personal characteristics of the child depend in part upon such aspects of his training as the age when he is required to begin his training, the speed with which he is required to learn his basic habits, the kinds of rewards and punishments used in his training, the relative self-control or impatience of his parents, and the basic love or hostility between parent and child.[2]

The culture that a child learns at home is sometimes called the *culture of the family*. Young children are influenced chiefly by the family culture; the peer group and the community will play more dominant roles later. The children you will be teaching and helping will have been shaped by the conditions of their homes. Culture and personality are learned within the circle of the family from human beings toward whom a child feels trust, fear, love, or hate. Just as a child learns from the family to speak their language and to eat the foods provided, the child also learns behavior and attitudes from the family.

The Role of the School Schooling is the means by which socialization is extended beyond the home, the means by which a child is introduced into the general culture in which he or she must live, work, and play. Because early education programs are many children's first encounter with this general culture, the child encounters many new and often conflicting customs. You as a teacher are an important factor in the child's transition from home culture to school culture. Parent education and involvement in the schooling of their children cannot be stressed enough as you come to realize that success in teaching depends on the cooperation, understanding, and support of all parents.

Cultures in the United States differ widely. Problems can arise in instruction if a teacher does not recognize those differences and individualize instructional methods and materials. The teacher must also recognize the

---

[2] Allison Davis and Robert J. Havighurst, *Father of the Man* (Boston: Houghton Mifflin, 1947), pp. 9–11.

The school brings together children of diverse backgrounds and cultures.

importance of both conformity and diversity. The varying cultures within any society need a certain amount of conformity to preserve equal opportunities for good health, for adequate education, and for satisfying daily and lifetime living conditions.

Flexibility and a respect for variation are important in developing a climate for growth and learning. Children come from widely different backgrounds and have experienced varying problems and life styles. They bring from home attitudes and abilities of varying effectiveness. They have begun to develop a sense of right and wrong, a code of living, and a set of standards for behavior. Their attitudes toward other humans are fairly well established; they know whether they view their environment as hostile or satisfying. A widening of experiences and the opportunities to talk about them are among the great values of early childhood education.

Cultural Differences

For many years the "melting-pot" concept of the American society was widely accepted. People from all parts of the world and all walks of life were expected to give up their cultures and become "American." This has not happened; there is an increasing acceptance for a multicultured society that seems likely to continue.[3] Differences in social customs, food, and even language are now valued, and overt pressures to end cultural differences are lessening. However, conflicting pressures — population growth, urban living, mechanization, and the mass media — promote conformity. Actually, factors that influence both the preservation of differences and conformity operate within our society. Rather than a "melting-pot," some people refer to the American society as a "tossed salad," in which every ingredient has maintained its own identity but added a new flavor to the whole.

Ethnic

Current immigration trends   When recent immigration reports are studied to discover how many immigrants came from which countries and where they settled, it becomes evident that few school systems in the United States are unaffected by the continued immigration of people from many cultures.

During the summer of 1980 more than 100,000 Cubans and thousands of Haitians immigrated to the United States. In addition, 14,000 Indo-Chinese are admitted each month. Under basic immigration laws 400,000 newcomers enter the United States each year, a number that doesn't include the refugees admitted under special laws. Table 4.1 summarizes a 1980 report issued by the Immigration and Naturalization Service that lists aliens who were registered for the year 1978.

Characteristics   What are the general characteristics of some of the major ethnic cultures with which you may be working?[4]

The Mexican-American home is frequently male-dominated. Sociologists relate that mothers will not ask their sons to go on errands or close a door, but cheerful acceptance of such responsibilities is expected of their daughters. This is especially evident in homes where the Spanish influence is dominant. It is less characteristic of homes with strong Indian attributes.

---

[3] For further reading on cultural differences, see J. W. Berry and P. R. Dasen, *Culture and Cognition Readings in Cross-Culture Psychology* (London: Methuen, 1973); Mary Ellen Durrett and Florence Profski, "Effects of Heterogeneous and Homogeneous Grouping on Mexican-American and Anglo Children," *Young Children*, 31, 6 (May 1976): 309–314; Mary Ellen Goodman, *The Culture of Childhood* (New York: Teachers College Press, Columbia University, 1970); Philip Jackson et al., "Perspectives on Inequality: A Reassessment of the Effect of Family and Schooling in America," *Haggard Education Review*, 43, 1 (February 1973): 37–164; Robert A. Levine, "Cross-Cultural Study in Child Psychology," in *Carmichael's Manual of Child Psychology*, ed. Paul H. Mussen (New York: Wiley, 1970); Lewis R. Tamblyn, *Inequality: A Portrait of Rural America* (Washington, D.C.: Rural Education Association, 1973); and Ann Cole, Carolyn Hoas, Elizabeth Heller, and Betty Weinberger, *Children Are Children* (Boston: Little, Brown, 1978).

[4] Velma Schmidt and Earldene McNeill, *Cultural Awareness: A Resource Bibliography* (Washington, D.C.: NAEYC, 1978).

Table 4.1 Immigrants and Where They Settled, 1978

Birthplace	Number	State of settlement	Number
Mexico	92,367	California	1,283,598
Vietnam	88,543	New York	796,454
Phillipines	37,216	Texas	392,094
Cuba	29,754	Florida	370,238
Korea	29,288	Illinois	287,777
China, Taiwan	21,315	New Jersey	275,852
India	20,753	Massachusetts	168,787
Dominican Republic	19,458	Michigan	135,522
Jamaica	19,265	Pennsylvania	109,200
Canada	16,863	Connecticut	94,032
Great Britain	14,245	Ohio	84,577
Colombia	11,032	Washington	73,388
Portugal	10,445	Hawaii	69,958
Guyana	7,614	Maryland	66,519
Italy	7,415	Arizona	63,583
Elsewhere	175,869	Elsewhere	708,901
		All registered aliens	1,980,480

Source: U.S. Bureau of the Census, *Statistical Abstract of the United States: 1980* (Washington, D.C., 1980), pp. 91–98.

The mother is dominant in homes where the Basque influence rather than that of southern Spain prevails.

Corporal (physical) punishment is not used on young children as an accepted means of discipline unless the family is influenced by the child-rearing practices of its Anglo neighbors. The extended family pattern is prevalent, with parents, grandparents, uncles, and aunts all sharing the responsibility for bringing up the children. Major decisions are seldom made by an individual — the extended family considers the problem, makes the decision, and accepts the responsibility. The family structure has built-in strength — and children of great creativity and promise come from the protection afforded them in their early years.

Many black and low-income Caucasian children are reared in homes where the mother or grandmother is the dominant personality. The father may not be present or, if he is, may consider the rearing of children to be exclusively woman's work. These families are frequently isolated — with roots in Appalachia, the deep South, or the plains states. The fact that it is frequently easier for women with few skills to get work than it is for men is a factor that disintegrates many homes. Some black and low-income

PROJECT
Identifying Cultures in Your Community

During your teaching you will have an excellent opportunity to study the cultures within the small community served by your individual school. The following activities will guide you in better understanding the children you will be teaching.

1. Draw a map of the total community — city, town, village, or rural area.
2. On this map designate by color or design:
   a. Type of area: Industrial sections, residential areas, shopping centers, schools, community agencies, and churches and synagogues.
   b. Housing: Single-family dwellings, three- or four-unit apartment buildings, multiple-family dwellings, public housing, and rental areas of single-family homes.
   c. Income levels (as identified by the local welfare office): Welfare, low income, middle income, high income, and nonworking rich.
   d. Cultural groups: By general numbers in area and/or by region within area.
3. List the children in your classroom. Pinpoint on your map where each child lives.
4. Read material collected for school records. Does the data collected by the school identify the child as a part of his or her immediate environment? Why? How?
5. What information in the school records will help you understand each child and will aid you in developing a learning environment for each child?

Caucasian children may enter school with less basic security than Mexican-American children because of the extended family structure typical of the latter group.

Many Vietnamese children are now in our schools. An understanding of their culture is important to teachers of young children if the children are to have a successful experience. A helpful pamphlet (*Handbook for Teachers of Vietnamese Refugee Students*, Ed 167 281) published by ERIC explains the child-rearing practices of families of the Vietnamese culture and provides suggestions for instruction of such children.

Class In addition to cultures based on ethnic origin, persons are identified with a specific class structure. Classes are usually identified as upper, middle, and lower class. These classes exist in nearly all ethnic groups and have clearly defined characteristics. Awareness of class differences has been increasing within the last decade. The news media have emphasized articles on middle-class and lower-class customs, providing opportunities for the general public to be aware of cultural differences.

Patterns of child rearing vary culturally. Some children from lower-income homes have a more permissive upbringing than those from middle-class backgrounds, although in a few cases the opposite may be true. This permissiveness may encourage children to be unruly in the classroom. Insistence on early control of bodily functions and on cleanliness may be rigorous or inconsistent. The children may come from homes where reading and use of oral standard English are limited, and they may be deficient in language development.

Persons of widely different racial and ethnic groups who have lived in poverty for many years or generations have come to share a set of attitudes and values that actually constitute a *culture of poverty*. Typical of this culture is the tendency to see each experience as a separate event and not to relate it to other occurrences. Another is the relative inability to defer gratifications. If you don't know what is likely to happen tomorrow and have little hope that it will be an improvement on today, why wait? It also becomes easier not to try than to try and fail again, and again, and again. These repeated failures frequently lead to outbursts of anger and violence and to a loss of trust in anyone or anything.

Language One important factor, that of language, may handicap all children of minority cultures. Incomplete sentences, dropped word endings, added endings, corrupted pronunciation of vowel or letter sounds, and other-language use — whether Spanish, Vietnamese, Italian, or Japanese — may interfere with learning in a regular classroom setting. If you are going to teach in an area where the children's language will be a factor in their learning, study the known research data on the language problems and become proficient in understanding their language. In 1976 the U.S. Department of Health, Education, and Welfare estimated that between 1.8 and 2.5 million children needed bilingual instruction.

Although foreign-speaking children will have a greater language handicap, most children in culturally different areas will have a different language than standard English. You must remember that hardly anyone in the United States speaks standard English, but we all have to *read* standard English in textbooks, newspapers, magazines, and other forms of printed material. When teaching children the mainstream language, your plan should be to ensure that they fully comprehend what is being said orally and in print by the mass media. The idea is not to replace or belittle their native language but to extend their knowledge and skill to include the use of standard English. Remember that language development and the formation of ideas go together. Freeing and encouraging children to speak is an important function of early childhood education if we want them to function at their full potential.

Cultures are complex. Cultural diffusion and acculturation proceed at different rates in different geographical situations and with different individuals. Cultures can change and have changed, but these changes can only be helped by teachers who are clear in their own purposes and ready to experiment: teachers who can be creative, accepting, and knowledgeable.

VALUES

In one kindergarten classroom the children were discussing what they would do in several different events. The events were suggested by the teacher, based on behavior problems that had arisen during the previous few days.

"What would you do if you found a beautiful red marble in the sandbox?" the teacher asked. Answers: "I'd put it in my pocket." "I'd give it to Mary (her best friend)." "I'd sell it." "I would throw it away." "I'd give it to you." After the last answer, the children said they would give it to the teacher, the aide, or the principal.

"What would you do if someone on the bus accidentally shoved you and made you fall down?" Answers: "I'd hit him." "Cry." "Tell the bus driver." "Tell my father and he'd beat him up." "I'd tell my big brother." "Knock his block off." "I'd tell the principal and he'd spank him."

"What would you do if John had a new baseball bat and wouldn't let you play with it?" Answers: "I'd tell the teacher on him because you're supposed to share." "I'd take it when he wasn't looking." "I don't want a baseball bat." "I'd hit him with it." "I wouldn't let him play with anything."

The teacher then changed the type of questions. "What would you do if you lost a big red marble while you were playing?" Answers: "I'd tell the teacher." "I'd tell the principal." "I would look for it." "I'd cry." "My mother would buy me a new one." "I wouldn't care."

"What would you do if you accidentally pushed Alice down on the playground?" Answers: "Say I was sorry." "Run." "Tell her I was sorry." "Go tell the teacher."

As the children began to get restless the teacher ended the session with the comment, "Tomorrow we'll talk some more about what we'd do when we have to make a choice." This was this teacher's approach to beginning to help children develop values and make moral judgments of right and wrong.

What is a value? A *value* is the degree of importance or usefulness an individual puts on an idea, an action, or an object. What does "moral" mean? *Moral* relates to the principles of right and wrong behavior.[5] As a

---

[5] Martin L. Hoffman, "Moral Development," in *Carmichael's Manual of Child Psychology*, ed. Paul H. Mussen (New York: Wiley, 1979).

teacher you must plan opportunities for children to form values and to make moral judgments. Children who have these opportunities should begin to establish reasons and logical behavior for their actions and thoughts.

What are some of the concepts about values and moral judgments that children should know and understand for successful experiences in life? One authority has listed the following concepts that need to be started during a child's early years. Remember, you are only the initiator; the child will not master these concepts all at once.

Individuals must make choices.
Habits can be useful and they can be harmful.
Seeing is not always believing.
The same word can mean different things to different people.
The idea of need relates to what people must have to survive.
The values of goods or services are related to needs, wants, scarcity, and abilities.
The values and customs of the society in which an individual lives are the primary determiners of his behavior.
Differences in ways of living should be viewed in the light of the values and customs that underlie them.
Institutions such as the family, school, and church pass on, clarify, and sometimes change beliefs, values, and customs from generation to generation.
The use of the terms "good" and "bad" usually implies some standard or some desired end or purpose.
The importance of natural resources depends on what the individual values and to what uses he desires the resources to be put.
Values which people have sometimes vary with new situations.
People usually behave in terms of what they believe to be true.
People usually classify or group their fellow beings into some kind of categories based on what they believe and value.
The way people earn a living has a relationship to the goals and values they hold.[6]

Sometimes teachers have difficulty organizing activities to accomplish value teaching. In the book *Values and Teaching,* Louis Raths and his associates discuss choosing freely, choosing from among alternatives, choosing after thoughtful consideration of the consequences of each alternative, prizing and cherishing, affirming, acting upon choices, and repeating the previous six processes.[7] These processes are influenced by what the authors call "value indicators." These indicators include goals or purposes; aspirations; attitudes; interests; feelings; beliefs and convictions; activities; and worries, problems, and obstacles. Teachers can improve their teaching of values by using these criteria in planning their activities for children and establishing their goals for teaching.

---

[6] Martin L. Hoffman, "Moral Development."
[7] Louis E. Raths, Merrill Harmin, and Sidney B. Simon, *Values and Teaching* (Columbus, Ohio: Charles E. Merrill, 1966), pp. 28–33.

PROJECT
Knowing Yourself

> To be adult means to be able to manage cognitive dissonance, to tolerate ambiguity, to cope with the illogic of the world . . . to have knowledge of one's limits as well as of one's assets: to know that one is not all-powerful and yet to know at the same time that one is never negligible.
>
> Karl W. Deutsch

Before you can teach others to acquire values and make moral decisions, you must know and understand your own values and moral principles. Here are some activities to do and discuss with others.

1. Make a list of everything you value and list the reasons why they are valuable to you.
2. Ask your parents what they value and why.
3. Outline the differences in your values and your parents' values. Can you identify the reasons for the differences?
4. Discuss and compare your values with those of other persons your age. Can you trace the reasons for basic differences?
5. Watch three old movies on television and identify the values and morals presented.
6. Analyze the most recent movie you have seen and contrast and compare the values and morals presented in the recent movies with those presented in the old movies you saw.
7. List ten behaviors you feel are wrong. Do you believe your list of wrongs should be "wrong" for everyone?

Additional information and materials for value and moral teaching are provided in Chapter 7 in the section on socialization. The additional readings at the end of this chapter include books concerned with pertinent problems on moral and value issues that will help you develop appropriate lessons for young children.

GOALS AND OBSERVATION

Goals of Teachers and Children

What is a goal? A *goal* is the knowledge or skill that you hope to obtain from teaching the lesson, or the knowledge or skill you hope the children will learn from participating in the lesson. Teachers have goals and children have goals. Each set of goals has an impact on the learning that takes place in the classroom.

Teachers can provide children with a continuity of experiences that will promote their acquisition of physical, social, and mental skills. These skills are broadened and enriched through vigorous and realistic foundation activities based on common sense and a thorough knowledge of the needs of children.

Before planning the presentation of specific curriculum areas, teachers must set broad general curriculum goals. A satisfactory curriculum is one that provides opportunities for augmenting and reinforcing the following lifetime goals of children:

- Positive self-concept
- Knowledge of people, experiences, and things
- Competence in language and social skills
- Competence in body mastery
- Ability to control emotions
- Competence in reliance and self-directiveness
- Ability to think critically and to solve problems
- Expression and appreciation of aesthetic events and activities
- Social and cultural values

After you have set broad general goals for your curriculum planning, you need to analyze and organize the goals or needs of children in more precise, concrete tasks. In establishing your organized list of tasks for children, remember that children differ in their ability to perform the tasks: in their timing of accomplishing the tasks, in their valuing of performing the tasks, and in their mastery of the tasks. Also, since these goals are lifetime ones, children must have opportunities in their daily lives to pursue them.

The following list of goals for children will help you develop opportunities for accomplishing these goals.

Opportunities for optimum accomplishment of children's goals

- A child must have the opportunity to become independent.
- A child must have the opportunity to love, to be loved, and to be secure.
- A child must have the opportunity to make judgments and decisions to become self-disciplined, self-guided, and self-directed.
- A child must have the opportunity to understand the physical environment through curiosity, reasoning, and problem solving.
- A child must have the opportunity to give, to share, and to receive.
- A child must have the opportunity to work and to play with others.
- A child must have the opportunity to develop and to understand his or her body.
- A child must have the opportunity to develop an oral vocabulary through social and intellectual experiences.

An excellent pamphlet, which was recently published by the Institute for Early Childhood Education, lists fifty-two goals or responsibilities for teachers and twenty-nine goals related to productive living for children.[8] This pamphlet is a valuable guide for teachers in setting their priorities before they begin to teach.

Observation

The visual observation of young children at work and play in a classroom setting is very important in helping teachers evaluate the growth in learning that is taking place. It is impossible to give the very young standardized achievement tests because of their lack of reading ability and short attention spans. Even the giving of oral tests has its limitations because of the child's

---

[8] B. J. Barnes et al., *Accountability: Taking Account of Human Value* (Fullerton, Calif.: Institute for Early Childhood Education, 1978).

curiosity about each topic, the long discussions that usually occur, and the difficulty in keeping the child's interest on the task.

Techniques There are several ways to observe children. The most common is the use of an anecdotal record. In this method, while observing the child or after an important incident has occurred, the teacher records (usually on a 3" × 5" card) the observation or incident for later evaluation and recommendations.

Another common way to observe young children is the use of a standard list of performances that have been taught to the children or that the children have had an opportunity to learn through working and playing in self-directed activities. The Evaluation of Individual Differences charts in Part Three of this book are good examples of this procedure. A standard list given to all teachers can be detrimental to a program, however, if teachers think that all children have to perform each task at the same level of performance and at the same age.

An observational procedure that is becoming more common is the use of published texts on observational settings with established goals, materials, procedures, and evaluation techniques. When applied with common sense these materials can be helpful. In using such materials you need to be sure that children have had an opportunity to learn the information or skills. A good application of this form of observation is to use the procedure as a diagnostic instrument. In this way the information gained will be regarded as the basis for further teaching rather than as an end result.

In all observation activities, you need to establish goals for observation before you begin. The results obtained may be used for "grading" the ability of a child or for evaluating the need for reteaching or introducing new material.

Observation and the Assessment of Goals If as a teacher you have established a list of goals for you and your children (which you should put in writing), you will need to verify whether you and the children are accomplishing these goals. Verifying or assessing both your progress and the children's progress is a very important aspect of teaching. One of the major problems that beginning teachers encounter is that children forget. They have to have many opportunities to learn something before it can be mastered and used again or before it can be transferred to another setting and used to learn something new. One way to assess the progress of the children is by means of the type of observation guide shown in Table 4.2.

Observation Forms At times during your career as a teacher of young children, you will have opportunities to observe the classrooms of other

Table 4.2 A Guide for Observational Ratings of Goals

DATE: _____ TIME: _____ TO: _____

Goal	Mary Adams — Activity (example)	Materials used	Jack Jones — Activity (example)	Materials used
List the activities each child did while you watched.	1. Listened, went to listening station, put record on player, listened. 2. Left listening station and went to easel, and so on.	Records, record player.	Listened, went to block and truck center, built a road, "drove" a truck, talked to two boys also building and "driving" trucks.	Blocks, trucks.

Goal	Mary Adams — Yes	No	Jack Jones — Yes	No
Did each child have freedom to move about and set up own learning environment?	Yes. Teacher checked to see if record player was on correct speed.		Yes. Aide asked children to lower their voices three times.	
Was the child helped to understand the relationship of the activity to previous learning or to group living.		No. Mary was told to listen to record.	Yes. Aide explained why they needed to lower their voices.	
Were questions and talking encouraged?	Yes		Yes	
Was the child expected to be quiet and to stay in one spot?		No		No
Were adults available for help and discussion?	Yes		Yes	

Table 4.2 (cont.)

	Mary Adams		Jack Jones	
Goal	Yes	No	Yes	No
Did the child converse fluently?		No	Yes	
Does the child relate well to children and/or to adults?	Yes		Yes	
Does the child have special friends?	Yes		Yes	
Does the child have special, recurring interests that appear in almost every activity—art, stories, discussions?		Not apparent in this activity.	Yes. "Drove" his dog wherever he "drove" his truck.	
What physical skills did the child use?		None except sitting.	Crawling, use of hands and arms for pushing.	
Were these physical skills controlled and mastered?			Yes	
Did the child approach a new problem or situation with curiosity and a willingness to try?	Yes		Yes	
What are the next steps needed for this child to grow physically, emotionally, socially, and intellectually?	Shorter listening activities.		Smaller trucks and replica stores, gas stations, bridges.	

teachers. On some occasions you'll wish to observe your own children. To do this successfully a printed form probably will be valuable. The three forms shown here have been used by many teachers and seem to include the information that classroom teachers find helpful. Use the one that best suits you.

Analysis of Classroom Activities

Number of children _____

Subject _____

Teacher personality, planning, etc. _____

_____

Physical learning environment (good? bad? why?) _____

_____

Student activity _____

Interest level _____

Is learning taking place?/How do you know? _____

_____

What did you learn that can apply to your own teaching? _____

_____

_____

Observation Sheet

What did the teacher teach?

What did the children learn?

How do you know?

Observation of Cognitive Learning

Observer's Name _____ Group Observed _____
Date _____ Time _____
Directions: Observe children in _____ activities.
Activity: _____
Describe teacher's and aide's roles (verbal and nonverbal).

Describe materials to be used, their arrangement, location, availability to all children in group, and quantity.

Describe integrating cognitive learnings (math, science, social studies, language arts, and aesthetics).

SUMMARY

The study of cultures, values, and goals establishes a social setting for the creation of a curriculum program that will deal with children on additional levels of individuality. Knowledge of the influences of culture, the development of values and goals for both teachers and children, and the use of observation in the assessment of goals, will enable you to plan activities, choose materials, and plan lessons especially designed for your children.

ADDITIONAL READINGS

Arizona State Department of Education. *Some Hints to Work with Vietnamese*. ED 133 383. Urbana, Ill.: ERIC Clearinghouse on ECE, 1976.

Bloom, B. S. "New Views of the Learner: Implications for Instruction and Curriculum." *Childhood Education*, 56 (October 1979): 4–11.

Borke, H., and Sue S. Borke. "Perception of Emotional Responses to Social Interactions of Chinese and American Children." *Journal of Cross-Cultural Psychology*, 3 (1972): 309–314.

Burmark, L., and H. Kim. "The Challenge of Educating Vietnamese Children in American Schools." *Integrated Education*, 91 (1978): 2–8.

Chang, T. S. "The Self-Concept of Children in Ethnic Groups: Black American and Korean American." *Elementary School Journal*, 76, 2 (1976): 157–164.

Frazier, Alexander. *Values, Curriculum and the Elementary School*. Boston: Houghton Mifflin, 1980.

Gallimore, R., J. W. Boggs, and C. Jordon. *Culture, Behavior and Education: A Study of Hawaiian-Americans*. Beverly Hills, Calif.: Sage Publications, 1974.

Grand, Carl A., ed. *Multicultural Education*. Washington, D.C.: ADCD, 1977.

Kriger, S. F., and W. H. Kroes. "Child-Rearing Attitudes of Chinese, Jewish and Protestant Mothers." *The Journal of Social Psychology*, 86 (1972): 205–210.

McHale, Cardell Magda, John McHale, and Guy F. Streatfield. *Children in the World*. Washington, D.C.: Population Reference Bureau, 1979.

Morfield, Sheila. *Nonsexist Learning and Teaching with Young Children*. ED 154 932. Urbana, Ill.: ERIC/EECE, 1979.

Scharf, Peter, ed. *Readings in Moral Education*. Minneapolis, Minn.: Winston Press, 1978.

Steward, M., and D. Steward. "The Observation of Anglo-, Mexican-, and Chinese American Mothers Teaching Their Young Sons." *Child Development*, 44 (1973): 329–337.

Van Camp, Sarah S. "The World Through 5 Year Old Eyes." *Childhood Education*, 54:5 (1978): 215–221.

Werner, Emmy E. *Cross-Cultural Child Development*. Monterey, Calif.: Brooks/Cole Publishing Co., 1979.

CHAPTER 5

Organization: The Physical Setting for the Curriculum

Exploration Tasks

After studying this chapter, you should be able to complete these tasks:
- Discuss the factors influencing the general organization of a classroom.
- Develop time schedules appropriate for the activity planned and for the children involved.
- Write lesson plans that are clear, concise, accurate, and appropriate for the children being taught.
- Identify two types of individualization and plan individualized activities.
- Group children according to varying criteria.
- List appropriate activity centers for an early childhood room and describe some activities and materials for each center.
- List and select useful, well-constructed, permanent equiment for early childhood rooms.

The school's physical environment should be organized to encourage all children to explore the range of learning opportunities available and to provide symbols that affirm the contributions, values and potentials of females and males of all social, ethnic and social class groups.

    Shirley D. McCune and Martha Matthews

OVERVIEW

Organization is important for all successful teaching and learning. The cluttered, messy room is distracting and confusing to children. Unplanned and disorganized activities tend to make teaching a haphazard event. Too many or not enough materials or equipment bewilder and disturb both children and teachers. Every individual in the room, children and teacher, should know what is happening in the classroom and what supplies are available.

But organization of materials, equipment, ideas, and activities is a means to an end and not an end in itself. Neat and beautifully written lesson plans or a spotlessly clean room and all the latest shiny equipment do not guarantee the creation of an effective learning environment. The effectiveness of planning, scheduling, and selection of equipment depends on the ends sought and on the teacher's understanding of how best to meet the needs of each child.

Sometimes teachers are too concerned with the task of fitting the child into the curriculum and into the organization of the classroom. They should instead fit the organizational patterns of planning, scheduling, and equipment selection to the individual interests and learning needs of each child.

This chapter is designed to help teachers plan daily schedules and lessons, individualize activities, and group children according to their needs and interests, as well as to aid teachers in organizing their rooms efficiently and in selecting appropriate equipment and materials.

FACTORS INFLUENCING ORGANIZATION

Many factors influence children's learning potential in any classroom organization. These factors include the number of children within a given space; the number of adults assisting the children; the ages of the children; and the location of the early childhood room in relation to bathrooms, food areas, outside doors, and water. The time of year and the daily weather also limit or expand use of space and equipment. The philosophy of the directors, principals, and school system is a powerful influence on teachers and their development of organizational plans for the individuals and groups.

The general organization of an early childhood program can start with a positive approach if you include some of the following suggestions at the beginning of the school year.

- Plan a staggered attendance of the children for the first week.
- Organize a shortened schedule for the first two weeks.
- Ask a parent to help the first few days.
- Signal to get the children's attention by playing a chord on a piano, ringing a bell, or flipping the light off and on.

- ✔ Start good social habits on the first day such as putting away toys, washing hands, lining up, and walking in a line.
- ✔ Participate in activities with the children.
- ✔ Provide name tags for each child so you can begin by calling each child by name.
- ✔ Make your room attractive, colorful, and usable before the children arrive.

SCHEDULES AND PLANS

Daily Schedules

Every teacher has to have general overall curriculum plans for the year as well as a general schedule for the activities of each day. Early childhood programs are influenced by starting times, bus schedules, availability of outdoor space, lunch times, availability of resource people, and building accommodations. Daily schedules should vary in length of time blocks according to the needs of the children being taught and the activity planned. All curriculum subject areas are not taught each day; teachers therefore need schedules showing variation in lengths of time devoted to the activity. If a teacher is successful in integrating the various subject areas into common activities, the teacher will not need as structured a schedule as those teachers who have difficulty in balancing the seven instructional areas.

To give you some knowledge of daily schedules, how they are organized, and how they vary, six examples are included in this chapter.[1]

Schedule 1: Full-day program

8:15 Teacher and aide greet children, take lunch money, check the children's health.

8:15 Children have free choice of activities:
Art Center: Children use easel, clay, crayons. Teacher introduces string pictures to small group.
Homemaking: Teacher adds mirror and health "tools."
Woodworking Center: Children complete projects.
Block Center: Children continue to play with transportation toys.
Manipulative Center: Closed.
Library Center: Children look at transportation books.
Science Center: Children look at books, pictures, and models that illustrate a variety of wheels.

---

[1] See pages 14–17 for additional typical schedules.

Music Center: Children listen to tapes for sounds of moving vehicles in city. The aide is at this station for the morning.

9:00 Opening exercise. Teacher takes attendance, introduces calendar activity, and checks weather. Children salute flag and sing opening song.

Teacher chooses helpers for the day.

9:15 Snack. Children discuss how many cups to use and what kind of juice to have.

9:30 Outdoor play. Teacher introduces the scooter and supplies bean bags and ropes.

10:00 Children rest and listen to the story record "Little Toot."

10:15 Music and Rhythms: Introduce "Wheels on the Bus."

10:30 Teacher and children get ready for lunch. Children go to lunch by color of clothes.

10:45 Lunch. Teacher orally reviews table manners.

11:15 Children rest on cots.

12:30 Children have free choice of activity.
Teacher closes block center and opens manipulative center.
Art Center: Children make pudding fingerpaint pictures and use easels only.
Woodworking Center: Closed.
Film Center: All other centers continue as children view filmstrip on wheels (seen by group yesterday).

1:00 Outdoor play. Children play with balls and scooter.

1:30 Teacher reads story "Too Many Names" and relates it to transportation unit.

2:00 Children play action games.
Teacher uses games to review body parts.
Teacher introduces and supervises tip-toe game.

2:15 Children and teachers prepare for dismissal and discuss the day's events.
Children take home circle picture.

2:30 Teacher dismisses each child individually.

Schedule 2: Full-day program

8:15 Teacher greets children.

8:30 Children engage in free play.
Block Center: Trucks and farm animals.
Home Center: Children continue previous play.

Manipulative Play Center: Children choose from sewing cards, puzzles, and peg boards.
Book Center: Children can look at and read a variety of pet stories.
Art Center: Children use chalk and construction paper.

9:15 Quiet time. Teacher reads a story about pets and discusses pets of children.

9:30 Children prepare to go outside. Teacher tells children how and where to go on playground.

9:40 Recess. Children play on swings or sandbox.
Teacher introduces jump rope.

10:00 Children wash hands and get drinks.

10:10 Snack time. Teacher discusses table manners with children.

10:20 Children rest while listening to record.

10:30 Quiet time.
Teacher introduces new math shapes: square, circle, and triangle. Teacher emphasizes circle and points out examples of a circle in the room.

10:45 Children wash hands and prepare for lunch.

11:00 Lunch.

11:30 Children practice art and math by cutting out circles.
Children play bean bag game by throwing bean bags through holes cut in a plywood clown.

11:45 Children rest while looking at books.

12:45 Children view film "The Three Little Pigs."
Children review language arts skills of listening and speaking.

1:00 Teacher plays exercise record. Moving different parts of body by name.

1:15 Recess. Children continue jumping rope activity.

1:45 Children engage in free play, continuing morning play center activities.

2:30 Teacher and children review day's activities, preview tomorrow's activities, and clean up the room.

Schedule 3: Half-day program

8:30 Teacher and aide greet children.
Teacher collects and counts lunch and milk money.
Teacher chooses helpers for the day.

8:45 Children engage in free play activities.
Family Center: Children learn how to set table.

Block Center: Teacher adds zoo animals to center.
Art Center: Teacher introduces straw blowing using straws, water colors, and paper.
Music: Teacher plays record about fall.
Library Center: Children read special books on the seasons.
Science Center: Children look at picture books on fall seasons.
Children play at feeling box with leaves, acorns, nuts, and so on.

9:15   Children listen to record and discuss what fall means to them. Teacher decorates bulletin board with pictures of fall scenes.

9:40   Outside play. Each child looks for something about fall season. They play on playground equipment.

10:00 Play guessing game — "What is it?" (describe animals)

10:05 Snack. Teacher and children discuss taking turns. Children wash hands, count cups, and name the colors of the cups.

10:20 Quiet time. While children rest on rug, teacher reads story on fall.

10:40 Children wash hands and go to rug for fingerplays.

11:00 Lunch.

11:30 Quiet time. Children prepare to go home.

Schedule 4: A typical day of a teacher and aide of three year olds

8:15   The teacher and aide review plans for day.
       The teacher and aide check availability of materials and supplies to be used.

8:30   Teacher and aide greet children, help with clothing, and talk to children.

8:45   Teacher and aide listen to, encourage, and observe children.
       Children engage in free play in family living center, truck and block area, dress-up area, and picture book corner.
       Teacher reads story to those who wish to listen.
       Aide helps other children select an activity.
       Teacher leads or helps children lead singing.
       Aide prepares snack.

9:45   Snack. Children help serve, teacher and aide converse with children.

9:55   Outdoor play. Teacher and aide supervise and play with children.

10:25 Children wash hands.

10:30 Children rest while listening to recorded music.

10:45 Round robin of activities: free play, art, record.
       Teacher helps children fingerpaint.
       Aide helps children listen to records about helping mother.

11:10 Unit topic: The weather and clothes we wear. Teacher leads discussion and shows pictures. Aide cleans up art center.
Children discuss, share, and act out walking in the rain and snow and playing in the sun.

11:35 Toilet.

11:45 Teacher helps children review the morning.
Aide prepares notes to be pinned on children.
Children discuss their day.

11:50 Teacher leads going-home song while helping children dress.
Aide helps children dress and get materials.
Children sing and prepare for going home.

12:00 Teacher sees that each child gets in the right car; aide helps.

12:15 Teacher and aide have lunch.

12:45 Teacher and aide straighten room.
Teacher and aide plan activities for tomorrow and identify their roles.
Teacher and aide gather materials for next day.
Teacher and aide discuss children's behavior and make anecdotal cards.
Teacher makes a new apron for art center.
Aide mixes more paint and puts out fresh clay.

3:00 Teacher checks mail box.
Aide checks bathrooms for paper and soap.

3:15 Teacher and aide leave.

Schedule 5: A typical day of a teacher and aide of five year olds

8:15 Teacher and aide review plans for day.
Teacher and aide check availability of material and supplies to be used.

8:30 Teacher and aide greet children, help with clothing, and talk to children.

8:45 Teacher and aide listen to, encourage, and observe children.
Children engage in free play: family center, block and truck area, water play area, woodworking area, and manipulative center.
Teacher assists children in learning how to use manipulative materials.
Aide assists children in woodworking.

9:30 Teacher teaches new song.
Aide sets up filmstrip projector and screen.

9:40 Teacher shows filmstrip with record or tape.
Aide prepares snack.

Children watch and listen to story. Then children "tell" story while viewing filmstrip.

10:00 Outdoor play. Teacher and aide play with and supervise children.

10:30 Snack. Children serve food.
Teacher and aide eat with children.

10:45 Children compose and dictate a thank-you letter to the telephone lineperson who came to show and tell them about his or her work. Children draw pictures about what they learned from their vistor. Teacher writes dictated letter.
Aide prepares materials to paint boats made by children in the woodworking center.

11:20 Children paint boats with teacher and aide assistance.

11:40 Children perform to movement records; teacher directing.
Aide cleans up paint area.

12:00 Toilet.

12:10 Lunch.

12:30 Rest time. Children may look at books or play with small toys on their mats or cots.
Teacher watches children and reads professional magazine.
Aide gets records from office.

1:00 Free play.
Teacher and aide assist children in learning to tie, button, and zip.

1:30 Children play counting game.
Teacher directs game.
Aide prepares notice of valentine party to be pinned on children.

1:45 Children prepare to go home.
Teacher and aide help with clothing and pin notes on children.

1:55 Teacher, aide, and children sing songs while waiting to leave.

2:00 Children leave, teacher and aide supervise.

2:15 Teacher and aide straighten room, plan for next day, prepare materials for next day, and construct a new bulletin board for the month of February.

3:15 Teacher and aide leave.

Schedule 6: A typical day of a teacher of six year olds

8:15 Teacher reviews plans for day.
Teacher checks board, chart, and handout materials.

8:25 Teacher greets children.

8:30 Sharing time. Teacher calls roll and takes records, lunch money, milk count, and attendance sheet to office.

8:45　Pledge.
Singing for enjoyment.

9:00　Teacher teaches four reading groups; oral reading, workbook page on comprehension, skill review lesson on board, maintenance lesson on a handout sheet.

10:15　Outdoor play. Teacher observes and plays with children.

10:35　Toilet.

10:45　Milk break and conversation.

10:55　Teacher teaches two groups of math; oral lesson with teacher, problems in workbook, and review lesson from chart.

11:40　Teacher reads story.

12:00　Toilet.

12:10　Lunch.

12:30　Art.
Teacher demonstrates how to make a pinch pot.
Children make pinch pots.

1:00　Outdoor play. Teacher introduces new game.

1:20　Teacher reads social studies text.
Children discuss, share ideas, and dictate letter to fire chief.

2:05　Film on colors of fall leaves, followed by discussion.
Assignment: Bring colorful leaves tomorrow.

2:30　Children move to music for total muscle usage.

2:40　Teacher reads poem to children.
Children practice their best manuscript in printing their name while listening.

2:45　Teacher prints a new letter on board.
Children practice printing new letter.

2:55　Children get belongings and sing songs they enjoy.

3:00　Children leave.

3:15　Teacher writes plans for next day.
Teacher gets new materials ready and checks supplies.
Teacher takes home two sets of math papers. (All workbooks and other papers were checked on completion.)

Lesson Plans

How long is a lesson plan? Although there isn't one specific length that guarantees adequate planning, good lesson plans do have certain characteristics. The following suggestions will help you develop plans that will permit creativity, flexibility, and accuracy in instruction.

- Each plan should be complete enough to be of value to a substitute teacher or to be used for review teaching.
- Plans should contain clear-cut objectives stated in terms of realistic individualized performances.
- Every plan should be written to evoke *active* participation on the part of the children.
- Activities of the lesson plan should be organized according to the time allotted for the activity.
- Each plan should anticipate possible questions by the children and behavior problems that may occur during the activity.
- Every plan should be flexible in time, response, and participation.
- Each plan should be based on the children's past experience and provide a basis for future learning.
- Plans should provide for interactions between children as well as between children and the adults in the room.
- Plans should always include opportunities for the children to be successful and to receive praise for their efforts.

Since young children are physically active and very verbal, plans should be designed to include many opportunities for learning how to be successfully involved — physically and verbally — in a group setting.

The actual form for writing lesson plans differs according to individual teacher needs. Some teachers use commercially prepared books, others use dittoed forms, and some prefer looseleaf notebooks. Any form is satisfactory as long as it provides enough space for inclusion of the needed materials and can be stored in a sequential format.

INDIVIDUALIZATION AND GROUPING

Individualizing Activities

There are two methods of individualizing activities for children.[2] One method is to determine a task that should be accomplished by all children at some time. (The task may be counting to ten, tying their shoes, sharing toys in a play situation, or some other expectation.) The task is rigid; the individualization is accomplished by permitting variation in the rates and the methods of learning the tasks. This method requires the use of many diagnostic activities to determine specifically each child's abilities, interests, and readiness for the tasks. The teacher must also have an understanding of the sequence of steps involved in achieving the tasks.

[2] The ideas and materials used in this and the following section were developed by A. Montgomery Johnston, Professor of Education at the University of Tennessee-Knoxville.

The second method of individualizing activities for children is to provide materials, equipment, and media that foster differences in performance. In this method, the only purpose of an activity is for the child to interact with the environmental stimuli. Such interaction takes place with many of the Montessori materials, art materials, dramatic play costumes, and free play activities.

The following lists of do's and don'ts will help you develop creative responses from your children.

Do's

Goals

Encourage individual goals.
Remove ceilings from learning for the bright.
Ensure success for all.
Encourage individual interests.
Foster creativity in all subjects.
Diagnose individual needs.
Identify unique ability differences.

Methods

Give individual tasks.
Let children talk.
Form interest groups.
Form invitational groups.
Form ephemeral-needs groups.
Provide many work centers.
Schedule individualized task times.
Allow individual learning styles.

Evaluation

Have individual conferences.
Set flexible time goals.
Transgress grade level allocations.
Test individually or in small groups.
Keep individual records of needs, interests, gains.

Don'ts

Have bright children wait for others.
Demand unattainable goals for some.
Keep group together.
Expect conformity to teacher's norms.
Assume common needs.
Set one goal for all at one time.
Prejudge individual potentials.

Give intellectual crutches as needed.
Let the able take shortcuts.
Give same tasks to all children.
Do all the talking yourself.
Form rigid ability groups.
Require common work activity.
Demand one process for all.
Demand all steps of a task by all children.

Talk only to the group.
"Grade" or "correct" all work.
Demand time deadlines for all tasks.
Stick to assigned grade topics.
Give same evaluation to all.

Grouping

How do you form a group? Many factors must be considered before children are grouped. Time, space, and materials need to be structured to provide a rich variety of alternatives to meet the unique learning patterns of individual children. Large blocks of time are usually required for the flexibility needed to develop the particular interests of the children. This allows for a relaxed flow of involvement in an activity. Space needs to be open and flexible to permit changes in its structure and the forming and termination of learning centers. Materials must be concrete, manipulative, movable, and appropriate for many different uses.

When you have arranged the time and space and provided the materials to permit creativeness and individuality in performance, you may group the children by any one of several ways. The teacher may act as a guide, advisor, observer, provider, and catalyst to one child or several. Material may be collected and situated in one place, providing diversity in manipulation, construction, and exploration. Game development may stimulate activity and varied responses. Materials may be gathered together in one place, based on the interests of the children. Physical and oral involvement in joint projects initiated by children may be encouraged. Cooperative enterprises may be initiated by problems that need to be solved. One child may help another child or a group of children. Parents may be invited to be actively involved in classroom projects.

Groups of children will form naturally on some occasions because of interests, friendships, needs, and types of activity. If all children wish to participate in the same activity, the teacher will have to devise a round-robin structure so that no child will be left out. At times when children have very special needs, the teacher will have to insist on the child's participation in the activity.

A Child's Participation

To give you an idea of how an early childhood program can contain both individualized and group activities, let us look at the experiences of a specific child. The child in this sequence — Charlie — has been in a class for four year olds for four weeks.

The day begins with Charlie wandering around the room — first the science area, then the book corner. Next he becomes fascinated by the guinea pig and decides to feed him. The teacher has to stop Charlie from dumping the whole box of food in the pen. The teacher suggests that Charlie help her put clean water in the tadpole pan. They discuss the tadpoles and the teacher sends Charlie to her desk for a book on tadpoles. The teacher flicks the lights off and on to signal all the children to go to the rug area. The teacher reads about tadpoles from the book Charlie brought her and the children discuss what they learned. After the discussion, the children select an activity for the morning work session. Charlie chooses cooking and helps cut the butter into thirds. He holds the measuring cup while another child pours the sugar, then watches while other children prepare the flour, eggs, and flavoring for the cupcakes. Charlie butters his cupcake pan. The batter is poured into the pans and the teacher puts the cupcakes into the oven. Charlie wanders to the dress-up corner and puts on the fire hat. Then he joins his special friend Jack in the block area and they play quietly. The teacher asks the children to put away what they are doing. When they have done so, they proceed to the playground where the aide teaches some of them to jump rope while the others play. Charlie tries to jump rope, but he jumps at the wrong time. The aide helps him but Charlie decides it is too hard and goes to the swings. Play time is soon over and the whole group has orange juice and crackers. Charlie helps give out the napkins. The teacher reads *The Gingerbread Man* to the group. Charlie plays with his shoe strings while she reads. The children choose an activity from six suggestions from the teacher. Charlie chooses to dictate a story about his trip to a lake. The aide writes the story as Charlie tells it to her. Lunchtime arrives. All the children wash their hands and pick up their trays and carry their trays to a table. Charlie and Jack decide to put two rolls in their mouths at the same time. The teacher looks at them and shakes her head. After lunch all the children lie down; some look at books, some sleep, and some just rest. Charlie "curls" his hair and opens and closes his eyelids with his hands. After rest time, the teacher and aide set up four centers: (1) making a drum out of a milk carton, (2) painting the stages of tadpoles at the easels, (3) listening to tapes of a visit to a farm in preparation for a field trip, (4) and a table with puzzles, pegboards, and a game. Each child is to participate in each center's activity. Charlie is in the "blue" group and begins in center 3, listening to the tapes. When the end of the day comes, Charlie has not finished his drum so he puts it on a shelf for completion next day. The children discuss the day's events and Charlie takes his story home.

ROOM ORGANIZATION

General Guidelines

A few general rules will help you establish a room that is functional, allows for freedom of movement, gives responsibility to children in caring for their room, and provides you with concrete suggestions on "where to put what."

✔ Place materials and equipment used most often close together to encourage constructive activity.

- Group quiet activities together, away from avenues of traffic, to encourage creativity, experimentation, and exploration.
- Arrange equipment and centers so children may move from one activity to another to lessen possibilities for misbehavior and provide opportunities for an easy transition and balance between quiet and active play and work.
- Have a quiet nook or cranny for a child to be alone for a while.
- Remember not to put out all material and equipment at one time.
- Establish basic centers. Add and subtract supplementary ones as the need occurs and common sense dictates.

Activity Centers

Figures 5.1 and 5.2 show groups of children at work and play in three different settings of two floor plans. These suggestions will guide you in organizing and placing your own centers in the classroom and in grouping children with similar interests or needs. With minimal movement of furniture you will be able to change center topics and control the movement of children from one center to another. As you can see, all children do not participate in each center during any specific day. The basis for placing individual children in the centers is evaluation, based on the kind of checklists for mastery of skills that appear at the end of each chapter in Part Three.

Activity centers in the classroom are useful for meeting individual differences in needs, interests, abilities, and learning styles; for diagnosing interests and abilities; for fostering self-actualization (role exploration, self-realization); and for facilitating interests, motivation, and discipline while the child is achieving significant accomplishments in specific subject areas. Work and play centers are not the cure-all for classroom organization and should be only one of many approaches used. Learning through individual personal experience, through doing, and through activity are the major values of activity centers. They may be used as icing on the cake for a specific task requirement, they may be the major focus of a unit or individualized project, or they may be the principal resource for a structured task. The teacher has some curriculum control by designating the centers established and exercises further control by the materials and activities available within each center. Further curriculum control is exercised by the teacher's guidance role, yet significant options are left to the learner to select the center to work at, the activity to carry out within the center, and the details of working out the activity chosen. This sharing of curriculum choices is an asset of the activity center approach.

Children must be carefully taught several things about their centers: what is in them, what purposes the materials might serve, appropriate and inappropriate uses, safety precautions, clean-up procedures, and times to use

Organization: The physical setting for the curriculum / 119

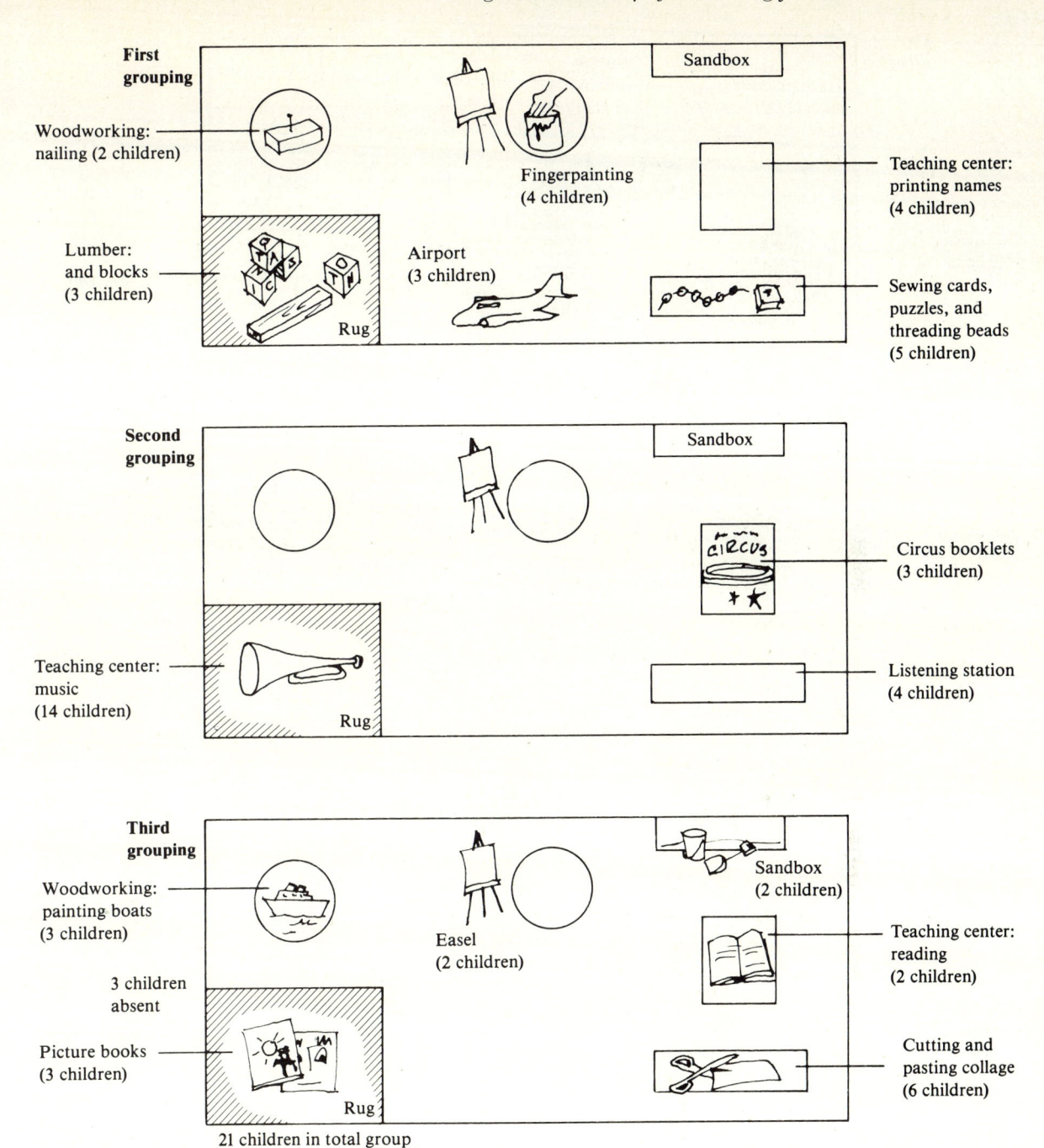

First grouping

- Woodworking: nailing (2 children)
- Lumber and blocks (3 children)
- Fingerpainting (4 children)
- Airport (3 children)
- Sandbox
- Teaching center: printing names (4 children)
- Sewing cards, puzzles, and threading beads (5 children)
- Rug

Second grouping

- Sandbox
- Circus booklets (3 children)
- Teaching center: music (14 children)
- Listening station (4 children)
- Rug

Third grouping

- Woodworking: painting boats (3 children)
- 3 children absent
- Picture books (3 children)
- Easel (2 children)
- Sandbox (2 children)
- Teaching center: reading (2 children)
- Cutting and pasting collage (6 children)
- Rug

21 children in total group

Figure 5.1
Activity Centers I

120 / *Settings*

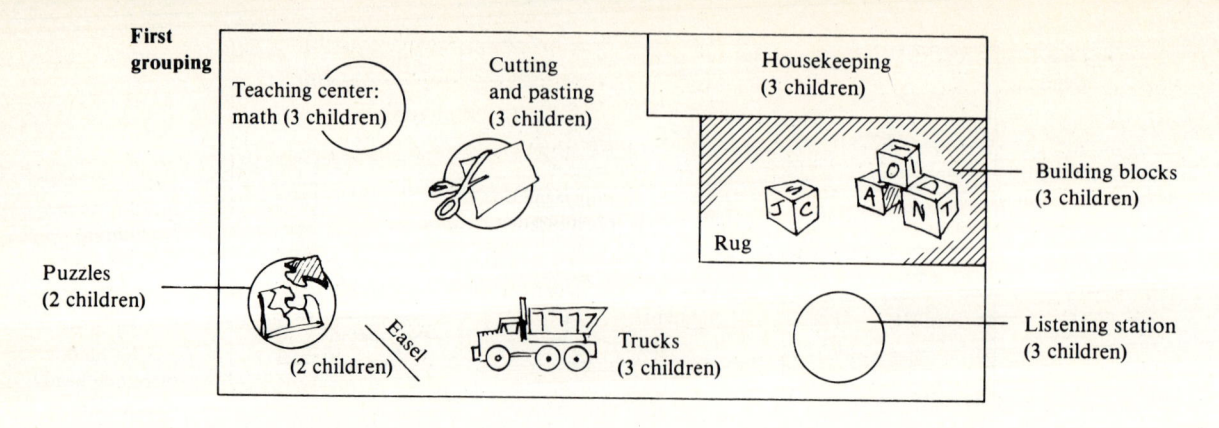

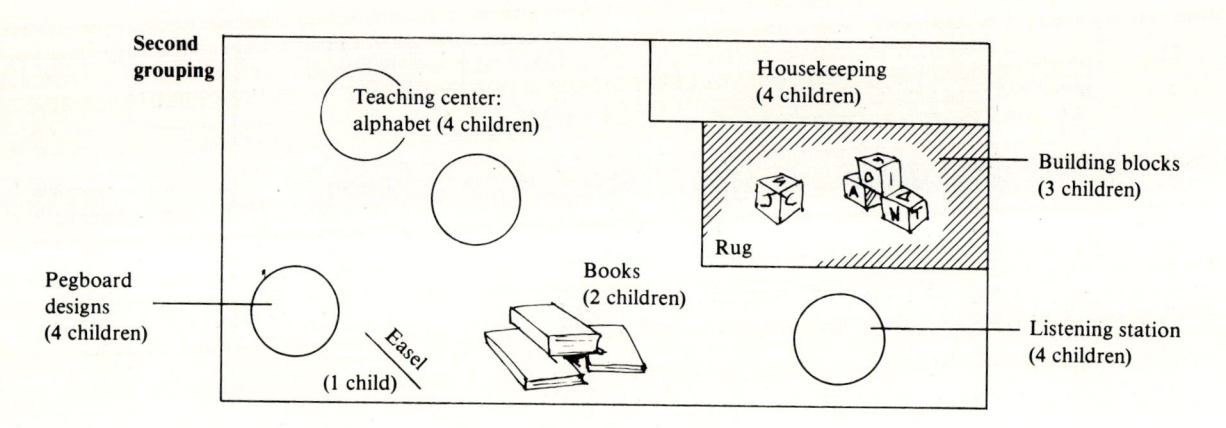

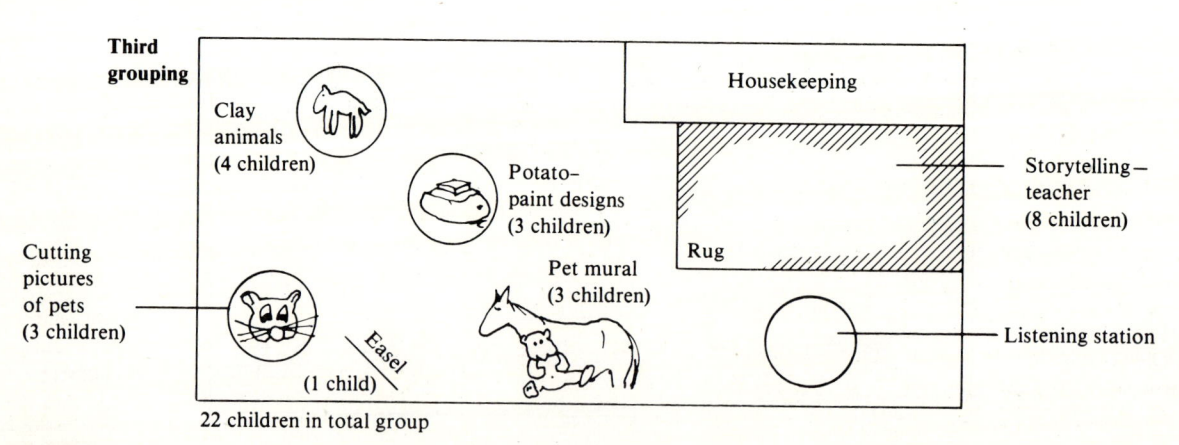

First grouping

- Teaching center: math (3 children)
- Cutting and pasting (3 children)
- Housekeeping (3 children)
- Building blocks (3 children)
- Rug
- Puzzles (2 children)
- Easel (2 children)
- Trucks (3 children)
- Listening station (3 children)

Second grouping

- Teaching center: alphabet (4 children)
- Housekeeping (4 children)
- Building blocks (3 children)
- Rug
- Pegboard designs (4 children)
- Easel (1 child)
- Books (2 children)
- Listening station (4 children)

Third grouping

- Clay animals (4 children)
- Potato-paint designs (3 children)
- Housekeeping
- Storytelling—teacher (8 children)
- Rug
- Cutting pictures of pets (3 children)
- Easel (1 child)
- Pet mural (3 children)
- Listening station

22 children in total group

Figure 5.2
Activity Centers II

each center. While children are using the centers, teachers and aides should move about — observing, conferring, and instructing as needed. Some teachers may wish to introduce one learning center at a time to make sure that the children know why and how to use it effectively and efficiently.

Center usage may be scheduled to fit a variety of teaching styles. Minimum usage might include one hour in the morning whenever group activity begins; during rest period after lunch; in scheduled activity periods; and while waiting for the bus. More extended usage might include any time a given child is not involved in total or small-group instruction — perhaps as much as half of the day. A particular center might be used all day, but a given child might use it for only 30 minutes. While a group of ten may be meeting with the teacher, some of the remaining students might use one or more of the centers.

It would be very nice if boards of education would provide all the equipment, materials, and space for every kind of center conceivable — and this is certainly a direction to explore for financing. However, teachers realistically have always had to be good scroungers; and to obtain many of the materials needed for these centers, they are likely to need to continue to scrounge.

Sharing between teachers can help immensely. When one teacher stops the weaving center, the teacher might lend the looms and materials to another teacher. Parents are often an unexpected resource, if they know exactly what is needed — even in poorer neighborhoods. Local businesses are generally very good about donations if the teacher makes a specific and personal appeal for a particular item. Children, too, can collect and improvise if they know specifically what is needed. Teachers are urged to decide precisely what they want and then explore several ways to obtain the things the need. Equipping, operating, and instructing in some centers can be greatly aided by scheduling parents to help two or three times each week in specific centers.

The following suggested list of ideas for centers have been found to be useful to several teachers. The equipment, materials, and activities in these centers should be varied to fit pupil maturity, teacher's curriculum and strategies, and available space.

Reading Center Made up of books and space to sit or lie to "read." Magazines and newspapers are also appropriate. Include a rug, pillows, shelves, display racks, bulletin boards, and a rocking chair. Space should have minimum traffic and noise.

Creative Writing Center Made up of tables, chairs, writing materials. Might include paper, pencils, typewriter (if available), crayons (for illustrating and writing), display space for finished projects. Children can make up their own writing technique or can dictate to the aide or teacher.

Listening Center   Made up of audio equipment, headphones and jacks, recordings, blank tape cassettes, storage shelves (for phonographs, tape players, recordings). Recordings may include music for appreciation, story records, teacher-recorded books on tape, or teacher-recorded individual activities. Commercially prepared audio materials are also appropriate. Blank tapes for children to record on should be included. This is one way a story can be shared with other children.

Viewing Centers   Made up of a television set, 8 mm and/or 16 mm projectors, 35 mm filmstrip viewers, several headsets and jacks, and a small screen recessed from light as much as possible. Storage space for films, strips, and equipment is needed. A Systems 80® machine would be appropriate for this center.

Creative Dramatics Center   Made up of props useful for acting and storage space for them. Clothes could include old hats, coats, dresses, shoes, canes, gloves, scarfs, aprons, and such. Children should be encouraged to dramatize stories and poems, role play their problems, and engage in exploratory movement.

Mathematics Center   Made up of mathematical activities, math games, math puzzles, geometric tools and materials, or books with math activities and puzzles in them.

Painting Center   Made up of easels, paints, brushes, smocks, and bulletin board for display. Paints may include (according to age) tempera, finger paint, chalk, water color, polymer, or oils. Children should be encouraged to illustrate creative stories and real events, to prepare posters and murals, and to produce individual creative expressions.

Clay Center   Made up of a study table, a crock of ready-to-use clay, a drying rack, a wire for cutting clay, and a few simple tools for shaping. A kiln would be helpful but not essential. Children should be encouraged to express themselves in three-dimensional form as well as two. Illustrations of stories, books, models, and artifacts as well as creative expressions should be encouraged.

Craft Center   Made up of work table, storage space, materials, and tools. Activities might include origami, kirigami, collages, paper sculpture, wire sculpture, or soap carving. Children should be encouraged to explore a variety of media and materials for creative expression. Developing relevant mobiles to hang over each center might add interest. Mobiles should be changed every two to three months.

Sand Table Center Made up of 3-foot × 5-foot (or larger) table with 4- to 6-inch sides, lined with galvanized tin, and half filled with fine sand. Children should be encouraged to portray ideas and problems visually. Projects can include a map of the community, a model of a conservation project, or creative expressions.

Garden Center Made up of sunny ground where children can plant and tend flowers and vegetables — where they can learn biology and responsibility — and where some can find their own expression. Try scheduling a parent or two to help here two or three times each week in season.

Games and Puzzles Center Made up of space to spread out a variety of games and storage space for them. A wide variety of games and puzzles suitable for the range of abilities and interests of the children should be available.

Biological Science Center May include an aquarium, a terrarium, a cage of gerbils or mice, seedlings and plants, specimen collections of any sort of biological phenomena, a microscope and slides, materials for conducting biological examinations and experiments, a bulletin board, field manuals.

Physical Science Center May include materials to conduct experiments in electricity (batteries, wires, magnets, switches, bells, lights), mechanics (levers, pulleys, wheels, pliers, screwdrivers), sound, light, hydraulics, or chemistry; observations in geology and astronomy. A work table, storage space, idea books, and bulletin board would be useful.

Construction Center Made up of a work bench (with vise), tools (hammers, saws), expendable materials (nails, glue, sandpaper, paint, wood, plastic, wire, metal). Children should be encouraged to make specific things the class needs (a birdhouse, an easel) and to be creative in making decorative items (a wood, wire, or metal sculpture; a mobile). Cabinet makers and lumber companies will usually donate wood scraps to teachers. Fathers or mothers may be willing to help here two or three times a week.

Block Center Made up of appropriate size blocks for the age group in sufficient quantity; bins for storage; and flat, clear space for building. Blocks are a creative learning device for all ages.

Cooking activities require a special area in the room.

Toy Center Made up of a variety of toys appropriate for the age group: trucks, cars, trains, dolls, cradles, doll house furniture. Playing with toys is a most valuable way of learning for children, and we should not expect them to grow out of it too early. Children should not feel that they are wasting their time when playing.

Cooking Center Made up of a one- or two-burner hotplate, pans, utensils, paper towels, paper plates, and so on. Cooking center activities can be extended by the use of ovens and sinks in the cafeteria. Materials and ingredients needed in specific activities can be brought the day needed to avoid spoilage and insect problems. Boys should be encouraged to use this center as well as girls. Try scheduling a mother or father to help.

Sewing Center Made up of cloth remnants, needles, thread, buttons, scissors, pins. A cast-off sewing machine would be nice but not essential. Supplies for knitting, crocheting, crewel, needlepoint, and embroidery would add options. Boys should be encouraged to use this center.

Weaving Center Made up of a variety of simple hand looms, cardlooms, inkle looms, yarns of various sizes and colors, string, and scissors. Boys as well as girls need to see and experience making a variety of woven materials to appreciate the many such materials in our culture. Some will develop a creative outlet.

Current Events Center Made up of a bulletin board, daily newspapers, magazines, contemporary posters, radio, and television.

Unit Centers Made up of centers specific to the particular unit under study. A center to go with a unit on pioneers might include replicas of pioneer-day objects, pictures, costumes, or models.

EQUIPMENT AND MATERIALS

What are some general guides in selecting equipment and materials? First, remember the objectives. Then ask yourself the following questions. Is the equipment sturdy and well constructed? Is the equipment free from sharp edges and painted with nonpoisonous paint? Is it easily cleaned? Can the equipment be used for various activities? Does the equipment promote use by small groups, large groups, and individuals? Does it serve the needs of growing and changing children?

Uses

After you have studied the equipment in the room, it is helpful to analyze the equipment and materials in light of their purpose and use. The checklist in Table 5.1 may prove an aid in analyzing activity centers, equipment, and materials and can also serve as an inventory for possible suggestions for changing or adding to your own room.

Permanent Equipment

An early childhood room for twenty children should include the following permanent equipment. See Figures 5.3 and 5.4 for some typical classroom designs utilizing this equipment.

Tables and Chairs *Tables* should be made of wood and lightweight metal with silencers on legs and with water-resistant tops. They should be selected with regard for the size of children to be served.

2 tables 20″ and 24″ high with 24″ × 36″ tops
3 round tables 20″, 22″, and 24″ high and 36″ in diameter

Table 5.1 Center/Equipment/Material Checklist

	All of these	Additional items	Items needed
General use Tables and chairs of varying heights, shelves, clothes, lockers, bulletin boards, low screens			
Family center Stove, refrigerator, table, chairs, cupboards, ironing board, iron, mops, broom, dustpan, telephone, television, dolls, doll bed, sink, cooking utensils, dress-up clothes, mirror, table dishes and utensils			
Block center Solid unit blocks of various sizes, small blocks, wooden boards, large hollow blocks, and accessories for use with the blocks — trucks, cars, phones, animals, signs, human figures			
Art center Double easels with trough, clips for paper, brushes, drying rack, paints (poster paint, fingerpaint, water colors), clay, paste, crayons, newsprint, construction paper, scissors			
Music and rhythm area Piano, phonograph, records, tape recorder, tapes, record and tape storage holders, tone blocks, drums, triangles, sticks, tambourines			
Science materials Magnets, compass, thermometer, magnifiers, measuring cups and spoons, hourglass, animal cage, fish bowl, terrarium			

Table 5.1 *(cont.)*

	All of these	*Additional items*	*Items needed*

Library corner
Picture books, easy-to-read books, books to read aloud, a listening station, tapes, records

Woodworking
Workbench with vise; tools such as hammers, saws, planes; materials such as dowels, soft pine lumber, large-headed nails, paint, brushes

Water play
Plastic bottles, cups, and spoons; bowls; sponges; egg beaters; wooden spoons; pitchers; squeeze bottles

Large muscle play
Crawl-through kegs, wagons, tricycles, climbing steps

Small muscle play
Puzzles, pegboard and designs, design cubes, nestled blocks, picture lotto games, Tinkertoys®, logs, pipes and wrenches, sorting boxes

Washing and toilets
Low basins and toilets, drinking fountain, low mirror, low paper towel holders, liquid soap dispenser

Eating
Low tables and chairs, dull-tined forks, smooth-edged spoons, flat-bladed small knives with rounded end (butter knives will do), unbreakable glasses and dishes

Resting
Individual pads with washable covers and blankets, individual cots (if program is for a full day), storage for pads and cots

PROJECT
The School's Physical Environment

A school's physical environment should encourage all children to learn.

1. Visit a school and draw a room design of the permanent equipment in the room. Measure the open spaces in the room that allow children to move freely about the room.
2. Observe a group of children at work in a classroom and make a list of the materials they are using.
3. Observe a teacher teaching and list the materials being used.
4. Visit several schools and draw diagrams of their playgrounds and outdoor equipment.

Block play needs ample space.

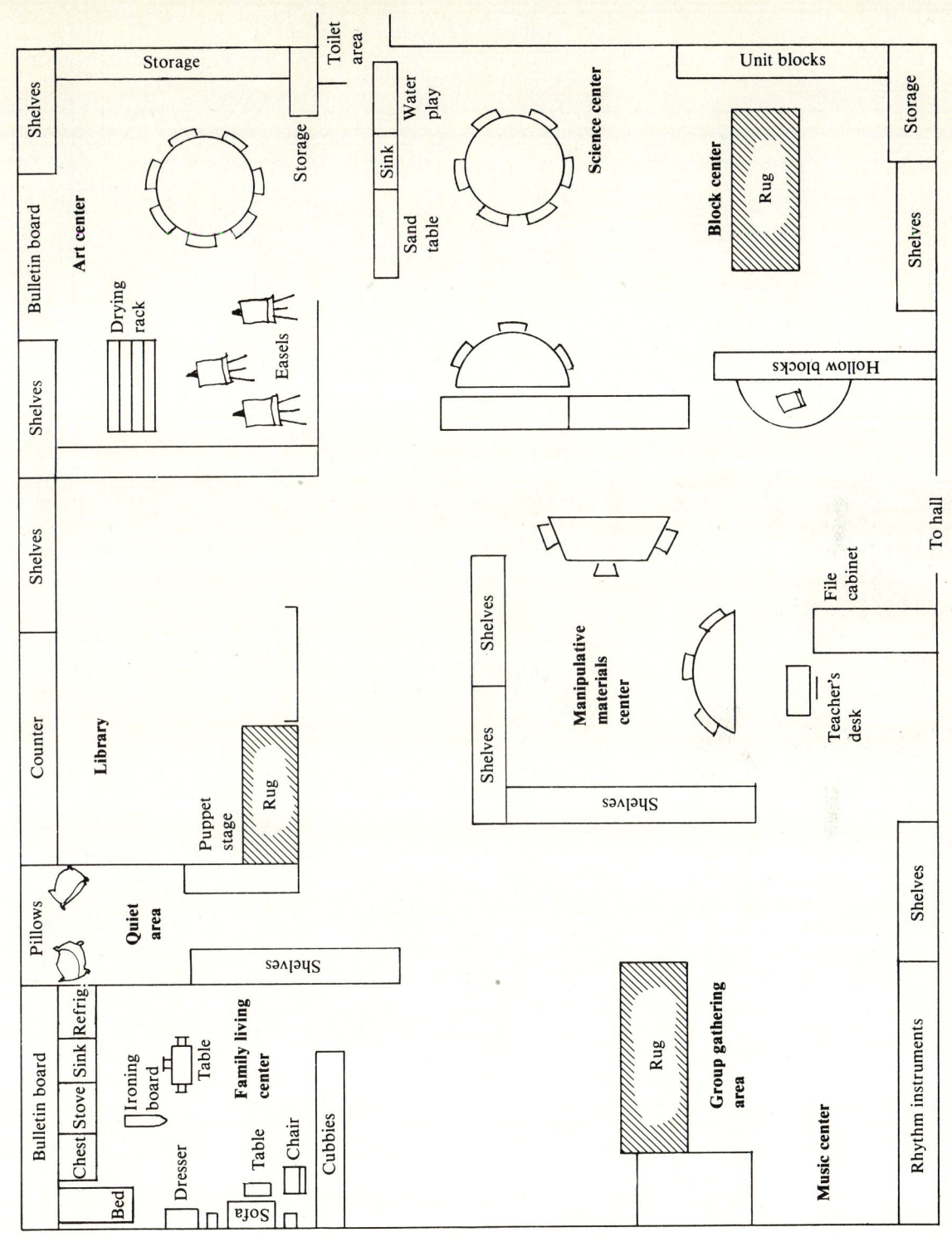

Figure 5.3 A Typical Classroom Design for Three Year Olds

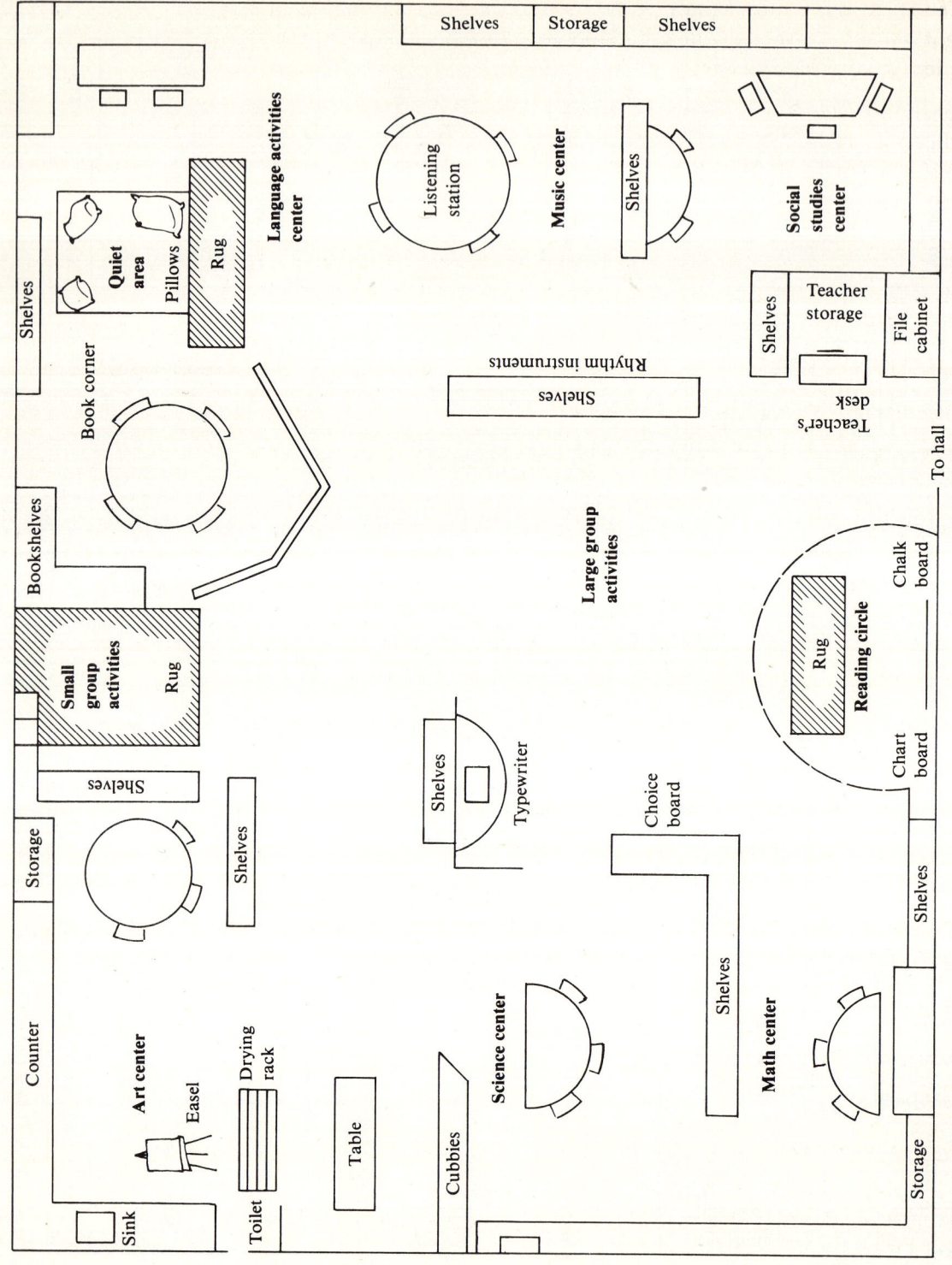

Figure 5.4 A Typical Classroom Design for Six Year Olds

Chairs designed to promote correct sitting posture and varied in seat height to provide for individual differences. Stackable chairs are desirable and legs should be equipped with silencers.

12 chairs with seats 10″, 12″, and 14″ high
3 adult chairs
1 small rocking chair
1 small beanbag chair

Storage and Display   *Storage space* should include sectional shelving light enough to be moved and adaptable for changing room space as children's interests change. Open shelves for blocks and other equipment frequently used by children should be easily accessible. Shelves containing toys that might roll out should have doors. Individual compartments should be available for each child's personal belongings.

12 individual cubicles 48″ high, 6″ wide, and 10″ deep with hooks and a shelf
6 cabinets 48″ long, 14″ deep, and 36″ high with open shelves
2 cabinets for teacher storage

Chalkboard should be at child's eye level.
Bulletin boards (3) made of cork should be at child's eye level.
Picture files should include cardboard, single-drawer file cabinets, metal phonograph record holders, or folding manila folders. These provide durable storage space to protect flat pictures.
Bookcases should have differing shelf heights. Children's books come in varying heights and widths.

2 bookcases 48″ long, 14″ deep, and 48″ high

Resting Equipment   *Resting equipment* is needed. The constant activity of young children and the stimulation of group interactivity necessitates provisions for rest. Lightweight, stackable cots are recommended. Quilted pads may be substituted for cots but they should have washable covers. Each child should have own washable blanket.

20 cots 48″ long, 26″ wide, and 12″ high
20 washable blankets
Storage for cots and blankets

Audio-visual Equipment   *Projection equipment* should include

16 mm motion picture projector with sound equipment
Combination filmstrip machine with 2″ × 2″ slide projector, slide carrier, and lift-off case

PROJECT
Remembering Your Own Early Childhood Education

One way to become a better teacher is to compare what you have personally experienced in your own education to current educational practices.

1. If you went to school before first grade, draw a diagram of how you remember the classroom.
2. Make a list of the furniture, toys, equipment, and materials you remember using or seeing in the room.
3. Describe the playground equipment you played on.
4. Write a paragraph on your favorite toys, equipment, or materials at age four or five.
5. Make a list of typical class activities in the order in which they were scheduled during the day.
6. Compare and contrast your recollections with your findings in the project on page 128.

Opaque projector
Projector stand
50" × 50" portable screen, stand type

Sound equipment, in the listening station, consisting of

2-speed tape recorder with microphone jack
AM/FM radio
Television set

Teacher's Materials   *Teacher's materials* are kept at the teacher's desk or wherever appropriate around the room.

Pair of 12" shears
Stapler
Paper punch
Adhesive tape
Masking tape (¾")
Clear tape
Thermometer (inside) with large figures
Thermometer (outside) with large figures
5 boxes of tissues

Tape measure
Straight pins and safety pins
Spoons
Yardstick
Foot rule
Green soap and adhesive bandages
Broom and dustpan
Wastepaper baskets
5 plastic sponges
U.S. flag

Equipment does not have to be expensive. Many of the items can be made from cardboard boxes or inexpensive materials. Some can be shared by several groups of children.

SUMMARY

Classroom organization is the physical "glue" that holds the subject area activities together. In this chapter we have presented ideas, suggestions, materials, and room designs to enable you to organize your own room for successful teaching. Classroom organization covers many different aspects, including factors influencing organization, planning and scheduling, individualizing and grouping activity centers, room settings, and permanent equipment. Even the best curriculum development and the best materials and equipment will not provide a good program for young children unless the teacher plans well, has developed a sequential, logical schedule of events for the day, and has organized the material and equipment in the room to provide opportunity for their use.

ADDITIONAL READINGS

Almy, M. *The Early Childhood Educator at Work*. New York: McGraw-Hill, 1975.

Bolgehold, B. D., et al. *Education Before Five*. New York: Bank Street, 1977.

Hendrick, Joan. *Total Learning for the Whole Child*. St. Louis, Mo.: C. V. Mosby, 1980.

Seefeldt, Carol. *A Curriculum for Preschools*. 2nd ed. New York: Charles E. Merrill, 1980.

Stevens, J. H., and Edith W. King. *Administering Early Childhood Education Programs*. Boston: Little, Brown, 1976.

PART THREE
Curriculum

A subject area guide for teaching young children, for developing materials for instructional use, for ordering supplies, for planning appropriate activities, and for comparing and contrasting the skills and content of the primary years.

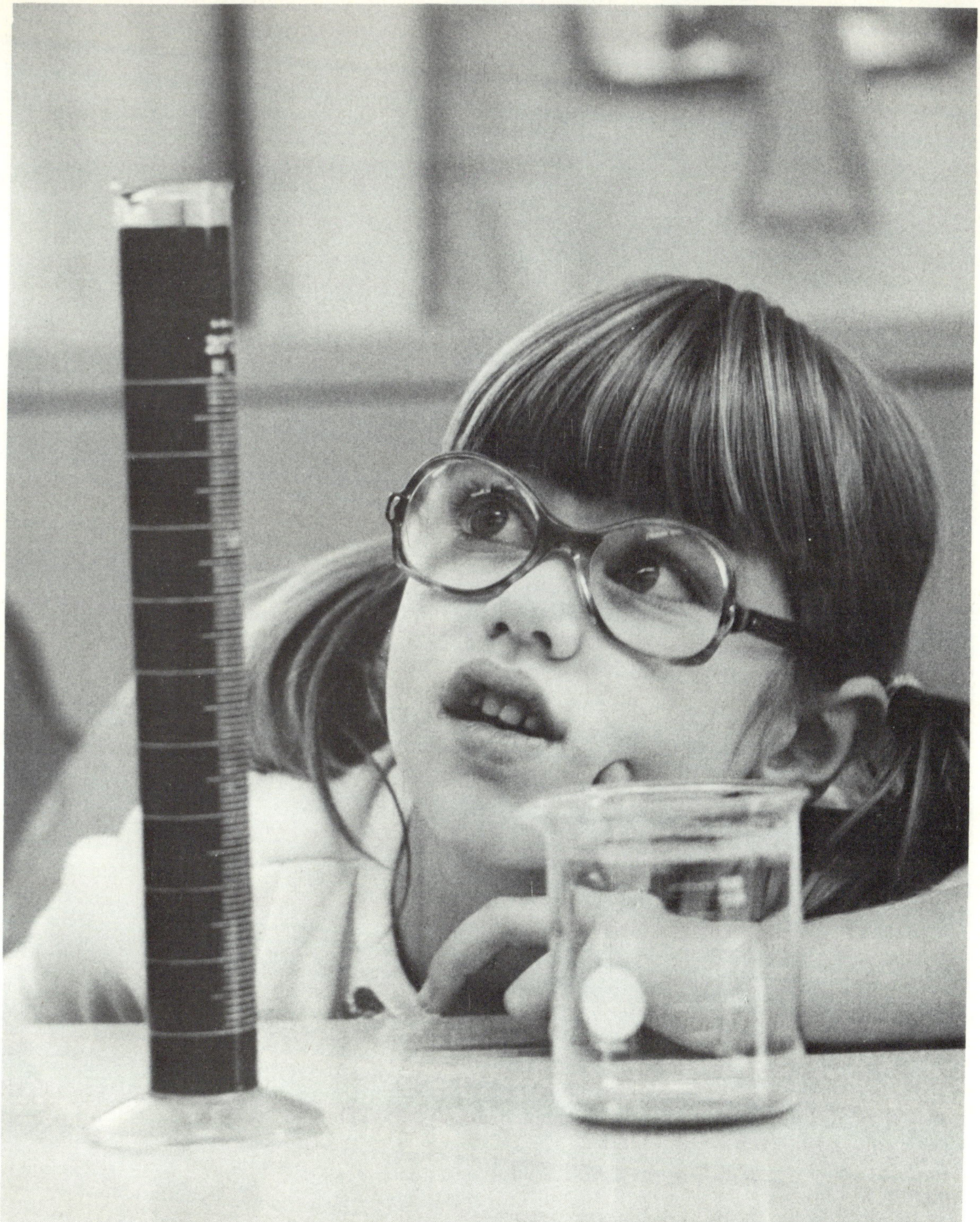

CHAPTER 6
The Language Arts

Focusing on goodness of fit between a particular child and a particular program recasts the issue of quality into a concern for individualization.

Elizabeth Prescott

Exploration Tasks

After studying this chapter, you should be able to complete these tasks:
- Identify and define each of the language arts.
- List the four major methods used to teach the language arts.
- Describe some of the different aspects influencing the development of oral language in children.
- Describe what children learn through the use of fingerplays.
- Define dramatization for young children.
- List the audiovisual aids used in a program for young children.
- Define manuscript writing and list ways teachers use it in a classroom.
- Describe how spelling is taught during the early years.
- Identify and discuss three elements of a reading program for young children.
- List the skills that are needed for reading readiness.
- Make a list of good books for young children.
- Discuss why young children like poetry.
- Describe a language experience chart.

OVERVIEW

The language arts furnish the most important skills taught in early childhood education. Although they are the major skills taught, they are usually taught in the context of one of the subject areas: science, social studies, math, or physical education. The language arts include development of listening skills, facility in oral language use, grammar structure, writing ability (both form and creative), spelling readiness, reading readiness, and (sometimes) reading ability. These skills are developed through the use of literature; dramatization; discussion; role playing; study trips; and the use of experience charts, fingerplays, listening stations (recorder, tapes, radio, TV, and so forth), puppetry, games, directions and explanations, pantomiming, interpreting pictures, and construction.

THEORETICAL CONTEXT

There are four major methods used to teach the language arts. One method requires the teacher to identify the child's specific weaknesses and problems in the various aspects of communication and then to "correct" them by direct instruction. Another method endorses the idea of providing a stimulating environment greatly enriched by materials and based on traditional activities found in upper-class private schools. These activities include the teaching of classical mythology and traditional folk tales, fairy tales, poetry, and children's songs. This subject matter is viewed as being beneficial to all children regardless of individual needs. A third method also advocates providing a stimulating environment, but that environment is used in two special ways: (1) for exploration and "idea" development by the children, which the teacher then builds upon and (2) for developing a preplanned sequence of events and activities for the children, a sequence that the teacher designs and controls. A fourth method combines certain features of the previous three; it seeks to meet individual needs by introducing activities, ideas, and materials appropriate for the child being taught.

At present there are two basic ways used to teach early reading. One is called skill orientation and the other ideational orientation. *Skill orientation* is based on the idea that reading is related to alphabetic writing as tokens of speech forms or aspects of linguistics. In this approach the child masters such things as learning letter names and sounds of letters. This is the approach that the TV program "Sesame Street" uses. In contrast to this approach, the *ideational orientation* approach develops oral language use with emphasis on content and meaning. Teachers use the child's own language and ideas and emphasize content and meaning. The teaching of reading to young children is not new nor are these two approaches, but what is new is the amount of basic research being conducted in this field by impartial researchers.

There are many aspects involved in teaching the language arts. Each of the language arts is discussed in detail in the remaining sections of this chapter.

ORAL LANGUAGE

Development of Speech

Speech does not occur suddenly, but develops gradually from many prelinguistic experiences.[1] From the first vocalization of the first real word, the child passes through a series of development stages while learning to talk. Each child goes from one stage to the next according to his or her own rate of development. Although all children do not speak at the same rate, speech generally follows a developmental pattern that is continuous, progressive, and predictable from birth to seven or eight years of age. Vocabulary and other language aspects continue to develop throughout a person's lifetime. Factors that may retard speech development include low mental ability, poor speech standards at home, and certain sibling positions in the family.

During the prelanguage period children cry, coo, gurgle, and babble, using almost all the vowel and consonant sounds in speech. By the seventh or eight month, vocalization occurs; that is, children are listening to and imitating their own sounds. By the tenth month, they begin to imitate sounds in their environment. At about the twelfth or fourteenth month, they speak their first words. Up to eighteen months they learn more words. From one and a half to two years, children begin to understand spoken language and respond to simple directions. They begin to acquire new words rapidly and they join the words to form sentences.

At three years of age, children are talking. They listen more attentively and use words with greater intelligence. Their sentences contain three or four words.

Four year olds enjoy talking and experimenting with words. "Why?" is often heard. Children like to listen to explanations, which increases their speaking and listening skills.

The average five year old is likely to have a wide vocabulary. A five year old is capable of forming six- and eight-word sentences, but may have difficulty with certain articulated sounds. At this stage the child's hearing mechanism should be sufficiently developed to hear speech sounds adequately.

---

[1] Information for this section was taken from Willard W. Hartup, ed., *The Young Child Reviews of Research*, Volume 11, No. 207 (Washington, D.C.: National Association for the Education of Young Children, 1972).

By age six vocabulary has increased to two or three thousand speaking words and to over seventeen thousand listening words. Sentence structure is more complex and reflects a variety of concepts, interests, and experiences.

Most children can make the speech sounds of *p*, *b*, *m*, *h*, *w*, and the sounds of the vowels by age three and a half; they can say the sounds of *t*, *d*, *n*, *k*, *g*, *ng*, and *y* by age four and a half; and they can say the sounds of *f*, *s*, and *z* by five and a half. By the time they are six and a half, they can use *ch*, *j*, *sh*, *th*, *l*, *r*, *wh*, *ht*, and all of the blends.

The majority of speech "defects" in young children are not really defects but are aspects of speech in the process of development. They usually disappear with maturation. Some children do have speech problems that cannot be corrected by a combination of maturity and opportunities for speaking and listening. To solve these problems a child will need help from a specialist; the teacher will need help in reinforcing the specialist's suggestions.

Listening

A child who listens is always listening to something. Listening, therefore, is not taught as a separate subject as science is but as a skill integrated into the content areas. At times during the entire daily program you will ask questions such as "John, where did we say a horse lives?" "What happened to Georgie and the ghost?" "Who remembers our rules for good manners on the bus?" You will also provide activities in all the classroom centers that require children to listen to other children. In addition, equipment and materials such as tapes, records, Systems 80®, Language Masters®, films, and television all require listening in their use. All lessons, whether taught by teacher or aide, require listening.

As a teacher of young children you should remember three important aspects of listening: plan for listening activities; know how to evaluate listening comprehension; and communicate to parents, other teachers, and other school personnel when and how you are providing opportunities for children to master this important skill. Children need to listen accurately and to be accurate listeners. If you as a teacher keep in mind the following suggestions, you will develop good listeners:

- Establish a classroom climate that is stimulating not only for "doing" but for "talking."
- Give accurate, clear, and precise directions, explanations, and examples.
- Be a good speech model in pronunciation and enunciation. Adjust the volume of your voice for individual, small-group, or whole-class discussions; for examples; and for directions.
- Provide many opportunities for children to talk to each other.
- Tell children the names of the things they use or observe and provide

them with a variety of descriptive words to relate their reactions and feelings.
- Be a patient, courteous, and attentive listener.
- Plan for introducing new words and their meanings as you plan units and select new books or new material.

Detailed research, methods, and activities will be discussed in your required language arts methods course.[2] As activities and experiences are presented in other chapters in this book, you will be reminded that listening is part of teaching.

A child's use of oral language is closely related to listening habits. In the following section we will discuss the environmental, mental, physical, emotional, and social factors that affect use of oral language and that also affect an individual's ability to listen.

Factors Affecting Oral Language

My mamma bought a new dress and my daddy got mad and my mamma wouldn't cook us anything to eat and my daddy got mad and he slammed the door and broke the glass and my mamma got mad and we went to my grandmamma's.

Young children like to talk. They enjoy "trying out" words and sounds. They will talk to anyone who will listen or to no one in particular. Some children, however, are reserved and withhold their comments until they feel completely secure. Their talk is of many things — an imaginary event, a happening at home, an exciting moment, or a serenely beautiful moment.

Children are individuals in their use of speech just as they are in other aspects of their individuality. Some talk in compound and complex sentences while others use single words and simple sentences. Some understand and precisely enunciate hundreds of words, while others have limited vocabularies and slur their words.

Environmental Differences If a child has always lived in a high-rise tenement, his or her experiences, interests, and, consequently, language will differ from those of a child who has lived in an upper-income suburban home and has taken many vacation trips. Where a child lives, whether it is a city, a coal-mining town, a migrant camp, a small farm, or a year-round home near a lake, affects language patterns.

Other environmental factors also affect a child's language: economic and cultural conditions, the number of children in the family, nationality, and religion. The child adopts the idioms and colloquialisms used by adults. If parents do not encourage questions, the child learns few words and doesn't know how to formulate a question. If all those around the child speak nonstandard English, teachers' expectations of the child's use of standard English in school are hopeless unless the child can be motivated by rewards and success.

---

[2] For review in this area, consult Paul C. Burns and Betty L. Broman, *The Language Arts in Childhood Education*, 4th ed. (Chicago: Rand McNally, 1979).

The language a child brings from home is called *primary language*. In some cases this is a nonstandard form of English. Often, however, the language at home may be Spanish, Japanese, Italian, or Greek; English in this case is considered a *second language*. These two conditions create two distinctly different problems.

Deprivation of opportunity to learn standard English Many children in the United States use a nonstandard, alternate form of English. While this is especially true of black slum children and white Appalachian children, other regional differences also exist in the United States. Use of pure, standard English is difficult to find. As you select your school community, learn to understand the English dialect spoken there. Plan activities that will enable the children to begin to understand and to use standard English. Your modeling of what standard English sounds like will be a strong, influential factor.

This complicated problem has three sides. You must be a good model so that the children have an opportunity to hear and imitate standard English. At the same time, you must use familiar words and expressions to refer to objects, places, and activities. Finally, the whole process of education is based on the idea that schooling provides opportunities for new learning. The old saying "start where the child is" provides a very valid and valuable guide in language development. Important learnings for three, four, and five year olds will be discussed in each of the subject chapters; but one good suggestion for beginning to expand children's oral language abilities is to start with concrete objects and activities rather than abstract situations.

Problems of non-English-speaking children The non-English-speaking child, like other children, may have had many opportunities or very limited opportunities. He or she has been exposed to more or less the same family relationships as other children: having been accepted, loved, and cared for matter of factly as another member of the family; having been merely tolerated; or having been rejected. He or she may be an only child or one of many children. The child has the same wants and the same needs as English-speaking children. The child is either a success or a failure in the environment. Problems, if they arise, usually occur when the young child is placed in a setting that is more or less representative of the general culture of the United States — white, English speaking, middle class, and (generally) Protestant.

Young children are probably aware of the larger community in which they live and may be at odds with its existence. A public school is the first enforced cultural conflict for many non-English-speaking children. Discrimination of one kind or another is practiced in varying degrees throughout the country. The first school experiences can be traumatic for any child; the child who encounters discriminatory practices has an even more difficult adjustment.

The bilingual and bicultural child The bilingual and bicultural child entering early childhood classes, lives in two worlds. Even the child who already is successful and comfortable in two languages and two cultures meets the usual problems of learning, physical growth, health, mental development, and social development. The teacher has an important responsibility in teaching this child to value more than one cultural heritage.

Mental Differences The use of oral language is closely related to mental development. Words represent ideas; the complexity of the ideas children understand or create is controlled to a large extent by their ability to think. The children in a classroom are not all three, four, or five at the same time; even if they were, the normal or average language development would vary greatly in any group.

Physical Differences Some children are full of vim, vigor, and vitality — alert and eager to learn. They have normal sight and hearing, enunciate distinctly, and pronounce words correctly. They get adequate nourishment, rest, and exercise to keep their energy level high all day. Other youngsters have these traits in varying degrees. A few have none of them.

Emotional and Social Differences Some children have learned that the world is a happy, pleasant place, while other children's experiences have instilled fear and suspicion. In many instances, children's feelings about themselves and their world influence language fluency.

Some children may have learned to get along with adults and other children and to talk easily to new acquaintances. They have learned to give and take in conversation. Other children may not have had an opportunity to socialize with adults and children outside their immediate families. This lack of social adjustment will affect language growth.

Grammar

In early childhood education grammar is taught so that children will become good users of language. As a teacher you are not only a model of good language, you also provide opportunities for children to grow in their use of language. For instance, you might ask a question and have the children reword the question to make it a statement: "Margaret, would you like to water the plants?" becomes "Margaret, water the plants, please." You can plan activities in which the children add modifiers to nouns or verb phrases to make their language more specific: "I like ice cream," becomes "I like chocolate fudge ice cream"; "Ann went home" becomes "Ann walked and ran home."

Games such as "I see something," descriptions offered during sharing time, discussions of out-of-school experiences, role playing with dress-up costumes, observations of nature, and science-related activities are a few of the many opportunities you will have to encourage children to become good users of language. Children must talk to extend their language ability. Reading literature to children will enrich their vocabulary; writing their dictated stories will supply opportunities to use it.

Activities for Developing Oral Language

Fingerplays Why use fingerplays? Fingerplays have little literary value; their purpose is not to establish a background in poetry. Probably the main reason for using fingerplays is to provide the teacher with visual clues of a child's comprehension and auditory memory.

Fingerplays require thinking; comprehension; and physical control of fingers, hands, arms, and other parts of the body. They are often carefully directed activities. Listening, the most difficult skill to teach, seems to be the most difficult to acquire; fingerplays provide enjoyable activities that require the children to make responses that are visually discerned by the teacher. Teachers can use this simple evaluation tool to check two activities at once — listening and comprehension.

The following fingerplays, by unknown authors, are commonly used by teachers. For more fingerplays, consult the books for teachers at the conclusion of this section.

Little Jenny Wren

As little Jenny Wren
Was sitting by her shed,
She waggled with her tail,   (Shake hips.)
And nodded with her head.   (Nod head.)
She waggled with her tail,   (Repeat above.)
And nodded with her head,
As little Jenny Wren
Was sitting by her shed.

Robin Redbreast

Little Robin Redbreast   (Thumb and little finger extended.)
Sat upon a rail.
Niddle, noddle went his head   (Move thumb.)
And wiggle, waggle went his tail. (Move little finger.)

My little kitten

My little kitten ran up a tree	(Fingers running up arms.)
And sat on a limb to look at me.	(Hands rest on opposite shoulder.)
I said, "Come kitty," and down he ran	(Fingers running down arms.)
And drank all the milk	(Hand cupped, with opposite finger drinking from pan.)
I poured in his pan.	

Pig

I had a little pig	(Fist with thumb up.)
And I fed it in a trough.	(Make cup of left hand.)
He got so big and fat,	(Make circle of arms.)
That his tail popped off!	(Clap both hands and knees.)
So, I got me a hammer	(One hand is hammer.)
And I got me a nail,	(Hammer on thumb of other hand.)
And I made the pig	(Continue to hammer.)
A wooden tail!	

My dolly

This is how my dolly walks,	(Children walk around circle, stiff-legged with arms raised.)
This is how she walks, you see.	
This is how my dolly runs,	(Run stiff-legged.)
This is how she runs, you see.	
This is how my dolly talks,	(Bend over, say, "Mama, Mama.")
This is how she talks, you see.	

Hands

On my head my hands I place,
On my shoulders, on my face,
On my lips, at my side;
Quickly at my back they hide.

Five little rabbits

Five little rabbits	(Show five fingers.)
Under a log.	(Cover with other hand.)
One says, "Hark, I hear a dog!"	(Show one finger, hand behind ear.)
One says, "Look, I see a man!"	(Point, indicating eye.)

Little hands

Open, shut them; open, shut them,	(Do motions as poem suggests.)
Give a little clap;	
Open, shut them; open, shut them;	
Lay them in your lap.	
Creep them, creep them slowly upward	
To the rosy cheek;	
Open wide the shining eyes	

Through the fingers peek.
Open, shut them; open, shut them;
To the shoulders fly;
Let them like the birdies flutter,
Flutter to the sky.
Falling, falling slowly downward,
Nearly to the ground;
Quickly raise them, all the fingers
Twirling round and round.
Open, shut them; open, shut them;
Lay them in your lap.

Five little kittens

There were five little kittens.   (Hold left hand up; with right hand, fold the
One little kitten went to sleep.   left-hand fingers into the palm, one by one,
Two little kittens went to sleep.   starting with little finger.)
Three little kittens went to sleep.
Four little kittens went to sleep.
Five little kittens went to sleep.
All the kittens were fast asleep.

Night and morning

The little boy is going to bed;   (First finger of right hand in palm of left.)
Down on the pillow he lays his head;   (Thumb of left hand is pillow.)
Wraps himself in the covers tight —   (Fingers of left hand closed.)
This is the way he sleeps all night.
Morning comes, he opens his eyes;
Back with a toss the cover flies: (Fingers of left hand open.)
Up he jumps, is dressed and away.   (Right index finger up and hopping away.)
Ready for frolic and play all day.

Quacking ducks

Five little ducks went out to play.   (Hold up five fingers on one hand.)
Over the hills and far away.   (Make fingers run away.)
Mama duck said,   (Make quacking motions with thumb
"Quack, Quack, Quack."   and four fingers.)
Four little ducks came running back.   (Four fingers run back.)

Going to sleep

Some things go to sleep in such a
funny way —
Little birds stand on one leg and   (Stand on one leg.)
tuck their heads away.   (Tuck head.)
Little chickens do the same a-
sitting on their perch.

Little mice lie soft and still as if
they were in church.
Little kittens all curl up in such a
funny ball.
Sleepy children all stretch out,   (Stretch and stand tall.)
so they'll grow straight and tall.

Five little astronauts

Five little astronauts	(Hold up fingers of one hand.)
Ready for outer space.	
The first one said,	(Hold up one finger.)
"Let's have a race."	
The second one said,	(Hold up two fingers.)
"The weather's too rough."	
The third one said,	(Hold up three fingers.)
"Oh, don't be gruff."	
The fourth one said,	(Hold up four fingers.)
"I'm ready enough."	
The fifth one said,	(Hold up five fingers.)
"Let's Blast Off!"	
10, 9, 8, 7, 6, 5, 4, 3, 2, 1	(Start with ten fingers and put one down with each number.)
BLAST OFF!!!!	(Clap loudly with "Blast Off!")

Some especially useful books on fingerplays include:

Cromwell, Liz, and Dixie Hibner. *Finger Frolics: Fingerplays for Young Children*. Livonia, Mich.: Partner Press, 1978.

Glazer, T. *Eye Winker, Tom Tinker, Chin Chopper: A Collection of Musical Finger Plays*. New York: Doubleday, 1972.

Scott, Louise Binder, and J. J. Thompson. *Rhymes for Fingers and Flannelboards*. St. Louis: Webster, 1960.

Steiner, Biolette G., and Roberta Evatt Pond. *Finger Play Fun*. Columbus, Ohio: Charles E. Merrill, 1970.

Dramatization   There is a difference between dramatizing a story and dramatic play. Since this chapter is devoted to the language arts, this discussion will be limited to dramatizing a story. Dramatic play will be discussed in the chapters on play and social studies because many of the events in both situations include role playing and acting out life styles.

Dramatization integrates the curriculum in a program for young children. As a new teacher you will want to be cognizant of the many interrelated activities within your planning.

Some stories lend themselves to being acted out by young children. The younger the child the less activity by the "acting child." At times the teacher or aide will read the story slowly as the children act out the story. At other times one child will tell the story while others do the acting. A tape of the story might be used, although teachers who have used this technique have discovered that often the children do not "act" in tempo with the tape. As a teacher you will want to watch the children and read or tell the story at their speed.

The books, nursery rhymes, and stories in the following list are probably available to you as a student teacher or aide or as needed for your lab experience. They have proven to be favorites of young children.

Caps for Sale
Do You Move as I Do?
Theodore Turtle
The Little Fir Tree
The Snowy Day
Mud! Mud! Mud!
On a Summer's Day
"*Humpty Dumpty*"

"*Hickory, Dickory, Dock!*"
Gingerbread Boy
Jack and Jill
The Three Pigs
The Three Bears
The Three Billy Goats Gruff
The Little Red Hen
Chicken Little

Puppetry Though puppetry is a fun experience, it is also a learning one. Usually a limited number of youngsters are physically involved in the activity — one, two, or three at the most. Because of the small size of most puppet stages, you will want to plan short events or one event with several short scenes so that the puppeteers can be changed or the "watchers" can move about. This will be a listening and watching occasion for most of the children. The use of puppets is a quiet-time activity that should be balanced by an active experience when you are planning for the day.

Puppets may be purchased or they may be made by the teacher and children. The puppets can be made from socks, sacks, sticks, flannel, papier maché, plastic bottles, or paper plates.

Usually you will want a selection of finger puppets, hand puppets, or stick puppets. Finger puppets can provide several characters on one hand and are good for scenes with several characters. Hand puppets that fit over the hand are generally made of sacks, flannel, or papier maché. Two or three children can use hand puppets at the same time on most puppet stages built for young children. Stick puppets are held by the hands and do not move. Finger and hand puppets can nod heads, clap hands, and grasp objects.

The use of puppets not only encourages oral language, but also develops listening skills, reinforces grammar usage, and provides another activity that correlates the language arts aspect of a program with other subject areas.

Flannelboards Flannelboards may be used in any subject area, but are exceptionally useful in the language arts program. An inexpensive flannel-

Puppets help stimulate conversations.

board can be made from any stiff, flat material (cardboard, plastic, plywood, or tagwood). A piece of flannel is placed over the flat surface. In selecting the flannel for the background, you will want to analyze the purposes of the board. Teachers usually make several boards of varying sizes and colors. To tell a story to a small group, you may need a small board to place on a chair or on your lap. At other times you will need a large flannelboard to relate an event requiring many characters or using objects that require a large space. Children will use a flannelboard to make up their own stories, depicting events of importance to them.

Characters or objects are easily made from felt, flannel, dress interfacing, or paper. A piece of sandpaper glued on the back of the figure will make it stay in place on the board.

While commercial boards and figures are available, as an observer and student teacher you will have an opportunity to see, discuss, and make your own materials. If you are selective in your construction, you will soon have several sets of flannelboard figures and background boards.

Activities for a flannelboard include telling a story in sequence, vocabulary development, concept building, creating new stories, reinforcing the reading of a story with concrete visual objects, oral discussions of character action, and assessments of listening comprehension through children's participation in the activities.

Books on flannelboard use include the following:

Anderson, Paul S. *Storytelling with the Flannel Board*. Minneapolis: Denison, 1963.

Scott, Louise Binder, and J. J. Thompson. *Rhymes for Fingers and Flannelboards*. St. Louis: Webster, 1960.

Wagner, Joseph Anthony. *Flannelboard Teaching Aids*. Palo Alto, Calif.: Fearon, 1950.

Records and Tapes Listening centers in early childhood classrooms are now very common. Usually the center consists of a tape recorder or record player with several headphones. Children in many situations operate the station themselves. Children can use the listening station without the help of a teacher or aide if tapes and records have identifying pictures glued to them. In this way children can make their own choices.

Many commercial records and tapes are available. Tapes can also be easily made by a teacher while reading aloud.

The following records and tapes have proven to be favorites of children:

"Angus and the Ducks." Weston Woods (LTR 039). Cassette (PBP 109/109c).
"The Big Snow." Weston Woods (LTR 025c). Cassette (LTR 025c).
"The Biggest Bear." Weston Woods (LTR 010). Cassette (LTR 010c).
"Blueberries for Sal." Weston Woods (LTR 041). Cassette (LTR 041c).
"Bruno Munari's ABC." Weston Woods (LTR 050). Cassette (LTR 050c).
"Bruno Munari's Zoo." Weston Woods (LTR 097). Cassette (LTR 097c).
"The Camel Who Took a Walk." Weston Woods (LTR 011). Cassette (103c).
"Caps for Sale." Weston Woods (LTR 012). Cassette (104c).
"A Child's Garden of Verses." Caedmon (TC 1077). Cassette (CDL 51077).
"The Circus Baby." Weston Woods (LTR 013). Cassette (LTR 013c).
"Complete Version of Ye Three Blind Mice." Weston Woods (LTR 060). Cassette (LTR 060c).
"Curious George Rides a Bike." Weston Woods (LTR 017). Cassette (PBC 105c).
"Danny and the Dinosaur." Weston Woods (LTR 067). Cassette (PBC 116c).
"Don't Count Your Chicks." Weston Woods (LTR 043). Cassette (LTR 043c).
"Fish in the Air." Weston Woods (LTR 078). Cassette (LTR 078c).
"The Five Chinese Brothers." Weston Woods (LTR 018). Cassette PBP 105c).
"Frank Luther Sings Lois Lenski Songs." Wack (WA 1A-1B).
"Gilberto and the Wind." Weston Woods (LTR 104). Cassette (PBP 124c).

"Happy Birthday to You and Other Stories" (Dr. Seuss). Caedmon (TC 1287). Cassette (CDL 51287).

"The Happy Day and Where Does the Butterfly Go When It Rains." Weston Woods (LTR 096). Cassette (LTR 096c).

"The Happy Owls and The Three Robbers." Weston Woods (LTR 063). Cassette (PBP 115c).

"The Hare and the Tortoise and The Lion and the Rat." Weston Woods (LTR 102). Cassette (LTR 102c).

"Harold and the Purple Crayon." Weston Woods (LTR 044). Cassette (PBP 112c).

"Hercules." Weston Woods (LTR 002). Cassette (LTR 002c).

"Hey Diddle Diddle, Baby Bunting and The Milkmaid." Weston Woods (LTR 034). Cassette (PBP 109c).

"In the Forest." Weston Woods (LTR 019). Cassette (LTR 109c).

"It Looked Like Spilt Milk and Sleepy Book." Weston Woods (LTR 098). Cassette (TWR 22c).

"Jenny's Birthday Book." Weston Woods (LTR 020). Cassette (PBP 105c).

"Johnny Crow's Garden." Weston Woods (LTR 021). Cassette (PBP 106c).

"Josie and the Snow." Weston Woods (LTR 094). Cassette (LTR 094c).

"Just Me." Weston Woods (LTR 106). Cassette (LTR 106c).

"Little Bear's Visit." Weston Woods (LTR 083). Cassette (LTR 083c).

"Little Tim and the Brave Sea Captain." Weston Woods (LTR 047). Cassette (PBP 111c).

"Little Toot." Weston Woods (LTR 016). Cassette (LTR 016c).

"Madeline and Other Bemelmans." Caedmon (TC 1113). Cassette (CDL 51113).

"Magic Michael." Weston Woods (LTR 022). Cassette (LTR 022c).

"Make Way for Ducklings." Weston Woods (LTR 0003). Cassette (LTR 003c).

"Mike Mulligan and His Steam Shovel." Weston Woods (LTR 004). Cassette (LTR 004c).

"Millions of Cats." Weston Woods (LTR 005). Cassette (PBP 101c).

"Mr. Rabbit and the Lovely Present." Weston Woods (LTR 082). Cassette (LTR 182c).

"The Mother Goose Treasury." Weston Woods (LTR 109). Cassette (LTR 109c).

"The Owl and the Pussy-Cat and Wynken, Blynken and Nod." Weston Woods (LTR 076). Cassette (LTR 076c).

"Peter and the Wolf" (Leonard Bernstein). Educational Record Sales. Record or cassette.

"Peter's Chair." Weston Woods (LTR 107). Cassette (LTR 107c).

"Petunia." Weston Woods (LTR 045). Cassette (PBP 111c).

"Play With Me." Weston Woods (LTR 046). Cassette (LTR 046c).

"Sing a Song of Sixpence and Queen of Hearts." Weston Woods (LTR 038). Cassette (LTR 038c).

"Old Mother Hubbard and Her Dog." Weston Woods (LTR 037). Cassette (PBP 109c).

"The Old Woman and Her Pig." Weston Woods (LTR 040). Cassette (PBP 109c).

"The Story about Ping." Weston Woods (LTR 008). Cassette (LTR 008c).

"Sun Up." Weston Woods (LTR 095). Cassette (LTR 095c).

"The Tale of Benjamin Bunny." Weston Woods (LTR 069). Cassette (TWR 17c).

"The Tale of Peter Rabbit." Caedmon (TC 1314). Cassette (COL 51314).

"The Tale of Mr. Jeremy Fisher." Weston Woods (LTR 070). Cassette (TWR 17c).

"Three Little Pigs and Other Fairy Tales." Caedmon (TC 1129). Cassette (COL 51129).

"A Tree is Nice." Weston Woods (LTR 032). Cassette (LTR 032c).

"Umbrella." Weston Woods (LTR 105). Cassette (LTR 105c).

"Whistle for Willie." Weston Woods (LTR 065). Cassette (PBP 116c).

Sources for ordering tapes and records

Caedmon Records and Tapes
D. C. Heath and Company
2700 North Richardt Avenue
Indianapolis, IN 46219

Weston Woods Records and Tapes
Weston Woods Studios, Inc.
Weston, CN 06880

Educational Record Sales
New York, NY 10007

Pictures Whether they come from a commercial set, are photographs, are drawn by the teacher, or are clipped from magazines, pictures can be used effectively in several ways with young children. The pictures should always be simple and clear in detail. If they are not already laminated or mounted on a stiff cardboard, do so before you use them in teaching. Children enjoy touching and holding pictures; therefore, each picture should be in such condition that it cannot be damaged easily.

Attractive bulletin boards are a must. Pictures help create interest and discussion whenever a new one is added to the board. Pictures held by teachers or aides will help children develop creative stories and relate events that have happened to them and will stimulate responses to questions asked by the teacher or aide. Oral language experiences are initiated, additional listening opportunities are provided, vocabulary is broadened, and word meaning is enriched by the use of pictures. As a potential student teacher you will want to begin a file collection of pictures.

Television Television requires both listening and viewing and, therefore, involves a language arts skill. The influence of television is easily observable by listening to children's discussions. Television does not seem to change speech patterns, but does change the content of oral discussions, probably because viewing is a passive activity that does not require the child to speak.

It is this author's view that television viewing in a formal program for young children should be limited. In the learning situation children need more active and social oral experiences than viewing television — experiences not usually provided in a home setting.

A booklet, "General Guidelines for Selecting Television Programming for Children," may be ordered from the nonprofit Committee on Children's Television, Inc., 1511 Masonic Avenue, San Francisco, CA 94117. This booklet is revised annually to include the latest research on televison programming and its effects on children.

READING

The teacher had made a chart of classroom activities. Beside each activity the teacher had placed an envelope to hold the name cards of the children in the room. In the morning before free play, each child chose his or her first activity; the teacher placed the child's name card in the appropriate envelope. After several weeks of this, the teacher began encouraging individuals to be the "teacher" and to place the cards in the envelope as the children made their choices. One day Laura announced she would like to make the assignments. After choosing her activity and putting her card in

Do you teach three, four, and five year olds to read? The answer is yes, no, and sometimes. Any discussion of the teaching of reading to young children touches on many controversial, emotion-laden issues. We must be careful not to turn out a world of youngsters who were turned off from reading because they were forced to do something that was too hard for them. When it is possible to identify a hundred or more "sure" approaches to the teaching of reading, as Aukerman does in *Approaches to Beginning Reading* (1971), the problem is even more confusing.

The first step in trying to settle the problem is to define *reading*. One group of educators defines reading as a decoding process; that is, children learn the relationships between written symbols (letters/words) and spoken sounds (letters/words). They believe that once these relationships have been mastered, the children are reading. These educators also believe that beginning readers already have a large oral vocabulary and know the meanings and concepts of the vocabulary words. Therefore, teachers do not need to stress word meaning and concepts but should stress the letter-sound associations that unlock the printed symbol.

Another group of educators agrees that reading is a decoding process, but they insist that deriving meaning from the printed symbols is of greatest importance and decoding is secondary. They believe that for genuine reading to occur, word recognition must be accompanied by word comprehension. Every experience and activity that you plan for the children in your room develops in some way a background for learning to read. Whether or not a child will learn to read printed symbols in a book or on a worksheet, a chart, or a chalkboard depends on individual ability and skill and, above all, on reading readiness.

Reading Readiness

Reading readiness is the stage at which a child is ready to begin formal reading instruction. This "stage" occurs at various times in children's early years. Generally, children are thought to achieve readiness for reading late in their fifth year or early in their sixth year. Most research shows that children age five and over can learn to read to some extent.[3] The research also shows that in most cases these children do not learn to read any better than their counterparts who are not reading at age five. There is also research that indicates that the majority of those reading by age five do not surpass their classmates in reading ability at the third-grade level.

An understanding of how children learn to read is very important for the teacher of young children. Even if you do not have children in your classroom who are ready to read, or if you teach in a community where teaching of reading is prohibited for anyone under age six, you need to know the basic foundation steps for developing good readers whenever they are ready to read. Many of the activities and experiences a child has in an early childhood program are reading-readiness oriented.

The Reading Process

The amount of time and money spent on the teaching of reading in public schools indicates the complexity of learning to read. The process involves attitudes, habits, skills, backgrounds of ideas, varying meanings of words, cultural differences, and children's differing capacities to learn to read.

Reading is a two-way process. A child brings meanings to printed symbols; when these printed symbols are put in a certain sequence to make a statement or question, the child receives a new meaning, an added meaning, or a reinforcing meaning of the symbols. To know the meanings of oral words, the child must have many experiences that broaden and give depth to the words. Accumulated experiences help individuals express and receive ideas. As the words are "read" the child "hears" each word and brings to it the background knowledge she or he has received through listening and speaking. All activities that require listening or speaking or both in a program for three, four, or five year olds are therefore readiness-for-reading activ-

that envelope, she puzzled over the other cards for a while and then sputtered, "Oh, fiddle! I wish I could read." (Whereupon the teacher began the first lesson in configuration.)

Mother: "What did you learn in school today?"

Mike: "To read."

Mother: "What did you read?"

Mike: "Boys."

Mother: "Boys? What does boys mean?"

Mike: "It means girls can't go in there."

---

[3] The classic studies on which reading readiness is based may be found in Arthur I. Gates, "The Necessary Mental Age for Beginning Reading," *Elementary School Journal*, 37 (March 1937): 497–508; Arnold L. Gesell, *The Mental Growth of the Preschool Child* (New York: Macmillan, 1925); and M. V. Morphett and Carleton Washburne, "When Should Children Begin to Read?" *Elementary School Journal*, 31 (March 1931): 496–503.

Table 6.1 Reading Content Spiral in Two Preprimers

Level 4: *This Is for Me*

Topics (word and sentence content and concepts)	Picture illustrations (to add to meaning of printed symbols)
Outside activities (having friends, jumping rope, rolling a tire, jumping in and out)	Window, brick wall, sidewalk, fall season, doves, tires, brick house, wooden fence
Getting dressed	Bedroom furniture, closet, desk, kitchen furniture, living room furniture
Walking to school with friends	School building
Meeting friends on way to school	Hallway of home, doll
Time to go to school	Umbrella, grandfather clock
What to see on way to school	Schoolyard activities, city street
Work of construction workers (construction machines)	Construction machines, fenced school yard
Riding a bicycle	School books, satchels
A classroom surprise	A rabbit
Walking home	A tree with fence guard
Sharing a picture with family	Potted plants in window

Level 5: *Like You and Me*

Topics (word and sentence content and concepts)	Picture illustrations (to add to meaning of printed symbols)
Visiting friend who lives in apartment house	Window, hat box, elevator, stairs, wig
Visiting a library	Books, shelves, librarian, desk
Seeing a fire engine at a fire	Fire engine, police, skyscraper
Buying groceries	Grocery store, clerk
Visiting a pet store	Pet store window, cages, rabbits, puppy, parrot
The work of a tugboat	Harbors, ships, iron fence, dock, iron and wood bench
Identification of math figures	Chalkboard, chalk
A lost puppy	City street, book shelf, sign, newspaper, living room
A visit to a museum	Bus, blue whale, rock crab, starfish, octopus, dinosaurs

Table 6.1 (cont.)

Level 5: *Like You and Me* (cont.)

Topics (word and sentence content and concepts)	Picture illustrations (to add to meaning of printed symbols)
An ugly duckling	Ducks, pond, grass, hen, fall leaves, storm, snows, swans, sun
A pet puppy	Fall, leaves, rake
Growing up	Basket, police officer, firefighter, newspaper reporter, photographer, doctor

ities.[4] The sample reading content spiral in Table 6.1 will help you understand the content knowledge needed before a child will read with ease. A reading content spiral progresses from the simplest of pictures, words, and concepts to the more complex meanings of pictures, words, and sentences.

When reading is recognized as developmental, growth will be based on previous learning, will be continuous, and will be unified in other content areas. Reading is not a series of unrepeated steps. The process is repeated each time a new experience occurs. As a child has more experiences in reading, the process becomes faster.

Reading Readiness Skills

Several aspects of learning to read are natural occurrences in programs for young children. As a teacher of these children you should be able to classify the activities in your program that will develop these necessary skills.

Vision Development The act of reading requires perpetual visual power. The two aspects of vision involve the eye as an organ and the performance of the eye. When a child has reading problems, some eye specialists examine the eyes only for problems in the interior and exterior parts of the eye, problems in the ability of the eye to focus on small letters at twenty feet, and problems in the optical systems in both eyes. These are problems of the eye as an organ. Vision also includes the performance of the eye — the focus of both eyes on an object, the speed of this focus, the accuracy of the change in focus from one word to another word, and the ability to maintain these skills continuously at various reading distances. All of these visual skills do not develop equally or at the same time in all children. Therefore, some children will have visual problems other than those identified by an eye specialist. Because of the complexity of the development of perpetual

---

[4] *Harper & Row Design for Reading* (New York: Harper & Row, 1972). See the first two preprimers.

visual power, many educators prefer to wait until the child is six and a half years old before teaching reading. Physicians have identified this as the age by which most children have developed sufficient visual power to read printed symbols.

Gross Difference Discrimination What are gross differences? They are differences that are immediately obvious in like items, such as differences in size, shape, color, or texture. In selecting materials and equipment for classrooms, vary the size, shape, and color of like items. Large and small blocks of varying colors; large and small cars and trucks of varying shapes; collections of paper, cloth, plastic, leather, wood, and so on of varying sizes, shapes, and colors; and dolls, furniture, puzzles, books — all may be compared by gross differences.

Repeated experiences with environmental surroundings — whether people, objects, or things — will reinforce the child's knowledge of gross differences. As a teacher you must relate the names, uses, and comparisons among like items so that, when the child is taught beginning reading skills, he or she will comprehend the oral language concepts needed to use those skills to learn to read. Vocabulary can then be expanded to include various definitions of the same word.

After a rather difficult small-group session on trying to teach the vowel sounds to kindergarteners who were over six years of age, a teacher and aide were standing together in the play yard planning snack time. A toothless six year old dashed up, hugged the teacher's legs, and said, "Teacher, you want to hear my bowel sounds?" "What?" the teacher asked, somewhat taken aback. "You know," replied Randy, "A, e, i, o, u. A, e, i, o, u."

Auditory Discrimination Young children love to talk and play games that involve clapping, skipping, jumping, and running to music at varying tempos, volumes, and rhythmic patterns. All the experiences that bring the child satisfaction also reinforce the experience. As a child continues to encounter oral language related to objects, persons, actions, and situations, the child develops a range of word meaning that is almost limitless. Later, when the child reads the printed symbols for these spoken words, he or she will know the meaning of the word in context.

Finer Differences in Discrimination As children experience more activities and events, they begin to notice finer differences in the materials already being used. They add location words (*near the top, in the middle, by the door,* and so on) and description words (*square, round, circle, long, short, wide,* and so on) to their oral vocabulary and to their visual discrimination abilities.

Picture Recognition and Interpretation Visual skill in interpreting and recognizing pictorial symbols usually begins before a child is three. In homes where parents read to children, take pictures of their children, and have magazines lying about, the children are exposed to many reinforcing experiences of picture "reading." In programs for three, four, and five year olds, experiences with pictures in all forms (books, magazines, films, television, slides, commercial picture sets, and drawings) extend the children's ability to associate meaning with visual stimuli.

Recognition of Similarities Among Objects, Persons, and Events As children gain experience and maturity, they are able to distinguish finer characteristics of objects. They are also able to associate things that appear alike in size, shape, color, location, and function. If this skill is well developed by the time the teacher introduces the basic beginning reading skills (sight words and individual letter sounds), the child has mastered the listening vocabulary necessary for accepting and comprehending directions, explanations, and examples.

Make your statements clear and easy to follow. You may wish to tape record directions for an activity while you are actually telling the children what to do. You may also write the directions for an activity in your lesson plans and, after several days, compare your vocabulary of various lessons to see if you are precise, direct, and saying what you mean.

Cause-and-Effect Organization As the child has increased opportunities to experience relationships among many different stimuli, he or she will begin to perceive situations in light of the causes of events and the effects the events have on the environment. This process evolves from associating a previous experience with a new experience, whether it is physical, social, emotional, or intellectual.

Ideas in Sequence The child's ability to comprehend situations and retain ideas increases with maturity. He or she will begin to put the action part of stories or events in order. As this happens the child will be able to anticipate the stages in a process, the adventures in a story, or the order of occurrences in a personal experience.

Meanings and Ideas Related to Written Symbols In early childhood classrooms children will observe teachers and aides as they use printed and written symbols to complete reports; label children's work; write letters to parents; read stories; or read directions for cooking, science, or art activities. The children will also begin to discover gross differences in words they see, such as children's names on paintings and names or labels on cracker and cookie boxes used for snack time. With more and more experiences in seeing printed symbols, they begin to develop a sight vocabulary.

Books for Teaching Visual Discrimination

Books are a good source of material to develop visual discrimination, which is one of the major factors in achieving reading readiness. As a teacher of young children you should have many opportunities to read to children. The following books will help you provide enjoyable occasions for the children and extend their opportunities to develop their visual discrimination skills.

Anno, Mitsumasa. *Anno's Alphabet Book*. New York: Crowell Publishers, 1975. Two pages are devoted to each letter of the alphabet. The first page has a wooden letter in the foreground and the adjoining page shows a picture of an item that begins with the letter being introduced. The picture has some unusual quality that can be discussed. Hidden in the border for both pages are other examples of words beginning with the new letter. There are at least two objects in each border designed to be located by the reader.

Aruego, Jose. *We Hide, You Seek*. New York: Greenwillow, 1979. The animals of East Africa play a game of hide and seek while the red rhinoceros tries to find them. In one double-page spread, the animals are hidden, and on the next two pages the animals identify their hiding places. At the end of the book, the red rhino has all the animals look for him among a herd of rhinos.

Charlip, Remy, and Jerry Joyner. *Thirteen*. New York: Parents Magazine Press, 1975. Thirteen individual pictures are contained on a two-page spread. Any one of these pictures can be followed throughout the book as it changes. If you flip the pages over quickly, the reader can create a motion picture effect.

dePaola, Tomie. *Charlie Needs a Cloak*. Englewood Cliffs, N.J.: Prentice Hall, 1973. An extra, unexpected character adorns the pictures in the book, as a mouse creates a series of adventures for himself. There is a story within a story for the alert reader.

Karlin, Nurit. *The April Rabbits*. Illustrator David Cleveland. New York: Coward, McCann and Goezbegan, Inc., 1978. On each page rabbits appear as the month of April evolves. There is a direct correlation between the day of the month and the number of rabbits in the illustrations. The reader has to search very carefully to find *all* the rabbits.

Lewis, Stephen. *Zoo City*. New York: Greenwillow Books, 1976. City machinery can be matched with an animal that looks just like the machine in shape. The pages of this book are cut in half. A match must be made between machines and animals. The pictures that belong together are not side by side but must be found in different sections of the book.

Livermore, Elaine. *Find the Cat*. Boston: Houghton Mifflin, 1973. A dog and a cat play a game of tag. The reader must try to find the hidden cat as the dog searches for it in vain. Every once in a while, the dog and the cat meet, only to begin the search again. In the end the dog succeeds in finding both the cat and his lost bone.

―――. *Lost and Found*. Boston: Houghton Mifflin, 1973. Two related pictures are placed side by side. One picture is complete, while the other has one missing item that the careful observer must find. All the action takes place on a park bench where a bird is taking items to use to build a nest. All of the borrowed things are returned at the end of the story.

Rothman, Joel. *Which One Is Different?* Garden City, N.Y.: Doubleday, 1975. There are varied groups in which one member is different. The reader must find the member that doesn't belong. Solutions are given at the back of the book.

Wildsmith, Brian. *Puzzles*. New York: Franklin Watts, 1970. Colorful animal pictures are found in each double-page spread. A question asks the reader to find something unusual in each picture.

Teaching the Alphabet

Do you teach the alphabet to young children? Teaching the alphabet is a controversial topic. Many educators believe that there is no reason to teach the sequential order of the letters of the alphabet to three and four year olds and that it is not the first stage of teaching the names of the letters to five year olds.

The alphabet has two parts: individual letters and a sequential order. The ability to form and recognize individual letters is a necessary skill for regular first-grade instruction in writing and reading. Pressure is being placed on kindergarten teachers to teach recognition, order, and form. After the middle of the year, most five year olds can recognize the form of several letters, especially those letters in their names. They also easily learn the letters in the names of friends or family members. After a child can recognize over half of the letters of the alphabet (not write, but recognize and name), he or she probably can learn the rest of the alphabet.

Learning to say the alphabet orally in sequential order may be beneficial at this time, but not earlier. Alphabet songs break the list of letters into units, making it easier for the children to remember them. Numbers are easier to remember in units (614–555–1770 is easier to remember than 6145551770); this is also true of the letters of the alphabet. If you review the chapter on how children learn, you will understand how this principle works. The alphabet is not used in sequential order until children use a dictionary, generally in the second grade. Therefore, the sequential order of the letters is secondary in importance, even though it may help children remember the letters.

Many five year olds should be able to recognize and name the letters of the alphabet by the end of the kindergarten year, but all of them will not be able to recognize and name all twenty-six letters. Remember, children differ in this ability as they do in the ability to tie their shoes, follow directions, talk in complete sentences, or retell a story in sequence. Recognizing, naming, and forming the letters of the alphabet are all necessary skills to be attained before a child can write or read successfully. Because of this, pressure by parents and some teachers to teach the "alphabet" will continue. Correct instruction on your part will help your children become more successful and will lessen the pressure to some extent.

Alphabet picture books are included in this chapter, alphabet songs are included in the music chapter, and alphabet materials are included in the general classroom equipment list.

Parents and Reading

As one of the child's first teachers, you must provide the child's parents with a fairly clear understanding of the reading process. Many parents look upon reading as a decoding or word recognition process. You need to help them understand that reading is primarily a thinking process, activated by visual symbols. Having a parent recognize the difference between word recognition and comprehension may be helpful. Print a nonsense word (for example, *stum*) and point out that although the word can be pronounced, it doesn't have any meaning. The parent has had no experience with it, has never heard it, and has never spoken it. Next, print a word the parent does know (and one a young child would learn; for example, *come*) and ask the parent to pronounce it, use it in a sentence, and tell the meaning of it.

This should help the parent understand that the art of reading is built upon previous experience and language skills the child already has and uses. More information for parent involvement will be provided in Chapter 13 on the parents' role in educating their children.[5]

Dialect and Reading

Many programs for young children emphasize the speaking of standard English. These programs were developed because the United States has many minority cultures, and the children from these cultures have often had difficulties in learning to read. In trying to pinpoint the causes for these difficulties, educators, psychologists, and linguists have conducted research studies on the language the child brings to school and the effects it may have on the teaching of reading and the other language arts. From these studies have come systematic information on the dialects of blacks, Spanish Americans, Appalachian Caucasians, American Indians, and other minority groups.

Some programs for young children have taken the same research and developed commercial material using the nonstandard English spoken by the children in the classroom. An alternative to this commercial material is the *language experience approach*, which uses the children's own language printed by the teacher. This recording of the children's language is then used to help the children see and hear the relationship of what was said to what they are reading. Because of the differences in the English we use in different situations, the language experience approach is probably more satisfactory. Also, when children read what they have personally experienced and spoken, they find it easier to comprehend the printed symbols.

One very important factor to remember in using a child's speech in beginning reading experiences is that there is often a significant difference between the language being produced by the speaker and the language being received by the listener. Production and reception do not operate in the same way. A child's reception ability precedes production acquisition. Children can understand many aspects of what they hear before they are able to produce it themselves.

To illustrate, if you studied a foreign language, you may remember that in the beginning it was easier to understand the language than to speak it. You also understand many different dialects of American English, although you may have difficulty in reproducing most of them. When you travel from one geographic region to another, you adjust to new and different features of a dialect and soon have perfect reception. As you teach, remember that children also have the same abilities.

---

[5] For further information, read Nancy Larrick, "Home Influences on Early Reading," *Today's Education* 64 (Nov.-Dec. 1975): 77–79.

Picture Books For Beginning Readers

Byars, Betty C. *Go and Hush the Baby*. New York: Viking, 1971.
Daugherty, James. *Andy and the Lion*. New York: Viking, 1966.
Freeman, Don. *Corduroy*. New York: Viking, 1968.
Heymans, Margriet. *Cats and Dolls*. Reading, Mass.: Addison-Wesley, 1976.
Keats, Ezra J. *Goggles*. New York: Macmillan, 1969.
Mayer, Mercer. *Frog Goes to Dinner*. New York: Dial, 1974.
Pearson, Susan. *Izzie*. New York: Dial, 1975.
Rey, H. A. *Curious George Learns the Alphabet*. Boston: Houghton Mifflin, 1963.
Schmiderer, Dorothy. *Alphabeast Book: An Abecedarium*. New York: Holt, Rinehart and Winston, 1971.
Steig, William. *CDB!* New York: E. P. Dutton, 1968.

Recommended reading for teachers in this area includes:

Durkin, Dolores. "A Six Year Study of Children Who Learned To Read in School at the Age of Four." *Reading Research Quarterly*, 10 (1974–1975): 961.
Goetz, Elizabeth M. "Early Reading: A Developmental Approach." *Young Children*, 34 (July 1979): 4–11.
Pflaum, Susanna. *The Development of Language and Reading in the Young Child*. Columbus, Ohio: Charles E. Merrill, 1974.
Strickland, Dorothy. "Pre-Elementary School Reading." In *Projections for Reading: Preschool Through Adulthood*. Edited by B. Calkins, et al. U.S.O.E./H.E.W. (1978): 7–16.
Teale, William H. "Early Reading: A Comprehensive Annotated Bibliography. Occasional Paper Number 2." ED166 683, ERIC/EECE, (1979).

LITERATURE

"Once upon a time" and "they lived happily ever after" are trademarks of stories for young children. For an individual who grew up with bedtime stories read by parents or grandparents, gifts of books for special occasions, and trips to the library for a weekly supply of "reading" material, children's literature is probably the most "fun" part of teaching. Telling or reading a story to young children is a pleasure because their responses are natural. They laugh, giggle, express surprise, say "Let me see," and ask you to read it again. Enjoying literature and developing a literary heritage for leisure hours is the most important part of a literature program.

Literature for its own sake should not be confused with realistic texts written to give information. Literature for young children includes stories with humor, stories about animals, realistic stories, folk tales, nursery rhymes, poetry, nonsense rhymes, fairy stories, and fanciful or make-believe stories. There are other books for young children whose main purpose is to give information. These books will be described, and recommended lists provided, in each of the chapters where the content of the book is pertinent.

The Teacher's Role

Experiences with literature during early childhood are the first steps in formulating children's later attitudes and interests in learning to read. Attitudes are usually "caught" from adults or other children. The teacher, therefore, is responsible for selecting books and stories appropriate for the children's level of maturity and interest, for becoming a good reader or teller of stories, for organizing the room and program to integrate the literature aspect of the curriculum into the entire daily program, and for selecting different literature activities.

Selecting Books and Stories   What are the characteristics of literature that appeals to young children? Children respond to books that have large, simple, and brightly colored pictures. The content should be about familiar objects with short, descriptive sentence text or no text at all. They enjoy rhymes or nonsense verses that stimulate their auditory senses through rhythmic word-sound repetition. They like definitive action and illustrations that reinforce the story. Often they like books of varying sizes — tall-thin, square-small, oblong-big, or "feeling" texture pages. In selecting books, your first responsibility will be to study and list the available books that have the following characteristics:

- Stories about animals
- Rhythms and rhymes
- Make-believe or fanciful stories
- Folk tales or Mother Goose stories
- Humorous tales
- Familiar settings and familiar experiences
- Characters resembling the children themselves
- Elements of surprise, action, or suspense
- Brightly colored illustrations in simple detail
- Simple, direct language
- Symbols and pictures large enough for satisfactory visual discrimination
- Content that builds on previous knowledge while extending experience

Because children mature at varying stages, as a teacher you will want to be careful in your selection of books for the age or ages you teach. Children also differ in their needs and interests in literature as they do in other subject areas.

164 / Curriculum

What is it like to be a three-year-old listener? Three year olds like to hear about everyday experiences and enjoy vicarious experiences with animals. Their attention span will be increased if you read a story to a small group or to an individual (they like to be involved). Repetition of the same story is often preferred over a new story. They like simple jingles and guessing stories. Most children will want to "stop" the story for discussion and comments. Many children will want to "read" to others the stories they have heard many times.

Four year olds assimilate content faster than three year olds and will listen as members of a larger group. They will make up silly language from a new word. They begin to enjoy rhyming poetry and they love exaggerated characters or events. They are at the "why" stage and enjoy books that show and tell answers about their environment.

Five year olds have grown in understanding and interests. They want more kinds of stories — adventure, make-believe, realistic, and stories of long ago. The child of five likes to choose his or her own book and often will "read" a picture book alone.

Becoming a Good Reader or Teller of Stories A good story or book may be appreciated by a poor reader by listening to a good storyteller. One of your goals as a potential teacher of young children should be to become an excellent storyteller. The following suggestions will help you become an "expert" early in your career.

One of the best ways we can encourage the lifetime pleasures of leisure reading is by becoming good storytellers ourselves. The following suggestions are designed to provide a starting place for storyteller-beginners. They may also serve as a prod to other adults who want to recapture some of the joys of story-telling.

Before telling a story, we need to give thought to such matters as acquiring familiarity with the material; mastering the development or succession of events, so as to give emphasis to the high-interest points, the climax, and the conclusion; knowing the story so well that answers to children's questions can be incorporated into the telling — through the use of gestures, synonyms or explanatory phrases — without spoiling the flow of the story; or selecting the most appropriate stopping point in a story that requires more than one sitting.

The "told" story must be short enough to match the audience's listening span. In reading aloud the story may be much longer, but each chapter or selection should serve as natural conclusions for the moment and yet be open-ended so that the listener "can't wait" to hear more. Language that is precise and vivid and that provides imagery of the action and events is especially desirable. Children should not become dependent upon unusual props. On the other hand, in picture books for young children the story is confirmed, complemented, and enriched by the accompanying illustrations.

In preparing a story for telling, try the following specific suggestions:

Selecting an appropriate story encourages concentrated listening.

Read your story aloud three or four times.
Record the story on a tape.
Analyze your recording as to enunciation, pronunciation, rate of speech, and sentence phrasing.
Write (or at least think through) a short introduction to the story.
Now practice telling your story again, incorporating your own contrived introduction.
Record the story again and compare it with the first tape.
Sit or stand in front of a mirror and tell your story aloud; watch your facial expression and body position. If you are sharing the illustrations from a book, analyze what the children see at various distances from you, depending on where they are sitting in the room.
If possible, share your story with a friend and get his/her reactions to your telling.
When you have mastered your story, try various means of illustrating it such as: role-playing, flannel boards, chalktalks, puppets, and cutouts.
Try the same procedures with groups of other ages in other rooms. Analyze the results.

Formulate an overall plan for enhancing the experience of storytelling, incorporating the following principles:

Remember to include a variety of types or forms of literature in your year's program.

Schedule a daily period for storytelling for children ages three to nine and at least three occasions a week for older children.

Remember that not all children will be interested in all stories and that quiet, parallel activities such as drawing, reading another book, or writing will not distract those who are listening.

Review some of the classic texts listed.

Then "sit loosely" and let your storytelling be a mutually enjoyable fun-time.[6]

Organizing Your Room and Program One of the most important aspects of teaching is the organization of equipment and materials within the room so that your planned program objectives can be met. An organization that inhibits use of supplies very often also inhibits or changes the expected outcomes of instruction. In addition, children may misbehave because of inadequate space, inaccessible materials, or inability to follow the directions given by the teacher.

Each room should have a center where children may look at books and magazines whenever they wish. This is a permanent center, although you may occasionally change the location of the center in the room. Each room should also have several books of collections of stories for the teacher's use. Although the children can handle the books, they are usually too heavy. These books can be stored on higher shelves, leaving the lower shelves for books the children will use more often.

Books may be put with science collections or in the family center for the children to "read" to their "children" as they play house. Books may also be placed in the block and truck area for ideas on building and play experiences. Holiday books may be placed near art activities to be read by an aide to the children.

At times, the children may use books and individual filmstrips with records. Tapes made by teachers or aides may encourage the children to look at a book as they listen to the story on tape.

Nancy: "How come we gotta sit on the floor?"

Teacher: "I am going to read a story."

Nancy: "I am not supposed to."

Teacher: "We all sit on the floor for storytime."

Nancy: "I can't. My mamma told me not to get dirty."

Children need comfortable "spots" for sitting or lying. A footstool, a small rocker, a beanbag chair, a rug, an overstuffed chair (if your room is large enough), several large pillows, and on special occasions an Indian tepee, an Eskimo igloo, a bear's "cave," or a pup tent will provide a private place for reading. Remember, this special place will need to have a top opening for adequate light.

Selecting Materials and Equipment Literature comes in many forms. Films, filmstrips, records, tapes, and videotapes are all media by which

---

[6] Adapted from Betty L. Broman, "Storytelling, the Frosting on the Cake," *Childhood Education*, 51, 6 (April/May 1975): 323.

literature may be conveyed to youngsters. Often the teacher or aide will have to start the use of these materials but, as children gain experience with the media, they will be able to handle more of the equipment by themselves. Some machines the children can use combine two or more of these media and make listening to a story comparable to watching a television set. Examples are Systems 80®, LaBelle Courier®, and several models of cassette automatic sound filmstrip viewers.

The Child's Part

What do the children do in a literature program? The most obvious answer is "listen," and of course they do. Children do many other things, though. The child who has the opportunity to use books at leisure soon becomes a selector of what he or she likes and what is of interest. With many opportunities, the child will become a browser each day to reinforce and remember old pleasures and to discover new pleasures.

The child is also a sharer of books and stories. Books from home may be brought to school for the teacher to read to the whole class. If a "curling up" spot large enough for two is provided, children will read to each other.

Children will soon play parts in stories they have heard. Usually this occurs in the dress-up area, family center, or block and truck area. Puppets and puppet stage can be the arena for many folk tales and nursery rhymes. Large dolls and stuffed animals are favorite companions for small rocking chair storytimes. To enjoy literature fully, children must have freedom to move, talk, and be creative in their interpretation of literature.

Storybooks for Young Children

Do you talk about books for young children or stories for young children? For lay persons this can often be confusing. Usually a story for a young child is complete in one book. There are also excellent collections of stories in (large) book form. For the classroom, single-story books are purchased by children and teachers. Books of collections of stories provide more stories to read to children at a reasonable price. They are usually too heavy for children and are held by teachers as they read aloud.

In most instances, as an observer, a student teacher, or an experienced teacher, you will be in an established school, not a new one. Therefore, all our lists of books include old as well as recent favorites. These lists will be helpful in all three of your beginning teaching activities as guides for developing experiences for children and for comparison with the card catalog in your school and public library. As a teacher, you will probably have an opportunity to order books. These lists will aid you in establishing a well-balanced collection. The books that follow are suitable for three, four, and five year olds.

Imaginative stories

Aruego, Jose. *Look What I Can Do*. New York: Charles Scribner's, 1972.
Baum, Arline, and Joseph Baum. *Know What? No. What?* New York: Parents Magazine Press, 1964.
Bemelmans, Ludwig. *Madeline*. New York: Simon & Schuster, 1939.
Bollinger-Sovilli, Antonello. *The Knitted Cat*. New York: Macmillan, 1971.
Burningham, John. *Mr. Gumpy's Outing*. New York: Holt, Rinehart and Winston, 1971.
Burton, Virginia Lee. *Mike Mulligan and His Steam Shovel*. Boston: Houghton Mifflin, 1939.
Candell, Rebecca. *Did You Carry the Flag Today, Charlie?* New York: Holt, Rinehart and Winston, 1966.
Cleary, Beverly. *The Real Hole*. New York: William Morrow, 1960.
Concord, Ellen. *Impossible Possum*. Boston: Little, Brown, 1971.

De Brunhyoff, Laurent. *Babar and the Wully-Wully*. New York: Random House, 1975.
Devlin, Wende, and Harry Devlin. *Old Witch and the Polka-Dot Ribbon*. New York: Parents' Magazine Press, 1970.
Dickens, Frank. *Fly Away Peter*. New York: Scroll Press, 1970.
Duvoisin, Roger. *Petunia's Treasure*. New York: Knopf, 1975.
Ets, Marie Hall. *Talking Without Words*. New York: Viking, 1968.
Flack, Marjorie. *Ask Mr. Bear*. New York: Macmillan, 1932.
Freeman, Don. *Corduroy*. New York: Viking Press, 1968.
Hoff, Syd. *Barkley*. New York: Harper & Row, 1975.
Kalan, Robert. *Blue Sea*. New York: Greenwillow Books, 1979.
Keats, Ezra Jack. *Hi, Cat*. New York: Macmillan, 1970.
Kellogg, Steven. *Much Bigger Than Martin*. New York: Dial Press, 1976.
Kroll, Steven. *The Tyrannosaurus Game*. New York: Holiday House, 1976.
Label, Arnold. *A Treeful of Pigs*. New York: Greenwillow Books, 1979.
Lionni, Leo. *Pezzettino*. New York: Pantheon, 1975.
Margolis, Richard J. *Big Bear to the Rescue*. New York: Greenwillow Books, 1975.
Mayer, Mercer. *Ah-Choo*. New York: Dial, 1976.
McCloskey, Robert. *Blueberries for Sal*. New York: Viking, 1948.
———. *Make Way for Ducklings*. New York: Viking, 1941.
Meyer, Renate. *Hide and Seek*. Scarsdale, N.Y.: Bradbury, 1972.
Minarik, Else Holmelund. *A Kiss for Little Bear*. New York: Harper & Row, 1968.
———. *Little Bear's Friend*. New York: Harper & Row, 1960.
Ormondroyd, Edward. *Theodore*. Oakland, Calif.: Parnassus, 1966.
Potter, Beatrix. *The Tale of Mrs. Tiggy-Winkle*. New York: Frederick Warne, 1950.
Rand, Ann. *Sparkle and Spin: A Book About Words*. New York: Harcourt, Brace, Jovanovich, 1957.
Rey, H. A. *Curious George*. Boston: Houghton Mifflin, 1941.
Salus, Naomi P. *My Daddy's Mustache*. Garden City, N.Y.: Doubleday, 1979.
Sawyer, Ruth. *Journey Cake, Ho!* New York: Viking, 1953.
Sendak, Maurice. *In the Night Kitchen*. New York: Harper & Row, 1970.
Seuss, Dr. *Oh, the Thinks You Can Think*. New York: Random House, 1975.
Thaler, Mike. *Magic Boy*. New York: Harper & Row, 1961.
Withrop, Elizabeth. *Bunk Beds*. New York: Harper & Row, 1972.

Adventures of animals

Allard, Harry. *I Will Not Go To Market Today*. New York: Dial, 1979.
Asch, Frank. *Moon Bear*. New York: Charles Scribner's, 1978.

Binki, Witali. *Humphrey Goes Hunting*. Chicago: Children's Press, 1969.
Brown, Margaret Wise. *The Little Island*. Garden City, N.Y.: Doubleday, 1946.
Delton, Judy. *Rabbit Finds a Way*. New York: Crown, 1975.
Duvoisin, Roger. *Petunia*. New York: Knopf, 1950.
———. *Petunia, Beware!* New York: Knopf, 1958.
Fatio, Louise. *The Happy Lion's Treasure*. New York: McGraw-Hill, 1970.
Friskey, Margaret. *Seven Diving Ducks*. Chicago: Children's Press, 1969.
Goodall, John S. *The Ballooning Adventures of Paddy Pork*. New York: Harcourt, Brace, Jovanovich, 1969.
Hutchins, Pat. *Rosie's Walk*. New York: Macmillan, 1968.
Keats, Ezra Jack. *Maggie and the Pirate*. New York: Four Winds, 1979.
Lobel, Arnold. *Frog and Toad Are Friends*. New York: Harper & Row, 1970.
———. *Owl at Home*. New York: Harper & Row, 1975.
McCloskey, Robert. *Make Way for Ducklings*. New York: Viking, 1941.
Potter, Beatrix. *The Tale of Benjamin Bunny*. New York: Frederick Warne, 1904; reprint 1977.
———. *The Tale of Jemima Puddle Duck*. New York: Frederick Warne, 1908; reprint 1977.
Quinn-Harkin, Janet. *Peter Penny's Dance*. New York: Dial, 1976.
Rey, H. A. *Curious George*. Boston: Houghton Mifflin, 1941.
Roy, Ron. *Three Ducks Went Wandering*. New York: Seabury Press, 1979.
Sharmat, Marjorie Weinman. *The 329th Friend*. New York: Four Winds, 1979.
Steig, William. *Amos and Boris*. New York: Farrar, Straus & Giroux, 1971.
Ueno, Noriko. *Elephant Buttons*. New York: Harper & Row, 1973.
Waber, Bernard. *Lovable Lyle*. Boston: Houghton Mifflin, 1969.
Watson, Clyde. *Tom Fox and the Apple Pie*. New York: Thomas Y. Crowell, 1972.
Wildsmith, Brian. *Python's Party*. New York: Franklin Watts, 1975.
Yashima, Mitsu. *Momo's Kittens*. New York: Viking, 1961.

Alphabet books

Ahlberg, Janet, and Allen Ahlberg. *Each Peach Pear Plum: An "I Spy" Story*. New York: Viking, 1979.
Anno, Mitsumasa. *Anno's Alphabet*. New York: Thomas Y. Crowell, 1975.
Baskin, Hosea; Tobias Baskin; and Lisa Baskin. *Hosie's Alphabet*. New York: Viking, 1972.
Broomfield, R. *The Baby Animal ABC*. New York: Penguin Books, 1976.
Burningham, John. *John Burningham's ABC*. Indianapolis, Ind.: Bobbs-Merrill, 1964.
Emberley, Ed. *ABC*. Boston: Little, Brown, 1978.

Fujikawa, Gyo. *Fujikawa's A to Z Picture Book*. New York: Grosset & Dunlap, 1974.

Greenaway, Kate. *A Apple Pie*. New York: Frederick Warne, 1975.

Rey, H. A. *Curious George Learns the Alphabet*. Boston: Houghton Mifflin, 1963.

Scarry, Richard. *Early Words*. New York: Random House, 1976.

Schmilerer, Dorothy. *The Alphabet Book: An Abecedarium*. New York: Holt, Rinehart & Winston, 1971.

Weisgard, L. *My First Picture Book*. New York: Grosset & Dunlap, 1977.

Wildsmith, Brian. *Brian Wildsmith's ABC*. New York: Franklin Watts, 1963.

Folk tales and fables

Aardema, Verda. *Why Mosquitoes Buzz in People's Ears*. New York: Dial Press, 1975.

Ambrus, Victor G. *The Sultan's Bath* (folk tale). New York: Harcourt, Brace, Jovanovich, 1972.

Aruego, Jose. *A Crocodile's Tale: A Philippine Folk Story*. New York: Charles Scribner's, 1972.

Association for Childhood Education International. *Told Under the Blue Umbrella*. New York: Macmillan, 1962.

Babt, Jan. *The King and the Broom Maker*. New York: Delacorte, 1968.

Brown, Marcia. *Once a Mouse* (fable). New York: Charles Scribner's, 1961.

Ciardi, John. *John J. Plenty and Fiddler Dan*. Philadelphia: Lippincott, 1963.

de LaFontaine, Jean. *The Hare and the Tortoise*. New York: Franklin Watts, 1966.

———. *The Lion and the Rat*. New York: Franklin Watts, 1963.

Ets, Marie Hall. *Elephant in a Well*. New York: Viking, 1972.

Galdove, Paul. *Old Mother Hubbard and Her Dog*. New York: McGraw-Hill, 1960.

———. *Old Woman and Her Pig*. New York: McGraw-Hill, 1960.

———. *The Three Bears*. New York: Seabury, 1972.

Ginsburg, Mirra. *The Chick and the Duckling* (Russian). New York: Seabury, 1972.

Hirsh, Marilyn. *How the World Got Its Color* (Oriental). New York: Crown, 1972.

Hogrogian, Nonny. *One Fine Day* (American). New York: Macmillan, 1971.

Kingsley, Emily; David Korr; and Jeffrey Moss. *The Sesame Street Book of Fairy Tales*. New York: Random House/Children's Television Workshop, 1975.

Lobel, Anita. *King Rooster, Queen Hen*. New York: Greenwillow Books, 1975.

Humorous books

Asch, Frank. *Sand Cake*. New York: Parents' Magazine Press, 1978.
Barrett, Judi. *Animals Should Definitely Not Wear Clothes*. New York: Atheneum, 1970.
Blegrad, Lenore. *This Little Pig-A-Wig, and Other Rhymes About Pigs*. New York: Atheneum, 1978.
Carle, Erie. *Do You Want To Be My Friend?* New York: Thomas Y. Crowell, 1971.
Cheney, Richard E. *Really Eager and the Glorious Watermelon Contest*. New York: E. P. Dutton, 1970.
Cole, William. *Oh, What Nonsense*. New York: Viking, 1976.
Copp, Jim. *Martha Matilda O'Toole*. Scarsdale, N.Y.: Bradbury, 1969.
Dauer, Rosamond. *Bullfrog and Gertrude Go Camping*. New York: Greenwillow Books, 1980.
Duvoisin, Roger. *Petunia*. New York: Knopf, 1950.
Eastman, Philip. *Are You My Mother?*. New York: Random House, 1960.
Freeman, Don. *Dandelion*. New York: Viking, 1964.
Gag, Wanda. *Millions of Cats*. New York: Coward-McGann, 1928.
Horworth, Betty. *Be Nice to Josephine*. New York: Franklin Watts, 1970.
Leaf, Munro. *The Story of Ferdinand*. New York: Viking, 1936.
Mayer, Mercer. *Boy, Was I Mad*. New York: Parents' Magazine Press, 1969.
McPhail, David. *Bumper Tubbs*. Boston: Houghton Mifflin, 1980.
Raskin, Ellen. *Spectacles*. New York: Atheneum, 1968.
Sandburg, Carl. *The Wedding Procession of the Rag Doll and the Broom Handle and Who Was in It*. New York: Harcourt Brace Jovanovich, 1967.
Seuss, Dr. *Horton Hatches the Egg*. New York: Vanguard, 1940.
Slobodkina, E. *Caps for Sale*. Glenview, Ill.: Scott, Foresman, 1947.
Smith, Kay. *Parakeets and Peach Pies*. New York: Parents' Magazine Press, 1970.
Tanz, Christine. *An Egg Is To Sit On*. New York: Lothrop, Lee & Shepard, 1978.
Ungerer, Tomi. *The Beast of Monsieur Racine*. New York: Farrar, Straus and Giroux, 1971.

Collections

Arbuthnot, May Hill, and Helton L. Root, Jr. *Time for Poetry*. 3rd ed. Glenview, Ill.: Scott, Foresman, 1968.
Association for Childhood Education International. *Bibliography of Books for Children*. ACEI, 1977.
Child Study Association of America. *Holiday Storybook Read Me Another Story. Read Me More Stories Read-to-Me-Storybook*. Child Study Association of America, no date.

———. *Told Under the Green Umbrella*. New York: Macmillan, 1935.
———. *Told Under the Magic Umbrella*. New York: Macmillan, 1967.
Cullinan, Bernice E., and Carolyn W. Carmichael, eds. *Literature and Young Children*. Urbana, Ill.: The National Council of Teachers of English, 1977.
Johnson, Edna, et al. *Anthology of Children's Literature*. 5th ed. Boston: Houghton Mifflin, 1977.
Rice, Eva. *Mr. Bimble's Hobby and Other Stories*. New York: Greenwillow Books, 1975.
Sutherland, Zena, ed. *The Arbuthnot Anthology of Children's Literature*. 4th ed. Glenview, Ill.: Scott, Foresman, 1976.

Paperback Books   Many good books are available in paperback editions and most publishers will send you a copy of their catalogue upon request.

Several publishers specialize in books for the young: Dover Publications, Inc., 180 Varick Street, New York, NY 10014 (facsimiles of favorites); Houghton Mifflin Co., 2 Park Street, Boston, MA 02107 (*Sandpipers* for preschool and up); Penguin Books, Inc., 7110 Ambassador Road, Baltimore, MD 21207 (*Puffin Picture Books*); and The Viking Press, 625 Madison Avenue, New York, NY 10022 (*Seafarer Books*).

The following publishers publish series of cardbook, cloth, and plastic books: Dean's Rag Book Company; Golden Press, Grosset and Dunlap, Platt and Munk, and Rand McNally.

Poetry   Jingles, rhymes, and repeated phrases with catchy repetitions are beginning activities for introducing poetry. Humorous poems are fun to repeat and are easily remembered. Enjoyment of poetry is the main purpose of teaching and sharing poems in an early childhood program.

Some poems are taught because they are part of a child's literary heritage ("Rain," "Now We Are Six," "Twas the Night Before Christmas"). Others are shared for pure enjoyment. Memorizing poems should be an individual activity that a child wants to do. Whole-group reciting or singing of a poem may be fun and also will allow the more timid child to participate without feeling self-conscious.

The following collections of poems and rhymes are proven favorites of children and teacher:

Alderson, Brian, ed. *Cakes and Custard*. New York: William Morrow, 1975.
Association for Childhood Education. *Sung Under the Silver Umbrella*. New York: Macmillan, 1962.
Berenstein, S., and J. Berenstein. *Berenstein Bear's Nursery Tales*. New York: Random House, 1973.
Book, L. Leslie, illus. *Ring O'Roses*. New York: Frederick Warne, 1966.

PROJECT
Attitudes Toward Reading

Love of reading is nurtured throughout childhood and starts even before a child learns how to read.

1. Were you read to as a young child? What were your favorite books?
2. Were you told stories as a young child? If yes, were they fictional or were they about real people (for example, you, your parents)? Which kind did you prefer? Do you still remember any of these stories?
3. How old were you when you got your first library card? Describe your early experiences and attitudes toward using the library. What did your library look like? Did you set aside a special time for visiting it on a regular basis?
4. Did you own many books as a child? How did you primarily acquire these books — as presents selected by others or as purchases that you yourself made?
5. What were your attitudes toward books and reading as a child? As an adult? Do any of the experiences discussed in questions 1 to 4 account for these attitudes? In what way?

Briggs, Raymond, illus. *The Mother Goose Treasury*. New York: Coward-McCann, 1966.

Ciardi, John. *The Reason for the Pelican*. Philadelphia: J. B. Lippincott, 1969.

Cole, William, comp. *The Birds and the Beasts Were There* (Anthology). New York: Philomet, 1963.

DeAngeli, Marguerite, illus. *Book of Nursery and Mother Goose Rhymes*. Garden City, N.Y.: Doubleday, 1954.

Field, Eugene. *Wynken, Blynken, and Nod*. New York: Hastings House, 1964.

Fisher, Aileen. *Feathered Ones and Furry*. New York: Thomas Y. Crowell, 1971.

Fujikawa, Gyo. *A Child's Book of Poems*. New York: Grosset & Dunlap, 1969.

Greenaway, Kate. *Under the Window*. New York: Frederick Warne, 1910.

Hopkins, Lee Bennett, comp. *Good Morning to You, Valentine*. New York: Harcourt Brace Jovanovich, 1975.

Kuskin, Karla. *The Bear Who Saw the Spring*. New York: Harper & Row, 1961.

Languer, Nola. *Miss Lucy*. New York: Macmillan, 1969.

Lear, Edward. *The Quangle-Wangle's Hat*. New York: Franklin Watts, 1969.

Lenski, Lois. *City Poems*. New York: Henry Z. Walck, 1971.

Lobel, Arnold. *Gregory Griggs and Other Nursery Rhyme People*. New York: Greenwillow Books, 1978.
Milne, A. A. *The World of Christopher Robin*. New York: E. P. Dutton, 1958.
O'Neill, Mary. *Hailstones and Halibut Bones*. Garden City, N.Y.: Doubleday, 1961.
Prelutsky, Jack. *Toucans Two*. New York: Macmillan, 1970.
Rao, Anthony. *The Highlights Book of Nursery Rhymes*. Columbus, Ohio: Highlights for Children, 1974.
Reeves, James. *Pefabulous Animals*. New York: E. P. Dutton, 1960.
Rossetti, Christina. *Sing-Song*. New York: Macmillan, 1952.
Rothman, Joel, and Argentina Palacios. *This Can Lick a Lollipop/Esto Coza Chupando Un Caramelo*. Garden City, N.Y.: Doubleday, 1979.
Stevenson, Robert Louis. *A Child's Garden of Verses*. Illus. Brian Wildsmith. New York: Franklin Watts, 1960.
Wallace, Daisy, ed. *Monster Poems*. New York: Holiday House, 1976.
Watson, Clyde. *Father Fox's Penny-rhymes*. New York: Thomas Y. Crowell, 1971.
Weil, Lisi. *If Eggs Had Legs*. Garden City, N.Y.: Doubleday, 1976.
Wildsmith, Brian. *Brian Wildsmith's Mother Goose*. New York: Franklin Watts, 1964.
Zuromskis, Diane. *The Farmer in the Dell*. Boston: Little, Brown, 1978.

WRITTEN LANGUAGE

Many research studies on readiness, form, practice, and methods of handwriting provide teachers with adequate information for developing a functional writing program for young children.[7]

The one point the researchers agree on is that manuscript writing (printing) is the best form for beginning writing. Manuscript is a form of writing based on simplification of the Roman alphabet. Two basic strokes form capital letters and lowercase letters: a straight line and a circle. All letters are formed by these strokes or some combination of them (see Figure 6.1).

In manuscript writing, letters are placed close together to form a word unit. Words are separated by a space equal to a lowercase circle. The space between two sentences equals about two lowercase circles.

---

[7] Three examples are Dan W. Andersen, "Teaching Handwriting," *What Research Says to the Teacher*, No. 4 (Washington, D.C.: National Education Association, 1968, reprinted 1969); Carol Chomsky, "Write First, Read Later," *Childhood Education*, 47, 6 (March 1971): 296–299; and Pauline Whitsel, "Writing Readiness," *Instructor*, 85, 7 (March 1976): 107.

Figure 6.1
Manuscript Alphabet

Used with permission from *Creative Growth with Handwriting*, Second Edition. Copyright © 1979. Zaner-Bloser, Inc., Columbus, Ohio.

In the typical early childhood classroom the teacher will find that children vary in their interest and ability to write. Some children will want to start writing early and will have the coordination to do quite well. Other children will need additional time to gain greater control of their arm and hand muscles and to develop an interest in learning to write.

Many children enter school experiences knowing that there is a relationship between written words and expressed ideas or spoken words. Receiving letters and cards, watching television, and having books and stories read to them build this kind of understanding. Because parents and teachers alike realize the need for children to master the skill of writing, no one questions why we need to teach children to write. The question is how to begin teaching manuscript to the young in the best possible way.

The Teacher's Role

What must the teacher do to make learning manuscript an easy progression for children? First, the teacher learns the basics for successful manuscript form. Large muscles in the arm and smaller muscles in the hand must be developed through manipulative activities. The vocabulary necessary to understand directions must be mastered. Skill in using writing instruments must be acquired through practice in using pencils, crayons, or brushes in many expressive ways before formal instruction begins. The activities necessary to acquire these skills are integrated throughout the regular instruction program.

Second, the teacher studies the form of manuscript being used in the first grade. The teacher uses bold, accurate letter forms to print name cards, experience charts, and labels. As the teacher teaches children to print, she or he consistently uses standard forms that the children will use in first grade.

Third, the teacher enlists parents in the teaching process. The teacher does this by explaining to them how manuscript is taught and showing how this helps the child learn the new skill. Parents should understand the advantages in the child's learning to write correctly from the very beginning. When parents and teachers have the same goals, the child learns accurately and quickly.

Fourth, the teacher provides activities that help children develop eye-hand coordination. In learning to write more time may be lost through impatience than in any other way. Before any formal instruction begins children must have many experiences in tasks that require eye-hand coordination. They must have innumerable exercises to develop small muscles of the hands and larger arm muscles. For this development, the teacher builds into the program many interesting experiences.

Painting provides exercise for different muscles by the use of small brushes and fingers indoors and big brushes and a bucket of water outdoors. The same paint and paper provide different experiences as they are moved from table top, to floor, to easel. Puzzles and small pegboard games are good for eye-hand coordination as are the quite different activities of hammering and sawing. Finger muscles get a workout when modeling with clay — either the reusable plastic kind or permanent, fireable natural clay. Dough, either bread dough or that made just for play, offers excellent hand-arm muscle exercise. Coloring, cutting, and tracing activities help in both muscle development and hand-eye coordination. "Driving" small cars along block roads and dressing small dolls contribute to building readiness for writing.

Variety keeps life in the room exciting and stimulating and encourages children to continue working. A child who cannot be drawn into one activity may be captivated by the different textures, colors, or placement of similar material, which in itself offers opportunities for good muscle development.

Eye-hand coordination (manipulative) activities for three and four year olds include:

- Stringing flat enameled wooden rings, beads, or blocks on heavy cordlike string
- Stacking and building with multicolored cubes
- Lacing a large shoe
- Weaving laces on patterned lacing boards

- Pushing a large wooden needle through half-inch holes drilled in a wooden block
- Zipping, snapping, and buttoning clothes
- Pounding, screwing, and using wrench on miniature workbench
- Screwing jumbo-sized nuts on a large spindle
- Pounding tight pegs through holes on pounding bench

Eye-hand coordination (construct) activities for three and four year olds include:

- Snapping wooden blocks and wheels together to make simple figures
- Stacking and building with interlocking bricks
- Stacking and building with unconstructed posts
- Stacking and sorting H blocks
- Stacking and building with interlocking beams and boards
- Pushing and pulling dowels and forms in Tinkertoys®

These activities, used for muscle development and eye-hand coordination, can also be used to build the vocabulary necessary for manuscript writing. While giving directions, the teacher purposefully introduces relevant terms such as:

top	circle	cross
curve	slant line	space
clockwise	above	straight
half-way	bottom	dot
begin	left, right	in the center (middle)

In discussing projects with individual children, the teacher phrases questions that must be answered with these terms.

The Child's Part

Fulfillment of the activities listed is the teacher's responsibility. What is the child's part in the learning process? As the teacher writes, the children observe a good model. Often the first words children recognize in print are their own names, learned as the teacher writes the names on art work and other possessions. As children listen to books being read, they observe that specific printed words have meanings. As they see their own words written down in experience charts or as they describe something they have drawn, they learn that words are symbols for sounds. They observe that printed materials remain the same in content and can be read over and over. Through all these experiences children learn that learning to print has value.

Children are ready to profit from formal training in manuscript writing when they:

- Have mastered the vocabulary necessary to comprehend oral directions (*top, bottom, space*, and so on)
- Practice holding crayons and pencils in the correct manner for printing
- Use and maintain readiness skills previously taught
- Make straight and slanted lines
- Make circles, half-circles, and two-thirds circles
- Know the names of numbers or letters that they are going to print
- Know and recognize capital letters and small letters

Good writing skill is a lifetime asset. The time taken to prepare a child to become a good beginning manuscript writer cannot be better spent.

SPELLING

Should young children learn to spell words? The answer is yes and no! What is spelling? *Spelling* is the forming of a word by writing or by saying individual letters in a sequential order that is recognized nationally as the correct form of the word.

Children should not begin formal spelling activities (word lists, word patterns, prefixes, suffixes, and so on) until they are able to read — that is, pronounce and understand the meanings of the words — and write with ease the individual letters that form the word. These skills are usually acquired by the time the child is seven years of age or is in the second grade. Remember, though, that children differ in spelling ability as well as in other skills and that some children may have the ability to spell sooner, while others may not be ready for formal spelling until much later.

Many tasks in a program for young children are spelling-readiness activities. These activities promote good spelling skills that establish a basis for accurate spelling later. The following lists will help you recognize and identify spelling-readiness activities.

Spelling readiness integrated into classroom activities
Reading aloud to children
- Reading aloud enriches the child's vocabulary by providing new words to use.
- Listening to stories familiarizes the child with sentence structure and grammatical forms of words.
- Seeing and hearing the teacher read printed symbols creates a desire to write and create.

Listening
- Ability to spell depends to a considerable extent on a child's comprehension of spoken language.
- Hearing words spoken correctly helps the child recognize the same words in print.

Speaking
- A child can usually spell with greater ease those words that he or she uses in speaking.
- Through sharing, discussions, and role playing, a child reveals the scope of his or her vocabulary, which will be used later in spelling.

Writing
- The teacher's writing activities make the child aware of the need to learn to spell.
- A phonetic skill useful for writing will help the child to spell.
- Material composed and written by the teacher or aide makes spelling a personal necessity.
- Labeling of children's personal belongings gives the child opportunities to recognize how different names are spelled.

For additional activities and ideas for teaching spelling to young children, read the following sources:

Chomsky, Carol. "Beginning Reading Through Invented Spelling." *Selected Papers from the 1973 New England Kindergarten Conference*. Cambridge, Mass.: Lesley College, 1973.

Horn, Ernest. "Teaching Spelling." *What Research Says to the Teacher, No. 3*. Washington, D.C.: Association of Classroom Teachers of the National Education Association, 1954; reprinted 1971.

Read, Catherine. "Preschool Children's Knowledge of English Phonology." *Harvard Educational Review*, 41, 1 (February 1971): 1–34.

Rhea, Paul. "Invented Spelling in Kindergarten." *Young Children*, 31, 3 (March 1976): 195–200.

LANGUAGE EXPERIENCE CHARTS

Experience charts have many uses in early childhood classrooms. The main purposes of experience charts are to record in written form events, observations, stories, poems, and thoughts of the children; to present children's oral language in written form to help them become aware that printed symbols have meaning; and to have a written record of the experiences to be used at a later time, shared with parents, or studied by teachers to follow the language and concept development of the children.

Many types of language experiences may be recorded on these charts: a group experience the teacher wishes to record sequentially in the children's own language, an individual's comments about an experience; or the children's own stories and poems, which the teacher or aide writes out in manuscript form. An experience chart is adaptable for whole-group involvement, a small group, or individual comments and thoughts.

Charts can be purchased in several forms: a metal stand with large circular rings to support holed sheets of paper on a cardboard back; large sheets attached to a stiff cardboard back and cover that provides a triangle-shaped stand; a sheaf of large sheets of paper with a cardboard front and back that fits into slots cut in the top edges of a cardboard box; or a large cardboard-backed tablet of paper that can be placed in the chalk rail, on the floor leaning against the wall, or from which individual sheets of paper can be torn and taped to any flat surface. Large sheets of lined paper can also be bought in very inexpensive bulk form.

Sometimes the experience is not recorded on a chart as such but on a chalkboard, a 36" x 18" piece of newsprint or lined paper, a large piece of cardboard cut from the side of a box, a white window shade (be sure to use washable ink so that you can use the shade again), brown or white butcher paper, or pieces of paper salvaged from various sources (cardboard shirt liners, for instance).

SUMMARY

The language arts content area in an early childhood program covers many different subjects. Each of these subjects is important when planning an adequate daily schedule of activities. Because of the simplicity of the basic or foundation skills to be taught, the teacher must have a thorough knowledge and an in-depth background in each area. It is much more difficult to teach a student step by step, one skill at a time, than it is to teach a skill in concert with several other skills and not be concerned about which comes first.

In this chapter we have covered the following main topics of the language arts: Methods of teaching the language arts to young children; the influencing factors and the ways of teaching oral language; the "why" of teaching manuscript writing; the ways to teach spelling to young children; the teaching of reading; the processes of teaching the alphabet; books for a literature program; ideas for teaching poetry and fingerplays; ways of teaching dramatization to young children; audiovisual aids appropriate for classroom use; and the use of language experience charts in programs for young children.

DIFFERENTIATING AND INTEGRATING MINI UNITS

The danger of studying a book with separate chapters for each subject area is that you may forget that each subject area is integrated with every other subject area. The language arts — while skills — are taught within the subject areas of social studies, science, mathematics, art, music, and physical education to provide the content or context in which children may see an abstract concept applied and so learn the skill.

To help you understand the interrelation of the content taught at different ages, the spiral effect of skills and knowledge, and the integrating process that occurs, mini units have been developed for each chapter to teach listening and writing (telling) skills at various levels of a child's ability. Skills and knowledge are constantly expanding in a child's learning. Basic simple skills and knowledge are given depth as they are enriched and enlarged. Just as a simple word such as *run* has many definitions, other words or concepts have many meanings that depend on the context in which the word or concept is used. This expansion of skills and knowledge proceeds in a spiral — from one simple skill or bit of factual knowledge to a wider, more complex understanding.

Mini Units Differentiating and Integrating for **Three Year Olds**

	September	*January*	*May*
Topic	Environmental listening.	"The Story I Like Best" (literature).	"When I Was Little" (creative writing).
Objectives	To develop the skill of listening.	To provide an opportunity for the children to tell a story in sequence.	To provide an opportunity for children to see the relationship of oral language and printed symbols.
Materials	Radio, TV, door, window, record or tape of dog barking, car horn, rain.	A rug, a child's rocking chair, a listener (teacher, aide, parent, or older child), paper and pencil or felt pen.	Lined paper, felt pen, stapler, construction paper.
Procedures	Children name sounds they hear.	Read the story the child likes best; child then retells in own words.	Print on sheets of paper children's stories — as they tell them — of something that happened to them when they were little. Add construction paper covers, making books to send home to parents for rereading.

The language arts / 183

Mini Units   Differentiating and Integrating for **Three Year Olds** *(cont.)*

	September	*January*	*May*
Evaluation	Have children whisper to aide what they heard.	Listener records (writes) child's telling of story.	Rereading of story.
Integrating skills	Oral language practice. Concept building of objects for social studies or science.	Listening practice. Speaking practice. Grammar practice. Literature background.	Oral language practice. Recall. Listening. Establishing relationships of the skill of reading to oral language.

Mini Units   Differentiating and Integrating for **Four Year Olds**

	September	*January*	*May*
Topic	Talking games.	Creative drama (for any traditional literature).	Round robin poetry.
Objectives	To develop and expand use of nouns, verbs, prepositions, adjectives, and adverbs.	To develop and expand oral vocabulary, give action words meaning, and act out traditional literature.	To develop sense of rhyming words and to develop idea of a poem (words do not have to rhyme).
Materials	Small toys or objects.	Three cardboard box "houses," masks for pig and wolf.	Paper, felt pen, pictures of things that rhyme (for example, king, ring, sing, wing).
Procedures	The child names everything you touch and each action that you do — hop, skip, jump, and so on. Children use adjectives and adverbs to describe toys. They play hide and seek with items on, in, behind, over, and so on.	Children take turns playing pigs and wolf and act out the action words as they say them.	Teacher says "Once there was a king" (or any other rhyme word). The children develop the ideas of topic.
Evaluation	Listen to child.	Teacher observes and offers individual help to accomplish task.	Rereading of poem developed.
Integrating skills	Eye-hand coordination. Oral labeling. Visual discrimination.	Physical movement. Sequential development of ideas. Word meaning.	Listening development. Word meaning. Sentence and phrase formation.

Mini Units Differentiating and Integrating for **Five Year Olds**

	September	*January*	*May*
Topic	"My Five Friends" (oral creative stories).	"What Could I Do?" (oral discussion).	"I Know Your Name" (inventive spelling).
Objectives	To develop creative expression through storytelling.	To give children an opportunity to share ideas.	To develop an awareness that oral words have a printed form.
Materials	Have each child draw faces on five strips of paper approximately 2″ × 5″. Paste finished faces on toilet tissue rolls that have been halved.	A piece of string, a rubber band, a ribbon, a milk carton, a rock, paper, felt pen.	12″ × 18″ newsprint, crayons, name cards.
Procedures	Child names each face and places each on a finger and the thumb. These become characters in the story the child tells.	Say to child, "What could I do with this?" Print on paper child's suggestions. Read suggestions and discuss them.	Child draws pictures of classmates and prints the first letter of their names over their pictures. The pictures are shared with whole group.
Evaluation	Listen to child for accuracy of character portrayal. Observe drawing of face in relation to face of character.	Listen to responses for logical and creative answers.	Observe drawings for likeness to classmates and listen to explanations of shared pictures.
Integrating skills	Awareness of facial expression. Role playing. Character development. Oral language development. Sequential events.	Oral vocabulary development. Direction. Explanations. Concept development.	Ability to select right letter for labeling. Drawing. Eye-hand coordination. Letter identification. Oral sharing.

EVALUATION OF INDIVIDUAL DIFFERENCES

In the early years of childhood, evaluation is important — but not, however, for the same reasons that may be valid later. Evaluation is not performed to grade children or to measure them competitively. Rather, three, four, and five year olds are evaluated or assessed to diagnose problems and prescribe individualized instruction.

You are constantly accountable for your treatment of the children in your charge. Carefully kept records of the children's strengths and weaknesses can speak volumes whenever you are called upon to account for your recommendations and procedures. In addition, these records can form the basis for many helpful and positive parent conferences.

The evaluative checklists in the subject area chapters serve as examples. Experience, along with the advice of teachers and administrators, and careful consideration of the educational goals of your school will indicate how often and how many factors you should evaluate for your records. Review the lists as you come to them. See them as representing real children. Decide how you would group these children for effective instruction.

Many of the activities in programs for young children are "play" situations. Materials that are provided for children require them to perform some action on the material. The actions required often carry over to the reading process. Therefore, they are valid reading-readiness activities. The following evaluative checklists for relevant activities indicate how individuals may differ in their abilities to master some of the basic classroom activities.

Mastery of Puzzles   Young Three Year Olds (Age range 3.0 to 3.4 by October 1)

Name	October	January	May
Rosario	4 pcs.	10 pcs.	16 pcs.
Elizabeth	—	—	5 pcs.
Ivan	—	—	5 pcs.
Maria	—	6 pcs.	10 pcs.
Washington	6 pcs.	10 pcs.	10 pcs.
Eddie	—	—	5 pcs.
Keith	10 pcs.	16 pcs.	16 pcs.
Mike	—	4 pcs.	10 pcs.
Doug	—	5 pcs.	6 pcs.
Joy	4 pcs.	6 pcs.	10 pcs.
Ann	—	4 pcs.	6 pcs.
Betsy	—	—	4 pcs.
Amber	—	6 pcs.	8 pcs.
Leigh	5 pcs.	6 pcs.	10 pcs.
Mary	—	4 pcs.	6 pcs.
Ellen	—	—	4 pcs.
Roy	—	—	6 pcs.
Sam	—	—	—
Forrest	5 pcs.	10 pcs.	16 pcs.
Peter	—	6 pcs.	10 pcs.

Mastery of Stringing Beads Young Four Year Olds (Age range 4.0 to 4.4 by October 1)

Name	October	January	May
Graham	—	—	5 beads
Ed	—	—	—
Scott	—	—	—
Dana	—	6 beads	10-bead "necklace"
Valerie	4 beads	6 beads (all same color)	9 beads
Kay	—	5 beads	7 beads
Dee Ann	2 beads	7 beads	filled string — 16
Charles	—	2 beads	4 beads
Debbie	—	—	—
Jean	—	1 bead	4 beads
Jo Ann	—	—	—
Robert	—	—	3 beads
Susan	1 bead	5 beads	8 beads
Linda	3 beads	8 beads (all different colors)	10 beads
Lynn	—	—	—
John	—	2 beads	5 beads
Fred	—	—	—
Tom	—	—	3 beads
Frank	—	—	—
Monroe	—	—	2 beads

Mastery of Tying Shoes Young Five Year Olds (Age range 5.0 to 5.5 by October 1)

Name	October	January	May
Gigi	no	no	no
Alice	no	no	yes
Elizabeth	no	yes	yes

Mastery of Tying Shoes Young Five Year Olds (Age range 5.0 to 5.5 by October 1) *(cont.)*

Name	October	January	May
Jenny	no	no	no
Martha	yes	yes	yes
Sam	no	no	yes
Joe	no	no	no
Nancy	no	no	yes
Bill	no	no	no
George	no	no	yes
Francis	no	yes	yes
Judy	no	yes	yes
Guy	no	no	yes
Jason	no	no	yes
Jerry	no	no	yes
Kate	yes	yes	yes
Sharon	no	yes	yes
Earl	no	no	yes

The following is an example of how one teacher used the information gained from similar evaluative checksheets. She used the following code to set up groups for instruction and practice in the language arts skills:

Learning to count = C
Learning to print individual letter forms = W
Learning the alphabet = A
Learning to read whole words (sight vocabulary) = R

	Sept.	Oct.	Nov.	Dec.	Jan.	Feb.	Mar.	Apr.	May	June
José	C	C	CW	CWA	CWA	CWA	CWA			
Mary	CW	CW	CW	CW	CW	CWA	CWA			
Alice			C	CW	CW	CW	CW			
Burnett				C	C	CW	CW			
Rose	C	C	CW	CWA	CWA	CWA	CWA			
Ann	CW	CW	CW	CWA	CWA	CWA	CWA			
Yosef					C	C	CW			

	Sept.	Oct.	Nov.	Dec.	Jan.	Feb.	Mar.	Apr.	May	June
George			C	CW	CW	CW	CW			
Brice	C	C	CW	CW	CW	CW	CW			
Louise		C	C	C	CW	CW	CW			
Kathy		C	CW	CWA	CWA	CWA	CWAR			
Ray						C	C			
Elizabeth		W	CW	CW	CW	CW	CWA			
Linda	CW	CW	CWA	CWA	CWA	CWAR	CWAR			
Jack	C	C	CW	CW	CW	CW	CWA			
Pere					C	CW	CW			
Leo		W	CW	CW	CW	CWA				
Ruth					C	C	C			
Marshall	C	CW	CWA	CWA	CWA	CWAR	CWAR			
Saul				C	C	CW	CW			
Henry	CW	CW	CW	CW	CWA	CWA	CWA			

End of March status of children: 9 children, story memorization, learning the alphabet, learning to write; 3 children, learning to memorize stories; 7 children, story memorization and learning to write; 3 children, stories, alphabet, writing, and beginning reading.

LEARNING GOALS FOR CHILDREN

Keep in mind that every school system has explicit performance goals and standards for children before they leave the kindergarten. Your role as a teacher of young children is strengthened if you know how and in what measure you are contributing to the children's mastery of these exit skills.

- ✔ Children can discuss events of the day in a sequential order.
- ✔ Children can follow simple oral directions.
- ✔ Children can listen to a story for ten to fifteen minutes.
- ✔ Children can orally describe objects and happenings.
- ✔ Children can visually recognize a few printed symbols — name, signs, and such.
- ✔ Children have a repertoire of stories.
- ✔ Children can manipulate equipment and materials that develop eye-hand coordination and large and small muscles.

BASIC SKILLS SEQUENCE CHART

Whenever you are responsible for teaching children you must make several decisions. One, you must decide which theory of instruction you believe in. Two, you must decide what curriculum content is appropriate for the children you are teaching. Three, you must decide which of the skills related to the curriculum content you've selected (or is mandated by your school or school system) are inherent in the understanding of the content. The *crux* of teaching occurs at this point.

The skills basic to each curriculum content area are sequential in their development. Therefore, regardless of the age, or grade, or achievement level of the child you are teaching, you must know (or have available for your use) what comes first, second, and so on, in the skills expansion development that is inherent in the content being taught.

As a teacher of young children, your understanding of what will be taught in the following years is very important. Remember, while you may be the children's first teacher (other than their families), their schooling will go on for many years.

Skills sequence charts are included at the end of every chapter in Part Two to help you comprehend (1) the importance of the skills you are teaching to your children, (2) the relationship of what you are teaching to what will be taught, and (3) the meaning of the term "basic skills."

Use these lists wisely. They should prove valuable as you plan, evaluate, analyze, diagnose, and report to parents.

Language Arts Skills

Key symbols: (✔) Introduction (✔✔) Extension and reinforcement

Skill	Level 1	Level 2	Level 3
Auditory perception			
Discriminate the following conditions of sound: Loud-soft, noisy-quiet, high-low, fast-slow	✔	✔✔	✔✔
Locate sources of sounds (in room, outside, above, near, and so on)	✔	✔✔	✔✔
Identify sources of sounds (voices of children, teachers)	✔	✔✔	✔✔
Identify the tunes of songs	✔	✔✔	✔✔
Repeat the tunes of songs	✔	✔✔	✔✔
Reproduce simple rhythmic patterns	✔	✔✔	✔✔
Identify words that rhyme	✔	✔✔	✔✔

Language Arts Skills *(cont.)*

Key symbols: (✓) Introduction (✓✓) Extension and reinforcement

Skill	Level 1	Level 2	Level 3
Hear sounds at the beginning, end, and middle of words	✓	✓✓	✓✓
Produce various sounds and associate them with words	✓	✓✓	✓✓
Recognize differences among words with similar sounds		✓	✓✓
Discriminate sounds as to pitch and tune		✓	✓✓
Match sound/symbol with beginning consonant, final consonant, phonogram		✓	✓✓
Discriminate between words, phrases, and sentences		✓	✓✓

Auditory memory

Skill	Level 1	Level 2	Level 3
Imitate a sound produced by another person or an object	✓	✓✓	✓✓
Reproduce a rhythmic pattern after hearing it once	✓	✓✓	✓✓
Repeat nonsense words or simple sentences verbatim	✓	✓✓	✓✓
Repeat a sequence of directions or events in a story	✓	✓✓	✓✓
Follow two or three simple directions in sequential order	✓	✓✓	✓✓
Retell the essential elements of a story that has been told or read	✓	✓✓	✓✓
Name the days of the week and months of the year in sequence	✓	✓✓	✓✓
Walk across rows, up and down columns, and so on, according to visual patterns and verbal instructions		✓	✓✓

Language development in listening

Skill	Level 1	Level 2	Level 3
Listen without being distracted (roll call, announcements, show and tell)	✓	✓✓	✓✓
Respond correctly to directions	✓	✓✓	✓✓
Listen to answer a question	✓	✓✓	✓✓
Relate what is heard to personal experience	✓	✓✓	✓✓
Enter imaginatively into the experience, setting, and feelings of the characters in a story being told	✓	✓✓	✓✓
Carry out directions for delayed assignments		✓	✓✓
Follow two-step directions (vocal, tapes, and so on)		✓	✓✓
Listen with appreciation to more refined selections (concerts, poetry, films, recordings, and so on)			✓
Listen with appreciation and show mental and emotional enjoyment (storytelling, films, recordings, etc.)			✓
State a purpose for listening			✓

Language Arts Skills (cont.)

Key symbols: (✔) Introduction   (✔✔) Extension and reinforcement

Skill	Level 1	Level 2	Level 3
Oral expression			
Dictate ideas for a group experience chart	✔	✔✔	✔✔
Describe objects in terms of color, shape, or size	✔	✔✔	✔✔
Make up simple endings for a story	✔	✔✔	✔✔
Tell a story about a picture	✔	✔✔	✔✔
Dictate stories for charts and booklets	✔	✔✔	✔✔
Give personal information — address, telephone number, parents' names	✔	✔✔	✔✔
Express ideas in complete thoughts	✔	✔✔	✔✔
Read orally with expression	✔	✔✔	✔✔
Express how a story or situation makes him or her feel	✔	✔✔	✔✔
Read clearly, distinctly, and with expression		✔	✔✔
Describe feelings and emotions		✔	✔✔
Distinguish between telling and asking sentences		✔	✔✔
Read so that listeners enjoy the story		✔	✔✔
Begin to use correct phrasing			✔
Complete a rhyme with correct word			✔
Dictate a sentence telling what happened in a story	✔	✔✔	✔✔
Begin with a general statement, then dictate sentences that are increasingly specific (Example: This is an animal. This is a dog. This is a black dog.)	✔	✔✔	✔✔
Accurately observe punctuation when reading			✔
Give a short oral book report			✔
Express to an audience the meaning and feeling of a particular selection			✔
Keep eyes ahead of voice while reading			✔
Written expression			
Become aware of the use of the period, question mark, and exclamation point (introduced separately)	✔	✔✔	✔✔
Copy words correctly	✔	✔✔	✔✔
Write first and last names correctly	✔	✔✔	✔✔
Use capital letters correctly in proper names	✔	✔✔	✔✔
Copy words, phrases, and sentences correctly	✔	✔✔	✔✔

192 / Curriculum

Language Arts Skills (cont.)

Key symbols: (✔) Introduction   (✔✔) Extension and reinforcement

Skill	Level 1	Level 2	Level 3
Space words correctly	✔	✔✔	✔✔
Become aware of the use of a comma	✔	✔✔	✔✔
Copy stories from experience charts legibly in manuscript	✔	✔✔	✔✔
Write a sentence describing a picture or object	✔	✔✔	✔✔
Write simple sentences from dictation		✔	✔✔
Organize ideas into sequence		✔	✔✔
Use a period, comma, question mark, and exclamation point in writing		✔	✔✔
Write a story with the help of a picture and a list of key words		✔	✔✔
Continue to use capitalization correctly — first word in a sentence, proper names, days of week		✔	✔✔
Recognize, understand, and use the structural parts of words (Example: adding *ed*, *ing*, and so on)		✔	✔✔
Capitalize correctly months of the year, holidays, names of places		✔	✔✔
Punctuate the following correctly: Commas for words in a series, dates, greeting, and closing of a letter; apostrophe in contractions and apostrophe to show possession		✔	✔✔
Use abbreviations correctly			✔
Write short invitations or thank-you notes			✔
Distinguish between sentences and phrases			✔
Know the correct use of punctuation marks in sentences			✔
Begin to study paragraph make-up (indentation, central theme, and so on)			✔
Begin to compose compound sentences			✔
Practice the mechanics of a paragraph			✔

Sequence

	Level 1	Level 2	Level 3
Complete a simple task in logical order	✔	✔✔	✔✔
Arrange a number of objects and pictures in order	✔	✔✔	✔✔
Recognize sequence of events as to what happens first, second, third, and so on	✔	✔✔	✔✔
Arrange sentences to illustrate what happened first, next, and last		✔	✔✔
Recognize the order of events by such key words as *first, next, earlier, finally, yesterday, today,* and *tomorrow*			✔
Give directions for others to follow		✔	✔✔
Follow oral and printed direction found in workbooks, tests, project sheets, games, puzzles, and so on			✔
Follow written and oral directions for making things			✔

Language Arts Skills (cont.)

Key symbols: (✔) Introduction   (✔✔) Extension and reinforcement

Skill	Level 1	Level 2	Level 3
Follow sequence for solving two-step problems: Study pictures, read first and last sentences carefully, reread entire set of directions, recall steps of direction in sequence			✔
Classification			
Identify and name several objects belonging to the same class	✔	✔✔	✔✔
Sort objects and pictures of objects into classes	✔	✔✔	✔✔
Understand that words belong in certain categories (action words, descriptive words, and naming words)	✔	✔✔	✔✔
Group characters and events into particular classes		✔	✔✔
Interpretive: Inferential			
Interpret feelings and actions of story characters	✔	✔✔	✔✔
Use picture clues to supplement information read or heard	✔	✔✔	✔✔
Become aware of colorful language in a story	✔	✔✔	✔✔
Begin to translate figurative language and become aware of rhyme and rhythm			✔
Use capitalization as a clue to infer importance, exaggeration			✔
Interpretive: Pictorial			
Become aware of meaning of symbols on a simple picture map	✔	✔✔	✔✔
Begin to understand picture maps and graphs	✔	✔✔	✔✔
Begin to interpret simple picture maps	✔	✔✔	✔✔
Begin to read simple charts and diagrams	✔	✔✔	✔✔
Interpret symbols on more complicated charts, maps, diagrams			✔
Interpretive: Predicting outcomes			
Suggest outcomes and alternate outcomes for actions observed in a picture	✔	✔✔	✔✔
Predict the weather giving reasons for predictions	✔	✔✔	✔✔
Predict outcomes of stories and events		✔	✔✔
Anticipate a solution to a problem or climax to a story			✔
Interpretive: Drawing conclusions			
Draw conclusions from stories heard	✔	✔✔	✔✔
Develop ability to form a mental image after reading a selection		✔	✔✔
Select evidence for conclusions from phrases, sentences, or whole paragraphs			✔

Language Arts Skills (cont.)

Key symbols: (✔) Introduction   (✔✔) Extension and reinforcement

Skill	Level 1	Level 2	Level 3
Interpretive: Causation			
Use picture clues to determine what might happen (cause-effect)	✔	✔✔	✔✔
Tell why a story character reacts in a certain way	✔	✔✔	✔✔
Describe the possible effects of a given action	✔	✔✔	✔✔
Know who did what, when or where it occurred, and how and why it occurred		✔	✔✔
Critical: Analysis			
Recognize nonsense (limericks, imaginative poetry)	✔	✔✔	✔✔
Make judgments (orally) as to whether story is real or imaginary	✔	✔✔	✔✔
Make judgments about character's behavior	✔	✔✔	✔✔
Distinguish opinions from facts found in a given selection		✔	✔✔
Understand types of words used to arouse emotions		✔	✔✔
Become aware of exaggerated statements in advertisements, pictures, oral and written material			✔
Critical: Evaluation			
Express orally a personal reaction to a situation, character, or event	✔	✔✔	✔✔
Become aware of humor in materials read or heard	✔	✔✔	✔✔
Know when sentences are true, exaggerated, or misstated		✔	✔✔
Become aware that changes occur in the retelling of stories			✔
Compare and contrast concepts with own experiences and various sources			✔
Creative			
Tell personal experiences that relate to certain parts of a story (Example: family customs or relationships)	✔	✔✔	✔✔
Plan dramatization of stories read (pantomiming)	✔	✔✔	✔✔
Develop appreciation by: Identifying with feelings expressed in a poem Identifying with a character and understanding character's point of view	✔	✔✔	✔✔
Role play a story situation		✔	✔✔
Compare the story situation with a real-life experience		✔	✔✔
Express the theme of the story through a puppet show		✔	✔✔
Tell imaginary stories		✔	✔✔

Language Arts Skills (cont.)

Key symbols: (✔) Introduction   (✔✔) Extension and reinforcement

Skill	Level 1	Level 2	Level 3
Compare the story situation with a real-life experience in both oral and written communication		✔	✔✔
Word recognition			
Develop a sight vocabulary	✔	✔✔	✔✔
Identify words by picture clues	✔	✔✔	✔✔
Identify words by configuration	✔	✔✔	✔✔
Read words with capital and small letters	✔	✔✔	✔✔
Phonic analysis			
Recognize that initial consonants have different sounds	✔	✔✔	✔✔
Recognize words that do not begin with the same sound	✔	✔✔	✔✔
Continue to supply a missing word in material heard when given an initial consonant sound	✔	✔✔	✔✔
Recognize the sound/symbol association of some initial consonants	✔	✔✔	✔✔
Use the known initial consonant sound plus the context to figure out unknown words	✔	✔✔	✔✔
Blend separate sounds into words	✔	✔✔	✔✔
Begin to determine whether a given consonant sound is heard at the beginning, middle, or end of a word (*b*oy, ta*b*le, ca*b*)	✔	✔✔	✔✔
Recognize the short vowel sound heard in one-syllable words	✔	✔✔	✔✔
Recognize the long vowel sound heard in words	✔	✔✔	✔✔
Discriminate between long and short vowel sounds when heard	✔	✔✔	✔✔
Be aware of initial consonant blends and digraphs	✔	✔✔	✔✔
Write the letters of the alphabet as dictated by the teacher (not in sequence)	✔	✔✔	✔✔
Become aware of the soft sounds of *c* and *g*	✔	✔✔	✔✔
Become aware that consonants in a word may be silent (nigh*t*, *k*nit, bal*l*, lam*b*)	✔	✔✔	✔✔
Recognize the sounds represented by the consonant digraphs and less difficult blends		✔	✔✔
Begin to hear syllables in words		✔	✔✔
Become aware that *y* functions as a consonant or a vowel		✔	✔✔
Begin to use the sound of some consonant digraphs and blends in the initial position plus the context to figure out new words		✔	✔✔
Use two or more consonant letters together to form a blending of the sounds (blends-clusters)		✔	✔✔

Language Arts Skills *(cont.)*

Key symbols: (✔) Introduction   (✔✔) Extension and reinforcement

Skill	Level 1	Level 2	Level 3
Know *r* controlled vowels (*ar, er, ir, or, ur*)		✔	✔✔
Know that *l* and *w* affect the vowel sound (ball, saw)		✔	✔✔
Make new words by substituting initial consonant blends and digraphs			✔
Recognize the consonant blend or digraph heard at the end of words			✔
Begin to recognize the vowels heard in words of one or more syllables			✔
Become aware of the diacritical marks for the long and short vowels			✔
Become aware of the *schwa* sound that may be spelled with any vowel			✔
Recognize the sound/symbol association of the vowel digraphs and diphthongs			✔
Recognize the vowels heard in one or more syllables			✔
Use the diacritical marks for the long and short vowels			✔
Recognize that a vowel in a syllable often follows the same principle as the vowel in a one-syllable word			✔
Know the most common vowel principles that give clues as to which sound the vowel will use			✔
Recognize that the vowel combinations *aw* and *au* usually represent the same sound (*saw, fault*)			✔
Realize that spelling patterns are clues to vowel sounds			✔
Recognize that words with spelling patterns *ght, ind, ild, old, olt* and *ost* are clues to long vowel sounds			✔

Structural analysis

Skill	Level 1	Level 2	Level 3
Practice and expand ability to use plurals, verb forms, comparison, and possessives in oral language	✔	✔✔	✔✔
Recognize the root word within a derived word (prefix or suffix)		✔	✔✔
Know that simple endings denote tense (*ed, ing*), number (*s, es*), person (*s, es*), and possession (*'s*)	✔	✔✔	✔✔
Recognize the two words for which a contraction stands		✔	✔✔
Be aware that the spelling of a root word often changes when an ending or suffix is added		✔	✔✔
Recognize syllables in written words		✔	✔✔
Identify prefixes and suffixes in derived words		✔	✔✔
Understand that prefixes have action meaning		✔	✔✔
Know the meaning of prefixes and suffixes (show grammatical function) that occur in reading materials			✔

Language Arts Skills (cont.)

Key symbols: (✔) Introduction (✔✔) Extension and reinforcement

Skill	Level 1	Level 2	Level 3
Write the two words for any given contraction			✔
Use hyphenated compound words			✔
Identify the apostrophe in reading and make the distinction between the possessive form and the contraction			✔
Understand and apply the principles of syllabication			✔

Contextual application

Identify words by use of rebus	✔	✔✔	✔✔
Supply missing words when sentences or stories are read and/or heard	✔	✔✔	✔✔

Comprehension: Vocabulary

Begin to use action and naming words in concrete situations	✔	✔✔	✔✔
Understand meaning of words used in written directions	✔	✔✔	✔✔
Begin to understand words of opposite meanings (antonyms)		✔	✔✔
Extend the use of action and naming words in concrete situations		✔	✔✔
Recognize homonyms		✔	✔✔
Recognize synonyms			✔
Begin to identify words that give clues to the organization of materials read such as *classification*, *sequence*, *causation*, and *comparison*			✔
Identify words that give a clue to the organization of materials read such as *classification*, *sequence*, *causation*, and *comparison*			✔
Identify signal words that occur in materials read			✔

Comprehension: Main idea

Give a title for a story	✔	✔✔	✔✔
Recognize main ideas of a short story or rhyme heard or read	✔	✔✔	✔✔
Find the topic sentence in a given paragraph		✔	✔✔
Identify the central theme of stories read			✔

Comprehension: Details

Become aware of details that note time, place, and the major characters in a story	✔	✔✔	✔✔
Find details to support main idea of a short story or poem	✔	✔✔	✔✔
Differentiate between descriptive words, action words, and name words		✔	✔✔
Select words or phrases that describe a person, place, or thing		✔	✔✔

198 / *Curriculum*

Language Arts Skills (*cont.*)

Key symbols: (✔) Introduction   (✔✔) Extension and reinforcement

Skill	Level 1	Level 2	Level 3
Comprehension: Following directions			
Follow oral directions	✔	✔✔	✔✔
Observe simple written directions	✔	✔✔	✔✔
Repeat directions	✔	✔✔	✔✔
Follow simple written directions for independent work-type activities	✔	✔✔	✔✔
Locational: Dictionary			
Use a dictionary to locate words	✔	✔✔	✔✔
Begin to learn sequence of letters	✔	✔✔	✔✔
Arrange pictures in alphabetical order	✔	✔✔	✔✔
Tell which letter precedes and which letter follows in the alphabet	✔	✔✔	✔✔
Know that dictionaries are arranged in alphabetical order		✔	✔✔
Arrange words in alphabetical order using second letter		✔	✔✔
Realize that indexes, card catalogs, and reference books are arranged in alphabetical order		✔	✔✔
Begin to understand the purpose and use of guide words		✔	✔✔
Determine in which third of the dictionary a word may be located			✔
Be familiar and have practice with guide words as an aid to locate words			✔
Recognize the types of information included in a standard dictionary (syllabic division, pronunciation, meaning, pictorial aids)			✔
Locate any given word in the dictionary			✔
Use guide words as a helping aid in locating words			✔
Become aware of the pronunciation key given at the bottom of the page			✔
Recognize that words have various meanings			✔
Locational: Parts of a book			
Locate title page and identify title	✔	✔✔	✔✔
Use table of contents to find page numbers	✔	✔✔	✔✔
Locate the page number of a given title	✔	✔✔	✔✔
Read the titles of stories as listed in the table of contents		✔	✔✔
Find page numbers quickly		✔	✔✔
Know that some books are divided into chapters		✔	✔✔
Understand titles and subtitles		✔	✔✔

Language Arts Skills (cont.)

Key symbols: (✔) Introduction (✔✔) Extension and reinforcement

Skill	Level 1	Level 2	Level 3
Begin to use glossary and index		✔	✔✔
Be skillful in locating and using the major parts of a book: title, page, table of contents (stories, units, chapters), glossary, index			✔
Recognize that italicized or boldfaced words may be found in the glossary			✔

Locational: Library resources

Skill	Level 1	Level 2	Level 3
Become familiar with the library and the work of the librarian	✔	✔✔	✔✔
Become aware that various types of material are found in the library		✔	✔✔
Identify alphabetical arrangement of the fiction books		✔	✔✔
Begin to find library books independently		✔	✔✔
Be familiar with the resources of the library (card catalog, atlases, encyclopedias, general references, periodicals, and so on)			✔

Use of pictorial aids

Skill	Level 1	Level 2	Level 3
Use pictorial aids for word recognition and word meaning	✔	✔✔	✔✔
Use simple picture maps	✔	✔✔	✔✔
Begin to get information from pictures, maps, globes, graphs, and diagrams		✔	✔✔

Organizational: Outlining

Skill	Level 1	Level 2	Level 3
Recognize which sentence tells what the paragraph is about		✔	✔✔
List the major events in the paragraph		✔	✔✔
Understand and use these in a book report: title, author, favorite part of book, where to find the book		✔	✔✔
Become familiar with the form of a topical outline		✔	✔✔
Become aware of the types of paragraph organization: details of supporting main idea, sequence, causation, classification, comparison			✔
Become aware of key words in topic sentences that indicate the type of paragraph being read			✔

Organizational: Summarizing

Skill	Level 1	Level 2	Level 3
Retell a sentence in own words	✔	✔✔	✔✔
Summarize the major points and events of a story previously read (may use pictures)	✔	✔✔	✔✔
Summarize the story by paragraph units		✔	✔✔

Language Arts Skills (cont.)

Key symbols: (✔) Introduction   (✔✔) Extension and reinforcement

Skill	Level 1	Level 2	Level 3
Note taking			
Draw illustrations to use as notes when telling a story		✔	✔✔
List words to use as notes when telling a story		✔	✔✔
List phrases to use as notes when telling a story			✔
List simple sentences to use as notes when telling a story			✔
Study techniques			
Recall information		✔	✔✔
Read to answer questions		✔	✔✔
Recognize important details			✔
Become aware of the importance of memory aids			✔
Rate			
Begin to scan to find the answer to a specific question	✔	✔✔	✔✔
Scan a page to find a sentence that has been quoted		✔	✔✔
Practice reading words, phrases, and sentences at various rates		✔	✔✔
Scan a selection to find answers to a list of questions as quickly as possible			✔
Skim a book to find out if you would like to read it			✔
Time and spatial skills			
Understand time	✔	✔✔	✔✔
Place happenings in chronological order	✔	✔✔	✔✔
Develop numerical sequence	✔	✔✔	✔✔
Analyzing and evaluating information			
Interpret titles	✔	✔✔	✔✔
Reread for clarification	✔	✔✔	✔✔
Differentiate between fact and fiction	✔	✔✔	✔✔
Obtain accurate details		✔	✔✔
Arrange and organize information and ideas		✔	✔✔
Secure reliable sources of information		✔	✔✔
Evaluate information for specific purposes			✔

ADDITIONAL READINGS

Aukerman, Robert C. *Approaches to Beginning Reading*. New York: Wiley, 1971.

Baker, Augusta, and Ellin Greene. *Storytelling: Art and Technique*. New York: R. R. Bowker, 1977.

Bettelheim, Bruno. *The Uses of Enchantment: The Meaning and Importance of Fairy Tales*. New York: Knopf, 1976.

Cullinan, Bernice E. "Changing Perspectives in Black English and Reading." *Reading Instruction Journal*, 18 (January 1975): 32.

Cullinan, Bernice E., Angela Jagger, and Dorothy Strickland. "Language Expansion for Black Children in the Primary Grades: A Research Report." *Young Children*, 29 (January 1974): 98–112.

Kaye, E. *How to Treat TV with TLC: The ACT Guide to Children's Television*. Rev. ed. Boston: Beacon Press, 1979.

Lundsteen, Sara W. *Listening: Its Impact on Reading and the Other Language Arts*. Urbana, Ill.: National Council of Teachers of English, 1979.

Ollila, Lloyd O., ed. *The Kindergarten Child and Reading*. Newark, N.J.: International Reading Association, 1977.

Pflaum-Conner, S. *The Development of Language and Reading in Young Children*. Columbus, Ohio: Charles E. Merrill, 1978.

Schimmel, Nancy. *Just Enough to Make a Story: A Sourcebook for Storytelling*. Berkeley, Calif.: Sisters' Choice Press, 1978.

Somers, Albert B., and Janet Evans Worthington. *Response Guides for Teaching Children's Books*. Urbana, Ill.: National Council of Teachers of English, 1979.

Tiedt, Iris M. *Exploring Books with Children*. Boston: Houghton Mifflin, 1979.

CHAPTER 7
Social Studies

Exploration Tasks

After studying this chapter, you should be able to complete these tasks:
- Identify the content of a social studies program.
- Describe the teacher's role in the socialization process.
- Describe and plan an affective education program for three, four, and five year olds.
- Identify several books that will help children improve or understand social living experiences.
- Explain and plan activities for the dramatization process for young children.
- Write units of work on appropriate topics.
- Plan a field trip.
- Select appropriate resource people, materials, and equipment.

Because responsibility has two faces, individual and social, we must see it not as an opposite of freedom but rather as a necessary companion.

Alice Miel

OVERVIEW

What is social studies for young children? The basic content of a social studies program for young children is the same as a program for any other age — with elements of anthropology, economics, geography, history, political science, and sociology. As a teacher of young children, however, you will not have twenty minutes of anthropology on Thursday; you will have a story and a discussion about children from other lands or other parts of the country. When you do, you will have begun a study of anthropology. You will not teach economics every Monday or geography every Friday; but sometime during the week the children in the family center will go to the "store" to buy groceries and the trucks in the block center will be "driven" to a parent's office past the bank, past the airport, and over the bridge into the city.

Social studies is one of the two *content areas of instruction*, which emphasize the learning of facts and information (the other is science). Therefore, whenever you teach a *skill subject*, which emphasizes the learning of processes (language arts or math, for example), you generally teach social studies at the same time. Social studies is the "glue" that bonds the elements of the curriculum for young children.

There are definite units of work in social studies as well as integrating daily activities. This chapter has three main divisions: the first division explains the socialization process, the second discusses the process of integration of content areas, and the third suggests books and equipment appropriate for three, four, and five year olds. The chapter begins with a look at some general approaches to teaching social studies.

THEORETICAL CONTEXT

The two main theories of teaching social studies are the self-realization or child-centered approach and the cognitive process approach, which has standard goals and content that all children should learn. Currently the cognitive process approach is prevalent. This is probably occurring for several reasons: (1) public schooling for many very young children is comparatively new, (2) most adults do not understand how children learn through play, (3) early educational experiences do not necessarily make children advanced first graders, and (4) many adults do not wish to pay for schooling that does not show immediate testable results. All these factors have led some educators to adopt a cognitive approach, which utilizes behavioral goals, workbooks and other printed seatwork, formal instruction (generally in a first-grade atmosphere), and the testing of children on what they have learned.

In the cognitive process approach to teaching social studies, the curriculum is "subject matter centered." The teacher, or more likely a committee, decides what is to be taught, how it is to be taught, and often when it is to be taught. The subject matter may be presented in various ways, with teachers being able to choose how it is taught.

Behavioral goals may be an advantage for teachers. One of the major problems in teaching young children is establishing activities that are sequential in nature, have a purpose, are appropriate for the age taught, are interesting to the children, and are play situations based on the individual needs of a child. However, one problem of having a systemwide or statewide program is that unthinking or literal-minded school personnel may view the topics included in such a program as the only acceptable content for classroom social studies programs.

A self-realization or child-centered approach requires in-depth planning, many materials, and content selection, just as the cognitive process approach does. The child-centered concept, however, usually starts with a child's or a small group's needs and interests. From these needs and interests, activities are developed for the classroom. Teachers using the child-centered approach also develop units or themes for all children to participate in at their various ability levels. Some teachers let the children's interests dominate the instructional program. There is no need for children to spend three months of the school year on the zoo just because one or two children become aggressive in their interest in the zoo. Remember, you are the teacher, and part of your responsibility is to guide and select the content and the process by which the children are to learn. Another difficulty that may arise is that teachers tend to plan activities in which they (the teachers) excel. Unless you plan carefully, your social studies program will be unbalanced and express your interests rather than the children's.

Which is the better approach? Probably both are equally acceptable, depending on the content to be taught. The child-centered approach can provide the spontaneity for high interest and participation. The cognitive process approach is subject-matter concentrated; its behavioral objectives and well-developed plans provide accurate opportunities for step-by-step learning. You'll want to try both ways in your beginning teaching experiences.

SOCIALIZATION

All human beings have certain responsibilities — self-control, self-respect, and self-reliance; independence in thought and action; and respect and appreciation of the rights, worth, and contributions of others. No one lives an isolated life uninfluenced by other human beings. The world is a human world and the results of a person's interaction with other people and their physical environments control all functions of life.

For each individual this process starts in the home and is maintained by parents or other adults within the home environment for many years — sometimes for a lifetime. Because educating a child is a joint endeavor, parents and teachers must work together in a understanding way so that each knows his or her own role as well as the other's role. As a teacher you are responsible not only for providing accurate individualized instruction; you are also responsible to parents for explaining what, why, and how you are providing certain learning experiences. In turn, parents have an obligation to you to reinforce and maintain these educational goals at home. There is no more important aspect of a child's education than the contribution of the educational experience to socialization.

Paul: "Watcha got?"
Janie: "Somethin."
Paul: "Let me see it."
Janie: "No."
Paul: "I'll tell!"
Janie: "I don't care!"
Paul: "Teacher —! Janie won't let me see what she's got."

The Teacher's Role

As a teacher you have several responsibilities for developing the socialization process of each child. The first of these responsibilities is to develop techniques that will encourage social interaction of children — sharing times, joint work responsibilities, creative play situations, construction activities, discussions, and events for going into new environments and meeting new people. A second responsibility is to provide flexibility in each of these activities to allow for individual differences as well as individual growth patterns. A closely related responsibility is that of providing a variety of experiences, materials, and equipment that not only meets the needs of the individuals but also maintains previous learnings, introduces new learnings, and creates new possibilities for additional learnings. The fourth responsibility for the teacher is to utilize the neighborhood environment and community service people so children may have first-hand experiences as participating members of their world. The fifth responsibility is to provide sexually unbiased activities that allow children to express their feelings and behavior without stereotypical limitations. An interesting pamphlet of activities published by ERIC Clearinghouse on Elementary and Early Childhood Education (ED 154 932) provides a good beginning for developing your own activities.

Affective Education

In recent years, educators have come to realize the importance of individuals communicating their feelings to develop a better understanding of themselves and others. Because the very young are honest in expressing their feelings, the early childhood years are the logical time to acquire a clear understanding of themselves and their own behaviors. The objectives of an *affective education* program at this early age include the development of communication skills, respectful human relationships, and appropriate social behavior. As a teacher of the young you have two main responsibilities in this area: to understand the feelings of children and to provide the children with opportunities to understand their own feelings.

To help you understand the feelings of children, read and study the following books, pamphlets, and journals:

Books

Ginott, Haim. *Teacher and Child*. New York: Macmillan, 1972.
Gordon, Thomas. *Parent Effectiveness Training*. New York: Wyden, 1970.
———. *Teacher Effectiveness Training*. New York: Wyden, 1975.
Greenberg, Herbert M. *Teaching with Feeling*. New York: Macmillan, 1969.
James, Muriel, and Dorothy Jongeward. *Born to Win: Transactional Analysis with Gestalt Experiments*. Reading, Mass.: Addison-Wesley, 1971.
———. *Transactional Analysis for Moms and Dads: What To Do with Them Now That You've Got Them*. Reading, Mass.: Addison-Wesley, 1975.
Kübler-Ross, Elisabeth. *Questions and Answers on Death and Dying*. New York: Macmillan, 1974.
Satir, Virginia. *Peoplemaking*. Palo Alto, Calif.: Science and Behavior Books, 1972.

Pamphlets

Wold, Anna W. M., "Helping Your Child To Understand Death"; Weingarten, Violet, "The Mother Who Works Outside the Home"; and Arnstein, Helene S., "When a Parent Is Mentally Ill: What To Say To Your Child." Child Study Association of America, 9 East 89th Street, New York, NY 10028.

Journals

Journal of Divorce. Haworth Press, 174 Fifth Avenue, New York, NY 10010.
The Single Parent. The Journal of Parents Without Partners, Inc., International Headquarters, 7910 Woodmont Avenue, Bethesda, MD 20014.

To fulfill your second obligation of helping children express their feelings, the following published materials are available:

DUSO (Developing Understanding of Self and Others) by D. Dinkmeyer (1970). Order from American Guidance Service, Inc., Publishers Bldg., Circle Pines, MN 55104. The "DUSO Kit" is an excellent source of materials for feelings commonly experienced by young children. Materials included in the kit are a teacher's manual, posters, picture-story books, records or cassette tapes, puppets and props, and a durable metal carrying case. The materials in the "DUSO Kit" help children have a keener awareness of their own feelings and needs. The kit also trains children in group discussion procedures, emphasizing an attitude of acceptance.

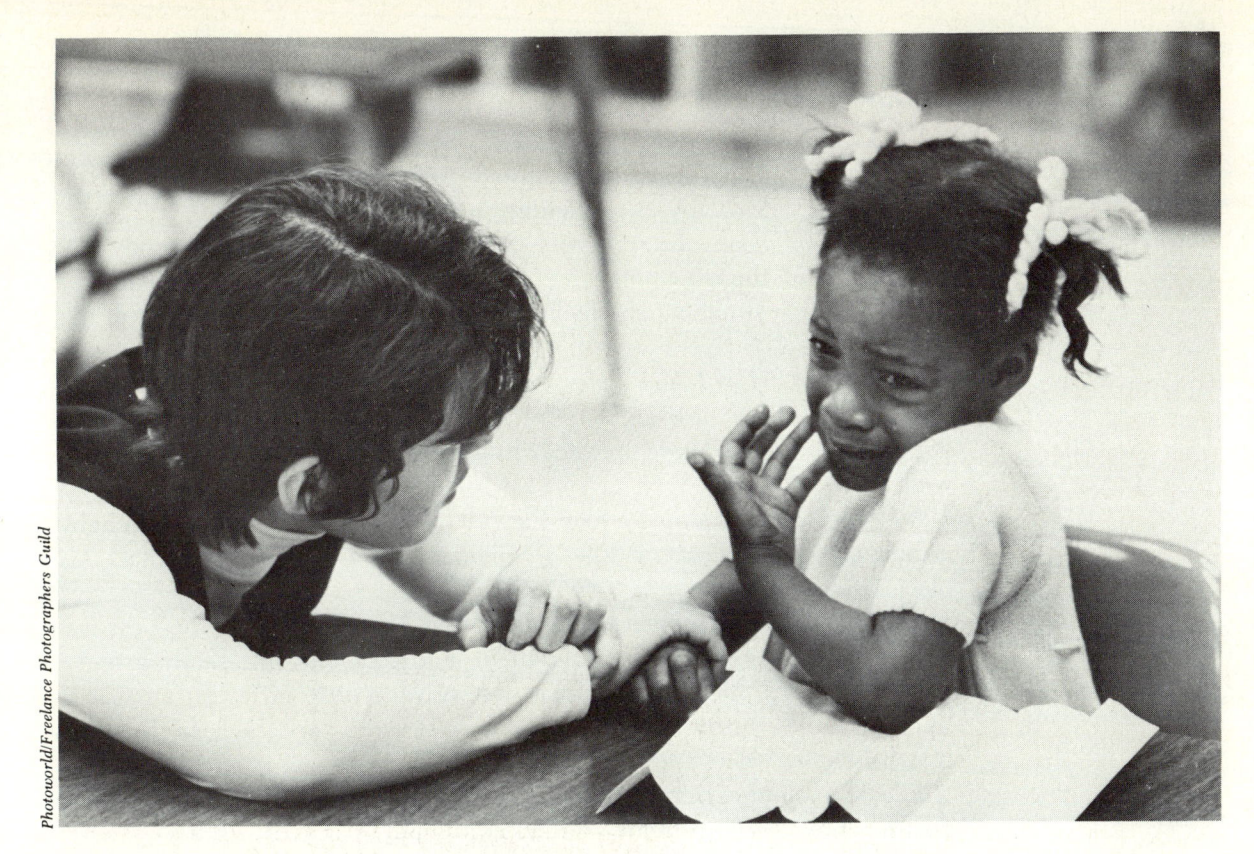

Freedom to express emotions is important.

Methods in Human Development by H. Bessel and V. Palomares (1967). Order from Human Developing Training Institute, San Diego, CA. *Methods in Human Development* is a curriculum program consisting of two parts: theory manual and activity guides. The Theory Manual describes the scope, procedures, and objectives of *Methods in Human Development*. It also provides for the teacher a conceptual framework within which to recognize, label, and understand the behaviors of children at different age levels. Four Lesson Guides provide a planned program that focuses on the themes of *Awareness* — understanding thoughts, feelings, and actions; *Mastery* — knowing one's abilities and how to use them; and *Social Interaction* — knowing other people. The program is implemented by a group discussion technique called the "Magic Circle." In the Magic Circle, thoughts, feelings, and social behavior are expressed and shared by group members.

T.A. for Tots (and other Prinzes) by Alvyn M. Freed, Ph.D. (1974). Order from Tap Co., 391 Monroe St., Sacramento, CA 95825. Designed to help children get acquainted with themselves and to promote understanding of others, *T.A. for Tots* is directed at preschool and first-grade children. Also available is the Tot-Pac, an audiovisual program designed for classroom use. Contents of the Tot-Pac are: Leader's Manual, *T.A. for Tots*, slide sets, record, posters, and Warm Fuzzies and Cold Pricklies.

The following books may be ordered from Behavioral Publications, 72 Fifth Avenue, New York, NY 10011:

Billy and Our New Baby by Helene S. Arnstein: Aimed at helping a child adjust to the new baby in the family.

I Have Feelings by Terry Berger: Seventeen different feelings, both good and bad, and the situations that precipitated each one. Each feeling is presented by a situation, the feeling that results, and an explanation of that feeling.

One Little Girl by Joan Fassler: Because she is somewhat retarded, grown-ups call Laurie a "slow child." But Laurie learns that she is only slow in doing some things. There are other interesting things that she can do quite well.

All Alone with Daddy by Joan Fassler: Ellen is a little girl who delights in being with her daddy. While her mother is away, Ellen tries to take her place.

The Boy with a Problem by Joan Fassler: David discovers the best way to cope with a problem is to talk about it to someone who really listens.

Don't Worry, Dear by Joan Fassler: A very little girl with an understanding mother grows out of thumbsucking, word-repeating, and bedwetting habits.

The Man of the House by Joan Fassler: The story of a little boy who assumes the Daddy role for a few days.

My Grandpa Died Today by Joan Fassler: A boy learns about death for the first time.

Lisa and Her Soundless World by Edna S. Levine: After Lisa and her parents learn about her deafness, she learns to hear sounds with a hearing aid and is finally able to say words.

Things I Hate by Harriet Wittles and Joan Greisman: Tackles the normal frustrations of most children who have to do things that are sometimes disagreeable.

The Hospital Is Where compiled by Grace Smith: A collection of writings and drawings by children who have experienced hospitalization.

Children must learn to cope with divorce, severe illness, or death within their immediate family. Research indicates that only when adults have adjusted reasonably to these problems can they deal adequately with the emotional reactions of children. Research also indicates that adults are inhibited when talking about divorce, severe illness, and death.[1] Children should be included in the varying aspects of life's problems as they occur.

---

[1] J. Fassler, *Helping Children Cope: Mastering Stress Through Books and Stories* (New York: Free Press, 1978).

They should not be forced to participate in any of the events. A teacher should present only basic truths of such events that children can understand and expand upon as they mature.

Affective Education Books for Children

As you will remember from the discussion in the literature section of the language arts chapter, many books for children are written about problems and events a young child experiences. These books can often be used for more than one purpose. They are listed here because it is often difficult for beginning teachers to select books for special topics. The following list should be a valuable resource during your teaching.

Alexander, Martha. *Bobo's Dream*. New York: The Dial Press, 1970.
———. *Nobody Asked Me If I Wanted a Baby Sister*. New York: The Dial Press, 1971.
———. *Sabrina*. New York: The Dial Press, 1971.
Anglund, Joan Walsh. *A Friend Is Someone Who Likes You*. New York: Harcourt Brace Jovanovich, 1958.
———. *Love is a Special Way of Feeling*. New York: Harcourt Brace Jovanovich, 1958.
Baldwin, Ann Norris. *Sunflower for Tina*. New York: Scholastic Book Services, Four Winds, 1970.
Barrett, Judi. *I Hate to Take a Bath*. New York: Scholastic Book Services, Four Winds, 1975.
Blaine, Marge. *The Terrible Thing That Happened at Our House*. New York: Parents Magazine Press, 1975.
Bond, Jean. *Brown Is a Beautiful Color*. Chicago: Franklin Watts, 1969.
Borack, Barbara. *Grandpa*. New York: Harper & Row, 1967.
———. *Someone Small*. New York: Harper & Row, 1969.
Brandenburg, Franz. *No School Today*. New York: Macmillan, 1975.
Bright, Robert. *Georgie*. Garden City, N.Y.: Doubleday, 1959.
———. *Georgie to the Rescue*. Garden City, N.Y.: Doubleday, 1956.
Brown, Margaret Wise. *The Dead Bird*. New York: William R. Scott, 1958.
Bulla, Clyde Robert. *Daniel's Duck*. New York: Harper & Row, 1979.
Candill, Rebecca. *A Pocketful of Cricket*. New York: Holt, Rinehart and Winston, 1964.
Cohen, Miriam. *Best Friends*. New York: Macmillan, 1971.
Cole, William. *That Pest Jonathan*. New York: Harper & Row, 1970.
De Bruyn, Monica. *The Beaver Who Wouldn't Die*. Chicago: Follett Publishing Co., 1975.
Ehrlich, Amy. *Zeek Silver Moon*. New York: The Dial Press, 1972.
Ets, Marie Hall. *Bad Boy, Good Boy*. New York: Thomas Y. Crowell Co., 1967.

―――. *Just Me*. New York: The Viking Press, 1965.

Farber, Norma. *As I Was Crossing Boston Common*. New York: E.P. Dutton, 1975.

Fassler, Joan. *Howie Helps Himself*. Chicago: Albert Whitman, 1975.

Flack, Marjorie. *Angus Lost*. Garden City, N.Y.: Doubleday, 1941.

―――. *The Story about Ping*. New York: The Viking Press, 1933.

Freeman, Don. *Will's Quill*. New York: The Viking Press, 1975.

Gackenbach, Dick. *Do You Love Me?* New York: Seabury Press, 1975.

Gag, Wanda. *Millions of Cats*. New York: Coward-McCann, 1938.

Goldman, Susan. *Grandma's Somebody Special*. Chicago: Albert Witman, 1976.

Guilfoile, Elizabeth. *Nobody Listens to Andrew*. Chicago: Follet Publishing Co., 1957.

Hazen, Barbara Shook. *Why Couldn't I Be an Only Kid Like You, Wigger?* New York: Atheneum, 1975.

Hoban, Russell. *A Baby Sister for Frances*. New York: Harper & Row, 1964.

―――. *A Bargain for Frances*. New York: Harper & Row, 1970.

―――. *Best Friends for Frances*. New York: Harper & Row, 1969.

Hoff, Syd. *Barkley*. New York: Harper & Row, 1975.

Hurd, Edith Thacher. *Catfish*. New York: The Viking Press, 1970.

Hunter, Mollie. *The Third Eye*. New York: Harper and Row, 1979.

James, Elizabeth, and Carol Barkin. *Sometimes I Hate School*. Chicago: Childrens Press, 1975.

Kantrowitz, Mildred. *I Wonder if Herbie's Home Yet*. New York: Parents Magazine Press, 1971.

Keats, Ezra Jack. *Louie*. New York: Greenwillow Books, 1975.

―――. *Peter's Chair*. New York: Harper & Row, 1967.

―――. *The Snowy Day*. New York: The Viking Press, 1962.

―――. *Whistle for Willie*. New York: The Viking Press, 1964.

Kellogg, Steven. *The Mystery of the Missing Red Mitten*. New York: The Dial Press, 1974.

Kroll, Steven. *Is Milton Missing?* New York: Holiday House, 1975.

Larsen, Hanne. *Don't Forget Tom*. New York: Thomas Y. Crowell Co., 1978.

Lenski, Lois. *Blue Ridge Billy*. Philadelphia: J. B. Lippincott, 1946.

―――. *High Rise Secret*. Philadelphia: J. B. Lippincott, 1966.

―――. *Project Boy*. Philadelphia: J. B. Lippincott, 1954.

Levine, Edna S. *Lisa and Her Soundless World*. New York: Human Sciences Press, 1974.

Lexau, Joan. *Benjie on His Own*. New York: The Dial Press, 1970.

―――. *Emily and the Klunky*. New York: The Dial Press, 1971.

Litchfield, Ada B. *A Button in Her Ear*. Chicago: Albert Whitman, 1976.

Lobel, Arnold. *Frog and Toad Are Friends*. New York: The Viking Press, 1970.

Mack, Nancy. *Tracy*. Chicago: Childrens Press, 1976.

Mallett, Anne. *Here Comes Tag-Along*. New York: Parents Magazine Press, 1971.

Marzollo, Jean. *Close Your Eyes*. New York: The Dial Press, 1978.

Mayer, Mercer, and Marianna Mayer. *Mine!* New York: Simon & Schuster, 1970.

McCloskey, Robert. *One Morning in Maine*. New York: The Viking Press, 1952.

McNutty, Faith. *The Elephant Who Couldn't Forget*. New York: Harper & Row, 1980.

Miles, Miska. *Annie and the Old One*. Boston: Little, Brown, 1971.

Oakley, Graham. *The Church Mice Spread Their Wings*. New York: Atheneum, 1976.

Peter, Diana. *Claire and Emma*. New York: The John Day Co., 1976.

Peterson, Jeanne Whitihouse. *I Have a Sister/My Sister Is Deaf*. New York: Harper & Row, 1977.

Peterson, Palle. *Sally Can't See*. New York: The John Day Co., 1977.

Politi, Leo. *May May*. New York: Charles Scribner's Sons, 1960.

Potter, Beatrix. *Story of Peter Rabbit*. New York: Frederick Warne & Co., 1902; reprinted 1977.

Preston, Edna Mitchell. *The Boy Who Could Make Things*. New York: The Viking Press, 1970.

Raskin, Ellen. *Spectacles*. New York: Atheneum, 1968.

Rice, Eve. *Oh, Lewis!* New York: Macmillan, 1974.

———. *What Sadie Sang*. New York: Greenwillow Books, 1976.

Rogers, Helen Spelman. *Morris and His Brave Lion*. New York: McGraw-Hill, 1975.

Schick, Eleanor. *Making Friends*. New York: Macmillan, 1969.

Schlein, Miriam. *The Girl Who Would Rather Climb Trees*. New York: Harcourt, Brace, Jovanovich, 1975.

Simon, Norma. *I Was So Mad*. Chicago: Albert Whitman, 1974.

Skorpen, Liesel Moak. *Michael*. New York: Harper & Row, 1975.

Slobodkin, Esphyr. *Caps for Sale*. Reading, Mass.: Addison-Wesley, 1947.

Smaridge, Norah. *The Big Tidy-Up*. New York: Golden Press, 1970.

Sobol, Harriet Langsam. *My Brother Steven Is Retarded*. New York: Macmillan, 1977.

Steptoe, John. *Stevie*. New York: Harper & Row, 1969.

Udry, Janice. *Mary Jo's Grandmother*. Chicago: Albert Whitman, 1970.

Viorst, Judith. *Alexander and the Horrible, No Good, Very Bad Day*. New York: Atheneum, 1972.

———. *The Tenth Good Thing About Barney*. New York: Atheneum, 1971.

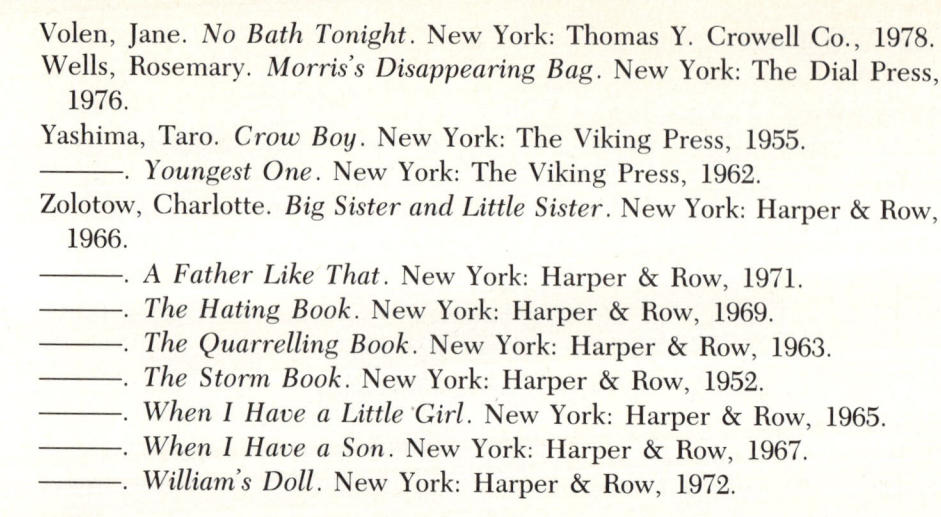

Volen, Jane. *No Bath Tonight*. New York: Thomas Y. Crowell Co., 1978.
Wells, Rosemary. *Morris's Disappearing Bag*. New York: The Dial Press, 1976.
Yashima, Taro. *Crow Boy*. New York: The Viking Press, 1955.
———. *Youngest One*. New York: The Viking Press, 1962.
Zolotow, Charlotte. *Big Sister and Little Sister*. New York: Harper & Row, 1966.
———. *A Father Like That*. New York: Harper & Row, 1971.
———. *The Hating Book*. New York: Harper & Row, 1969.
———. *The Quarrelling Book*. New York: Harper & Row, 1963.
———. *The Storm Book*. New York: Harper & Row, 1952.
———. *When I Have a Little Girl*. New York: Harper & Row, 1965.
———. *When I Have a Son*. New York: Harper & Row, 1967.
———. *William's Doll*. New York: Harper & Row, 1972.

Affective Education Activities

Children need activities that encourage awareness of their own feelings and the feelings of others. The activities should not only help them become aware of their feelings but also provide appropriate behavior models. Many discipline problems can be avoided if a teacher anticipates those occasions when a child may be jealous, mad, frightened, or apprehensive.

The following activities should be planned for early in the school year. Not all the activities should be introduced at once and some are more appropriate for three and four year olds than for five year olds.

Listening to Records and/or Singing Songs Children can share common feelings and frustrations and recall past happenings by listening or singing together. Group discussions of such problems will help shy children express their feelings. The record *You Are Special* (Mr. Rogers, Small World Records) contains songs about fear and frustrations common to the very young. Another Mr. Rogers record, *Let's Be Together Today,* provides songs about anger and insecurity. *Ramo*, by Phillis Hiller (Creative Materials Library, P.O. Box 12068, Nashville, TN) is a song-story about a small elephant who has many problems similar to those of young children.

Using a Flannelboard The flannelboard is a simple, easily available, and inexpensive tool that will serve for several different activities in a school program. A 36″ × 36″ board is preferable because it allows for large items (see Chapter 5 for construction and materials). For affective education use cut out a facial outline about 10 inches high. Then make a variety of facial expressions to put on the face: smile (happiness), tears (sadness), rounded mouth (surprise), frown (anger), tight lips (fear). Display one of the faces and have the children tell you what kind of a face it is (what it expresses).

After several such experiences, relate some classroom incidents and ask the children to place appropriate expressions on the flannelboard face. Children should be encouraged to share happy experiences when a smile appears on the flannelboard, unhappy experiences when the tears appear, and so on. This activity can be used by individuals or groups.

Using a Mirror A full-length mirror is a necessity in a classroom for young children. The mirror can be used to help children recognize the differences in their own facial expressions as they are displaying emotions such as happiness, sadness, or anger. The mirror is also helpful for improving personal appearance, for dramatization, and for real-life experiences.

Using Photos Snapshots of children in happy or positive situations will encourage children to behave in acceptable ways. Photos of children during misbehavior or in sad or angry moments can be embarrassing and cause resentment. Expressions of feelings and emotions are normal, natural occurrences and should be accepted as such. There are times when a sad face or tears are appropriate. Anger and frustration are also normal and children need to have acceptable outlets of behavior. Verbal or written expression (drawing) of anger and frustration should be encouraged.

Using Games Appropriate for Expressing Feelings Several inexpensive games can be made for a group for individual expression of feelings. A birthday cake made from a cardboard box covered with crepe paper can be used as a "I wish for a _____ for John." Children can be asked to close their eyes and make a wish for something that John would like. After they have thought of something, they tell John what they "wished" for him. The activity is a form of sharing and bringing happiness to someone else.

"Guess How I Feel!" can be played with one or several youngsters at the same time. The younger children can use the flannel-board face and features to portray how they feel, and older individuals can be given large sheets of newsprint and crayons or paint. The child relates how he or she feels that day and explains why to you (as the teacher), to the aide and/or to other children. A mirror will help the child who wants a "picture" of himself or herself.

A "Give a Gift" game can be made from several boxes of various sizes wrapped for different occasions — birthday, returning to school after an illness, or other events. The boxes have one end that opens so objects may be placed inside. The gift is not kept but used or kept for the day. This game helps children share and think of the feelings of others. A new child in the room might receive a welcoming gift from the whole group each day for a week.

Another game that helps children recognize their own fears as well as the fact that others also have fears can be made from construction paper, cut-out pictures, and poster board. This game may have various names — "Sometimes I Am Afraid," "Things That Are Scary to Me," or "Sometimes I Am Worried." You might start the game by saying, "When I was young I was afraid to (of) _____." From coloring books, workbooks, magazines, or used books, cut out pictures that depict an event or object children might be afraid of doing or seeing. These cutouts can be pasted on construction paper to fit into pockets on the poster board. Clip a paper label, such as "Sometimes I Am Afraid," to the top of the poster board. After you and the children have finished discussing the problems, place the completed poster board on an easel, chalk ledge, or other stand. The children should feel free to discuss the pictures at any time. The poster may be removed at the end of the day.

During the presentation of any of these games, the teacher should emphasize at least three ideas: fear is an acceptable feeling, sometimes other people share our feelings, and fears make us cautious and help us avoid dangerous or harmful situations. Children will be more comfortable with their fears by learning that adults and other children have fears; they will feel more secure when they are comforted and assured by others.

The list of affective education books in this chapter will provide several stories for introducing affective education in your classroom.

INTEGRATION OF CONTENT AREAS

In Chapter 3 you had an opportunity to analyze your children's physical, social, emotional, and intellectual needs, as well as exceptions to these generalizations because of handicaps. In Chapter 2 you read about the past and the present. In Chapter 4 you had an opportunity to study the role of cultural differences, values, and goals in a school setting. In Chapter 6 you delved into the integrating skills of the language arts. In this chapter you will learn how to put all this knowledge into use in the content area of social studies.

Dramatic Play

To most adults the word *dramatization* is associated with drama, literature, a play, or acting out a story. In educating young children the activities are slightly different and occur much more often. Young children do act out stories and they often have "parts" in a play (see Chapter 5). The characterizations are not rigid portrayals and the script is loosely followed, but the most important aspect of dramatization for young children occurs during play. What do children "play"? Children play house; play store; play driving a car, truck, or train; play characters such as a doctor, a police officer, a teacher, a nurse, a construction worker, or a telephone operator. The materials and equipment are small replicas of the real thing in adult life.

In this type of play, children are developing concepts basic to understanding their natural and social environment and are establishing concrete skills that will be used as foundation skills for later academic subjects.

There are two forms of play for young children. Dramatic play usually occurs in the classroom in the various centers set up in the room. Physical development play, which includes hopping, skipping, jumping, swinging, sliding, digging, pushing, and pulling, occurs mainly outside or in a recreational area in the school. If you have a large classroom some of these outdoor activities will occur in the room as well. (Physical development play is discussed in Chapter 11.)

The content of dramatic play is social studies in nature. Two aspects of the social studies, anthropology and sociology, were covered in the social-

Replica toys reinforce everyday experiences.

ization section of this chapter. These aspects plus geography and economic concepts are developed in dramatic play. The trip to the airport or the "drive" to the office in the truck center are beginning geography skills; buying stamps in the make-believe post office or a can of soup in the "supermarket" are beginning economic understandings.

Preparation As a teacher you must begin your planning for dramatic play long before the children arrive in the classroom. Three, four, and five year olds bring background knowledge and experience with them each day they come to school. Their knowledge and experience grow and change, not only through events at school but through home and community events. Therefore, the most logical starting point for social studies curriculum planning is the home and community.

Goals The teacher has four main goals for arranging dramatic play: to stimulate a child's desire to participate in activities and experiences; to provide equipment and material that will allow dramatic play; to provide adequate time and freedom of movement for full utilization of the activity and equipment; and to guide these activities so they are cumulative in nature and spiral in development of physical, social, emotional, and intellectual growth.

The Child's Participation Through dramatic play a child learns a variety of ways to understand the social and physical environment, to acquire new and useful information, and to maintain and enrich basic skills and knowledge. The manipulation of objects, trying things out, and general curiosity are natural reactions of young children; and, therefore, the act we label "play" is an easy means of learning.

When children have airplanes to play with, they will soon need an airport, a landing strip, a control tower, a pilot, a flight attendant, passengers, and cargo. All these requirements to operate an airplane develop language facility, an increased vocabulary, new concepts, and problem solving that includes planning and building the airport as well as traffic control. If play is to be a learning situation, the airplane must be in a suitable environment. That means that because airplanes do certain types of things, they are limited in several ways; airplanes give services and they require services. This extends to all toys in the early childhood classroom, where toys serve as models of the real world.

In play-learning situations the equipment helps provide for the child an integrated learning situation, advanced both horizontally and vertically by the self-impelling drives of the child involved.

Boats need harbors, lakes, docks.
Trains need tracks, stations, tunnels.
Doll beds need dolls, blankets, pillows.
Dolls need clothing, beds, chairs.

When children learn through play, they need to have some built-in behavior control. Through classroom organization, planning, and group rules, teachers help children learn to "play" successfully. Another way to help children learn about rules and about objects that move in real life is to use floor and table top designs. These may be painted, taped, or drawn on plywood, oilcloth, table tops, or the floor. The children then may learn the "rules of the road" for their cars, trucks, boats, airplanes. The designs in Figures 7.1 and 7.2 may help you create your own designs.

Young children reveal what they know through verbal interaction and by physical behavior. Therefore the activities of a child during dramatic play provide for the teacher an opportunity to observe and to check behavior that reveals incorrect or undesirable concepts. A child may always place the farm animals in a truck and dump them out, never placing them in a farm setting. That child may be using the animals as objects rather than as symbols of animals that are alive. Another child may exhibit undesirable

218 / *Curriculum*

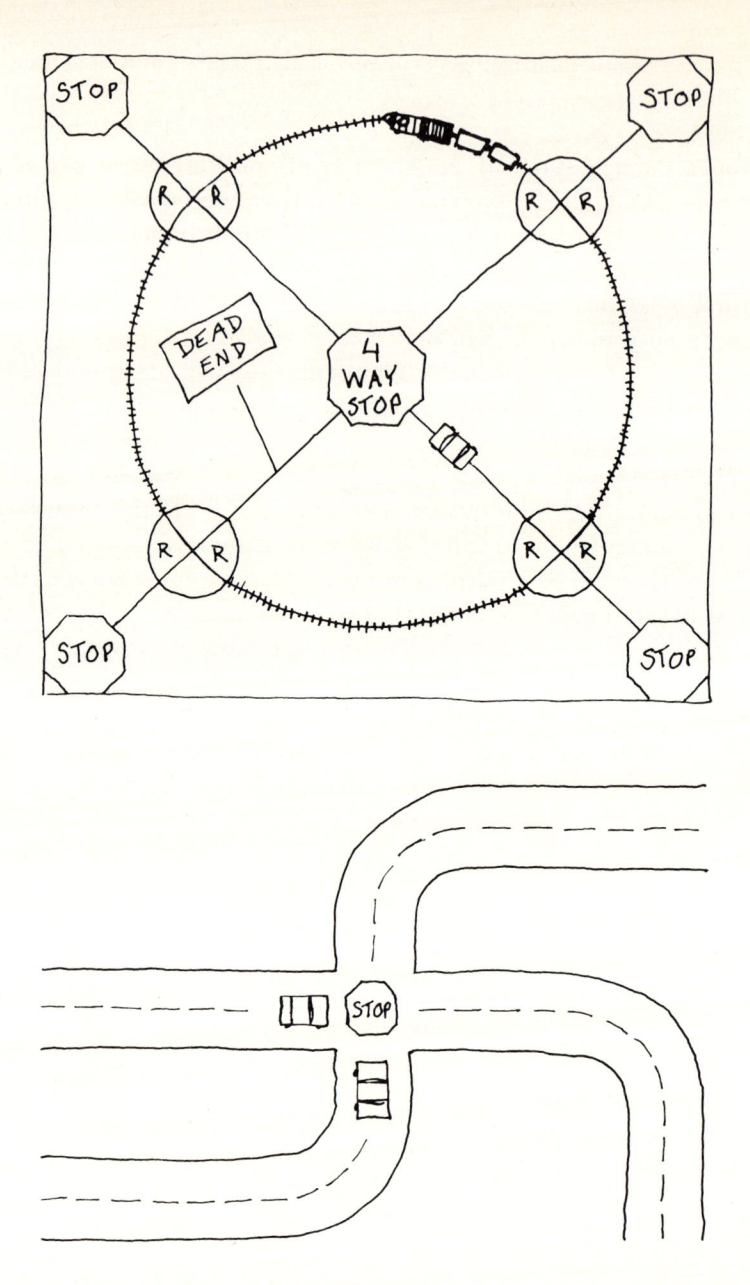

Figure 7.1
Alternative Floor Designs

concepts of living patterns, such as slapping the dolls, overturning the cooking pan, and crashing the cars.

Dramatic play provides many opportunities for children to become aware of the relationships of work, play, and social living. Interaction that occurs when the truck (from the truck and block center) delivers groceries from the "supermarket" to the family center involves three different centers. The doll in the doll buggy visiting the post office, the dress-up box, and the dentist's office involves three everyday life situations — mailing a letter, buying a new dress, and caring for family health.

Play situations can also be therapeutic. The child who fears the doctor's office because of a shot or stitches can role play a visit to the doctor's office to have eyes checked, ears looked into, a knee bandaged, or pulse taken — all of which are done by doctors but do not hurt. Other therapeutic situations occur daily in the family center where a child can "correct" a mother and father by scolding or sending them to their room, or by seating the baby away from mother at the table. These activities release feelings that arose at home that could otherwise build up over a period of time and become more hidden in very unacceptable behavior.

Units of Work

During the early years educational activities come in three forms: spontaneous play, teacher-planned units of work, and children-inspired activities. *Spontaneous play* occurs whenever children are allowed to interact with the materials and equipment in their environment. The teacher plans for this by selecting materials that encourage such play and by providing time for the interaction. *Teacher-planned units of work* are designed to provide continuity to a child's entire school experience and to introduce basic skills and knowledge in a logical sequence. Good planning and selection by teachers will help maintain skills and knowledge but will not be repetitious. *Child-inspired activities* often occur because of questions asked or by something brought home. The alert teacher will have many opportunities to provide exciting and interesting activities through development of the children's own needs.

Aiko: "You be the mamma and I'll be the daddy."

Maria: "You can't be the daddy, you're a girl."

Aiko: "OK. You be the daddy and I'll be the mamma."

Maria: "I can't be the daddy, silly. I'm a girl!"

Aiko: "Well, you be the mamma and I'll be the baby."

Figure 7.2
Table Top Design

Several activity books are available to teachers for guidance on appropriate topics and on units, materials, and equipment. As a potential new teacher you may wish to buy several to get you started with ideas. As you have more experience you may want your own activity book. A good time to start on your book is right now. Some teachers use large index cards filed in a container. Others use loose-leaf notebooks and paste ideas on indexed pages. Still others collect ideas by using file folders or large manila envelopes. Any form for collecting ideas is acceptable — *except* individual tidbits kept hither and yon.

The following list of topics will help teach you to identify which topics have already been taught and which will be taught later or by another teacher. You are a member of an educational team working together for appropriate learning experiences for children.

Social studies — Topics of work

People

Mother, father, sister, brother, grandmother, grandfather, aunt, uncle, cousin, neighbor, friend, friends of family, community helpers

Transportation

Rail, air, water, truck, automobile

Home

Family members, jobs, clothing, furniture, appliances, types of houses

Holidays

Halloween, Thanksgiving, Valentine's Day, George Washington's Birthday, Fourth of July

Community

School, post office, supermarket, doctor's office, dentist's office, drugstore, variety store, department store, museum, zoo, park, lake, river, harbor, airport, train station, bus depot, firehouse, police station

Animals

Pets, farm, jungle, woods, field, zoo (each in relation to humans). *Appropriate Animals:* Turtle, goldfish, guppies, tropical fish, rabbit, snake (garter, grass, or water), chick, duckling, gosling, cygnet, dog, cat, horse, squirrel, bear, groundhog, frog, bird (parrot, cardinal, robin, pigeon, bluejay, dove, sparrow), mice, mole, fox, elephant, lion, tiger, seal, porpoise, whale, giraffe, zebra, deer, guinea pig

Many social studies topics are closely related to science topics and should be taught as joint projects.

Self-concept unit

Concept	Activities	Materials
Every child is special and unique.	Explore individual differences through use of full-length or hand mirror.	Mirrors Cameras Charts
Every child is like other individuals in some way.	Examine skin, hair, nails with a magnifying glass.	Boy, Judy® puzzle Girl, Judy® puzzle
Each child is part of the group.	Compare weight and height of children by monthly weight and height chart.	*I See Me*, sequence pictures (Order from R. H. Stone Products, 18279 Livernois, Detroit, MI 48221)
Each child needs friends.	Take photographs of children. Make silhouettes of children.	*My Face and Body*. Instructs® flannelboard set
Each child differs in ability to do tasks.	Label children's possessions.	*Members of the Family*. Instructs® flannelboard set
Each child can perform in a school setting.		Self-help frames — button, zip, hook paper dolls.
Each child has privileges.		
Each child has responsibilities.		

Books Anglund, *A Friend Is Someone Who Likes You*; Ets, *Just Me*; Freeman, *Dandelion*; Gay, *What's Your Name?*; Simon, *If You Were an Eel How Would You Feel?*; Scheider, *While Suzie Sleeps*. Also look at the social living booklist in this chapter.

Songs See music chapter for sources. "Sometimes I Am Very Small," "Here We Are Together," "Sing Me Your Name," "Do You Know This Friend of Mine," "I Helped My Daddy," "I Can," "I Take My Little Hands."

Records "A Visit to My Little Friend," Children's Record Guild; "Every Day We Grow," Young People's Records; "I'm Dressing Myself," Young People's Records; "Me, Myself and I," Children's Record Guild.

Movement Rhythms *Creative Movement for the Developing Child* by Clare Cherry, hand and body movement pages 31, 45, 76–78, and 80. *Songs for the Nursery School* by Laura MacCarteney, hand and body movements pages 95, 96, 97, 102, 112, 115. (See Chapter 12 for additional sources and addresses.)

Thanksgiving unit

Concepts to be taught	*Activities*	*Materials*
Thanksgiving is a time for being thankful for all the things we have.	Read a story about the first Thanksgiving.	Books
		Pictures
		Foods
	Set up an interest center of related Thanksgiving items.	Wigwams
The Pilgrims and Indians were friends and they helped each other.		Buckle
		Churn
	Make a picture chart depicting the original and the present-day observation of Thanksgiving.	Candle mold
		Moccasin
We celebrate the friendship of the Pilgrims and Indians by inviting friends and family to dinner.		Bow and arrow
		Tomahawk
		Canoe
	Make a table top or sand box Indian village or early American village.	Drum
		Birchbark
The foods we eat are the same kind the Pilgrims and Indians ate.		Kettle
		Pumpkin
	Cook appropriate foods.	Cranberries
		Grapes

Books See book list in this chapter.

Songs See book list in Chapter 11.

Fingerplay

Mr. Turkey

Mr. Turkey's tail is big and wide.	(spread hands)
He swings it when he walks.	(move hands back and forth)
His neck is long, his chin is red,	(stretch neck and stroke)

He gobbles when he talks.   (gobble)
Mr. Turkey is so tall and proud,   (stand tall)
He dances on his feet.   (move feet)
And on each Thanksgiving Day,
He's something good to eat.   (pat stomach)

Field or Study Trips

Trips outside the classroom environment provide first-hand experience not available in a classroom. These trips do not need to be by bus or car. A walking trip in the school or in the neighborhood can be as beneficial as a thirty-minute ride to a department store. In fact, an in-school visit is the most logical type of field trip for three and four year olds. A visit to the principal's office to see and try out the typewriter will reinforce a play typewriter in a play center. A visit to the custodian will promote "Helpers in Our School" concepts and "Caring for Our Room" projects. A visit to the school library is often sufficient for understanding the importance of the library and the use of books.

The success of any trip depends on advance preparation by the teacher. What will the children see on the trip? What will they *hear?* What physical *involvement* will they have? How much time will the entire trip take? What rules of *behavior* will be needed?

Before you take a group on a trip, the whole class must function as a group. The children must understand the process of forming a line, following in a line, gathering together in a group or circle. They must be able to follow oral directions such as "Hold hands, step down (or up), walk, line up, and one at a time." Their toilet habits must be sufficiently mature to allow for the amount of time necessary for the trip.

If you plan to go out of the building, check the weather report first. Second, check the transportation pick-up and delivery procedures. Twenty to twenty-five wet and/or cold children can dissipate any and all positive features of a field trip.

Early in the morning is probably the best time for a trip because the children are rested. Do not let the children engage in active play before they leave. The children will be very excited about the trip and may become excitedly exhausted before getting out the door. Some children may be apprehensive about going to a new place and leaving the security of the known. Short trips in the school or neighborhood before a bus trip will lessen this excitement and apprehension.

Where do you go outside of the building? A walk around the school block is a natural way to start taking trips. In this way you can establish procedures and behavior patterns. Generally, something "extra" will happen — a friendly dog will join the group, a maple tree will be turning red, the telephone repair person may be working on a line, a parked car may have a flat tire, or the bakery may deliver bread to the school. Don't insist on walking around the block if something interesting is happening in the first hundred feet. The purpose of the trip is to understand the school neighborhood — not the feat of walking around the block.

When your group of children has learned to travel to nearby places, trips requiring transportation are in order. Where should you go? Farms: dairy, orchard, nursery, or vegetable gardens. Transportation facilities: airport, bus station, train depot, or a boat dock. Recreational areas: beach, park, zoo, museum, or woods. Construction sites: houses, bridges, or streets. Neighborhood service buildings: post office, firehouse, or police station. Mature five year olds may enjoy and learn from such experiences as visiting a bakery, an ice cream plant, a department store, or a supermarket. But do not take five year olds on an eight-hour field trip! Confine the whole trip — the getting there and back plus the visit — to a morning or an afternoon. Remember, young children have short attention spans and need variety in their physical activity.

How many trips do you take? Probably, at the beginning of the year three in-school trips may be necessary to establish general excursion behavior. Neighborhood walks may occur every other week as long as weather permits. Two or three longer trips may take place late in the school year. Remember, field trips occur at every level of the children's education. Your trips will probably not be their first or their last.

Resources: People, Objects, Animals

Not all adventures require going somewhere to see something. It is good to have a person visit the classroom; to have collections available for scrutiny; to have objects to handle or animals to feed, pet, and care for in the classroom.

Bela: "Let's build a house. You help me. I am the boss."

Juan: "I am the plumber."

Bela: "No, you have to hammer."

Juan: "Mrs. Wu said no hammering. I'll be the truck driver."

Bela: "You drive the little truck and I'll drive the big truck. I am the boss."

Sometimes resource people are available in the school when the school building is serviced. Plumbers, electricians, carpenters, and cooks are usually in a building sometime during the year.

The mail carrier, police officer, and firefighter often are more "real" singly in a classroom where the children can touch and talk to them individually and examine their equipment than when the group of children visits a building and sees several persons doing the same activity. Newspaper photographers, nurses, and artists (potters, painters, artisans) are also good resource people. Be selective in who you choose to be a community helper. Many individuals who help others provide their services for a fee, such as doctors, dentists, lawyers, or electricians. These people are not classified as community helpers. "Community helpers" are generally paid by taxes or charitable contributions.

MATERIALS, EQUIPMENT, AND BOOKS

Many of the materials and equipment placed in classrooms for young children are replicas of materials and equipment found in everyday life. Therefore, a play activity for a young child is an enactment of an environmental experience or a role-playing analogy of an experience that will occur in adult life. Frequently play involves fantasy roles such as pirates or princesses. These materials and equipment are usually called toys. Because parents and other lay persons do not recognize the toy-replica factor, as a teacher you will have the responsibility to explain the relationships of the facsimile, the experience, and adulthood.

In educating parents on the values of social studies play, be sure that you stress the factors of reading readiness — oral vocabulary development, word meaning, comprehension, and knowledge. As you read and study the following lists, analyze each item for its potential to teach a child something new.

The following lists are for teaching the social studies although some items may be used in other areas. Additional items will be listed in other chapters.

Remember, there are several ways of teaching concepts. For example, if you are teaching a unit on water transportation some forms of transportation will be taught by listening to a story; some will be taught by a film, filmstrip, or picture book; others by puzzles, flannel cutouts, or posters; still others will be taught by a field trip; and some will be taught by the replica material in the room.

If materials, equipment, and books can be shared with other teachers it may not be necessary to have each item in every classroom. These lists should be helpful to you as a beginning teacher not only for ordering purposes but for planning your instructional program.

Replica Toys

Boats Aircraft carrier, barge, cabin cruiser, canoe, cargo carrier, coast guard cutter, ferry boat, fireboat, houseboat, motorboat, rowboat, fishing trawler, tanker, tugboat, passenger ship, submarine, steamboat, paddleboat, sailboat.

Buses City bus, school bus, church bus, interstate bus.

Cars Sedan, coupe, convertible, station wagon, sports car, racing car, jeep, van, taxi, ambulance, limousine, patrol car, camper.

Trucks Dump truck, canteen truck, fire truck, semitrailer, tank truck, delivery truck, cement mixer, refuse truck, moving van, pickup truck, automobile carrier, livestock truck, swivel crane truck, wrecker, bulldozer, road grader.

Trains Passenger train: diesel engine, coaches, dining car, Pullman car, club car, baggage car, Vistadome car. Freight train: autocarrier, flat car, gondola car, tank car, box car, refrigerator car, cattle car, hoppers, caboose.

Airplanes Fighter jet, passenger plane, cargo plane, biplane, glider, sea plane, helicopter.

Other machines Motorcycle, bicycle, tricycle, scooter, wagon, snowmobile, lawn mower, milking machine, baler, thrasher, snow blower, cultivator, seeder.

Household items Refrigerator, range, vacuum cleaner, washer, dryer, blender, sewing machine, alarm clock, telephone, beds, dolls, tables, cooking set (teapot, saucepan, covered pot, frying pan, ladle, colander), flatware (forks, spoons, knives), luncheon set (plates, cups, saucers, serving bowls, platters, sugar bowl, creamer, salad bowls, glasses, coffee pot), housecleaning set (broom, dust mop, sponge, push broom, whisk broom), doll house (dining room set, kitchen equipment, bathroom accessories, bedroom set, playroom set), ironing board, iron, rocker, egg beater, wooden spoons.

Miscellaneous items Typewriter, radio, TV, doll carriage, stroller, cash register, doctor's kit, set of hats (cowboy hat, straw hat, construction helmet, derby, top hat, firefighter's helmet, baseball cap), shopping cart, mirrors.

Tools Hammer, screwdriver, pliers, wrench, drill, saw, ruler, tape measure, rake, hoe, shovel, spade, trowel, wheelbarrow.

Materials to help make the preceding meaningful Supermarket stall, crawl-in playhouse, bridges, puppet stage, bedding (mattress, pillow, blanket), doll clothes, play food, traffic signs (railroad, one way, crossroads, school, stop, speed limit, yield, exit, do not enter, bike route, no U turn, pedestrian), mailbox, clock, metal and paper money.

Costumes Cowboy, hobo, man, woman, bride, ballerina, pirate, clown, king, queen, and whatever roles are common in the community (for example, miner, farmer, factory worker).

The items you use may be made from cardboard, may be empty containers of the real object, may be the actual objects, or may be made by teachers or parents out of relatively inexpensive materials.

Commerical Materials and Equipment

Each item is listed by manufacturer if the item is known by its trade name. If the item is a common item made by several companies, the item does not have a manufacturer listed. The number of pieces in a puzzle are given to aid you in selecting puzzles for varying ages both chronological and mental.

Puzzles

Airfield: Childcraft, 1 pc.
Airplane: Judy, 14 pcs.
Airplane: Kiddiecraft, 6 pcs.
Astronaut: Judy, 11 pcs.
Baby chicks: Judy, 6 pcs.
Baker: Playskool, 16 pcs.
Birthday party: Playskool, 6 pcs.
Boats: Constructive Playthings, 11 pcs.
Boy: Judy, 6 pcs.
By the pond: Childcraft, 6 pcs.
Cakemaker: Playskool, 11 pcs.
Car: Judy, 13 pcs.
Delivery truck: Judy, 14 pcs.
Farm puzzle: Judy, 15 pcs.
Farmer puzzle: Judy, 10 pcs.
Fire engine: Judy, 12 pcs.
Fireman: Childcraft, 6 pcs.
Fruits I like: Playskool, 4 pcs.
For my bath: Playskool, 4 pcs.
Gas station: Childcraft, 6 pcs.
Garbage truck: Childcraft, 6 pcs.
Garage: Childcraft, 18 pcs.
Girl: Judy, 6 pcs.
Grocery shopping: Judy, 6 pcs.
Harbor: Childcraft, 16 pcs.
Harbor: Childcraft, 17 pcs.
Helicopter: Playskool, 10 pcs.
Horse and colt: Childcraft, 5 pcs.
House: Childcraft, 6 pcs.
Ice cream man: Childcraft, 6 pcs.
Johnny growing: Judy, 6 pcs.
Kitchen cupboard: Judy, 5 pcs.
Milkman: Childcraft, 6 pcs.
Mailman: Childcraft, 6 pcs.
Pickup truck: Judy, 13 pcs.
Policeman: Childcraft, 6 pcs.
Postman: Judy, 11 pcs.
Postman: Playskool, 19 pcs.
Puffy, the engine: Sifo, 10 pcs.
Speedy, the fire engine: Sifo, 10 pcs.
Sports car: Sifo, 16 pcs.
Ship: Childcraft, 5 pcs.
Steamboat: Playskool, 5 pcs.
Steamship: Kiddiecraft, 6 pcs.
Story of milk: Judy, 12 pcs.
Train: Alphabet Inlay Puzzles, 25 pcs.
Train: Judy, 20 pcs.
Traffic: Childcraft, 14 pcs.
Transportation: Childcraft, 5 pcs.
Truck: Sifo, 18 pcs.
Truck driver: Sifo, 16 pcs.
Tugboat: Judy, 16 pcs.
Vegetables: Sifo, 6 pcs.
Work with safety: Sifo, 6 pcs.

Flannelboard replicas and bulletin board forms

Air transportation: Instructo
Cars and trucks: Instructo
Holiday primary cutouts: Instructo

PROJECT
Understanding Community Participation

Before you can teach children to understand and participate in community activities, you need to have had experiences that help you to understand various forms of community participation.

1. Describe the community social events and resources in your present community that are especially suitable for young children (for example, fairs, parades, historical events and buildings, and so on).
2. As a child, did you participate in similar types of community events?
3. Write a unit on one of these events of your childhood as you remember it, and then add a supplementary unit on how your experience might have been improved.
4. List the replica toys that you used and the dramatic play activities that you engaged in as a young child to "play out" community events, activities, and occupations.
5. Interview one of your friends who grew up in a different type of community. List his or her favorite replica toys and dramatic play activities as a young child. Compare these toys and activities with your own list. Can you draw any conclusions?

Flannelboard replicas and bulletin board forms (*cont.*)

Community helpers: Instructo
Community workers: Instructo
Fall and Halloween (seasonal gummed back stickers): Dennison, Hallmark
Farm yard: Instructo
Foods: Instructo
Members of the family: Instructo

My face and body: Instructo
Simple transportation: Instructo
The community: Instructo
Vegetables and fruits (poster cards): Milton Bradley, Creative Playthings
Water Transportation: Instructo

Miscellaneous equipment

People to use as passengers
Animals to transport
Unit blocks to build roads, bridges, stations, garages, docks
Hollow blocks and building boards

Steering wheel
Wheel toys such as doll carriage, wagons, trikes, wheelbarrows
Metal and paper money kit: Childcraft
Change maker: Childcraft

Miscellaneous equipment (*cont.*)

Interlocking wooden train sets
Railroad with turntable: Child Guidance
Skaneatles train set
Hole punch
Multiplay screen
Riding train: Constructive Playthings
Plastic play foods: Childcraft
Balance scale: Childcraft
Play store and puppet stage: Childcraft
Farm fence: Childcraft
Table block farm: Childcraft
Coaster seat: Constructive Playthings
Wooden barn: Creative Playthings
Sculptured rubber animals and farm: Creative Playthings
Postal station mailbox: Playskool
Disguise kit: Creative Playthings
Animal playsacks: Creative Playthings
Hats, hats, hats: Creative Playthings
Girl's hats galore: Creative Playthings
Brother and sister dolls: Constructive Playthings
Drink-wet dolls: Constructive Playthings
Flexible doll family: Constructive Playthings (black and white)
Black and white families: Instructo flannelgraph sets
Dress me dolls: Rag doll for children to learn dressing skills
Self-help frames, buttons, zippers, hooks: Montessori

Materials and Equipment for Spontaneous Play

Materials and objects for the dress-up box can lead to dramatic play and role playing that will reinforce the content and concepts taught in several subject areas. A firefighter's hat, a police badge, a nurse's cap, a doctor's stethoscope, a plumber's wrenches, a salesclerk's uniform, a mail carrier's pouch, a carpenter's toolbox, a chef's apron, a waitress's or waiter's uniform, or a gas station attendant's jumpsuit will provide stimuli for in-class activities that are often as profitable as a field trip.

A Hat Rack of Careers To encourage role playing and to maintain concepts previously taught, a hat rack or replica of real apparel will provide instant re-enactment of learned concepts.

Make a hat rack about 4 feet high. Use a 4″ × 4″ stud for the post. At the top, nail a 2″ × 2″ × 20″ piece of wood with three coat hooks screwed into the parallel sides of the wood. A large (10″ diameter) tin can from the cafeteria filled with cement makes an appropriate base. On each side of the post, nail larger spikes about 8 inches apart. On this post hang:

Carpenter's cap and apron	Sailor's hat
Construction worker's hard hat	Golfer's hat
Firefighter's hat	Nurse's cap and cloak
Police officer's cap	Swimming cap
Baker's hat and apron	Space helmet
Chef's hat	Miner's hat
Pilot's hat	

A Treasure Chest of Role-playing Equipment

Boots	Doctor's bag
Stethoscope	Brief case
Badge	Mail carrier's bag
Shopping bags	Purses
Small suitcase	Serving tray
Paint brushes	

Remember that all of the suggested materials and equipment are not necessary, nor would it be appropriate for all of the items to be available at one time. Both the hat rack and the treasure chest items can be used in conjunction with the various centers and materials established or regular parts of the classroom.

The Zoo at School Small animals brought to the classroom for a short visit can take the place of an actual visit to their normal habitats. Rabbits, chickens, a piglet, ducks, tropical fish, mice, turtles, frogs, gerbils, hamsters, guinea pigs, or parakeets are all appropriate animals for a classroom. Large animals or animals with dangerous characteristics (geese, goats, some snakes, monkeys) should be seen in another setting.

A Plumber's Box Three, four, and five year olds will spend many happy hours assembling and reassembling pipes into many designs. The storage box or plumber's box should be of sturdy construction because of the weight of the pipes and fittings and needs a handle. Materials needed:

Short, wooden-handled, rubber-based plunger (1)
Striped bill caps (2)
Six-inch lengths of pipes one inch in diameter (5)
Ten-inch lengths of pipe two inches in diameter (5)
Twelve-inch lengths of pipe one inch in diameter (5)
Three-inch lengths of pipe two inches in diameter (5)

Fittings: crosses, elbows, bends, unions, couplings, adapters, to fit pipe sizes (30)
Small jar of plain petroleum jelly for rubbing threads of pipes so they will screw easily

Brick Laying   Outdoor play can be enriched by having ten to fifteen bricks, a gallon plastic bucket, and two trowels. The children mix water and sand until it looks and feels stiff. They then arrange the bricks in patterns and "cement" them together with the wet sand.

Woodworking   Constructing objects with wood and related materials is an excellent way to enhance dramatic play activities as well as to provide creative gifts to family members and personal playthings. The construction process and the manipulation of the tools and materials require constant supervision either by the teacher or aides. The experience of supervision can also be helpful to you as a student teacher.

Working with wood, paint, cloth, and various tools promotes eye-hand muscle coordination and involves large muscle development and control. The enjoyment of pounding, painting, sawing, and sewing provides enjoyment as well as satisfaction in a finished project. Three and four year olds enjoy pounding nails and painting precut short pieces of wood. Be sure the nails used are no longer than three-fourths the depth of the main board or you will have a board nailed to the workbench. Three and four year olds sometimes get carried away when pounding! Thinner pieces of wood are used on top or on the sides of the larger, thicker piece, and nails that will penetrate the wood are necessary. Also, the nails must have thin shafts so that the thickness of the nail will not split the wood. (See nail description.)

Because woodworking requires close supervision, only a few children can participate in the activity at a time. Usually four children can hammer, saw, drill, paint, and decorate their chosen projects at one time.

Space organization is a necessity for these activities. A woodworking bench, a work table, a painting table, a storage shelf for "wet" articles, a storage space for uncompleted objects, a chest for storage of the tools, a lumber "pile" or bin, and a supply shelf are all a permanent part of the classroom when woodworking is included in the program (see Figure 7.3). An ideal setup would include a small room where several groups of young children could participate at different times during the school year.

Equipment and supplies   Equipment for a woodworking center includes:

Workbench: a hardwood table approximately 44" long, 20" wide, and 25" high

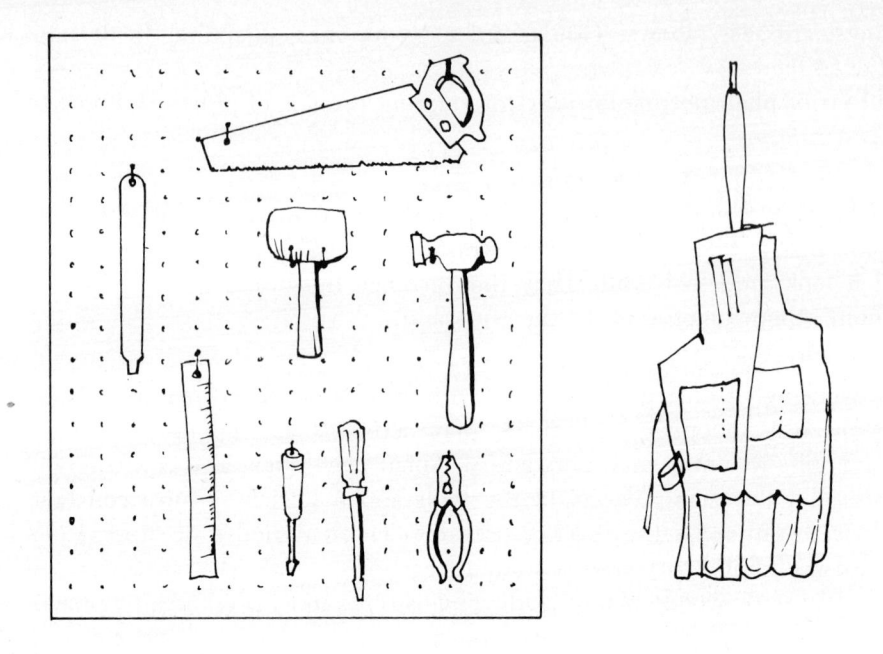

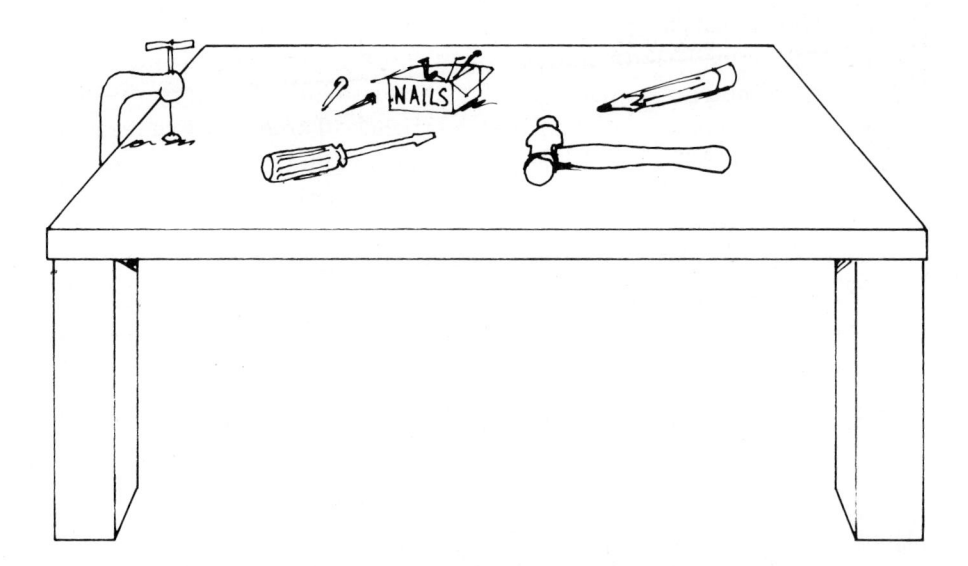

Figure 7.3
Woodworking Equipment

Tools: 8-inch file
 Set of 8 drill bits
 Hand drill
 Set of 5 auger bits
 Bit brace
 Chisel
 Pair of C-clamps

16-ounce hammer
7-ounce hammer (do not use a play hammer)
Block plane
6-foot ruler
Coping saw
Set of coping saw blades (6)
Screwdriver ¼″ blade and 4″ to 6″ long
Square
Pair of pliers
1-inch paint brushes (2)
2-inch paint brushes (2)
2½-inch paint brushes (2)
3-inch paint brush (1)

Supplies for an average kindergarten class of twenty-five for a year (reduce to three-fourths for classes of three and four year olds):

Paint (use only latex washable paints and nontoxic varnishes): 2 pints of red; 2 pints of blue; 1 pint each of white, green, yellow, brown, orange, black, pink; 1 quart clear shellac or varnish

Glue: Elmer's 1-quart size

Bonding cement: 2 eight-ounce tubes

Nails: 5 pounds of nails 1¼″ × 1½″ long (four-penny, six-penny, eight-penny, ten-penny, and two sizes of roofing nails are the most commonly used; a big head is necessary)

Sandpaper: 1 gross of mixed numbers

Dowel rods: three ¼″ dowel rods (30 or 40 inches long); three ½″ dowel rods; two 1″ dowel rods

Lumber: all lumber should be of soft wood (pine or poplar) and surfaced (sanded) on all sides
   30 ft. of ¼″ × ½″ strips (for fences, boat rails, airplane propellors, windmills)
   15 ft. of ¼″ × 2″ strips (for doll furniture, truck rails, boxes)
   15 ft. of ¼″ × 2½ strips (for airplane wings, furniture, sides of small pens)
   20 ft. of ¼″ × 4″ boards (for trains, boats, cars)
   25 pieces of ¼″ × 6″ plywood sheets (for building roofs)
   10 pieces of ¼″ × 24″ plywood sheets (for larger construction)
   15 ft. of 1″ × 3½ boards
   15 ft. of 1½″ × 2″ boards
   15 ft. of 1½″ × 3½″ boards
   15 ft. of 1½″ × 5″ boards (for boats, trains, cars, and various creations)

Chalk: 4 pieces, for marking measurements

Carpenter's pencils: 2, for marking measurements and designs

Other materials: fabrics, string, twine, rope, wire, leather, yarn, rubber, plastic, paper, rug pieces, tin and aluminum cans, bottle caps

An inexpensive mini unit Children need to practice manipulating tools and materials before they "create" something. Use of simple tools and pine logs will provide children an opportunity for this practice.

Goals: To give children an opportunity to use tools such as hammer, screwdrivers, and saw. To provide children with a soft wood appropriate for using nails and screws. To provide children with a soft wood for sawing.

Materials: Hammer, saw, screwdrivers (regular and Philips), nails (roofing, ten-penny, and spike), screws (varying in length and type with large heads), and three 8-inch-diameter pine logs approximately 20 inches long.

Teacher activities: Show children how to hold hammer. Show children how to start nail. Show children how to hold screwdriver. Show children how to start screw. Show children how to hold saw. Show children how to saw.

Children activities: Practice nailing nails into one log. Practice turning screws in the second log. Practice sawing the third log.

Books
General books

Adaff, Arnold. *Ma Dala*. New York: Harper & Row, 1971.
Asch, Frank. *George's Store*. New York: McGraw-Hill, 1969.
Baker, Eugene. *I Want To Be a Taxi Driver*. Chicago: Childrens Press, 1969.
Barton, Byron. *Wheels*. New York: Thomas Y. Crowell Co., 1979.
Beck, Barbara. *The First Book of Fruits*. New York: Franklin Watts, 1967.
Brown, Margaret Wise. *Country Noisey Book*. New York: Harper & Row, 1940, 1976.
―――. *The Pig War*. New York: Harper & Row, 1969.
Chapin, Cynthia. *Wings and Wheels*. Chicago: Albert Whitman, 1967.
Crawford, Mel. *The Cowboy Book*. New York: Golden Press, 1968.
Crews, Donald. *Freight Train*. New York: Greenwillow Books, 1978.
―――. *Truck*. New York: Greenwillow Books, 1980.
Dobbins, Dorothy Wyeth. *What Do You Do with a Drawbridge?* Reading, Mass.: Addison-Wesley, 1976.
Dugan, William. *The Sign Book*. New York: Golden Press, 1968.
Emberly, Ed. *Cockadoodle Doo*. Boston: Little, Brown, 1964.
Ets, Marie Hall. *Gilbert and the Wind*. New York: The Viking Press, 1963.
Flack, Marjorie. *The Boats on the River*. New York: The Viking Press, 1946.

———. *The Story About Ping*. New York: The Viking Press, 1935.
Flothe, Louise Lee. *Cowboys on the Ranch*. New York: Charles Scribner's Sons, 1959.
Fox, Charles. *Come to the Circus*. Chicago: Reilly & Lee, 1960.
Friskey, Margaret. *Indian Two Feet and His Eagle Feather*. Chicago: Childrens Press, 1967.
———. *Indian Two Feet and His Horse*. Chicago: Childrens Press, 1971.
———. *Indian Two Feet and the Wolf Cubs*. Chicago: Childrens Press, 1971.
Goble, Paul. *The Girl Who Loved Wild Horses*. Scarsdale, N.Y.: Bradbury Press, 1978.
Gramatky, Hardie. *Hercules*. New York: G. P. Putnam's Sons, 1940.
———. *Little Toot*. New York: G. P. Putnam's Sons, 1939.
Greene, Carla Baker. *I Want to be a Bus Driver*. Chicago: Childrens Press, 1969.
———. *I Want to be a Dairy Farmer*. Chicago: Childrens Press, 1957.
———. *I Want to be a Farmer*. Chicago: Childrens Press, 1963.
———. *I Want to be a Fireman*. Chicago: Childrens Press, 1957.
———. *I Want to be a Fisherman*. Chicago: Childrens Press, 1956.
———. *I Want to be a Mechanic*. Chicago: Childrens Press, 1959.
———. *I Want to be a Policeman*. Chicago: Childrens Press, 1958.
———. *I Want to be a Road Builder*. Chicago: Childrens Press, 1958.
———. *I Want to be a Storekeeper*. Chicago: Childrens Press, 1958.
Lenski, Lois. *The Little Auto*. New York: Henry Z. Walck, 1934.
———. *The Little Engine*. New York: Henry Z. Walck, 1946.
———. *The Little Farm*. New York: Henry Z. Walck, 1942.
———. *Papa Small*. New York: Henry Z. Walck, 1951.
———. *Policeman Small*. New York: Henry Z. Walck, 1962.
Lobel, Arnold. *Owl at Home*. New York: Harper & Row, 1975.
Mahy, Margaret. *The Boy Who Was Followed Home*. New York: Franklin Watts, 1975.
Moneure, Jane. *People Who Help People*. Chicago: Childrens Press, 1976.
Munari, Bruno. *Bruno Munari's Zoo*. New York: Philomet Books, 1963.
Munro, Muriel A. *Have You Seen Louie?* Racine, Wisc.: Western Publishing Co., 1970.
Nichols, Charles. *Danny Driver*. New York: Golden Press, 1968.
Olsen, Ib Spang. *The Marsh Crone's Brew*. Nashville, Tenn.: Abingdon Press, 1960.
Oppenheim, Joanne. *Have You Seen Roads?* Reading, Mass.: Addison-Wesley, 1969.
Palazzo, Tony. *Let's Go to the Jungle*. Garden City, N.Y.: Doubleday & Company, 1962.
Parish, Peggy. *Little Indian*. New York: Simon & Schuster, 1968.

Pfloog, Jan. *Farm Book*. New York: Golden Press, 1964.
Pineo, Craig. *Peter Policeman*. New York: Golden Press, 1968.
Risom, Ole. *I Am a Kitty*. Racine, Wisc.: Western Publishing Co., 1970.
———. *I Am a Puppy*. Racine, Wisc.: Western Publishing Co., 1970.
Rockwell, Anne. *My Dentist*. New York: Greenwillow Books, 1975.
———. *My Doctor*. New York: Greenwillow Books, 1976.
Rockwell, Harlow. *My Kitchen*. New York: Greenwillow Books, 1980.
Rogers, Helen Spelman. *Morris and His Brave Lion*. New York: McGraw-Hill, 1975.
Rojankovsky, Feodor. *Animals on the Farm*. New York: Knopf, 1962.
———. *Animals in the Zoo*. New York: Knopf, 1962.
Rosen, Winifred. *Henielta, The Wild Woman of Borneo*. New York: Scholastic Book Services, Four Winds, 1975.
Scarry, Huck. *Huck Scarry's Steam Train Journey*. New York: William Collins Sons & Co., 1979.
Scarry, Richard. *The Great Big Car and Truck Book*. New York: Golden Press, 1951.
Schick, Eleanor. *Andy*. New York: Macmillan, 1971.
Schlein, Miriam. *Heavy Is a Hippopotamus*. Reading, Mass.: Addison-Wesley, 1954.
Schuttlesworth, Dorothy. *ABC of Buses*. New York: Doubleday, 1965.
Sharmat, Marjorie Weinmann. *Burton and Dudley*. New York: Holiday House, 1975.
Skorpen, Liesel. *All the Lassies*. New York: Dial Press, 1970.
Thomas, Dawn C. *Mira! Mira!* Philadelphia: J. B. Lippincott, 1970.
Varga, Judy. *Circus Cannonball*. New York: William Morrow & Co., 1975.
Wildsmith, Brian. *Wild Animals*. New York: Franklin Watts, 1966.
Williams, Garth. *The Chicken Book*. New York: Delacorte Press, 1970.
Wright, Mildred W. *Sky Full of Dragons*. Austin, Tex.: Steck-Vaughan, 1969.
Yashimo, Taro, and Mitsu Yashimo. *Plenty to Watch*. New York: Viking Press, 1954.
Young, Miriam. *Beware of the Polar Bear*. New York: Lothrop, Lee & Shepard, 1970.

Special occasions

Abish, Roz. *T'was the Moon on Wintertime*. New York: Prentice-Hall, 1969.
Aichinger, Helga. *The Shepherd*. New York: Thomas Y. Crowell, 1966.
Anderson, Lonzo, and Adrienne Adams. *200 Rabbits*. New York: Viking Press, 1968.
Anglund, Joan Walsh. *Christmas is a Time of Giving*. New York: Harcourt Brace Jovanovich, 1961.
Armour, Richard. *The Adventures of Egbert the Easter Egg*. New York: McGraw-Hill, 1961.

Bailan, Lorna. *Humbug Witch*. Nashville, Tenn.: Abingdon Press, 1965.
Ballaglia, Aurelius. *The Reindeer Book*. New York: Golden Press, 1965.
Barry, Robert. *Mr. Willowley's Christmas Tree*. New York: McGraw-Hill, 1963.
Bolognese, Don. *A New Day*. New York: Delacorte Press, 1970.
Brown, Margaret Wise. *On Christmas Eve*. Reading, Mass.: Addison-Wesley, 1975.
———. *The Golden Egg Book*. New York: Golden Press, 1943.
Bruna, Dick. *Christmas*. New York: Doubleday, 1969.
Brustlein, Janice. *Little Bear's Christmas*. New York: Lothrop, Lee & Shepard, 1964.
Buckley, Helen E. *The Little Boy and the Birthdays*. New York: Lothrop, Lee & Shepard, 1965.
Burnett, Bernice. *The First Book of Holidays*. New York: Watts, 1974.
Carle, Eric. *The Secret Birthday Message*. New York: Thomas Y. Crowell Co., 1971.
Coppersmith, Jerome. *A Chanukah Fable for Christmas*. New York: G. P. Putnam's Sons, 1969.
Dohler, Lavinia. *National Holidays Around the World*. New York: Fleet Press, 1968.
Dolbier, Maurice. *Torten's Christmas Secret*. Boston: Little, Brown, 1951.
Duvoisin, Roger. *Easter Treat*. New York: Alfred A. Knopf, 1954.
Ets, Marie Hall. *Nine Days to Christmas*. New York: Viking Press, 1960.
Flack, Marjorie. *Ask Mr. Bear*. New York: Macmillan, 1958.
Geffner, Anne. *A Child Celebrates: The Jewish Holidays*. Sepulveda, Calif.: Double M. Press, 1979.
Hoban, Russell C. *A Birthday for Frances*. New York: Harper & Row, 1968.
———. *The Mole Family's Christmas*. New York: Parents Magazine, 1969.
Hoffman, Felix. *The Story of Christmas*. New York: Atheneum, 1975.
Hopkins, Lee Bennett (compiler). *Sing Hey for Christmas Day!* New York: Harcourt, Brace, Jovanovich, 1975.
Hou-tien, Cheng. *The Chinese New Year*. New York: Holt, Rinehart, and Winston, 1976.
Kaufman, Joe. *The Christmas Tree Book*. New York: Golden Press, 1965.
Keats, Ezra Jack. *The Little Drummer Boy*. New York: Macmillan, 1968.
———. *The Snowy Day*. New York: Viking Press, 1962.
Klein, Leonore. *Mud! Mud! Mud!* New York: Alfred A. Knopf, 1962.
Kroeber, Theodora. *A Green Christmas*. Oakland, Calif.: Parnassus Press, 1967.
Lenski, Lois. *On a Summer's Day*. New York: Henry Z. Walck, 1953.
Marcus, Rebecca B. *Fiesta Time in Mexico*. New York: Garrard Publishing Company, 1974.
Massey, Jeanne. *Littlest Witch*. New York: Alfred A. Knopf, 1959.

Moore, Clement Clark. *The Night Before Christmas*. New York: Random House, 1975.

Moore, Clement Clark (Tasha Tudor, illustrator). *The Night Before Christmas*. Chicago: Rand McNally, 1965.

Niessbaum, Hedda, ed. *Charlie Brown's Fourth Super Book of Questions and Answers About All Kinds of People and How They Live*. New York: Random House, 1979.

Scarry, Richard. *The Santa Claus Book*. New York: Golden Press, 1965.

Sechrist, Elizabeth. *Heigh-ho for Halloween!* Philadelphia: Macrae Smith, 1959.

Seuss, Dr. *How The Grinch Stole Christmas*. New York: Random House, 1957.

Showers, Paul. *Indian Festivals*. New York: Thomas Y. Crowell Co., 1969.

Slobodkin, Louis. *Trick or Treat*. New York: Macmillan, 1959.

Thayer, Jane. *Gus Was a Christmas Ghost*. New York: William Morrow, 1970.

Watson, Nancy Dingman. *Sugar on Snow*. New York: Viking Press, 1964.

———. *Tommy's Mommy's Fish*. New York: Viking Press, 1971.

Wells, Rosemary. *Morris's Disappearing Bag*. New York: Dial Press, 1975.

Zolotow, Charlotte. *The Bunny Who Found Easter*. Oakland, Calif.: Parnassus Press, 1959.

Yashimo, Taro. *Umbrella*. New York: Viking Press, 1958.

SUMMARY

When you begin designing your social studies program you need to start by knowing the theories of teaching the subject and the basic content of programs for young children as developed by early childhood specialists in the field of social studies. Once you have established the way you are going to teach and what you are going to teach, then you must select the books, materials, activities, and resources to help you meet your goals. This chapter is designed to guide you through each of those steps.

| DIFFERENTIATING AND INTEGRATING MINI UNITS | As is true with language arts skills, the content of social studies is integrated with the skill areas such as science, reading, math, art, and music. To help you remember the process of identifying all of the interrelated content areas and skills taught to children ages three to six, study the following spiral topics and the mini units. As we discussed in Chapter 6, conceptual learning |

is developed in a kind of spiral; that is, knowledge is acquired in stages of increasing complexity, progressing from the concrete to the abstract. It is the teacher's role to determine when the children are ready to progress in the spiral to a more complex application of a learned concept; facts are presented in widening perspectives, expanding the child's experiences continuously.

Spiral Topic 1 Human Beings, Relationships

Me		*Individuals*
Girl	Boy	Families
Children		Friends
Mother	Father	Neighborhoods
Women	Men	Communities
Sisters	Brothers	A state
Aunts	Uncles	A country
Grandmother	Grandfather	Or other lands
Friends		
Neighbors		
Community helpers		
Other people		
Minority groups		
People of other lands		

Activities. Look at self in mirror: play games learning parts of body and clothing: role play home life, visits, special events, and work.

Spiral Topic 2 Oral Vocabulary for Citrus Fruit Unit (children ages three to six — social studies in content and language arts in skill; a career education topic)

First stage	*Second stage*	*Third stage*
Orange	Tree	Picker
Lemons	Climate	Grader
Tangerines	Bees	Inspector
Grapefruit	Beekeeper	Warehouse personnel
Limes	Grower	Refrigerator personnel

Spiral Topic 2 (cont.)

First stage	Second stage	Third stage
Skin	Nursery worker	Trucker
Peel	Cultivator	Produce broker
Sections or segments	Fertilizer	Store manager
Smell	Sprayer	Produce clerk
Squeeze	Irrigator	Check-out
		You

Spiral Topic 3 Developing a Concept of Movement of Wheeled Vehicles

Content: Science activities related to social studies, language arts, art, and math.

Vocabulary: Wheel, pedal, push, pull, motor, tracks, tires, steam, electric, coal, gas, oil, big, little, tall, long, high, one, two, three, four, six, eight.

Concrete objects: train, trolley, ski lift, tractor, trailer, truck, wheelbarrow, bicycle, automobile, bus, tractor, tricycle, wagon, scooter

Spiral Topic 4 Houses

Fact: The surface of my house is painted white.

Concept: The surface of houses may be painted.
The surface of houses may be not painted.
The surface of houses may be brick.
The surface of houses may be stone.
The surface of houses may be black.
The surface of houses may be white.
The surface of houses may be red.
The surface of houses may be green.
The surface of houses may be yellow.
The surface of houses may be brown.
The surface of houses may be many other things.

Generalization: Houses have outside coverings, the coverings different in form and in color.

Subjects involved: Oral language, listening, art (color identification), science (paint, stone, brick, block, wood).

Social studies / 241

The continuity and integration of activities in the classroom is very important. Social studies experiences provide active, creative, individual responses from children. The following mini units will help you plan appropriately for young children. As you study the mini units, you will notice that each unit is planned for events during the school year, September to June, and is planned for the child as he or she matures. For example, the mini units for May require use of skills learned earlier as well as new skills that will be taught.

Mini Units Differentiating and Integrating for **Three Year Olds**

	September	*January*	*May*
Topic	A parade of workers.	A winter party.	A spring walk.
Objectives	To provide children an opportunity to walk in a line. To provide readiness opportunities for a field trip.	To provide children an opportunity to share, serve food, set a table, and eat preserved foods.	To provide a beginning geography lesson in distance and place location.
Materials	Dress-up materials from family center. Costumes for role playing. Hats depicting various careers.	Waxed apples, dried prunes, canned soup, frozen bread; paper plates, napkins, and bowls; plastic utensils.	A picture book, change to pay for items, a large sheet of paper, and a felt pen.
Procedures	Children select costumes and walk in a line around the room. Children say "I am a nurse," and so on. Children visit another classroom to show costumes and tell who they are.	Children are to help set the table, share pieces of apple, observe ways and methods of preserving foods, discuss what they are eating.	Select a store within walking distance of school. Walk to store, buy items, let children pay for them. Provide a rest stop on way home, read story at stop. Next day, draw trip on paper and discuss.
Evaluation	Performance of children.	Discussion, act of doing, and eating.	Discussion.
Integrating skills	Oral language development. Following directions (listening). Physical movement.	Good food habits. Science; preserving foods. Oral language development. Listening.	Math; money. Literature. Physical exercise. Oral language. Listening.

Mini Units Differentiating and Integrating for **Four Year Olds**

	September	*January*	*May*
Topic	My next-door neighbor.	A traffic pattern.	A rubber raft lake.
Objectives	To introduce children to the concept of visiting — behavior, sharing, manners.	To help children operate tricycles, wagons, and other small vehicles without mishap.	To introduce children to the idea of floating and sailing as a means of transportation.
Materials	Large cardboard box (a refrigerator carton is great), poster paint, and large shears.	Two-inch plastic tape, road signs, and vehicles.	A one-person rubber raft, water, boats, tiny dolls, animals.
Procedures	Cut door and windows in box at appropriate places. Have children paint "house." Place house near family center in room. Children "visit" new house and family center; have discussions and demonstrations of behavior, sharing, and manners.	Place tape on floor with road signs at appropriate places for traffic control. Children are to ride or push vehicles on tape and obey signs.	Blow up raft; use either indoors or out. Fill raft with about five inches of water. Discuss and describe boats to be used. Select dolls and animals for passengers. Children "transport" their passengers to various parts of raft.
Evaluation	Observation and discussion.	Success of movement of vehicles.	Observe children at play.
Integrating skills	Oral language development. Physical activity.	Physical activity. Following directions. Safety.	Vocabulary. Eye-hand coordination. Physical activity. Social behavior.

Mini Units Differentiating and Integrating for **Five Year Olds**

	September	*January*	*May*
Topic	A scribble table, "How I Feel Today."	People puppets.	News time.

Mini Units Differentiating and Integrating for **Five Year Olds** (*cont.*)

	September	*January*	*May*
Objectives	To give children an opportunity to express their feelings.	To introduce children to types of clothing worn by people in other lands.	To help children become aware of events at home, neighborhood, community, and areas where relatives live.
Materials	Brown or white butcher paper, crayons, and table.	Picture books, films, filmstrips, sample costumes, resource persons, cardboard, tongue depressors, and puppet stage.	24" × 36" lined paper, pad, felt pen, and bulletin board.
Procedures	Cover table with paper divided into 12" × 12" squares. Children may go to table at any time to draw how they feel.	Discuss and view films, filmstrips, and books. Have resource persons visit. Children draw child of another land and paste on cardboard. Staple tongue depressor to back of card for handle. Children stage a puppet show for parents.	Have children bring to school pictures from magazines or newspapers to share with others. Place these on bulletin board. Make classroom paper by having sharing time on "Where I've Been," "My Grandmother Lives in (Place)," "Last Night We (event)."
Evaluation	Individual discussions with children for understanding and explaining feelings.	Puppet show.	Discussion, bulletin board, and class newspaper.
Integrating skills	Art. Eye-hand coordination. Discussion; sharing.	Literature. Art. Oral language. Listening.	Oral language. Listening. Creative writing.

EVALUATION OF INDIVIDUAL DIFFERENCES

As you will remember from the language arts chapter, every group of children displays a wide range of ability and performance. Because social study units tend to be whole-group activities, teachers must be constantly aware of individual progress. The following checklists exhibit typical performances and the variance in attainment for ages three, four, and five.

Trace the progress of several children at different ages and you will see how widely children's social development varies.

Mastery of Social Behavior Mastery of Combative Traits Usual for Two Year Olds (Age Range 3.0 to 3.4 by October 1)

Name	October	January	May
Ben	no	yes	yes
Sherrie	no	yes	yes
William	no	no	yes
Cathy	yes	yes	yes
Bonnie	yes	yes	yes
Hans	yes	yes	yes
Linda	no	no	yes
Bob	no	no	no
Paul	no	no	yes
David	yes	yes	yes
Zeno	yes	no	yes
Louise	no	no	yes
Corrine	no	yes	yes
Elizabeth	no	yes	yes
Charles	yes	no	yes
Mona	yes	yes	yes
Phyllis	no	no	no
Rufus	no	no	no
Doug	no	yes	yes
Emanuel	no	yes	yes
Jack	no	yes	yes

Mastery of Social Behavior The Normal Trait of Self-assertiveness Has Lessened Significantly (Age Range 4.0 to 4.6 by October 1)

Name	October	January	May
Jane	no	no	no
Mike	no	no	yes

Mastery of Social Behavior (cont.)

Name	October	January	May
Rosemary	no	yes	yes
Alecia	no	no	no
Lillian	yes	yes	yes
Hyman	no	no	no
Penny	no	no	yes
Karl	no	no	no
Hilda	no	yes	yes
Mark	no	no	no
Bob	no	yes	yes
Richard	no	no	no
Sue	yes	yes	yes
Margaret	no	no	yes
David	no	yes	yes
Scott	no	no	no
Helen	no	no	yes
Elaine	no	yes	yes
Peggy	no	no	no
Myko	yes	yes	yes

Mastery of Social Behavior   The Trait of Frequent Arguments Has Lessened (Age Range 5.0 to 5.4 by October 1)

Name	October	January	May
Sharon	no	no	yes
Audrey	no	no	no
Barbara	yes	yes	yes
Theos	no	yes	yes
Henry	no	no	yes
Felix	no	no	no
Rosanna	yes	yes	yes
Carrie	no	no	yes
Colburn	no	no	yes

Mastery of Social Behavior (cont.)

Name	October	January	May
Ricky	no	yes	yes
Lamar	no	no	yes
Dan	no	no	no
Amy	no	yes	yes
Ann	no	no	no
Antonio	no	yes	yes
Marvin	no	no	yes
Sallie	no	no	no
Carolyn	yes	yes	yes
Terry	no	no	no

LEARNING GOALS FOR CHILDREN

Children are expected to have mastered certain skills before they are considered ready to leave kindergarten. Knowledge of these exit skills will help you teach the young children in your charge.

- ✔ Children discuss events and topics using correct terminology.
- ✔ Children exercise self-control, self-respect, and self-reliance; independence; they share and are courteous.
- ✔ Children express feelings and emotions in a socially acceptable manner.
- ✔ Children role play human behavior and actions through use of replica equipment.
- ✔ The child assumes responsibility for belongings and school property.
- ✔ Children ask permission before using the materials or toys of others.
- ✔ The child is willing to help others.
- ✔ The child sits with the group and participates cooperatively in planning, story telling, and the like.
- ✔ The child talks freely with a teacher or other child in small informal groups.
- ✔ The child completes a chosen task before moving to the next activity.
- ✔ The child asks questions and makes contributions to the group.
- ✔ The child interacts with a number of different children each day.
- ✔ The child is curious and responsive to new situations and new people.
- ✔ Given an opportunity voluntarily to show work, the child chooses to do so.

Social studies / 247

✔ The child participates in group activities without dominating the group.
✔ The child responds verbally to the greeting of a classroom guest.
✔ The child waits for turn.
✔ The child accepts criticism without becoming angry and resentful.

See page 189 for an explanation of how to use skills sequence charts. **BASIC SKILLS SEQUENCE CHART**

Social Studies Skills

Key symbols: (✔) Introduction   (✔✔) Extension and reinforcement

Skill	Level 1	Level 2	Level 3
Map skills			
Making map plans	✔	✔✔	✔✔
Understanding map language	✔	✔✔	✔✔
Learning, understanding, and using cardinal directions	✔	✔✔	✔✔
Interpreting and using map and globe symbols		✔	✔✔
Locating places on maps and globes		✔	✔✔
Interpreting topographic features		✔	✔✔
Determining distance between various places		✔	✔✔
Locational and acquisition skills			
Classifying information	✔	✔✔	✔✔
Using information gained from one situation in another situation	✔	✔✔	✔✔
Using appropriate captions	✔	✔✔	✔✔
Reading to discover relationships and to make comparisons	✔	✔✔	✔✔
Recording for information and ideas	✔	✔✔	✔✔
Using table of contents		✔	✔✔
Making outlines			✔
Using the dictionary, glossary, and index			✔
Using key terms in stating concepts, generalizations, and so on			✔
Using the library as a resource center			✔
Using multimedia materials			✔

248 / Curriculum

Social Studies Skills (cont.)

Key symbols: (✔) Introduction   (✔✔) Extension and reinforcement

Skill	Level 1	Level 2	Level 3
Organizing and arranging skills			
Keeping to the point	✔	✔✔	✔✔
Listing, categorizing, and classifying	✔	✔✔	✔✔
Outlining			✔
Using topic sentences			✔
Using key words, terms, and/or phrases			✔
Time and spatial skills			
Understanding time	✔	✔✔	✔✔
Utilizing time vocabulary	✔	✔✔	✔✔
Placing happenings in chronological order	✔	✔✔	✔✔
Developing numerical sequence	✔	✔✔	✔✔
Communicative skills			
Reporting, oral and written		✔	✔✔
Tactfully handling and reconciling differences and criticisms	✔	✔✔	✔✔
Answering questions and tactfully handling interruptions			✔
Reading for information, interpretation, and enjoyment	✔	✔✔	✔✔
Analyzing and evaluating information skills			
Interpreting titles	✔	✔✔	✔✔
Rereading for clarification	✔	✔✔	✔✔
Obtaining accurate details		✔	✔✔
Arranging and organizing information and ideas		✔	✔✔
Differentiating between fact and fiction	✔	✔✔	✔✔
Securing reliable sources of information		✔	✔✔
Utilizing alternatives		✔	✔✔
Evaluating information for specific purposes			✔
Human relation values and skills			
Taking turns	✔	✔✔	✔✔
Following rules	✔	✔✔	✔✔
Engaging in fair play	✔	✔✔	✔✔

Social Studies Skills (*cont.*)

Key symbols: (✔) Introduction   (✔✔) Extension and reinforcement

Skill	Level 1	Level 2	Level 3
Being cooperative in working with others	✔	✔✔	✔✔
Recognizing the necessity to extend good will to others	✔	✔✔	✔✔
Recognizing the worth of individuals regardless of race, creed, color, or physical or mental disabilities	✔	✔✔	✔✔
Accepting individual responsibilities	✔	✔✔	✔✔
Recognizing the value of resourcefulness, honesty, integrity, and self-discipline	✔	✔✔	✔✔
Participating effectively in group undertakings	✔	✔✔	✔✔

ADDITIONAL READINGS

Bandura, A., and R. Walters. *Social Learning and Personality Development*. New York: Holt, Rinehart and Winston, 1963.

Banks, J., ed. *Teaching Ethnic Studies*. Forty-third Yearbook of the National Council for the Social Studies. Washington, D.C.: NCSS. 1973.

Batten, T. F. *Reasoning and Research: A Guide for Social Science Methods*. Boston: Little, Brown, 1971.

Carpenter, H., ed. *Skill Development in Social Studies*. Thirty-third Yearbook of the National Council for the Social Studies. Washington, D.C.: NCSS. 1963.

Decardi, J. "Concept Teaching." *Social Education*, 37 (1973): 331–333.

Doland, D. J., and K. Adelberg. "The Learning of Sharing Behavior." *Child Development*, 38 (1967): 695–700.

Dunfee, M. *Elementary School Social Studies. A Guide to Current Research*. Washington, D.C.: Association for Supervision and Curriculum Development, NEA. 1970.

Geletka, J. "The Political Awareness of Preschool Children." Master's thesis. College Park: University of Maryland. 1973.

Hartup, W. W., and R. Coates. "The Role of Imitation in Childhood Socialization." In *Early Experience and the Processes of Socialization*. Ed. R. A. Hoppe, G. A. Milton, and E. C. Simmel. New York: Academic Press. 1970.

Johnson, H. *Children in "The Nursery School."* New York: Agathon Press. 1973.

Larkins, G., and J. P. Shaver. "Economics Learning in Grade One: The Use of Assessment Studies." *Social Education*, 33 (1969): 958–63.

Lee, J. R., and N. Stampfer. "Two Studies in Learning Geography: Implications for the Primary Grades." *Social Education*, 30 (1966): 627–28.

McKinney, J. D., and L. Golden. "Social Studies Dramatic Play with Elementary School Children." *Journal of Educational Research*, 67 (1973): 172–76.

Pagano, Alicia L., ed. *Social Studies in Early Childhood: An Interactionist Point of View*. Washington, D.C.: National Council for the Social Studies, 1978.

Portugaly, D. "A Study of the Development of Disadvantaged Kindergarten Children's Understanding of the Earth as a Globe." *Dissertation Abstracts*, 28 (1968): 4056-A.

Sheridan, J. M. "Children's Awareness of Physical Geography." *Journal of Geography*, 67 (1968): 82–86.

Spodek, B. "Social Studies for Young Children: Identifying Intellectual Goals." *Social Education*, 33 (1974): 40–45.

Wisniewski, R., ed. *Teaching About Life in the City*. Forty-second Yearbook of the National Council for the Social Studies. Washington, D.C.: NCSS. 1972.

CHAPTER 8
Science

Exploration Tasks

After studying this chapter, you should be able to complete these tasks:
- Identify and describe the three forms of science for young children.
- Describe the teacher's role in exploring, comparing, classifying, and experimenting.
- Develop sequential units appropriate to the age, ability, and knowledge of the children you teach.
- Describe how to select and care for science equipment, materials, and living things.
- Describe and plan for whole-group, individualized, and incidental classroom "experiments."
- Identify several science-related play activities.
- Plan mini units for maintaining a high interest level in science.

Only the complex mind and feeling of a human adult is a match for the complex mind and feeling of the human child. Neither workbooks nor teaching machines, textbooks nor computers can ever be flexible enough to deal with the unpredictability and unexpectedness of the demands for knowing of a curious child.

Dorothy H. Cohen

OVERVIEW

Science is a subject for which curiosity is an asset. Since young children are very inquisitive, science is easily taught, especially as it provides many exciting and interesting moments. Along with social studies, it is one of the two content areas within which skills are taught.

Young children are more interested in observing, handling, manipulating, exploring, comparing, and performing than in the actual knowledge gained from their actions. The freedom of movement, the many materials, the small adult-to-child ratio, the many opportunities for verbal interaction, and the opportunity for a listener lead them to be actively involved in science lessons.

Science in school takes three forms: formal acquisition of skills and knowledge, informal trying out and examining, and incidental learnings from events of interest. Formal science is usually planned by the teacher and taught to the whole group as experiments or demonstrations. Informal science is often taught through interest centers and displays of environmental findings by students and teacher. Incidental learnings result from natural phenomenon changes and related incidents in other teachings. For best management of incidental science learning, the teacher should have an inquisitive mind, a good science background, and adequate resources for information and materials.

THEORETICAL CONTEXT

Ruthie: "It's gonna rain."
Nancy: "No, it's not."
Ruthie: "Yes, it is. I see black clouds."
Nancy: "That don't mean nothing."
Ruthie: "Yes, it does. You're dumb."

In science there are two basic approaches. One is a content approach called *the discovery process*. As the children are exploring, observing, questioning, measuring, and hypothesizing, the teacher encourages and leads them on to more in-depth knowledge of the subject. A rich science-related environment is necessary; this is why you will need many science-related materials and pieces of equipment in your classroom. Many of the science happenings in this type of classroom are incidental and, as a teacher, you may have to "pull a rabbit out of a hat" on the spur of the moment. Therefore, you should know the materials in your materials center (library) and be aware of community resources. Because of the variety of potential scientific events that can occur in this approach, planning and evaluation have to be general in nature. Experience charts and sharing time are both ways to determine what children have learned, to organize their learning in a logical way, and to have a permanent record of the event for later reinforcement or recall of the pertinent facts.

The other approach to teaching science is called *the process approach*. Exploring, observing, questioning, measuring, and hypothesizing are involved in this approach also, but the beginning point differs from the discovery approach. In this approach the teacher selects the content to be taught, develops a unit based on what she or he wants the children to know, and usually develops objectives (behavioral) for the children to accomplish, which in themselves become an evaluation of what the children have learned.

Problem solving can and does occur in both approaches. Children seem to respond more alertly, with more interest, and for a longer period of time when they have the opportunity to find the answer for themselves. Being a good questioner will help the children think of more aspects of the activity. Be sure to give children plenty of time to respond between questions or you'll get yes and no answers.

THE TEACHER'S ROLE

What do you do as a teacher of science? Your first responsibility is to provide an interesting environment that will challenge each child's curiosity. As the children explore, compare, classify, and experiment, you must do three things: introduce activities, recognize and accept a wide range of abilities and skills, and individualize the instructional steps for grasping the content by speed of attainment and depth of acquisition. In addition, you must help children by listening, discussing, introducing, and planning.

Science is an ideal subject for field trips, since children learn best from concrete experiences. Reread the section on field or study trips in the social studies chapter before you plan a science excursion.

Planning

In science, as in every other area, the teacher must have a broad basic overview of what is age-appropriate for the students and what topics are pertinent. Science lends itself to adaptation to the seasons, and the natural season topics provide spontaneous leads into demonstrations and informal learnings in interest centers. The seasonal topic outline that follows will help you plan for the year's program, will aid you in selecting materials and equipment for your room, and will guide you in your purchases of books and expendable supplies for the year ahead.

Sequential seasonal topics

Autumn

Changes in plants: color, falling leaves, receding sap
Changes in animal habits: migration, storing of food
Harvesting: types of crops, ways of harvesting, ways of preserving food, ways of preparing food for eating

Changes in weather: variances in temperature; types of precipitation; effects of both on clothing, food, activities

Winter

Contrast and compare animal activities and species
Contrast and compare autumn and winter weather
Contrast and compare daylight and dark as season changes
Contrast and compare activities, clothing, and foods
Introduce need for heat: sun and artificial heat sources
Introduce drying and evaporation
Introduce light and color (soap bubbles, lenses, prisms)

Spring

Introduce and compare variance in weather, plant life, and clothing
Discuss baby animals, parenthood, and care
Demonstrate planting and observe new growth
Compare characteristics of water, sand, and mud; demonstrate evaporation; absorption; flow and force; and mixing, dissolving, and combining, using water and sand play
Introduce machines and their use: spring is usually the time for renewed construction and repair; lawns and gardens require the use of machines

Summer

Concepts about this season are taught in late spring and early autumn while school is still in session
Compare and contrast seasonal changes in weather, clothing, and activities
Show how plant life and animal habits change in winter, spring, summer, and autumn
Introduce insects, spiders, butterflies, moths, and worms
Compare fresh fruits and vegetables of summer to those harvested and stored in autumn (Autumn, late spring, and summer are good times to teach the food preparation activities discussed later in this chapter.)
Introduce concept of food, water, and sunlight for growth of plant life

Collecting and Ordering Supplies

After you have planned your broad general approach to teaching science another responsibility you will have as a teacher will be to collect and order materials and equipment appropriate for the ages, interests, and abilities of the children you teach. Lists of the basics for science teaching can be a little overpowering to a new teacher; and perhaps you will be discouraged when you visit your own classroom and discover that many of the listed items are not available. The lists we provide are "idea" suggestions; they give you direction and help in selecting essential items first and are a guide for filling in and adding to at a later time. Specialized equipment and materials will be discussed and listed under the appropriate topics such as sand and water play, food preparation, environmental play, and interest center activities.

General classroom science materials

Animals Guinea pigs, rabbits, birds (for older children), setting hen (or incubator), chicks, ducks, land snails, frogs, toads, salamanders, hamsters

Aquatic animals Goldfish, minnows, polliwogs, catfish, snails

Insects Butterflies, caterpillars, grasshoppers, katydids, ants, ladybugs (See equipment section for supplies.)

Plants Sweet potato vines; carrot ferns; "tree" grown from potato, carrot, and avocado seed; ivy; cacti

Seeds Green bean, corn, pumpkin, and sunflower for large seeds; rye (grass) and lettuce for small seeds

Bulbs Onion, narcissus, tulip, day lily, gladiola

Nonliving things (some were once living things) Rocks, seashells, coral, earth, dried specimen of flowers and weeds, twigs, branches, seed pods, leaves, preserved fish, starfish

Science equipment

Food for animals, fish, and marine life
Cages for animals and insects
Aquarium and terrarium: four- to five-gallon glass tank, aquarium net, plastic hose for draining
Birdbath, birdhouse, feeding station for birds and squirrels
Containers for small insects: clear plastic jars with holes for air in top; plastic, tin, and aluminum containers, two to six inches deep, with tops of screen or mesh (thin bands of an old inner tube make excellent fasteners for holding screen or mesh on containers)
Containers for plants and seeds: plastic pots, window boxes, metal or wooden planters, milk cartons, peat pots, clear plastic cups
Garden tools: rake, watering can, hoe, spade, trowel (can be brought from home or borrowed for the limited time they are used)
Pictures: purchased sets or cut from magazines, posters, charts, slides, filmstrips, films, video tapes

Records and tapes (see lists)

Metric measures: 10 ml, 100 ml, 250 ml, 500 ml, 1 liter, and 2 liter containers (aluminum); 125 cc, 250 cc, 500 cc, 1000 cc containers (plastic); plastic or aluminum with pour spout

Miscellaneous: calendar, thermometers, magnifying lenses (glass or plastic), magnets (bar and horseshoe), iron filings, sponges, string, rope, cord, shallow plastic dishes, funnel, ruler, tape measure (metric and English), rain gauge, hourglass, kaleidoscope, compass, prism, balance (scale), gravity ramp — to be set at different angles for changes in speed of rolling or sliding objects

Care of Living Things in the Classroom

A pet or animal is a common visitor or resident in early childhood classrooms. The selection and care of these living things is of primary importance for the health and safety of both the children and animals.

Because of the accessibility of pet shops and the great pleasure children receive from watching and holding animals, teachers and parents are often tempted to purchase undesirable pets for the classroom and home. The object of a pet at school or home is to provide the child with an opportunity to care for and learn about living things. Day-to-day responsibilities such as feeding, cleaning cages, and changing water are the rudiments of responsibility necessary for other aspects of life.

Although they are pretty and interesting, canaries and parakeets are not appropriate for the classroom because of the smallness of the bird and the intricacies of the cage. Small hands may squeeze the bird or leave the cage door unlatched.

The small turtle usually found in variety stores may be a carrier of salmonella and could cause children who handle the turtle to become seriously ill. The pet store iguana and monkey have no place in a classroom or home of young children. Both require year-round heat of over 80° and extensive cleaning of cages.

Wildlife such as raccoons and deodorized skunks, which on occasion are available at pet stores, often revert to wild behavior and emit strong odors. Wildlife is best observed in its wild state by providing grain and birdbaths. The grain will attract not only birds but squirrels, chipmunks, and in some instances raccoons and opossum.

Care Guide The following guide for care and feeding of appropriate living things for young children will aid you in selection and will also provide you with a resource for parent education.

Goldfish Feed twice daily, dry flake feed. Change the water every three days. If the water is chlorinated let the water stand for twenty-four hours. Water should be at room temperature.

Children need to learn how to care for animals.

Siamese fighting fish As easy to care for as goldfish and require the same food and water.

Guppies, mollys, swordtail, platies These fish reproduce by live birth rather than from eggs. Three years olds will be fascinated by these fish. Use a large tank with an air pump for regular use and keep a smaller tank for the offspring since the parent fish may swallow their young. Transfer young with a fish net and use an air stone for oxygen (no pump because it will suck up small fish). Feed twice a day, flake food at one time and freeze-dried fish food at the other time.

Tropical fish Red borles and silver angel fish are the least expensive and are very hearty. They swim in schools and you will need six to ten of each in a ten-gallon tank. You will need a heater, a pump, and a pH kit to test the water regularly so you can add the right chemicals to make the water acidic enough. Be sure to check with the pet store clerk about the aggressiveness of the tropical fish you buy. Some will attack and kill other fish. Plants are not necessary but do make the tank more attractive. You will need to check the pH content of the water after you have added any additional objects. Feed only twice a day; alternate flake food, freeze-dried foods, and frozen brine shrimp.

PROJECT

The Animals in Your Life

Young children are very interested and curious about all kinds of animals. Your interest in and acceptance of living things are desirable for a successful science program.

1. Write a short essay describing your family's pets and your responsibilities, relations, and attitudes toward them.
2. Did you ever have an experience with an animal that frightened you? Describe it. Did it change your attitude toward animals? Based on your own experience and your knowledge of children, how would you deal with a young child who had been similarly frightened?
3. Have you ever experienced the death of a pet? What were your feelings? How was the pet's death explained to you? How would you as a teacher handle the death of a classroom pet?

Box turtles The box turtle needs little care and can be picked up and carried about by a two year old. The turtle does not bite. Turtles eat greens, fruit, and ground meat. Turtles hibernate. If the room where it is kept becomes cool, the turtle will become sluggish.

Ants A purchased ant farm can provide many hours of entertainment and requires no special care after it is established.

Gerbils Four year olds love gerbils. They are gentle and friendly and will eat out of a child's hand if the child is gentle. Abusive behavior will cause the gerbil to bite, but the bite will not harm the child. Gerbils can chew plastic, wood, and cardboard and therefore need a metal or glass cage. Use torn newspaper for bedding; add a hollowed-out ball and an aluminum can for exploring activities. Gerbil females will eat their young if the babies are at all deformed. Crowding or extreme noise will also disturb mother gerbils, adding additional problems. Because of this don't enter the "mating game" — buy two of the same sex. They like dry seeds, grain, cereals, breads, grass, fruit, lettuce, and carrots. A hanging water bottle made for cages is best for providing liquid.

Guinea pig A guinea pig is a nonjumping, nonclimbing, talkative cuddler. They squeal and grunt whenever they are comfortable and at home. Guinea pigs need a steady warm temperature and must be in a well-lighted hutch, free of drafts. They are also gnawers, so thin wood, paper, or plastic cages cannot be used. Straw, wood shavings, or cat litter provide material for absorbing moisture. Clean hutch weekly. They are vegetarians, eating apples, lettuce, grass, or commercial rabbit food. They need a salt spool, a dish of water, and a small container of vegetable oil once a week. Two female guinea pigs are best for classrooms. Male and female mate when they are a month old but the female should be protected until she is six months old. Males may fight if they are in the same cage continuously.

The living things listed above are appropriate for classrooms. Dogs and cats are usually not, although we know one teacher who was most successful with one mother cat. (Of course, the cat may have been the successful one in this instance.) A handy book for your bookshelves is *How to Keep Your Pet Healthy* by Elizabeth Charles (1974). Order from Collier Books, New York.

Even with the best of care, most living things in the classroom have a short life expectancy. Although the death of an animal is tragic, the event can be a rather gentle introduction to the normal cycle of all living things. For more on handling the events of death that may occur in a child's life, refer to Chapter 7.

Juan: "Once we had two goldfish, but they got cooked."

Rita: "They got cooked?!"

Juan: "Un huh. My brother cleaned their bowl and filled it with hot water."

Plants for the Classroom

The following plants are relatively free from pests, adapt to almost any amount (or lack) of sunlight, thrive at ordinary classroom temperatures, endure irregular watering and feeding, and are not poisonous. Young children may "taste" leave or flowers, so be careful in your selection of plants for the classroom.

Common name	*Latin name*
Snake plant	*Sansevieria*
Philodendron	*Philodendron oxycardium*
Pepper plant	*Peperomia obtusifolia*
Cast iron plant	*Aspidistra elatior*
Peace lily	*Spothipyllum commutation*
Air fern	*Aerides*
Jade plant	*Crassula argentea*

THE CHILD'S PARTICIPATION

Although the teacher plans, gathers materials, and provides the time and space for a science environment, the child should be the active participator

260 / Curriculum

and learner. What do children do? They observe and they talk; they feel, taste, smell, hear, and talk; they collect, experiment, and talk. "Why?" "Let me see," and "Let me do it" are all normal reactions to science activities indoors and out. Young children are not passive watchers. They are active doers.

Whole Group

At times a teacher will plan a demonstration for the whole group. It must be brief but should provide opportunities for discussion and should encourage physical participation. The content should be accurate, even though the children may not have a complete, comprehensive knowledge of the reasons for the phenomenon they observe. Freedom of movement, freedom to handle objects, and adequate time for exploration and investigation on an individual basis will stimulate creative participation in whole-group experiments.

Eight of the most common and appropriate science "experiments" for young children follow. Purpose and objective are spelled out according to science procedures. The objectives are stated behaviorally and therefore include the participation activities.

Demonstration 1

Purpose   Color identification and color mixing

Objective   At the conclusion of the activity, the children should be able to:
Mix red and yellow and get orange.
Mix blue and yellow and get green.
Mix red and blue and get purple.
Identify each color by name orally.

Note   Use water colors, poster paints, or vegetable coloring.

Demonstration 2

Purpose   Identification of shapes

Objective   At the conclusion of the activity, the children should be able to:
Identify a square, a circle, a triangle, and a rectangle by visual observation and by touch.
Match these shapes regardless of size.

Note: Use commercially available shapes or cardboard cutouts.

Demonstration 3

Purpose   Identification of objects by their properties

Objective   At the conclusion of the activity, the children should be able to:
Identify like items by their color, shape, size, texture, and composition.
Differentiate items by color, shape, size, texture, and composition.

Demonstration 4

Purpose   Identification of the Five Senses

Objective   At the conclusion of the activity, the children should be able to:
Identify by smell the odor of apples, onions, lemons, cabbage, and other foods.
Identify by hearing the sound of dripping water, a closing door, a car, airplane, train, windshield wiper, cattle, horses, lion, and so forth.
Identify textures by feel (rough, ribbed, wavy, smooth, furry, and so on).
Identify by taste common foods such as peanut butter, apples, oranges, bread, and milk.
Identify by sight familiar items such as chairs, tables, desks, broom, and others.

Note   Place substance on cotton pad and "waft" under noses. Caution children not to taste unknown substances.

Demonstration 5

Purpose   Identification of the properties of air

Objective   At the conclusion of the activity, the children should be able to:
State that air moves by observing movement of clouds, trees, kites, flags, or smoke.
State that air takes up space after blowing up a balloon, blowing bubbles, or pumping up an air mattress.

Demonstration 6

Purpose   Identification of liquids and their properties

Objective   At the conclusion of the activity, the children should be able to:
Identify by sight and name five liquids.
Observe the mixing properties of liquid hand lotion and baby oil, liquid hand lotion and water, liquid food coloring and water, and liquid detergent and water.
Observe the mixing properties of liquid hand lotion and baby oil, liquid food coloring and baby oil, liquid detergent and baby oil.
State which liquids mixed and which did not.

> **Demonstration 7**
>
> *Purpose* Identification of evaporation property of water
>
> *Objective* At the conclusion of the activity, the children should be able to:
> Observe that the water disappeared when it was warmed.
> State that the sun or some form of heat soaked up the water (like a sponge).

> **Demonstration 8**
>
> *Purpose* Identification of the law of gravity
>
> *Objective* At the conclusion of the activity, the children should be able to:
> Observe that everything above the floor that is not attached, held, or otherwise supported falls to the floor.
> State that gravity is the force that pulls from the earth.

Individualized Science

The possibility for participating in a science-related activity is always present in classrooms for young children. A science table, center, corner, shelf, or box is created by the teacher and aide. Materials for this area are gathered from several sources and changed often. At the beginning the teacher will display interesting objects, toys, games, and equipment in the area. As the children become interested and alert to their environment, they too will add to the collection. Parents will often contribute special collections or help their child bring something of interest.

Children often work on their own in the science area with the teacher or aide available only by request. When something new is added to the area, the teacher does call the children's attention to it and on some occasions will whet their appetites by telling or showing them an unusual facet of the object. Usually though, children will become involved with this area every day. An individualized science program allows for creativity, freedom of involvement, and freedom to not participate at all times.

Incidental Science

There is absolutely no planning for incidental events that are scientific in nature. A violent windstorm leaves excellent examples of branches, leaves, and bark; a flock of robins decides to look for worms in the schoolyard grass; a spider makes a web in the corner outside the classroom window, and heavy dew then ladders the web; an inchworm finds its way into the classroom in a small bunch of child-picked dandelions. All of these are opportunities for incidental learning of science.

The teacher, of course, cannot answer all the children's questions about these wonders; therefore you as a teacher will need to have resource books and pictures available. Some of these books should be adult-level references for you and some should be pictorial, with few words, especially designed for small children. The incidental events in a classroom can be the spark needed to make the day a very special occasion.

PLAY OPPORTUNITIES

During the day's program for young children much of the time is spent in what most adults call play. Some of this play has a science base; through the play activities the child is actually learning scientific facts. As you will remember, play in the language arts was described as drama and the acting out of stories or portrayal of characters. In the social studies, play was described as role playing of family members or community helpers and as a way to solve personal problems. In science, play has a key role in helping children become aware of the environment, observing natural phenomena, and identifying the properties of certain elements.

As a teacher one of your most important objectives is to educate parents, other teachers, and the lay public about the importance of play and its many facets for learning. Sand and water play and food preparation are the two most common classroom play situations that are based on scientific skills and knowledge. Often the concepts and skills being taught and learned in these two activities are completely overlooked by lay observers of young children playing.

Sand and Water Play

Sand and water play can be provided in three ways. A sandbox, either inside or outside, is probably the most common means of presenting the properties of sand. Water play is usually provided indoors by the use of a large basin or a large plastic tub. Water play outside may be provided by hoses, tubs, bird baths, or small ponds. The third way is a combination of limited water and lots of sand and is usually "played" outside. The regular sand in a sand box needs to be moistened occasionally so that it doesn't become too dry for holding a form — road, house, or hill. The moisture will also keep it from becoming dusty.

Sand and water are flexible mediums that encourage creativity. The packing, scraping, patting, digging, wiping, splashing, and cleaning properties of sand and water tend to relax children. The activities are quiet and can be accomplished on an individual basis or with a friend. Individuals who have taught three, four, and five year olds for many years say that water and sand play seems to have a calming and soothing effect on children. The following equipment will aid the children in using this medium creatively.

Play Equipment The sand and water play table is usually about forty inches long, twenty-six inches wide, and nine inches deep. It is lined with heavy-duty plastic and has a drain. Some older tables are lined with tin. Some tables are for sand only or for sand with limited water. Equipment should include:

Molds of various designs
Cookie cutters, rolling pins, metric measures
Tools: rake, hoe, spade, with handles usually about 7 inches long
Sand combs: 1/8-inch plywood rectangles, 9 inches by 3 inches, with various designs cut in one side (scallops, triangles, squares)
Ice cream scoops, sugar scoops, or flour scoops
Containers of various sizes and shapes made of unbreakable plastic (include some with handles)
Small beach pails, nesting measuring cups, sand castle blocks
Small plastic cars
Wooden or plastic blocks for houses and other buildings

Water Play Other potential uses of water include floating and sinking "experiments"; the clean tepid water necessary for fish; soapy water for bubble blowing; bathing water for the dolls; use of the rain gauge; rainbow "experiments"; evaporating, freezing, and condensing "experiments"; and small ponds for sailing boats. A pail of water colored with food coloring makes a great "gallon of paint" for painting a cement bench, a table, or a brick wall. Do not "paint" wood with water because the wood finish will blister and the wood will soon rot. Equipment for water play should include:

Various types of boats
Pouring containers with spouts, plastic squirt and spray bottles
Small beach pails with handles of rope or plastic
Funnel, plastic tubing, sponges, wash cloths, and towels
Washable dolls
Plastic or vinyl aprons

Environmental Play If you have ever had a garden you may wonder whether "gardening" should be included under play; but gardening for the young is more play than work. The flower garden and the vegetable garden need only a small spot in the schoolyard. By digging in the dirt, planting the seeds, watering, and hoeing, children become more observant of their surroundings as protectors of growing things. Don't forget the possibilities of planting fruit trees that bear in early spring or in autumn. The beautiful

The use of soapless bubble bath oil can add a new dimension to water play.

blossoms, the early leaf buds, the bees, and the growth and the changing color of the fruit provide interesting environmental changes each year. Grass seed grown on a damp sponge in the classroom will create great interest and quick results. Comparison of this grass with outdoor grass makes each child more cognizant of what makes a lawn.

Classroom animals, birds, and fish can provide miniature environmental settings for their habitat and behavior. An aquarium is a miniature pond, a large cage can be a miniature living area, and a bird cage is a miniature aviary. Helping children observe and compare habitats and behavior in these small enclosures can help them understand and appreciate their own natural environment. Watching, discussing, feeding, watering, cleaning, and handling some of these animals lead to appreciating their importance to people.

Cooking and Other Food Activities

Activities using food are included in most programs for three, four, and five year olds. Food preparation and use are usually an exciting time for the children, as the activities require their participation and they have an opportunity to eat the end result. Children have many contacts with food in their daily lives and as most of these are pleasant, their activities involving foods are therefore highly interesting to them.

Cooking provides an introduction to the physical sciences because cooking is an easy way to see changes in a substance. Melting, dissolving, softening, thickening, and changing form and color — all occur in cooking.

Food does not have to be cooked. Preparing raw foods and combining ingredients also provide learning experiences. Very often the best beginning activities are those of frosting purchased cookies; flavoring milk; mixing punch; stirring instant pudding; and serving apples, oranges, crackers, and carrot and celery sticks at snack or lunch time.

The Teacher's Role A teacher does not have to be the "doer" in food preparation. The teacher provides the food, materials, and the setting for the activity. The teacher helps children in potentially dangerous situations, such as cutting or pouring hot liquid, and asks questions: "What if . . . ?" "How does . . . ?" "What happened?" "Why?" The teacher makes statements: "Try putting . . . ," "Mix the . . . ," and "Put in some more."

Your planning should provide many open-ended activities for the children to be as creative as they wish. But conforming activities are also necessary; too much water or milk added to the pudding mix doesn't make pudding. Suggest a variety of activities that will be challenging but not too difficult. Vary the type of activity so the children do not become bored.

Use inexpensive materials and small amounts. Spilling and dropping are normal with young children. Children should have an opportunity to experiment with and taste new foods. Things do not always taste good to all children and the teacher must not force children to eat what they have prepared. Although children's creative recipes are often inedible, they must not be made to feel guilty or ashamed of their efforts.

The Child's Participation Because the child is the active agent in food preparation, the activities are play oriented. New basic concepts are being formed, skills are being developed, and social skills are being promoted.

In basic concept development the children learn to describe things by naming shapes, comparing sizes, and describing colors. They learn to describe and differentiate tastes such as sweet, sour, or salty. Vocabulary is extended through use of descriptive words.

They learn that the change of appearance of food does not necessarily change its taste, as when a raw apple becomes applesauce.

In science play children learn that liquids and solids may change form; some solids become liquids, some liquids change to solids, and some liquids change to gases.

After a fall cooking unit on preparing autumn foods and making a cookbook for our parents, Billy dashed in one morning yelling, "Teacher, Teacher! Guess what!" "What's happened?" the teacher asked. "We ate my apple pie recipe last night!" Billy exclaimed.

Children learn to think more logically. Some actions can be reversed; that is, liquids can be poured into other containers and poured back to the original container. When an object changes place, it does not change its identity; milk in a cardboard container is still milk when it is poured into a glass, and it is the same milk. They learn that foods can be classified in many ways: milk may be cold or hot, may be frozen or liquid, and may vary in color. They learn that the amount of liquid poured does not change when the liquid is poured into varying sizes or shapes of containers.

As for physical skill development, children develop small-muscle coordination and eye-hand coordination through mixing, pouring, and grasping objects. They learn to recognize measuring equipment such as cup, teaspoon, and tablespoon.

Children also develop social skills. They take turns stirring, pouring, and serving. They learn to accept help to accomplish a task, to be successful with a pliable medium, and to continue an activity until it is finished.

Noncooking Suggestions Recipes are readily available, both from the special list of books at the end of this chapter and from cookbooks found in most homes. The recipes for the following foods are commonly found in any general cookbook: Waldorf salad, ambrosia, three-bean salad, snow ice cream, butter, cranberry-orange relish, colored milk, eggnog, and fruit juice shakes. In the blender try soups, peanut butter, and juices.

Cooking Suggestions There are several special cookbooks with children's recipes only. Books written for teachers of young children not only provide recipes but also give the procedures, cautions, and explanations of why cooking is an important part of growing up. The following books provide all of these functions and can be useful in your parent education program.

Association for Childhood Education International. *Cooking and Eating with Children: A Way to Learn*. Washington, D.C.: ACEI, 1974.
Early Childhood Education Council of Western New York. *Cooking with Children*. New York: The National Association for the Education of Young Children, n.d.
Goodwin, Mary T., and Gerry Pollen. *Creative Food Experiences for Children*. Rev. ed. Washington, D.C.: Center for Science in the Public Interest, 1980.
Kahan, Ellen House. *Cooking Activities for the Retarded Child*. New York: Abingdon, 1974.

Integration of Cooking with Other Subject Areas Figure 8.1, a concept spiral, provides an example of ways to integrate a food activity into a social

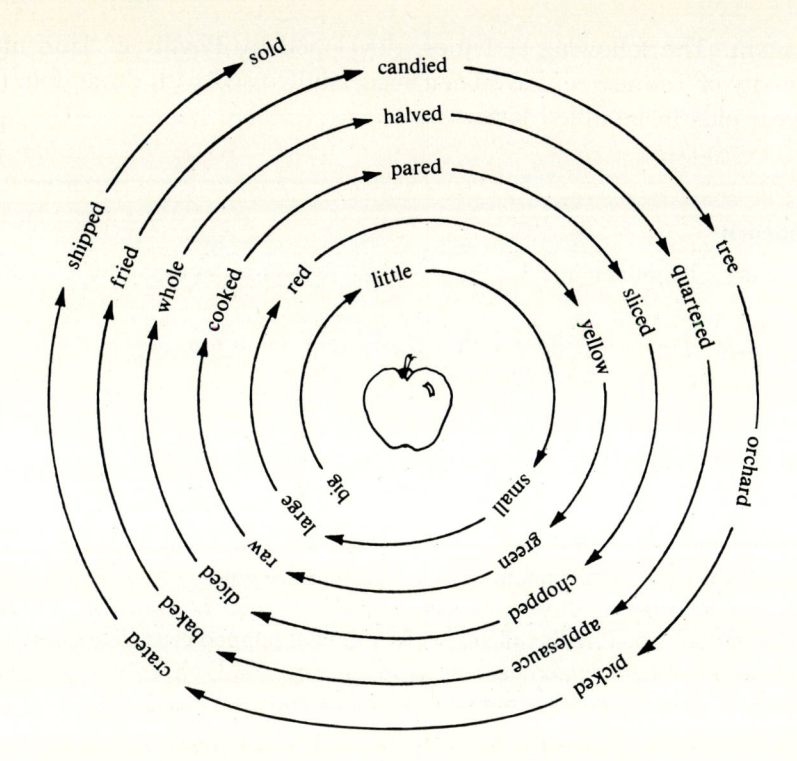

*Figure 8.1
Appleness Concept*

studies, language arts, science, or math unit. An apple is readily available several times during the school year for each child because of snack time or lunch at school. The apple is a unique resource for demonstrations that provide concrete examples for vocabulary and concept development in every curricular area. *Big, little, halves,* and *whole* are mathematic terms. *Crated, shipped,* and *sold* are terms used in social studies lessons. In this example of a concept spiral many of the activities associated with the apple involve preparation of the apple for eating.

Apple vocabulary

Raw	Whole	Red, green, yellow
Applesauce	Half	Big, little
Salad	Diced	Tree, branch
Fried	Sliced	Stem, skin
Apple pie	Quarters	Core, seed
Apple butter	Equal	Blossom

Senses Play Using the five senses to learn something new is usually great fun for your children because the activities require physical and oral involvement. The following activities, developed by Phyllis E. Huff of the University of Tennessee, have been successfully used with three, four, and five year olds in modified form.

Popcorn

Purpose: To actively involve the use of the five senses in exploring a familiar object.

Materials Popcorn popper with a transparent dome top, popcorn and seasonings, napkins to serve the finished product.

Procedure 1 Place the popcorn popper in a convenient place where all the children can see. Ask if they know what it is and how it works or is used.

Place the oil and the corn in the popper. Ask the children to infer what will happen as the oil heats. After a few inferences, ask them to keep those in mind and to be very, very quiet and find out what happens.

After the corn begins popping, ask what they have noticed so far. How did it fit the inferences? Be sure to have included seeing the corn pop, hearing the corn pop, smelling the oil get hot and the hot popped corn. Use questions such as "Was there something you could have noticed even if your eyes were closed?" "How many ways did you know that corn was popping?"

Procedure 2 An alternative introduction lends a little mystery. Put the popcorn popper in a concealed place but where it can be exposed to view easily, such as under a box, behind a screen, and so on. Just before the children arrive, set it up and plug it in. Making no reference, let the popping process start. When the children notice it, ask what they think is happening, how they can make the guesses (inferences) they are making. Then remove the cover and continue with the same procedure as above.

When the corn is popped, compare the volume before and after popping. Ask the children how else we might find out about the popcorn. Can we use any other part of our body besides our eyes, ears, and nose to find out?

Pass out the popcorn and have the children feel it. Ask them to describe how it feels, if all the kernels feel the same. Have them taste one or two kernels and describe how they taste.

Eat and enjoy the popcorn!

Correlate with Skills Studies For language arts, make popcorn balls or popcorn chains. Poems such as "Popcorn Song" (James Smith, *Creative Teaching of the Language Arts*) can be read by the teacher or used as choral-speaking activity. The activity is an excellent experience for the children to build upon and to compose their own story, poem, or song.

For art, make pictures and designs with popped corn; for movement learnings, pretend to be an unpopped kernel. Students are seated in a circle (popper). Slowly heat, then POP! (jump up).

Skeleton

Purpose To identify the major body parts and to stress importance of skeletal structure of the body.

Materials Skeleton model or paper skeletons such as those found at Halloween; or p. 136 of *Science Experiences for Young Children*.

Procedure Present the skeleton form to the class. Let them name the figure.

Using the name decided upon (for example, Boney), ask how Boney is like you. Some children will know they have a bone structure or a skeleton. Have them feel the bones in their own arms and hands.

Identify major body parts using the skeleton; head, arms, hands, legs, feet, and ribs. Ask them to locate Boney's head bones, then feel their own heads. Repeat with other listed parts.

Correlate with Skill Areas For music, use "Dry Bones." For language, read or compose stories about skeletons. For movement study, touch different bones; for math, measure bones. Using pieces of string, find the longest bone, the shortest bone, then find two bones the same length.

SCIENCE BOOKS FOR CHILDREN

Books, especially picture books, provide details, variety, and depth to science inquisitiveness. They are a must for every classroom. As a teacher you will need many sources for answering children's questions as well as many pictures to help them understand their science environment. The following books are recommended.

Adler, David A. *3D, 2D, 1D*. New York: Thomas Y. Crowell Co., 1975.
Aliki. *Corn Is Maize: The Gift of the Indians*. New York: Thomas Y. Crowell Co., 1976.
Armitage, Ronda. *The Lighthouse Keeper's Lunch*. New York: Elsevier Dutton, 1979.
Bester, Robert. *Guess What?* New York: Crown Publishers, 1980.
Branley, Franklyn M. *Light and Darkness*. New York: Thomas Y. Crowell Co., 1975.
Brewer, Mary. *What Floats?* Chicago: Childrens Press, 1976.
———. *Wind Is Air*. Chicago: Childrens Press, 1976.
Bruningham, John. *Seasons*. Indianapolis, Ind.: Bobbs-Merrill, 1971.
Busch, Phyllis S. *A Walk in the Snow*. Philadelphia: J.B. Lippincott, 1971.
Carle, Eric. *The Tiny Seed*. New York: Thomas Y. Crowell Co., 1970.

Carrick, Carol, and Donald Carrick. *The Blue Lobster: A Life Cycle*. New York: The Dial Press, 1975.
Carrick, Donald. *The Tree*. New York: Macmillan, 1971.
Clarkson, Jan Nagel. *Tricks Animals Play*. Washington, D.C.: National Geographic Society, 1975.
Cole, Joanna. *A Calf Is Born*. New York: William Morrow & Co., 1975.
———. *A Chick Hatches*. New York: William Morrow & Co., 1976.
Cosgrove, Margaret. *Wintertime for Animals*. New York: Dodd, Mead, 1975.
Daly, Kathleen N. *A Child's Book of Flowers*. New York: Doubleday & Co., 1976.
———. *Wild Animal Babies*. New York: Golden Press, 1970.
Domanska, Janina. *Spring Is*. New York: Greenwillow Books, 1976.
Duvoisin, Roger. *See What I Am*. New York: Lothrop, Lee & Shepard, 1974.
Fisher, Aileen. *Once We Went on a Picnic*. New York: Thomas Y. Crowell, Co., 1975.
Freschet, Bernice. *Grizzly Bear*. New York: Charles Scribner's Sons, 1975.
———. *Turtle Pond*. New York: Charles Scribner's Sons, 1971.
———. *The Web in the Grass*. New York: Charles Scribner's Sons, 1975.
———. *Where's Henrietta's Hen?* New York: G.P. Putnam's Sons, 1980.
Glauzman, Louis S. *Cats*. Washington, D.C.: National Geographic Society, 1974.
———. *Spiders*. Washington, D.C.: National Geographic Society, 1974.
Hoban, Tana. *Big Ones, Little Ones*. New York: Greenwillow Books, 1976.
Hoff, Syd. *When Will It Snow?* New York: Harper & Row, 1971.
Ipcor, Dahlou. *The Wonderful Egg*. New York: Doubleday, 1958.
Iwasaki, Chihero. *Staying Home Alone on a Rainy Day*. New York: Macmillan, 1968.
Jordon, Helene. *How a Seed Grows*. New York: Thomas Y. Crowell Co., 1960.
———. *Seeds by Wind and Water*. New York: Thomas Y. Crowell Co., 1960.
Kay, Helen. *Snow Birthday*. New York: Farrar, Strauss & Giroux, 1955.
Keats, Ezra Jack. *The Snowy Day*. New York: The Viking Press, 1962.
Kessler, Ethel, and Leonard Kessler. *All for Fall*. New York: Parents Magazine Press, 1974.
Krauss, Ruth. *The Carrot Seed*. New York: Harper & Row, 1945.
Lenski, Lois. *Now It's Fall*. New York: Henry Z. Walck, 1948.
Lerner, Sharon. *I Found a Leaf*. Minneapolis, Minn.: Lerner Publications, 1967.
Lewin, Betsy. *Animal Snackers*. New York: Dodd, Mead, 1980.
Lewis, Stephen. *Zoo City*. New York: Greenwillow Books, 1976.

McGovern, Ann. *Little Whole*. New York: Scholastic Book Services, Four Winds, 1978.
Mari, Dela, and Enzo Mari. *The Apple and the Moth*. New York: Pantheon Books, 1970.
———. *The Chicken and the Egg*. New York: Pantheon Books, 1970.
Memling, Carl. *What's in the Park?* New York: Parents Magazine Press, 1971.
Moncure, Jane. *Animal, Animal, Where Do You Live?* Chicago: Childrens Press, 1976.
———. *Thank You, Animal Friends*. Chicago: Childrens Press, 1976.
———. *What Will It Be?* Chicago: Childrens Press, 1976.
Morris, Robert A. *Dolphin*. New York: Harper & Row, 1975.
Parnall, Peter. *Alfalfa Hill*. New York: Doubleday, 1975.
Pfloog, J. *Animals on the Farm*. New York: Golden Press, 1977.
Schneider, Herman, and Nina Schneider. *Science Fun with a Flashlight*. New York: McGraw-Hill, 1975.
———. *Science Fun for You in a Minute or Two*. New York: McGraw-Hill, 1975.
Selsam, Millicent. *Egg to Chick*. New York: Harper & Row, 1970.
Shaw, Evelyn. *Octopus*. New York: Harper & Row, 1971.
Simon, Seymour. *Animal Fact/Animal Fable*. New York: Crown Publishers, 1979.
Tresselt, Alvin. *Autumn Harvest*. New York: Lothrop, Lee & Shepard, 1951.
———. *The Frog in the Well*. New York: Lothrop, Lee & Shepard, 1958.
———. *Hi, Mr. Robin*. New York: Lothrop, Lee & Shepard, 1950.
———. *Hide and Seek Fog*. New York: Lothrop, Lee & Shepard, 1965.
———. *I Saw the Sea Come In*. New York: Lothrop, Lee & Shepard, 1954.
———. *Johnny Maple Leaf*. New York: Lothrop, Lee & Shepard, 1948.
———. *Rain Drop Splash*. New York: Lothrop, Lee & Shepard, 1946.
———. *Sun Up*. New York: Lothrop, Lee & Shepard, 1949.
———. *White Snow, Bright Snow*. New York: Lothrop, Lee & Shepard, 1947.
Udry, Janice May. *A Tree Is Nice*. New York: Harper & Row, 1956.
Watson, Aldren. *My Garden Grows*. New York: The Viking Press, 1962.
Watson, Nancy. *Sugar on Snow*. New York: The Viking Press, 1964.
Webber, Irma. *Travelers All*. Reading, Mass.: Addison-Wesley, 1944.
Wheeler, Cindy. *A Good Day, A Good Night*. Philadelphia: J.B. Lippincott, 1980.
Wildsmith, Brian. *Squirrels*. New York: Franklin Watts, 1975.
Wolcott, Patty. *Tunafish Sandwiches*. Reading, Mass.: Addison-Wesley, 1975.
Wright, Dare. *Look at a Kitten*. New York: Random House, 1975.

274 / Curriculum

Zion, Gene. *All Falling Down*. New York: Harper & Row, 1951.
Zolotow, Charlotte. *Sleepy Book*. New York: Lothrop, Lee & Shepard, 1958.
———. *When the Wind Stops*. New York: Harper & Row, 1975.

Touch and Smell Books Children use all their senses to explore their environment. Several publishers have capitalized on their desire to touch and smell objects. These publishers include: Golden Scratch and Sniff Books; Golden Press/Western Series; Golden Press, Richard Scarry Books; and Random House, Sniffy Books.

SUMMARY

This chapter has presented the theories of teaching science and a selected basic science content for young children. The daily happenings in early childhood classrooms are always full of science-related events. Because of this, teachers have many opportunities to add to the content of their science programs. This chapter has covered basic materials and activities that can be adapted to the many science-related opportunities found in classrooms.

DIFFERENTIATING AND INTEGRATING MINI UNITS

Science is not taught in isolation but in a sequence of foundation basics. Because science is one of the two content areas, it serves as a framework for teaching other curricular areas and skill subjects. The following mini units will help you develop a basic foundation in science. Remember that each mini unit is designed to reinforce skills already learned and to provide new learning experiences as the children advance in maturity through the year.

Mini Units Differentiating and Integrating for **Three Year Olds**

	September	*January*	*May*
Topic	Seeds and how they grow.	Snow ice cream.	A pet rock.
Objectives	To provide children with the visual experience of sprouting seeds.	To provide children with an opportunity to eat frozen food.	To provide children with an opportunity to find a rock about the size of their own hands.

Mini Units Differentiating and Integrating for **Three Year Olds** (*cont.*)

	September	*January*	*May*
Materials	An aluminum pie pan, a sheet of paper toweling, one-half cup of water, twenty-five navy beans.	Ice cream mix for refrigerator tray, a cold snowy day.	Plastic eyes, Elmer's glue, various pieces of felt.
Procedures	Let children examine dry beans. Place the beans on the towel in the pie pan and pour water in pan.	Have children help prepare ice cream mix. Place in an aluminum dish or pan and cover. Have children place dish in snow.	Take children to a rocky area near school or provide a basket full of rocks. Compare sizes, shapes, and colors of rocks. Let children add features to make rock into "pet." Discuss care and feeding of pets.
Evaluation	Observation and discussion by children as the beans sprout.	Observe children's comparison of unfrozen mixture and frozen mixture.	Observe through listening what children know about pet care.
Integrating skills	Oral vocabulary building. Following directions.	Oral vocabulary building. Following directions read by teacher. Muscle control and development through mixing and pouring.	Math: comparison of shapes and sizes. Art: construction. Language: discussion and explanation.

Mini Units Differentiating and Integrating for **Four Year Olds**

	September	*January*	*May*
Topic	A shadow dance.	A zoo board.	A May Day picture.
Objectives	To help children understand principles of shadows.	To help children identify animals in a zoo.	To provide children with an opportunity to identify flowers.
Materials	Sunshine, assorted objects.	Books, pictures, films, filmstrips, toy zoo animals, paper, crayons.	"Flat flowers" such as vinca minor, pansies, or violets; pure white paper towels; thick, heavy books; manila 8" × 11" paper; Elmer's glue.

Mini Units Differentiating and Integrating for **Four Year Olds** (*cont.*)

	September	*January*	*May*
Procedures	Have children stand in sunlight so they cast a shadow. Play tag games with shadow.	Read stories to children. Show pictures, films, and filmstrips. Discuss the information and have children draw pictures.	Put fresh flowers between layers of toweling and place in books. Place heavy object on book. Press for seven to ten days. Glue on paper.
Evaluation	Observe children's action.	Place pictures on bulletin board. Observe children's discussions about own pictures.	Discussion and observation of skills.
Integrating skills	Physical exercise. Following directions.	Language development. Listening. Visual discrimination. Creative art.	Extension of verbal vocabulary. Physical exercise. Social skill of gift giving.

Mini Units Differentiating and Integrating for **Five Year Olds**

	September	*January*	*May*
Topic	Weed bouquets.	An inclined slide, gangplank, and ramp.	A pulley derrick.
Objectives	To provide children with an opportunity to observe, pick, and preserve weeds.	To expose children to the concept of an inclined plane.	To provide children with an opportunity to learn that a pulley allows weight to be lifted easily.
Materials	Weeds of any sort, one quart water, two tablespoons bleach, milk cartons with clay balls in bottoms.	Short and long boards, varying in width. Supports of varying heights. Small wheeled toys (not riding toys) and unwheeled toys.	Nail two large pullies to the bottom side of a large tree limb. Thread rope through each pulley. Tie knots in ends of rope so rope cannot be unthreaded.

Mini Units Differentiating and Integrating for **Five Year Olds** (*cont.*)

	September	*January*	*May*
Procedures	Pick a variety of weeds. Dip heads of weeds into water and bleach mixture until their color changes. Dry on newspaper and then place in containers.	Have children make various inclines and observe speed of wheeled toy.	Have children lift various objects using the rope. Have children lift objects without pulley. Discuss which was easier.
Evaluation	Observation of actions and finished products.	Discussion, observation, and participation.	Observation, participation, and discussion.
Integrating skills	Discussions. Physical exercise. Use of eye-hand coordination.	Physical exercise. General eye-hand coordination.	Physical exercise. Whole-body muscle development.

Levels of skill attainment in science will vary markedly in a group of children of the same chronological age and grade level. Mastery is sometimes linked to other skills, such as reading and mathematics. The following mastery lists show the varied skill levels in some typical classroom groups.

EVALUATION OF INDIVIDUAL DIFFERENCES

Mastery of Identifying Zoo Animals by Correct Name (Age range 3.1 to 3.5 by October 1)

Name	October	January	May
Alonzo	no	no	yes
Mary	no	yes	yes
Marian	no	yes	yes
Jackie	no	no	yes
Bruno	no	no	no
Margaret	yes	yes	yes
Wendell	no	yes	yes
Jo	no	no	yes
William	no	yes	yes
Wanda	no	no	no

Mastery of Identifying Zoo Animals by Correct Name (Age range 3.1 to 3.5 by October 1) *(cont.)*

Name	October	January	May
James	yes	yes	yes
Jess	no	no	no
Earl	no	no	yes
Tom	no	no	no
Emanuel	yes	yes	yes
Ruth	no	no	yes
Carmen	no	yes	yes
Nancy	no	yes	yes
Aileen	no	no	yes

Mastery of Identification that Water Remains Level Regardless of How Container Is Tipped (Age range 4.1 to 4.6 by October 1)

Name	October	January	May
Nolan	no	yes	yes
Gene	no	no	yes
Barbara	no	yes	yes
Curtis	no	no	no
Allen	yes	yes	yes
Crystal	no	no	yes
Alma	no	yes	yes
Louise	yes	yes	yes
Gerardo	no	no	no
Terry	no	no	yes
Harold	yes	yes	yes
June	no	yes	no
Bazdeo	no	no	yes
Tyrone	yes	yes	yes
Ray	no	no	yes
Suzanne	no	yes	yes
Eddie	no	yes	yes
Fred	yes	yes	yes

Mastery of Identification that Water Remains Level Regardless of How Container Is Tipped   (Age range 4.1 to 4.6 by October 1) (*cont.*)

Name	October	January	May
Sandra	no	yes	yes
Taisto	no	no	yes
Don	no	yes	yes

Mastery of Observation that Water Has Surface Tension   (Age range 5.0 to 5.4 by October 1)

Name	October	January	May
Eduardo	no	yes	yes
Edna	no	no	yes
Robert	yes	yes	yes
Juanita	no	no	no
Grace	no	no	yes
Bonnie	yes	yes	yes
Fred	no	no	no
Terry	no	no	yes
Mozelle	no	yes	yes
Albert	no	no	no
Warren	no	no	yes
Hyang	yes	yes	yes
Marjorie	no	yes	yes
Charles	no	no	no
Cecil	no	yes	yes
Mirzo	no	yes	yes
Bill	no	yes	yes
Robert	no	no	no
Michael	no	no	yes
Dorothy	yes	yes	yes
Roy	no	no	yes
Rickey	no	yes	yes

LEARNING GOALS FOR CHILDREN

Your school will have defined certain science-related skills each child is expected to master before leaving the kindergarten. Knowledge of the following general goals will help you become a better teacher of young children:

- ✔ The child can discuss science-related activities and events, using the correct terminology.
- ✔ The child can care for plants and animals in the classroom.
- ✔ The child can manipulate science equipment.
- ✔ The child shows interest in pictures of related science events.
- ✔ the child expresses a desire to share science-related objects and events.

BASIC SKILLS SEQUENCE CHART

See page 189 for an explanation of how to use skills sequence charts.

Science Skills

Key symbols: (✔) Introduction   (✔✔) Extension and reinforcement

Skill	Level 1	Level 2	Level 3
Space			
Describe apparent changes in the size of an object seen at various distances	✔	✔✔	✔✔
Estimate whether a known object is near or far by observing its apparent size	✔	✔✔	✔✔
Demonstrate how to measure and compare the distance between themselves and an object using linear devices	✔	✔✔	✔✔
Measure several objects using a standard measure		✔	✔✔
Write measurements in terms of a standard		✔	✔✔
Divide standards into equal parts		✔	✔✔
Measure dimensions in feet and inches using various devices		✔	✔✔
Identify a meter and a centimeter, and state that these are standard		✔	✔✔
Measure objects and communicate measurements in meters and centimeters		✔	✔✔
Identify processes in science and everyday life that involve measurement			✔
Name some common instruments used in measurement			✔
Use a measuring instrument to measure length, width, and height accurately			✔
Experiment with various materials to find their advantages and disadvantages as measuring devices			✔

Science / 281

Science Skills (cont.)

Key symbols: (✔) Introduction   (✔✔) Extension and reinforcement

Skill	Level 1	Level 2	Level 3
Measure common objects in English units (feet and inches)			✔
Relate units of the English system: inches to feet to yards			✔
Measure common objects in the primary metric units: meter, centimeter, and millimeter			✔
Distinguish situations in which accurate measurements are not needed			✔
Apply rough measuring techniques and estimate distances			✔
Use a spring balance			✔
Construct balances using simple materials			✔
Establish a standard for weight measurement			✔
Demonstrate that objects of equal weight can be balanced			✔

Time

Skill	Level 1	Level 2	Level 3
Arrange a series of related events in a logical sequence	✔	✔✔	✔✔
Compare two events to determine which takes longer	✔	✔✔	✔✔
Recognize that a week is made up of seven calendar days	✔	✔✔	✔✔
Identify that a month is longer than a week and that a year is longer than a month	✔	✔✔	✔✔
Describe regularly repeating events upon which some timepieces are based		✔	✔✔
Describe the energy sources needed to operate some timepieces		✔	✔✔
State the time on the hour, half hour, and quarter hour by observing a clock face		✔	✔✔
Name the units of time and state their relationships			✔
Time common events in seconds, minutes, and hours			✔
List the elements necessary to produce a shadow			✔
Experiment with various materials to produce shadows			✔
Infer the shape of an object by looking at its shadow			✔
Distinguish between opaque, translucent, and transparent objects			✔
List various sources of light			✔
Predict whether an object could be seen under specified conditions			✔
Recognize the apparent motion of the sun and moon over small periods of time			✔
Identify swirls or swirling objects in the enviornment			✔
Recognize that the apparent motion of an object may be the result of the movement of something else			✔
Demonstrate the relation of sunlight to day and night by experimenting with a simple globe			✔

282 / Curriculum

Science Skills (*cont.*)

Key symbols: (✔) Introduction   (✔✔) Extension and reinforcement

Skill	Level 1	Level 2	Level 3
Predict, with the help of a globe, where it is day and night at a particular time			✔
Observe that the sun is the source of almost all natural light on earth			✔
Recognize and explain that many of the objects we see reflect light			✔
Recognize that the apparent size of an object changes with distance			✔

Energy

Skill	Level 1	Level 2	Level 3
State that work has been done when an object has been pushed or pulled	✔	✔✔	✔✔
Construct simple machines using common objects	✔	✔✔	✔✔
Demonstrate the use of simple machines	✔	✔✔	✔✔
Recognize and identify the three simple machines used in familiar implements	✔	✔✔	✔✔
Describe a situation in which work has been done by naming the object moved and the force that caused the movement		✔	✔✔
Describe a situation in which application of a force does not cause work to be done, and explain why		✔	✔✔
Demonstrate that the force exerted by a moving object can cause another object to do work		✔	✔✔
Identify the energy supply that moves each object in simple instructions between one object and another		✔	✔✔
Name some sources of energy (food, fuel, electricity, moving air or water, and so on)		✔	✔✔
Identify the sun as the basic energy source for the formation of foods and fuels		✔	✔✔
Describe things that air can do			✔
Give evidence for the presence of air even though it is invisible			✔
Apply certain concepts about air, such as making a second hole in a can of liquid so that it will empty faster; tell why this works			✔
Demonstrate some effects of air pressure using everyday objects			✔
Describe how to lift a heavy object given an unlimited number of balloons			✔
Demonstrate that cooled air is heavier than the same volume of warmer air			✔
Demonstrate that warmed air is lighter than cooled air			✔
Infer that warmed air rises relative to cooler air by observing visible matter			✔
Demonstrate unreliability of human skin as a temperature sensor, to themselves and to others			✔
Measure temperature with a thermometer			✔
Make valid comparisons			✔

Science Skills *(cont.)*

Key symbols: (✔) Introduction   (✔✔) Extension and reinforcement

Skill	Level 1	Level 2	Level 3
Demonstrate expansion and contraction with changes of temperature in gases, liquids, and solids			✔
Apply the lesson's concepts to thermometers and to their general observations of the behavior of matter			✔
Construct a graph showing time and temperature change over a period of time			✔
Apply and demonstrate the concept of an insulator			✔
Distinguish between common conductors and common insulators			✔

Matter

Skill	Level 1	Level 2	Level 3
Identify an object from a description of its properties	✔	✔✔	✔✔
Sort and classify a collection of objects according to their physical properties	✔	✔✔	✔✔
Describe objects and infer the identity of an object from nonvisual observations	✔	✔✔	✔✔
Identify objects as matter in the form of solids, liquids, or gases		✔	✔✔
Demonstrate that familiar solids, liquids, and gases take up space		✔	✔✔
Define matter as anything that takes up space		✔	✔✔
Perform simple experiments in which matter seems to disappear or become invisible (dissolving, evaporating)		✔	✔✔
Demonstrate by taste or smell that tiny particles of matter are still present after a substance has been dissolved or evaporated		✔	✔✔
Infer from observations that matter is composed of tiny particles too small to be seen		✔	✔✔
Name some of the organisms involved in the decay of a log			✔
Begin to observe that life goes on in cycles			✔
Control variables in simple soil experiments			✔
Infer the importance of organic matter in soils from results of experiments			✔
Distinguish and name the main components of soil (rock, organic matter, water)			✔
Describe a simple community (lawn, desert, pond, seashore, vacant lot, woodland)			✔
Relate the existence and behavior of living organisms to the well-being of human beings or to the overall life community			✔
Recognize that "helpful" and "harmful" are arbitrary descriptions of organisms			✔
Apply the information in the lesson to observations made at home, play, and school			✔
Name and describe some of the life habits of selected organisms			✔

ADDITIONAL READINGS

Charles, Elizabeth. *How to Keep Your Pet Healthy*. New York: Collier Books, 1974.

Croft, J. Doreen, and Robert D. Hess. *An Activities Handbook for Teachers of Young Children*. 3rd ed. Boston: Houghton Mifflin, 1980.

Good, Ronald G. *How Children Learn Science*. New York: Macmillan, 1977.

Harlan, Jean. *Science Experiences for the Early Childhood Years*. 2nd ed. Columbus, Ohio: Charles E. Merrill, 1980.

Roche, Ruth L. *The Child and Science: Wondering, Exploring, Growing*. Washington, D.C.: Association for Childhood Education International, 1977.

Trojcak, D. A. *Science with Children*. New York: McGraw-Hill, 1979.

Victor, Edward. *Science for the Elementary School*. 4th ed. New York: Macmillan, 1980.

CHAPTER 9
Mathematics

Exploration Tasks

After studying this chapter, you should be able to complete these tasks:
- Discuss and identify the seven basic concepts to be taught to young children.
- Discuss Piaget's theory of mathematics readiness stages and describe two tasks that can determine a child's readiness.
- List some of the basic materials appropriate for mathematics teaching.
- Plan units and demonstrations that will enable you to present and evaluate instruction.
- Integrate mathematics activities with other curricular areas.

Children are not cars that you turn off an assembly line. Children come to us different; and if we do our job well, they should emerge from our experiences even more different, and not alike as one Ford is like the other.

Ira J. Gordon

OVERVIEW

Jim: "I can count to ten. Wanna hear me?"

Bob: "I can, too."

Jim: "One, two, four, six, seven, ten!"

Bob: "That's not right."

Jim: "Yes it is."

Bob: "No it's not. Teacher, Jim can't count to ten, can he?"

Mathematics is such an integral part of a young child's life that teachers and parents often do not realize the major role mathematical operations play in a child's daily existence. The child's oral language consistently reveals knowledge of comparisons, measurement, and number: "Give me the biggest!" "I want the round one!" "It costs a quarter." "I know my telephone number." "My grandmother lives two hours from here." "When the big hand is on the nine we go outside." "I have two dimes and a penny." "My brother gave me a nickel." "I am three and a half." "I have two new shoes." All of these statements divulge interest in and use of mathematical terms and concepts.

You can see from the children's comments in the preceding paragraph that mathematics is not taught in isolation, for good reason. Young children need concrete experiences in applying the use of the terms and concepts they are learning. As a teacher of young children you will need to plan and supply many activities and materials that will encourage mathematical skill development.

THEORETICAL CONTEXT

The basic theory for teaching young children mathematics is a sensorimotor approach. This approach requires that children have many opportunities to explore a rich mathematical environment; to have an opportunity to solve problems; and to have a well-planned, teacher-directed, organized mathematical program.

This organized mathematical program should include:

1. *Matching:* Matching sets containing the same number of objects, matching of coins
2. *Identification:* Identifying the larger of two groups containing unequal numbers of objects; associating numerals with corresponding groups of objects; associating the numeral 0 with an empty set; and naming coins — penny, nickel, dime, and quarter
3. *Sequencing:* Counting from 1 to 10; arranging numerals 1 to 10 in correct sequence; identifying objects in sequence using *first, last, next,* and *middle*; identifying objects in a sequence using ordinal numbers *first* to *fifth*; following directions to complete a task consisting of numbered steps

Piaget is an advocate of the sensorimotor approach to teaching math. In his book *The Child's Conception of Numbers,* Piaget stated that mathematical learning takes place in three stages: (1) coordination within the field of perception; (2) operations that go beyond the field of perception; and (3) transition from perception to deduction, progressive coordination of operations, and gradual development of reversibility. In Piaget's 1970 book

Science of Education and the Psychology of the Child (page 98), he stated that sensorimotor activities are a preparation for the logical operations — as logic is based on coordination of action before the level of language development.

For further information and research data on mathematical theories and content, read *Basic Skills in Kindergarten: Foundation for Formal Learning* edited by Walter B. Barbe (Columbus, Ohio: Zaner Bloser, 1980).

BASIC CONCEPTS

Vocabulary of Comparison

Because young children are very verbal, the development of a vocabulary of number concepts by comparison — of sizes, shapes, textures, temperatures, locations, and coin values — is comparatively easy. Children bring to the classroom many mathematical experiences from their home environment. These experiences, combined with planned environmental challenges in the classroom, are the basis for the development of a meaningful vocabulary of comparison. On the following pages we have listed a number of mathematical terms. If you use the list as a selector guide for activities and materials you will be able to extend your own vocabulary and establish centers that include mathematics.

Mathematical terms

Number	*Size*	*Shape*
All	Alike	Center
None	Different	Circle
Amount	Big	Corner
Single	Bigger	Large
Both	Biggest	Larger
Several	Cup	Largest
Few	Double	Long
Dozen	Equal	Short
Enough	Half	Round
Fewer	Height	Row
Fewest	Inch	Same shape
Gallon	Length	Shorter
How many	Little	Shortest
Many	Measure	Square
More	Tiny	Straight
Most	Huge	Curved
Pair		Tall
Whole		Taller
		Tallest
		Triangle

Location		
Upper	Lowest	Top
Up	Over	By
From	Under	Close
High	Above	Closer
Higher	Below	Closest
Highest	Before	Distance
Left	After	First

Mathematical terms (cont.)

Location
Right	Beside	Next
Low	Between	Last
Lower	Bottom	Middle

Coin-values — *Speed* — *Temperature*

Coin-values	Speed	Temperature
Cent-penny	Fast	Hot
Count	Slow	Cold
Dime	Crawl	Warm
Dollar	Walk	Cool
Nickel	Run	Boiling
Quarter		Frozen
		Chilly

Metric and English Standard Measure

Standard measure is an important part of mathematics taught to young children. As a child measures (or uses equipment that measures) the many things found in the learning environment, he or she experiences the exactness innate to measurement. As a skill, measurement is taught later in the school years. Nevertheless, some knowledge of measurement evolves because of use. Linear measure, time, capacity, weight, temperature, speed, quantity, and money are all parts of standard measure.

Introduction of Metric Measure Since the United States is gradually changing to the metric system, it is important that you as a teacher provide metric equipment, activities, and vocabulary. Children should learn the metric system naturally and should not be confused with conversion charts.

The following horizontal example shows the relationship between the six main prefixes used in everyday metric use.

1000	100	10	1/10	1/100	1/1000	Unit
kilo-	hecto-	deka-	deci-	centi-	milli-	meter
						liter
						gram

Time measure remains the same: 60 seconds = 1 minute, 60 minutes = 1 hour, 24 hours = 1 day, 7 days = 1 week, 365 days = 1 year, and 366 days = 1 leap year. A calendar month is 28, 29, 30, or 31 days long.

Money values remain the same, although the money standards of other countries are different from that of the United States.

Linear measure, capacity, weight, and speed will change: inches to centimeters, feet to decimeters, yards to meters, rods to dekameters, and miles to kilometers. In dry measure: pints to liters, quarts to liters, pecks to liters, and bushels to liters. In liquid measures: pints to liters, quarts to liters, gallons to liters, and barrels to liters. All dry and liquid measures become liters.

In weight measure, ounces become grams and pounds become kilograms.

In temperature, degrees Fahrenheit change to degrees centigrade. Speed changes from miles per hour to kilometers per hour. In quantity we will still use dozens and pairs.

As you plan food preparation activities for children you may need to convert old recipes to metric measures. The following equivalency chart will help you make the recipe successful:

1 tsp.	$\frac{1}{6}$ oz.	4.9 milligrams
1 tbsp.	$\frac{1}{2}$ oz.	14.8 milligrams
1 cup	8 oz.	2.25 deciliters
1 pint	16 oz.	4.5 deciliters
4 $\frac{1}{3}$ cups	35 $\frac{1}{6}$ oz.	1 liter (10 deciliters)

Measurement Activities Children's first experiences with measurement occur as they match things directly such as puzzle pieces or dominoes, fit certain shapes into corresponding holes, and build with blocks. Times are naturally associated with certain places (home, school, church, grocery store) and events (breakfast, lunch, dinner, bedtime, nap time, play time, story time). Five year olds will easily learn the sequence of the events of the classroom; a large clock (placed at their eye level) will provide many time-learning experiences as they match a toy clock for play time, clean-up time, music time, and so on. The concept of speed has been presented many times on the children's home TV sets. Although they don't have an accurate understanding of speed they have already established a large vocabulary of speed words. Many of the social studies activities in a regular classroom present miniature occasions for "playing" speed — transportation activities, films, filmstrips, field trips, and walks are only a few such activities. Capacity is also easily taught. Science activities are a natural outlet for using capacity, equipment, and material. Food preparation, pet care, experiments, and water and sand play all require capacity activities.

Weight is another measuring experience that children have encountered at home. They weigh themselves on the bathroom scales and are weighed by doctors or nurses for their medical records. They also see and hear their parents buying a pound of beans, ten pounds of potatoes, a pound of bananas,

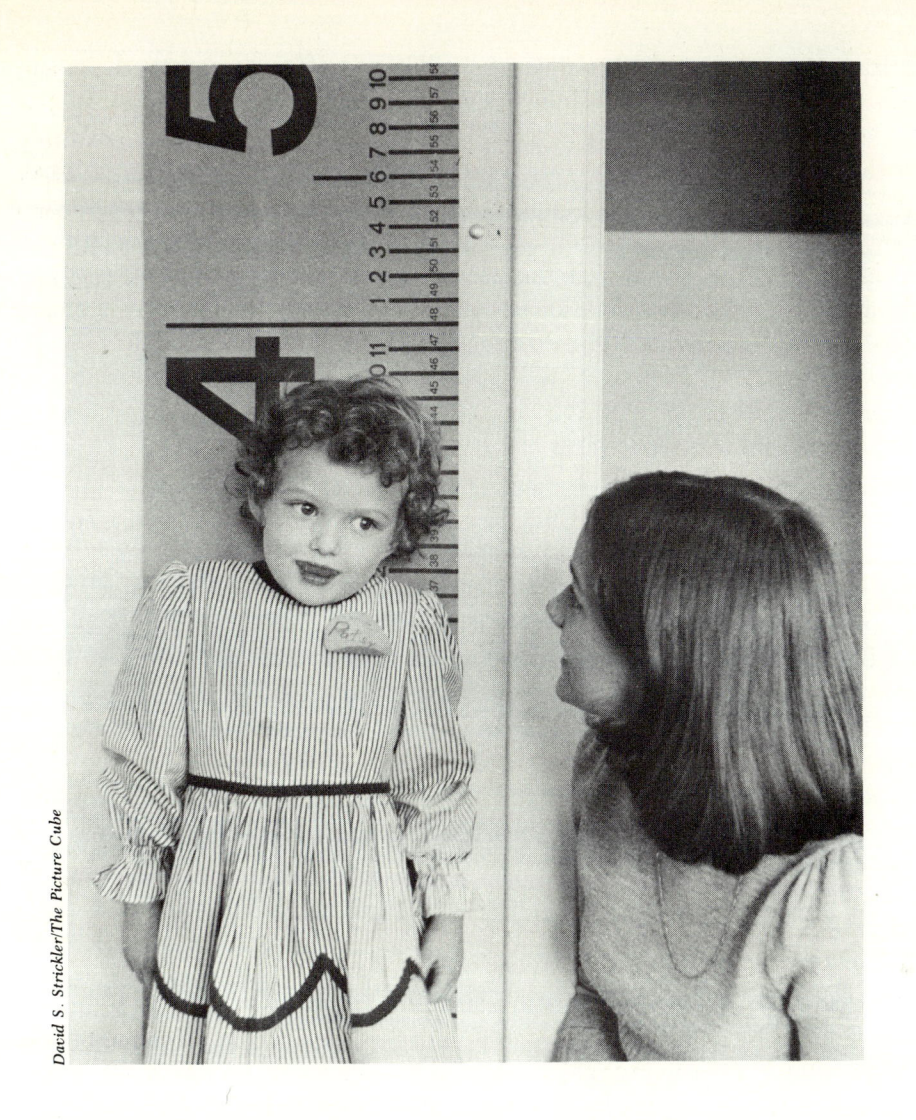

Children learn best through personal experiences.

a pound of candy. Classroom scales provide an opportunity for children to "see" how they grow; when coupled with a height chart display, the scale can help children visualize changes in their size.

Learning about temperature is a natural outgrowth of science teaching and environmental happenings. It is almost impossible not to have children learn about temperature. Money identification is also a normal process. Pennies, nickels, dimes, quarters, half dollars, dollars, and five dollars were all discussed in a recent three-year-old play situation with a cash register, play money, and a box full of classroom toys. Although they spoke the terms they did not know the related values. When the same play situation was set up in a five-year-old room the vocabulary increased to one hundred dollars, ten million, and variations on millions. As is apparent, the language was learned but not the value. Visual discrimination of a penny, nickel, dime, quarter, and dollar was accomplished by many of the four year olds in the same school setting. Quantitative measure is also introduced early in a child's life. At the supermarket they may buy a dozen eggs, oranges, lemons, or rolls. A new pair of shoes quickly includes the word *pair* in their vocabulary and in the winter the pair of mittens reinforces the use of the term. Young children do not have a number concept of what makes a dozen or a pair but do identify the vocabulary with items in their environment.

Numeration

Numeral functions occur in many of the everyday activities in a regular program for three, four, and five year olds. Numeral usage is common in a teacher's vocabulary: "It is 10 o'clock and time for us to go outside." "Put the balls in the first box." "Two children may paint at the easel." Furthermore, children use number functions as they distribute supplies, set a table, play games, or follow directions.

A full understanding of numeration is not accomplished during the early years but the vocabulary, the operations, and the materials are introduced. The skills of numeration include recognizing that numerals name numbers, associating word names with their corresponding numerals, reading and writing one-digit numerals, and associating numerals with intervals along a number line.

Number Concepts

The cardinal order of the numbers one through ten is taught by activities that require the children to count or determine how many. Ordinal numbers are taught by identifying which one — first, last, and so on. Recognition and use of the concepts of more, less, greater, smaller, few, and many are taught through comparison of numbers of concrete objects.

Sets

To understand what a number means, children need to comprehend vividly what a number means in relation to a group as a measurable whole made up of separate items. This is developed from experiences in one-to-one correspondence (pairs or matching) or collections of things (a set or subset). Objects belonging to a set are called *members* or *elements* and a set may have many, a few, or no members. A *subset* is a part of a set that has a common element not found in the other members of the set. For example:

The boys and girls of a kindergarten are a set. The boys are a subset of the set.

Conservation of Quantity

Young children like to pour water, sand, or any other material that has fluid properties. Conservation of quantity is begun in the sand and water play activities described in the science chapter. The object of teaching this concept is to understand that the quantity of the matter remains constant regardless of its shape.

Plane Geometry

As in most math activities the learning and teaching of plane geometry occurs through normal play and the activities planned by the teacher. Plane geometry includes identification of circles, triangles, squares, and rectangles as well as classifying objects by shape. Often lessons in identifying the color of an object include the geometric shape of the object. "Give me the blue circle," "Show me the red square," or "Put the yellow triangle on the green triangle."

MENTAL READINESS FOR MATHEMATICS

In Chapter 3 we reviewed the preoperational stage in children's intellectual development — ages 2–7 — as identified by psychologist Jean Piaget. In this stage, children reason and explain on the basis of intuition instead of logic, and because of this are very poor at understanding numbers and relationships. Piaget's research provided evidence that children cannot conceptualize number meaning until they understand classes and relationships. Piaget calls this the *ability to conserve*, that is, to realize that quantity or volume remains the same regardless of how it is divided into parts. Because children differ, however, chronological age is only a partial guide to the stages of ability. The tasks listed below are based on Piaget's tasks. After teaching these lessons in class you will understand the reasoning for his statements. Until a child can perform most of the following tasks successfully, it is doubtful that he or she is ready for addition and subtraction. It is also important to remember that Piaget is not talking about rote memory but true assimilation. Children often imitate without understanding.

Task: Conservation of Quantity

Materials Four *identical* transparent containers. Two of the four containers should be identical in capacity but different in shape–thinner or flatter. Two-quart containers of water: one quart with yellow food coloring added, one quart with green food coloring added. (Never use a coloring agent that could be harmful to a child. Always discourage children from drinking any liquids used in classroom tasks.)

Procedure Fill one of the four containers half full of the yellow water. Fill another container half full of green water. Ask the child, "Do the two containers have the same amount of water?" Be sure the child says that they are the same.

Pour half of the green water into another container and ask, "Do the containers with the green water have as much water as the container with the yellow water?"

Pour half of the green water from the two containers into the thinner or flatter container. Ask "Which container has more water, the new container or the container with the yellow water?"

Pour the green water back into the original container and ask "Is the amount of green water the same as the yellow water?"

Evaluation Generally children below the average mental age of seven (remember children differ in abilities) do not think that the quantity of water stays the same when it is transferred to various containers.

Task: Correspondence of Quantity

Materials Six blocks (all the same color). Six rods (about one-inch in diameter and six inches long so they can't be stuck into the nose or ear or be swallowed.)

Procedure Place the six blocks in front of the child. Tell the child "Pick up one rod for each block."

When the child is finished, say "Put one rod on each block."
(If the child can't do this stop here.)

Change the position of the blocks and put the rods in the spaces between the blocks. Ask "Are they the same now or are there more rods or more blocks?"

Rearrange the blocks and rods again and ask the same questions.

Evaluation Piaget believes that children do not have the basic concepts necessary for learning number operations unless there is understanding of permanence and equivalence of sets regardless of forms of display.

Task: Correspondence of Set Elements in a Series

Materials A 1-inch-diameter dowel rod 3 feet long. Cut the rod into ten pieces, making each piece ¼ inch longer than the one preceding it. Shortest piece should be 2¼ inches.

A ½-inch-diameter dowel rod 2 feet long. Cut the rod into ten pieces, varying the length of each piece by ¼ of an inch. Shortest piece should be 1 inch.

Procedure Place the 1-inch (diameter) rods in front of the child. Tell the child that each rod represents a child in the class. He or she is to put the "children" in a line, with the shortest child at one end and the tallest child at the other end. Each of the children in between should get a little bit taller. Leave these rods in place when the child has finished.

Next, place the ½-inch (diameter) rods in front of the child. Say that each rod represents a flag, and each child should have a flag that is "just his or her size." The smallest child should have the smallest flag and each child in line should have the right size flag, smallest to largest. Have the child arrange the rod flags in a row above the rods representing the children.

Change the order of the flags. See if the child can point to the smallest child and the smallest flag, and so forth.

Mix the rods up. Touch one rod and ask which flag that child will hold. Continue with several rods representing children.

Evaluation Piaget believes that "all correpondence presupposes seriation, and when seriation is not possible, neither is serial correspondence." This task determines whether or not a child can place objects in a series, make a one-to-one correspondence between two series, and maintain the correspondence.

Task: Conservation of Length

Materials Two dowel rods about 5 inches long. A piece of rope about 7 inches long. Two strips of thin cardboard 12 inches long and about ½ inch wide. Scissors.

Procedure Place the two rods side by side. Ask if the two rods are the same length or if one is longer than the other.

Remove one rod and replace it with the rope making sure the ends of the rope are aligned exactly with the ends of the rod (the rope has a bend in it). Ask the child if the rod and the rope are the same or if one is longer than the other.

Evaluation Measurement requires that the measuring device remains the same in length regardless of its position. Piaget's results from this task showed that 15 percent of children age 4½ answered correctly and 90 percent of the children age 5½ answered correctly.

PROJECT
Attitudes Toward Mathematics

If you analyze your own experiences in learning mathematics as a child, you will become more aware of the ways a teacher may influence the learning process.

1. Did you enjoy math activities as a young child? Why or why not?
2. Did you ever have difficulty in learning a new math concept? What was your teacher's response? How did you finally overcome this difficulty?
3. Did your attitude toward mathematics change as you advanced further in school? If yes, in what ways? What do you think accounted for these changes? If no, why do you think your early attitude persisted?
4. Taking into account current theories and methods relating to the teaching of mathematics (as discussed in this chapter), are there ways in which your early math experiences might have been improved? Write a paragraph describing these improved methods.

The preceding discussion on Piaget's findings of children's mental readiness for mathematics during the preoperational stage (ages 2 through 7) has been simplified to enable students to gain an insight into the importance of Piaget's studies. For complete preparation you should read the studies in full.

While Piaget is recognized by many leading educators as the foremost authority on a child's thought processes and mathematics, several other researchers have conducted studies of various components of mathematics and the young child. See the additional readings at the end of this chapter for a list of their works.

BOOKS, MATERIALS, AND EQUIPMENT
Math Books for Children

Aulaire, Ingrid. *Don't Count Your Chicks*. New York: Doubleday, 1973.
Berenstain, Stan, and Jan Berenstain. *The Berenstain Bear's Counting Book*. New York: Random House, 1976.

Brewer, Mary. *Which Is Biggest?* Chicago: Childrens Press, 1976.

Budney, Blossom. *A Kiss Is Round*. New York: Lothrop, Lee & Shepard, 1954.

Carle, Eric. *The Very Hungry Caterpillar*. New York: Philomel Books, 1969.

Froman, Robert. *Animals Are Easy as Pie*. New York: Thomas Y. Crowell Co., 1976.

Hall, Adelaide. *Let's Count*. Reading, Mass.: Addison-Wesley, 1976.

Hoban, Tana. *Count and See*. New York: Macmillan, 1972.

———. *Push-Pull, Empty-Full*. New York: Macmillan, 1972.

———. *Shapes and Things*. New York: Macmillan, 1970.

Hughes, Peter. *The Emperor's Oblong Pancake*. New York: Abelard-Schuman, 1976.

Ipcar, Dahlou. *Brown Cow Farm*. New York: Doubleday, 1959.

Langstaff, John. *Over in the Meadow*. New York: Harcourt Brace Jovanovich, 1967.

Mendoza, George. *The Scarecrow Clock*. New York: Holt, Rinehart and Winston, 1971.

Miller, J. P. *Big and Little*. New York: Random House, 1976.

Moncure, Jane Belk. *Magic Monsters Count to Ten*. Mankato, Minn.: The Child's World, 1979.

Poulet, Virginia. *Blue Bug's Treasure*. Chicago: Childrens Press, 1976.

Ruben, Patricia. *What is New? What is Missing? What is Different?* Philadelphia: J.B. Lippincott, 1978.

Schlein, Miriam. *Shapes*. Reading, Mass.: Addison-Wesley, 1952.

Shapp, Martha, and Charles Shapp. *Let's Find Out About What's Big and What's Small*. New York: Franklin Watts, Inc. 1975.

Shapur, Fredun. *Round and Round and Square*. New York: Abelard-Schuman, 1965.

Sugita, Yutaka. *Good Night — 1, 2, 3*. New York: Abelard-Schuman, 1971.

Weiss, Malcolm E. *666 Jellybeans! All That?*. New York: Thomas Y. Crowell Co., 1976.

Math Equipment and Materials

Many materials purchased for general use in a classroom may be used to present mathematical concepts. Math is taught both directly and indirectly; therefore, analyze all your equipment and materials in light of the math properties taught through normal use. Remember also that children differ in math abilities just as they differ in other abilities. Piaget's studies in math, described earlier in this chapter, will aid you in your selection of materials and activities.

Sorting and sequencing can be taught through play.

Equipment and material

Small blocks

Tactile numeral blocks
Colored counting blocks
Tactile domino blocks
Outdoor domino blocks

Rods and counters

Counting frames
Pegs and pegboards
Cuisenaire rods®
Counting sticks
Bead abacus
Stacking counters

Geometric and parquetry shapes

Bingo-type games that match shapes
Shapes: hexagon, square, oblong, triangle, circle: plastic or wood

Number operations

Cardinality, order, sequence, pairs, set, subset, plane geometry forms

Comparison, set, subsets, pairs, conservation

Set, subset, conservation, comparison, pairing and matching

Flannel cut-out shapes
Shape disks
Counting and sorting trays
Fraction disks
Fit-a-size-and-shape board
Parquetry design shapes

Equipment and material **Time and measurement**
Clocks

Large miniature clocks   Sequence and comparison of
Large clock with large black   numbers
  numbers
Small miniature clocks
Timer clocks

Calendars

Day-by-day movable date cal-   Sequence and comparison of
  endars   numbers
Regular calendars

Length measures

Height strips   Cardinality, sequence, com-
Yardsticks   parison of numbers
Beginner rules
Measuring tapes
Step-on floor tapes, 1 to 10
  feet long

Liquid or dry measures

Balance scale   Comparison of numbers and
Aluminum liquid measures   conservation of quantity
Unbreakable plastic capacity
  measures

Temperature measures

Indoor-outdoor thermometer   Order, sequence, comparison
Large educational
  thermometer
Plastic "thermometer"
  with adjustable degree band

SUMMARY

Mathematics in early childhood programs occurs in many different activities during the day. This chapter has presented a variety of theories, content areas, activities, and materials, appropriate for teaching mathematics to young children.

DIFFERENTIATING AND INTEGRATING MINI UNITS

As in the other curricular areas in a program for young children, mathematics is only occasionally taught as an isolated subject. Many opportunities will lend themselves to mathematical activities. These activities should be enjoyable, should require verbal responses, and should often involve physical activity. Develop more mini units, keeping in mind two standards: appropriateness of the lessons to the ability and maturity of the children and previous learning experiences.

Mini Units   Differentiating and Integrating for **Three Year Olds**

	September	*January*	*May*
Topic	An apple a day.	A cake walk.	Learning number words.
Objectives	To provide a basis for a beginning understanding of fractions.	To expose children to the idea that a whole object can be divided into many equal parts.	To provide children with an opportunity to hear and say number words.
Materials	Two apples and a knife.	Two boxes of prepared cake mix. Large rectangular baking pans. Frosting. A knife. Paper plates.	Anything that has more than one part, such as steps, blocks, silverware, candy.
Procedures	Cut apple in half. Have child put two parts together to make whole. Have child share half the apple with a friend.	Children mix cake mix and pour into pans. Children frost baked cakes. Count children, cut cake in that number of pieces. Place one piece of cake on a paper plate for each child. Place plates on floor in a circle.	Paint, step on, or touch objects and count them orally. Have child paint, step on, or touch and count with you.

Mini Units Differentiating and Integrating for **Three Year Olds** (*cont.*)

	September	*January*	*May*
		Have children walk behind cake circle while music plays. When music stops each child sits on floor and eats nearest piece of cake.	
Evaluation	Select another apple; have children tell you and show you how two children can share one apple.	Children count pieces of cut cake before served, then count the cake on plates. The whole doesn't change when cut in pieces.	Accomplishment of activity.
Integrating skills	Oral language. Listening. Sharing.	Oral language. Listening. Physical activity.	Oral language. Physical activity. Listening.

Mini Units Differentiating and Integrating for **Four Year Olds**

	September	*January*	*May*
Topic	Playing store.	Big and little shadows.	A parallel game.
Objectives	To introduce terms and visual identification of coins.	To introduce varying sizes of big and little.	To introduce the concept of parallel lines.
Materials	Table, two shelves, cash register. (Empty) containers of children's favorite foods, drinks, and candy. Small classroom toys. Play coins.	A sunny afternoon. Christmas wrapping ribbon. Scissors. Objects in the environment that cast shadows. Sheets of paper and a stapler.	Regular classroom furniture and equipment. Box of multicolored stars.
Procedures	Tape a play coin on each item to be sold. One child is storekeeper; others "buy" items by matching like coins.	Have children find shadows. Measure the shadow with lengths of ribbon. Cut ribbons and staple paper labeled as to which shadow it	Teacher identifies several objects in the room having parallel lines: train tracks, chair rounds, shelving, and so on. Children find similar

302 / Curriculum

Mini Units Differentiating and Integrating for **Four Year Olds** (cont.)

	September	January	May
		represented. Have children tell whether each is big or little.	lines and put stars matching in color on matching parallel lines.
Evaluation	Ability to match price coin taped on item with play coin.	Ability of children to identify size.	Ability of children to identify parallel lines in environment.
Integrating skills	Physical activity. Visual discrimination. Oral vocabulary extension.	Science. Physical activity. Oral language.	Oral language. Visual discrimination. Following directions. Physical activity.

Mini Units Differentiating and Integrating for **Five Year Olds**

	September	January	May
Topic	A penny candy store.	Number cards.	Counting surprises.
Objectives	To help children identify the penny coin and written symbols of 1¢, 2¢, 3¢, 4¢, and 5¢.	To help children identify number symbols by matching like numbers.	To help children count objects one through ten.
Materials	Pieces of candy in varying sizes. Labels of 1¢, 2¢, 3¢, 4¢, and 5¢. One hundred pennies, each marked with a dot of red nail polish (to identify "school" penny).	Twenty cards, numbered 1–10 twice.	Ten small blocks. Cards with directions prepared by teacher. Small pictures of prizes pasted on bottoms of blocks.
Procedures	Label each piece of candy in relationship to size: largest piece 5¢, smallest 1¢. Give each child five pennies. The child then buys candy until pennies are gone. Money is used again for another money game.	Deal five cards to each of two players. First player places a card on the table number up. Second player tries to match the number from his or her hand. First player puts down cards until the card is matched. Then the	Buy enough small items such as gum, or marbles for each child to win a prize. The directions are read from a card the child selects such as: "Count five blocks." If the child can count five blocks, the child wins the

Mini Units Differentiating and Integrating for **Five Year Olds** (*cont.*)

	September	*January*	*May*
		second player puts down a new card. Two hands of five are played. The first child to get rid of all cards wins.	prize on the bottom of the block.
Evaluation	Ability to give correct number of pennies for items for items bought.	Ability to match cards.	Ability to count number of blocks on command.
Integrating skills	Oral language. Visual discrimination. Physical activity.	Oral language. Following directions. Visual discrimination.	Listening. Eye-hand coordination.

EVALUATION OF INDIVIDUAL DIFFERENCES

Individuals differ in ability to understand and perform mathematical skills just as they do in other curricular areas. To enable you to evaluate the growth of children in this area develop similar evaluation sheets for the children whom you teach.

Mastery of Ordinal Numbers (first, second, third) (Age range 3.2 to 3.6 by October 1)

Name	October	January	May
Cheryl	no	no	no
Karen	no	no	yes
Vicki	no	no	no
Erich	no	no	yes
Barry	no	yes	yes
Robert	no	no	yes
Mabel	no	no	no
Kay	no	no	no
Taisto	no	no	yes
Franklin	no	yes	yes
Elizabeth	no	no	no

Mastery of Ordinal Numbers (cont.)

Name	October	January	May
Larry	no	no	yes
Pam	no	no	yes
Sïegurd	no	no	no
Sarah	no	no	no
Lee	no	no	yes
Debbie	yes	yes	yes
Scott	no	yes	yes

Mastery of Names of Cardinal Numbers (1 to 5) (Age range 4.0 to 4.5 by October 1)

Name	October	January	May
Peggy	no	yes	yes
Costos	no	no	no
Ruth	yes	yes	yes
Lebron	no	no	no
Clyde	no	yes	yes
Charles	no	no	yes
Susie	no	yes	yes
Catherine	no	no	no
Boyd	yes	yes	yes
Theodor	no	yes	yes
Charlotte	no	no	no
Harold	yes	yes	yes
Edward	no	no	yes
Rose	no	yes	yes
Thomas	no	yes	yes
Raymond	no	no	yes

Mastery of Pairing and Matching Sets (2 forks, 2 crayons, 2 pencils, 2 scissors) (Age range 5.2 to 5.4 by October 1)

Name	October	January	May
Val	no	no	yes
Dorothy	no	no	no
Maria	no	yes	yes
Judy	no	no	yes
James	no	no	no
Haakon	no	yes	yes
Andrew	no	no	yes
Vivian	no	no	no
Steve	no	no	no
Donna	yes	yes	yes
Ann	no	yes	yes
Samuel	no	yes	yes
Earl	no	no	no
David	yes	yes	yes
Louin	no	no	no
Gene	yes	yes	yes
Glenda	no	no	yes
Deborah	no	no	yes
Joyce	no	no	yes
Nolan	no	yes	yes
Claude	no	yes	yes
Nikolai	no	no	no
Ronald	no	no	yes

LEARNING GOALS FOR CHILDREN

Children are expected to be able to perform certain mathematics tasks before they leave kindergarten. Awareness of these goals will enable you to teach young children more effectively:

- ✔ The child can arrange objects according to size from largest to smallest.
- ✔ The child can recognize and name four basic shapes: circle, square, triangle, and rectangle.

306 / Curriculum

- ✔ Given a set of picture cards made up of matched pairs, the child can match the like cards.
- ✔ The child can count orally from one to ten.
- ✔ The child can make comparisons of more than and fewer than.
- ✔ The child can identify sets that have unlike members.
- ✔ The child can group like objects into sets.
- ✔ The child can use the idea of conservation by size and number.

BASIC SKILLS SEQUENCE CHART

See page 189 for an explanation of how to use skills sequence charts.

Mathematics Skills

Key symbols: (✔) Introduction   (✔✔) Extension and reinforcement

Skill	Level 1	Level 2	Level 3
Counting			
Count to 20	✔	✔✔	✔✔
Count to 100	✔	✔✔	✔✔
Count by 10s	✔	✔✔	✔✔
Count by 5s	✔	✔✔	✔✔
Count by 2s, 3s, 4s	✔	✔✔	✔✔
Count by 10s to 1,000	✔	✔✔	✔✔
Sets			
Form sets to 20	✔	✔✔	✔✔
Use 0 for empty set	✔	✔✔	✔✔
Match set with numerals 0–10	✔	✔✔	✔✔
Identify sets	✔	✔✔	✔✔
Identify sets and subsets		✔	✔✔
Identify number of sets	✔	✔✔	✔✔
Compare sets using concepts of more, less	✔	✔✔	✔✔

Mathematics Skills *(cont.)*

Key symbols: (✔) Introduction   (✔✔) Extension and reinforcement

Skill	Level 1	Level 2	Level 3
Numeration			
Recognize numerals to 20	✔	✔✔	✔✔
Recognize numerals to 200		✔	✔✔
Read numerals to 10,000			✔
Write numerals to 99	✔	✔✔	✔✔
Write numerals to 999		✔	✔✔
Write amounts for money			✔
Read numerals in any order	✔	✔✔	✔✔
Write numerals on print or number line	✔	✔✔	✔✔
Arrange 10s in order as number line		✔	✔✔
Name three-digit numbers on number line		✔	✔✔
Order numbers past 1,000			✔
Identify symbol in 1s and 10s places	✔	✔✔	✔✔
Name place values		✔	✔✔
Name three digit numerals		✔	✔✔
Understand 10	✔	✔✔	✔✔
Write expanded numerals		✔	✔✔
Rename 10s and 1s		✔	✔✔
Rename numbers		✔	✔✔
Round off numbers to nearest 10			✔
Read word names to 10	✔	✔✔	✔✔
Read word names for 10s		✔	✔✔
Identify first through fifth (ordinals)	✔	✔✔	✔✔
Identify first through tenth (ordinals)		✔	✔✔
Recognize ordinal words		✔	✔✔
Identify odd and even numbers		✔	✔✔
Compare numbers using *greater, less, equal*	✔	✔✔	✔✔
Compare numbers using symbols	✔	✔✔	✔✔
Read fractions		✔	✔✔
Compare unlike fractions			✔
Relate fractions to regions, sets, lines			✔

308 / Curriculum

Mathematics Skills (cont.)

Key symbols: (✔) Introduction (✔✔) Extension and reinforcement

Skill	Level 1	Level 2	Level 3
Operations			
Use 10s and 1s in two-place numbers	✔	✔✔	✔✔
Rename 1s as 10s and 1s		✔	✔✔
Use 10s and 1s		✔	✔✔
Add two numbers less than 18	✔	✔✔	✔✔
Add two numbers either way	✔	✔✔	✔✔
Subtract sets less than 18	✔	✔✔	✔✔
Choose addition or subtraction		✔	✔✔
Multiply two numbers 0–5			✔
Identify fractional parts		✔	✔✔
Add three numbers to 10	✔	✔✔	✔✔
Add three numbers to 12	✔	✔✔	✔✔
Add numbers up or down			✔
Recognize addition and subtraction as opposite operations		✔	✔✔
Use addition		✔	✔✔
Rename numbers 13 to 18	✔	✔✔	✔✔
Rename numbers 11 to 18		✔	✔✔
Check addition by subtraction			✔
Relate addition and subtraction facts			✔
Master addition and subtraction facts to 18		✔	✔✔
Add and subtract on number line		✔	✔✔
Add from right to left		✔	✔✔
Regroup 1s to 10s and 10s to 1s		✔	✔✔
Regroup three-digit numbers (addition)			✔
Regroup three-digit numbers (subtraction)			✔✔
Understand math vocabulary			✔✔
Count by 25, 35, 45, 55, 105 as preparation for multiplication		✔	✔✔
Use multiplication chart to 5			✔
Master multiplication facts to 5			✔
Name the product when two factors are given			✔
Name a missing factor when two factors are given			✔
Prepare for division			✔

Mathematics / 309

Mathematics Skills *(cont.)*

Key symbols: (✔) Introduction   (✔✔) Extension and reinforcement

Skill	Level 1	Level 2	Level 3
Master division facts to 5			✔
Use zero as a placeholder			✔
Sentences and problem solving			
Use objects for addition	✔	✔✔	✔✔
Choose correct subtraction problems	✔	✔✔	✔✔
Make up addition and subtraction problems	✔	✔✔	✔✔
Choose correct problems	✔	✔✔	✔✔
Choose correct operation	✔	✔✔	✔✔
Solve verbal problems		✔	✔✔
Solve two-step problems with money			✔
Solve multiplication and division			✔
Solve addition and subtraction problems with money		✔	✔✔
Solve rate problems of speed, distance			✔
Solve fraction problems			✔
Use greater than, less than, equal symbols		✔	✔✔
Use ( ) in problem solving		✔	✔✔
Solve problems	✔	✔✔	✔✔
Recognize shapes	✔	✔✔	✔✔
Recognize sizes	✔	✔✔	✔✔
Use words for amounts and heights	✔	✔✔	✔✔
Measurement and geometry			
Use measurement: inch	✔	✔✔	✔✔
Use measurement: centimeter		✔	✔✔
Use measurement: inch, foot, yard			✔
Use measurement: miles			✔
Make change to 99 cents		✔	✔✔
Recognize value of coins		✔	✔✔
Make change for dollars			✔
Measure volume: cup, pint, quart	✔	✔✔	✔✔
Measure volume: gallon			✔

310 / *Curriculum*

Mathematics Skills *(cont.)*

Key symbols: (✔) Introduction   (✔✔) Extension and reinforcement

Skill	Level 1	Level 2	Level 3
Measure weight: pound	✔	✔✔	✔✔
Measure time: hour	✔	✔✔	✔✔
Measure time: half hour	✔	✔✔	✔✔
Measure time: quarter hour		✔	✔✔
Measure time: minutes			✔
Measure time: reading clocks	✔	✔✔	✔✔
Use calendars: days of week, months, holidays, seasons	✔	✔✔	✔✔
Use calendar: months, days in week			✔
Measure temperature: weather	✔	✔✔	✔✔
Reproduce shapes		✔	✔✔
Recognize shapes: cube, sphere, cylinder, cone			✔
Make a shape: cube			✔
Recognize open and closed curves	✔	✔✔	✔✔
Recognize regions	✔	✔✔	✔✔
Understand vocabulary: segments, rays, angles, paths		✔	✔✔
Understand vocabulary: radius			✔
Understand vocabulary: right angles			✔
Understand vocabulary: symmetrical			✔

ADDITIONAL READINGS

Ames, L. B. "The Development of the Sense of Time in Young Children." *Journal of Genetic Psychology,* 68 (1946): 97–125.

Barbe, Walter B., ed. *Basic Skills in Kindergarten: Foundation for Formal Learning.* Columbus, Ohio: Zaner Bloser, 1980.

Copeland, Richard. *How Children Learn Mathematics.* 3rd ed. New York: Macmillan, 1979.

Corey, R., and L. P. Steffe. *An Investigation in the Learning of Equivalence and Order Relations by Four- and Five-Year-Old Children.* Research Paper No. 17. Athens, Ga.: University of Georgia Press, 1968.

Elkind, D. "Teaching Formal Operations to Preschool Advantaged and Disadvantaged Children." *The Ontario Journal of Educational Research,* 9 (1967): 3.

Gelman, Rachel. "Preschool Thought." *American Psychologist*, 34 (1979).

Ginsburg, R. *Mathematical Concept Learning by the Pre-School Child. Final Report* (ERIC) document no. ED065171). Washington, D.C.: National Center for Educational Research and Development, 1971.

Kennedy, Leonard M. *Guiding Children to Mathematical Discovery*. 3rd ed. Belmont, Calif.: Wadsworth, 1980.

Piaget, J. "How Children Form Mathematical Concepts." *Scientific American*, 189, 20 (1953): 74–79.

Piaget, J., B. Inhelder, and A. Szemenska. *The Child's Conception of Geometry*. New York: Basic Books, 1960.

Richardson, Lloyd I., et al. *A Mathematics Activity Curriculum for Early Childhood and Special Education*. New York: Macmillan, 1980.

Rothenberg, B. B. "Conservation of Number Among Four- and Five-Year-Old Children: Some Methodological Considerations," *Child Development*, 40 (1969): 383–406.

Uprichard, E. "The Effects of Sequence in the Acquisition of Three Set Relations: An Experiment with Preschoolers," *The Arithmetic Teacher*, 17 (1970): 597–604.

CHAPTER 10
Art

Exploration Tasks

After studying this chapter, you should be able to complete these tasks:
- Discuss the four major theories of teaching art to young children.
- Identify the forms of art appropriate during the early years.
- Make some basic, inexpensive art media.
- Identify and collect appropriate art materials.
- Select books for teaching color and shape.
- List a variety of instructive and creative art activities.

The artist is an adventurer, and the child working in art must learn to venture. Dangers and conflicts are always there, but the adventure is worth the 'errand into the maze' and the battle with the minotaur.

Nik Krevitsky

OVERVIEW

Young children delight in experimenting with the media of art activities — squeezing clay, swishing wide streaks of paint, smearing finger-paint, cutting, tearing, shaping, and constructing. All bring new and unexpected results that fascinate the child. Media exploration, identification, and use are the first introductory stages to the creative aspect of art.

Another aspect of art is the study or recognition of art products — paintings, sculpture, crafts, drawings — created by others. Although young children are not usually "taught" names of artists, the artists' products should be displayed, touched, and discussed; they should become part of a classroom's decor.

The teacher has five functions in the introduction of art into the classroom: to provide the media for use, to provide time for using the media, to schedule time for sharing the end result, to acquire and display books that encourage use of art materials and create interest, and to display objects of art created by others.

The Art Education Association has stated its primary goals for young children: the child should be able to see and feel visual relationships, make art objects, study works of art, and critically evaluate art.[1]

An object of art created by a young child is not evaluated by judging either the accuracy of imitation or the skill in use of the media. A teacher evaluates the experience and the finished product by answering four questions: Has the child had a pleasant and satisfying art experience? Does the finished product provide evidence of growth in the use of the media and the tools of art? Has the child shown an understanding of the uses and limitations of the media? Does the child express interest in forms, shapes, colors, textures, and designs?

THEORETICAL CONTEXT

For several years individuals have studied and analyzed young children and their use of art activities. These researchers have developed four basically different theories of how children develop their art abilities and what they are portraying in their objects of art. The theories are the developmental approach, the cognitive approach, the psychoanalytic approach, and the cognitive-developmental approach.

The Developmental Approach: How They Grow

Probably the most widely accepted theory of instruction in art is the developmental approach, which limits both direct instruction and any interference by the teacher in the child's work. The leading developmentalist,

---

[1] Cited in E. W. Lindermann and D. W. Herboz, *Developing Artistic and Perceptual Awareness* (Dubuque, Iowa: William C. Brown, 1974).

Viktor Lowenfeld, in his book *Creative and Mental Growth*,[2] has categorized five stages of children's growth in art. They are the scribbling stage (ages 2–4), demonstrated by self-expression; the preschematic stage (ages 4–7), characterized by representational attempts; the schematic stage (ages 7–9), shown by success in forming concepts; the gang stage (9–11), the beginning of realism; and the reasoning stage (11–13), or pseudorealism. In this approach the teacher is a guide, an attendant, and an inspirer.

The Cognitive Approach: What They Think

The cognitive theory is based on the idea that a child draws what he or she knows, not what is seen visually. Florence Goodenough is probably the principal art theorist who believes that children's art is more than a visual imagery and eye-hand coordination activity. According to Goodenough, art also includes the higher thought processes.[3] From this hypothesis, Goodenough and Dale Harris have developed the Draw-A-Man Test.[4] Research to test the validity of the cognitive theory approach shows that the Draw-A-Man Test is sensitive to various variables that influence the picture of the man the children draw.[5] From the author's own experience, over eight hundred first-grade children drew "sausage men" when told to draw a man because two weeks earlier they had received, through educational TV, instruction on "how to draw a man" using big and little ovals (called sausages by the instructor).

The Psychoanalytic Approach: What They Feel

The basis of the psychoanalytic theory approach is that children's art products reflect their own emotions rather than their intellectual knowledge, concepts, or general overall development. Lois Barclay Murphy and Katherine Baker Read, two advocates of this theory, have influenced many teachers of young children through their many articles and books.[6] The aspect of art most influenced by this theory is the extensive use of tactile materials such as fingerpaints and clay. Both media provide for the release

---

[2] Viktor Lowenfeld, *Creative and Mental Growth* (New York: Macmillan, 1947).

[3] Florence L. Goodenough, *Measurement of Intelligence by Drawings* (New York: Harcourt Brace Jovanovich, 1926).

[4] Dale Harris, *Children's Drawings as Measures of Intellectual Maturity* (New York: Harcourt Brace Jovanovich, 1963).

[5] See for example, E. B. Feldman, *Becoming Human Through Art* (Englewood Cliffs, N.J.: Prentice-Hall, 1970); H. J. McWhinnie, "Reviews of Recent Literature on Figure Drawing Tests as Related to Research Problems in Art Education." *Review of Educational Research* 41 (1971): 115–31; and J. R. Medinnus, D. Bobbitt, and J. Hullet, "Effects of Training on the Draw-A-Man Test." *Journal of Experimental Education* 35 (1966): 62–63.

[6] Two essential books are Lois Barclay Murphy and others, *The Widening World of Childhood* (New York: Basic Books, 1962) and Katherine Baker Read, *The Nursery School: A Human Relationships Laboratory* (Philadelphia: Saunders, 1966).

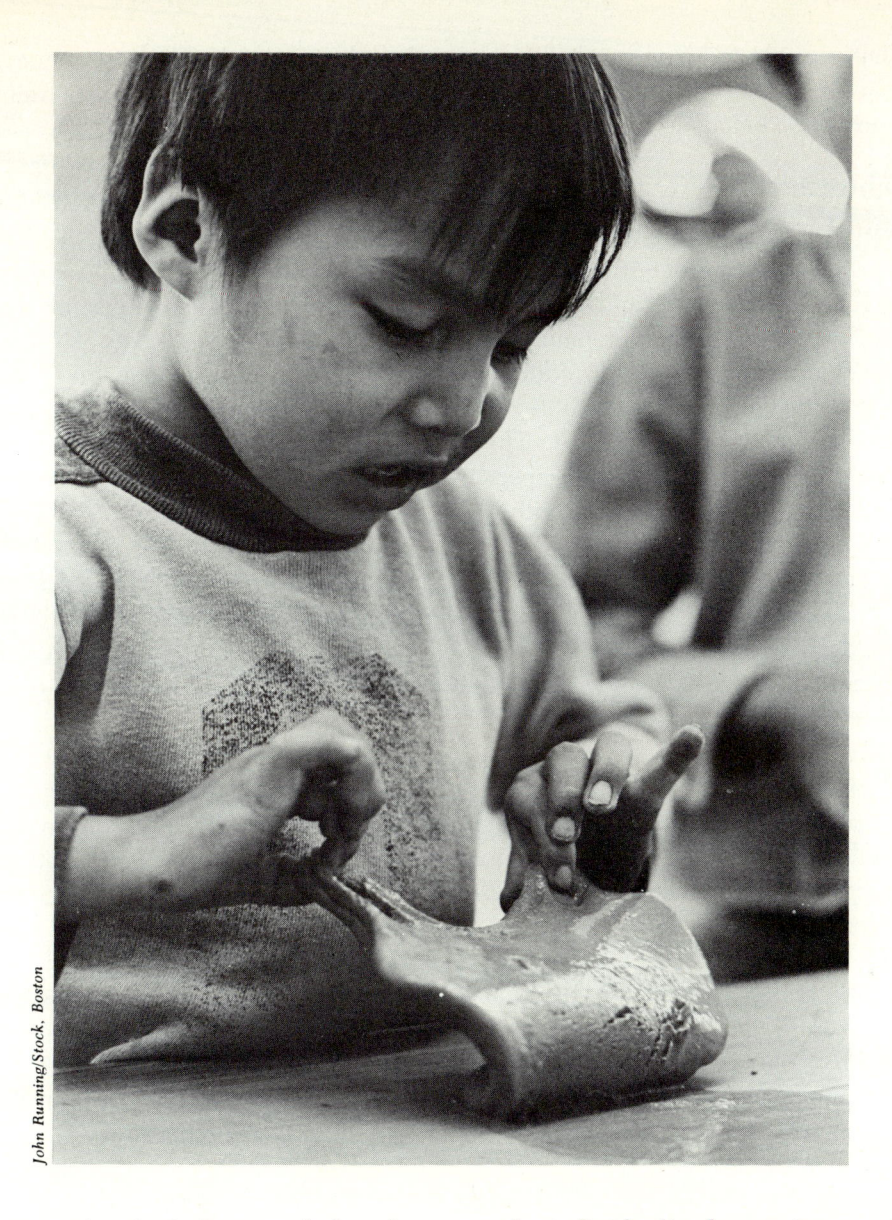

Clay takes many forms, and there are no mistakes.

of children's feelings and therefore provide individualized experiences of varying emotions.

Generally, however, research studies advocate caution in classroom teachers' use of children's art as a means of interpreting behavior.[7] Art activities

---

[7] See for example, R. Alschuler and L. B. Hattwick, *Painting and Personality: A Study of Young Children* (Chicago: University of Chicago Press, 1947); R. H. Lingren, "An Attempted Replication of Emotional Indicators in Human Figure Drawings by Shy and Aggressive Children." *Psychological Reports* 29 (1971): 35–38; D. Manzella, "The Effects of Hypnotically Induced Change in the Self-Image on Drawing Ability." *Studies in Art Education* 4 (1963):

that provide for emotional release are thought of as valuable experiences, but interpretation of the product in terms of understanding personality traits and social behavior should not be attempted by lay persons.

The Cognitive-Developmental Approach: How They Think and Grow

Piaget's experimental work in growth and development presents still another theory of why, how, and what children draw.[8] Piaget relates children's art to their ability to understand the permanent existence of objects. He believes that unless a child understands that objects are permanent the child has no imagery by which to recall the past and anticipate the future in the absence of the "real" object. This representation, according to Piaget, is the way children organize experiences to understand their environment. The representation requires either concrete or oral symbols: Imagery forms the concrete symbols; language forms the oral symbols.

Piaget lists three stages in a child's understanding of pictorial space as *synthetic incapacity* (partial and fragmental images), *intellectual realism* (the children draw what they know, not what they see), and *visual realism* (occurs about age 9; shows that the child understands the relationship of objects to their spatial coordinates).

Conclusions

At present the teaching of art is being scrutinized by researchers and many well-established practices are being questioned.[9] The four areas in question are: the "why" of what and how children draw or paint, the importance of selection of types of media, the diversity of the use of the media, and the role of the teacher in teaching techniques and motivation.

The author agrees with the theory of June King McFee, who advocates developing an art program based on many factors: the readiness of each child in physical, intellectual, and perceptual development as well as environmental settings and cultural influences acquired from the environment; the psychological atmosphere at home and school including rewards and

---

59–70; and R. S. Rogers and N. E. Wright, "A Study of Children's Drawings of Their Classrooms." *Journal of Educational Research* 64 (1971): 370–74.

[8] Reported in M. Brearly, *The Teacher of Young Children: Some Applications of Piaget's Learning Theory* (New York: Schocken Books, 1970). Also see: G. H. Luquet, *The Drawings of a Child* (Paris, France: F. Alcan, 1913); Jean Piaget, *The Child's Conception of Reality* (London: Routledge & Kegan Paul, 1955); and Piaget, *The Psychology of Intelligence* (London: Routledge & Kegan Paul, 1932).

[9] G. J. Clifford, "A History of the Impact of Research on Teaching." In *Second Handbook of Research on Teaching*, edited by R. M. Travers (Chicago: Rand McNally and Company, 1973); E. P. Cohen, "Does Art Matter in the Education of the Black Ghetto Child?" *Young Children* 24 (1974): 170–82; and E. W. Eisner, *Educating Artistic Vision* (New York: Macmillan, 1972).

punishment; the ability of the child to handle information — that is, general level of intelligence; and the child's ability to manipulate the media — creativeness and ability to design form.[10] Art education should be multi-faceted, including drawing, painting, sculpture, crafts, history, and a representation of an individual's culture.

As in the past, art education should provide a rich and stimulating environment, a variety of media, freedom to experiment, and, on an individual basis, some direct teaching of art techniques.

MEDIA

By the time most three year olds attend their first nursery school class they have experienced drawing and coloring. Pencils, crayons, and felt markers are found in many homes. One important reason for attending an early childhood program is that the child will have many opportunities for self-expression in various media. Some children may have acquired certain habits, such as coloring within lines, imitation, or another trait altogether — not thinking about color or form at all, making practically uncontrolled marks, or using the material in inappropriate ways.

Mary was standing back from the easel looking at her latest painting and said to the teacher, "You know, my mamma took me to the art gallery and they have pictures like this that real people have painted."

Forms

What forms of art are appropriate for children, ages three to six? Because of the flexibility of the creative materials used in art, most forms of art can be used with all ages. The results are not the same. Allowances have to be made for small-muscle development and length of time of the activity. The following forms of art will aid you in selecting activities that will be enjoyable and that will reinforce previous learnings.

Drawing
Painting
Pasting
Crafts: dying, flower preservation, sewing, embroidery, weaving, pottery

Cutting
Block printing
Sculpting

Children using these forms of art will vary in accomplishment according to age and other variables. Remember, this is the age of exploring and trying out.

[10] June King McFee, *Preparation for Art*, 2nd ed. (Belmont, Cal.: Wadsworth, 1970).

Classroom-Produced Media

For children to be creative, teachers must also be creative. Most extremely pleasurable activities cost little money but do require planning and knowledge. Recipes for art media should be prepared and tried out in advance. The recipes included here are basic ones that have been used by teachers of young children for years.

Finger-paint for One

Mix: ¼ cup liquid laundry starch
2 drops food coloring *or*
1 teaspoon powder paint

The preceding recipe will provide enough finger-paint for one experience for one child. If you wish to make a quantity of finger-paint, expand the recipe for each child to be included. A recipe for finger-paint for fourteen follows. A larger recipe for finger-paint may be stored by refrigerating in a tightly capped container. This recipe mixture may be divided and various food colorings added to provide several colors. Powder paints may be used for color, but the colors will stay on the children's hands if water is not easily accessible. Food coloring is a more appropriate coloring agent.

Finger-paint for Fourteen

Mix: ½ cup laundry starch
½ cup cold water
Add 4 cups boiling water, a cup at a time, and food coloring to obtain desired intensity of color.

For a different quality of paint add a half-teaspoon of liquid starch or a half-teaspoon of liquid detergent. Poster paints may also be made from one tablespoon of *clear* liquid detergent — use two tablespoons of powder paint and add water to get desired consistency. This makes a velvety mixture for one painting. Poster paint made from a pint of clear liquid detergent, a cup of powder paint and about a cup of water will give 15 four year olds an opportunity to paint each day for a month (one color).

Poster Paint

Mix: ¼ cup flour
1 cup water

Add water slowly to make paste. Heat about 4 minutes or until it begins to thicken, stirring constantly. Cool.

Mix: ¼ cup flour mixture
3 tablespoons powder paint
2 tablespoons water (You may need a little more water.)

Nontoxic Classroom Paste, Uncooked

Mix: ½ cup flour
½ cup water

Add flour to water so it won't lump.

Nontoxic Classroom Paste, Cooked

Mix: 1 cup flour
1 teaspoon salt
2 cups water

Add water slowly. Simmer about five minutes.

Thinned White Glue

Mix: ½ cup white glue
½ cup water

This will not be crusty when dry.

Flour Clay

Mix: 4 cups flour
1½ cups salt
2 cups water

Knead until smooth, adding food coloring if desired.

This clay can be colored with food coloring, or can be baked and painted with powder paints or acrylics. A fixative must be sprayed on painted objects. Because of the salt in the mixture the clay will dry the skin; to avoid this wet a washcloth with cooking oil and wipe each child's hands before using the clay.

Cornstarch Clay, Cooked

Mix: 2 cups baking soda
  1 cup cornstarch
  1¼ cups cold water

Cook mixture about five minutes, until it looks like mashed potatoes. Cover with wet paper towel to keep moist. When cool, knead until pliable, adding food coloring.

  Note: This clay must be refrigerated if it is to be reused because it will sour at room temperature.

Play Clay or Salt Clay

Mix: 3 cups salt
  6 cups flour
  3 tablespoons powdered alum
  6 cups boiling water

Cool, then add 1 tablespoon oil, knead. When dough is smooth add food coloring. Refrigerate when not in use.

Doll Clay

Mix: 2 cups flour
  1 cup salt
  1 cup water

Knead mixture, and bake on greased cookie sheet about two hours at 325° F.

This clay can be rolled about ¼ inch thick and cut with cookie cutters. For gingerbread men, paint brown and bake. Or try dolls or Christmas ornaments.

> **Papier-maché Paste**
> Mix: 8 cups wallpaper paste mix
>   10 cups water

This amount of paste will provide "dip" for five papier-maché objects about the size of a blown-up balloon (a good armature for small children).

> **Plaster for Molds**
> Mix: 8 cups patch plaster
>   5 cups water

This recipe will make enough plaster for four children for hand or foot molds. Plaster of Paris may be used but it dries very quickly and is difficult for young children to use. Patch plaster is inexpensive and takes at least thirty minutes to dry.

Crafts for the Preschool Classroom

Little children, with help, are able to produce many of their own projects. These activities give them a sense of pride in their accomplishment, and art is sure to be a positive experience. These projects include dying fabric, preparing some dyes from household materials, and preparing flower and foliage displays.

Dyes Dyes for young children are used in cool, not hot water, and fabrics will be likely to bleed unless first treated with a mordant. For cotton or linens, mix 1 gallon of water with 1 ounce of alum and ¼ ounce of washing soda. Boil the fabric in this mixture for about half an hour, rinse, and hang to dry (or dry in dryer). Synthetic fabrics do not take dye well. Old cotton sheets are ideal.

Onionskin dye can be made from the brown skins from about ten pounds of onions. (Onions can still be used.) Boil the skins in a quart of water for about a half hour. Add one tablespoon of salt to cooled dye. Goldenrod dye is another choice. Boil chopped flowers and stems of about thirty stalks of goldenrod in a quart of water for about a half hour. Add one tablespoon of salt to cooled dye. Cranberries also make a colorful dye. Boil a pound of cranberries in a quart of water for a half hour. Add one tablespoon of salt to cooled dye. These three natural dyes will provide brown, yellow, and red dyes for one dying experience for twenty children.

Flower Preservation Flower preservation is easy and fun. Children can hunt for flowers to use.

Cured flowers Select hardy field flowers, long stems, small flowers, never petaled flowers. Remove all leaves and hang upside down in a warm, dry place for two weeks.

Pressed flowers Choose flowers that have only one or two layers of petals. Pick them on a warm, dry day. Place flowers between white tissue in a book that is room temperature. Place a heavy object on book and leave for two weeks.

Dried flowers Select fresh flowers except violets, petunias, or bulb flowers. Remove leaves and stem. Make new stems from florist wire with a hooked end to hold wire in head of flower. Cover wire with florist tape. Put a layer of the mixture in a tall container with lid. Place flowers head down in top of mixture. Do not let flowers touch each other. Cover with more mixture, adding flowers and mixture until the end wires can be bent into the container and the container closed. Keep warm and dry. Leave about four days. Some flowers take up to two weeks to dry because of their thickness and size of the seed pod.

> Mix: 5 pounds corn meal
> 2 pounds borax

For foliage preservation you need fresh-cut green foliage of deciduous hardwoods, such as oak, maple, or birch. Holly, forsythia, and rhododendron are also good. Crush the bottom two or three inches of each stem with a hammer. Mix one cup of glycerin and three cups of very hot water. Place the foliage in the hot water and leave until the foliage feels oily — about three days. The foliage will change color and the color becomes permanent. The mixture can be reheated later and used again.

Art Materials

Art materials are so diversified that no discussion or listing can be complete. Although the formal aspects of art are somewhat limited in material, the crafts create open-ended experiences and therefore almost anything will do. This list can be used as inventory for materials you will need during the year.

Glazed paper
Oil cloth
Newspapers
Magazines
Newsprint
Wrapping paper
Construction paper
Finger-paint
Dry powder paint
Poster paint
Acrylic paint
Paste
Glue
Pencils
Crayons
Chalk
Felt markers
Left- and right-handed scissors
Clay
Plaster mix
Stiff bristle brushes, various sizes
Paper cutter
Felt materials
Small brooms
Popsicle sticks
Plastic pails
Design stamps
Scissors holder
Coat hangers
Cloth scraps
Tile
Glitter
Cottage cheese containers
Cotton puffs
Glass jars
Tin cans
Milk cartons
Easels
Sponges
Cloths
Paper towels
Aprons
Old shirts
Fixatives
Six-inch squares of bound screen
Toothbrushes
Straws
String
Yarn
Roll-on deodorant bottles
Eye droppers
Plastic bottles
Salt shakers
Sand
Clothespins
Corks
Wax paper
Wax
Burlap
Plastic darning needle
Pans of various sizes
Glass wax
Measuring cups and spoons
Berry baskets
Tacks
Corn meal
Plastic spoons
Masking tape
Punches
Rulers
Staplers
Seeds
Colored tissue paper
Feathers
Sequins
Dry cereals
Pine cones
Seed pods
Buttons
Styrofoam
Wood
Wire
Pipe cleaners
Macaroni
Juice cans
Stryrofoam meat trays
Leaves
Rocks
Shells
Cookie press
Pastry tube
Rubber bands
Dishpan
Paper cups
Drying rack
Tagboard
Corrugated paper
Nails

Teachers must be constantly watching for discarded objects that will provide materials for a creative experience in art. Each room should have at least two storage boxes for discards — one box for large items and another box for small items.

INSTRUCTION AND ACTIVITIES

Activities that involve children physically in their accomplishments are the best ways for children to learn. As John Dewey said, "Children learn by doing." Art, therefore, is easily adapted to the many phases of an early education program. Art occurs in relationship to the language arts, science, and social studies experiences planned for young children and, therefore, as a teacher you should analyze your plans to be sure that art activities are in balance with other experiences such as free play, music, and literature.

Art activities vary according to individual needs and performance. They also provide opportunities for creativity. Because of the relationship between creativity and instruction, teachers should plan for direct "how to" lessons with time for creative uses of the instruction and materials as well as many occasions for just creative responses to the materials. To help identify the instruction necessary for use of materials appropriate for young children and possible creative uses of the materials after the children know how to handle them, this section of the art chapter is divided into two parts — instruction and creative activities.

Instruction

Finger painting   This is one of the easiest forms of painting. The paint is placed directly on the paper and the design is made by smearing the paint with fingers, whole hands, arms, design stamps or objects, palm, side of palm, fingernails, or knuckles. To teach children to use finger-paint, wet the paper first with a sponge and drop small amounts of paint directly onto the wet paper. The paint can also be applied to dry paper, but this approach uses more paint. A third way is to wet the paper first, then add dry paint in spots. If the wet, finished finger-painting is placed on newspaper to dry the painting will curl. Young children "paint" over edges; if the wet paper is placed on the newspaper before painting, the paint sticks to the newspaper and holds the painting.

Poster or tempera painting   These types of paint are most commonly used at easels. The paint is of a creamy consistency and does not "run" or "bleed" when brushed on paper in an upright position or put next to another color. Paints are applied with long-handled brushes of varying widths. Children need to be taught how to handle the brush for painting and they need to be taught to wash the brushes after using them or at clean-up time. Although the paint may be left on brushes until the end of the day without hardening, children need the responsibility of caring for materials they use.

Chalk drawing   Chalk adds interest to drawing activities because it comes in so many hues not available in crayons or paints. Chalk is made in square

Art / 325

Sometimes paintings are color expressions.

or round sticks of different thicknesses and may be used either as a pointed object or as a wide object. Chalk may be used on either dry or wet paper. Chalk drawn on wet paper has a sheen finish and the colors blend together. When children finish using chalk they should wash their hands thoroughly. On completion, the chalk drawing should either be covered with paper or sprayed with a fixative. A good fixative can be made of equal parts of liquid starch and water, sprayed from a container made for a window washer.

Crayon drawing Crayon drawing is often limited to paper although crayons can be used on cloth, wood, or plastic. Children usually have several coloring books at home and they are encouraged to color within the lines. While they are in an early childhood program their experiences should be of a more creative nature and unstructured as to form and color. Children need to be taught how to hold a crayon, to fill in the whole sheet with their ideas, and to have the opportunity to see other children's drawings that are not replicas of another picture or taken from a coloring book.

Clay modeling Beginning experiences with clay include pounding, poking, pushing, rolling, pinching, and breaking off small pieces. After the general manipulation of the clay, children begin to roll and pat the clay into crude forms. Gradually these forms become recognizable as pots, dishes, letters, animals, or other objects. Children should be shown how to roll the clay between their palms for a round ball or on a table to make a long roll. They should be shown how to make a pinch pot. Once they have learned the basic ways of making a hunk of clay into these forms, they will create their own forms.

Weaving Weaving is the process of interlacing one set of strings or strips of cloth, plastic, yarn, or straw with another set of materials on a form that provides a loom. The first material put on the loom is called the *warp*. The warp is woven back and forth lengthwise around the nails or pegs on the frame of the loom. After the warp is on the loom the *weft* materials are woven crosswise of the warp, alternately over and under the threads. Each weft thread is pushed against the last weft thread to make a solid surface. Strawberry baskets are good for beginning weaving; the structure furnishes the warp and the child adds the weft.

Cutting and pasting Almost everything a young child cuts is also pasted. There are a few exceptions but not many. As a teacher you will need left- and right-handed scissors with rounded ends. Let the child select the scissors most comfortable for cutting. Plastic egg cartons taped closed with holes punched in one side provide an upright handle-up storage place for scissors. Usually two such storage containers are needed — one for an art activity and one for children doing other activities that might require cutting. Children need to be shown how to cut out things in magazines, newspapers, or sheets of paper. Objects do not need to be cut out "on the line." A simple circle cutting of the entire object is quite satisfactory.

Pasting of the cut-out object may be done on old magazines, plain paper, newspaper, wood, plastic, and so forth. Paste should be applied to the middle of the cut-out object and spread to the edges. Paste should be used sparingly. Children can paste many materials besides cut-out or torn paper:

yarn, cloth, cardboard, ribbon, sequins, cotton, string, buttons, weeds, and grasses.

Sewing Children can make their own sock puppets by sewing on button eyes, cloth circle noses, and red felt lips or tongues. Precut forms of hand finger puppets can be basted around the edges with yarn. Hot-plate mats for gifts and doll bed quilts can be quilted with yarn. Large plastic needles are available for yarn sewing.

Creative Activities

After basic skills and knowledge of the properties of the materials are introduced, children should have many opportunities to be creative. Since there are several books on the market with the processes, techniques, or procedures to help children be creative, the following activities grouped by chronological age of children are open ended — they have no exact end product. The reason for grouping the activities by chronological age is that many teachers have used these activities and found them to be successful, happy experiences for children at the age level where they are placed. Because children differ, individuals within each age level will vary in their performances in the activities.

Arts and Crafts for Three Year Olds

Collage Children can make collages by tearing, cutting, and pasting newspaper, colored tissue, crepe paper, construction paper, bits of cloth, plastic, tape, buttons, yarn, bottle caps, or wood.

Easel painting Painting bright bold colors on unprinted paper is very satisfying to three year olds. Newspaper is sometimes used, but children will request "clean" paper. Based on many observations of experienced teachers, children are more eager to paint the unprinted paper clipped to the easel than newspaper that is clipped to the easel.

Finger-painting Finger-painting by three year olds is really misnamed. They use their palms, fists, arms, and whole body movement. Generally the product is finished when the children are tired of manipulating the paint.

Printing Three year olds are fascinated by dipping an object in paint and then making a print with it on paper. Thick slices of carrots or potatoes cut with wedges or semicircles have proven to be interesting stamps. See Figure 10.1 for some examples.

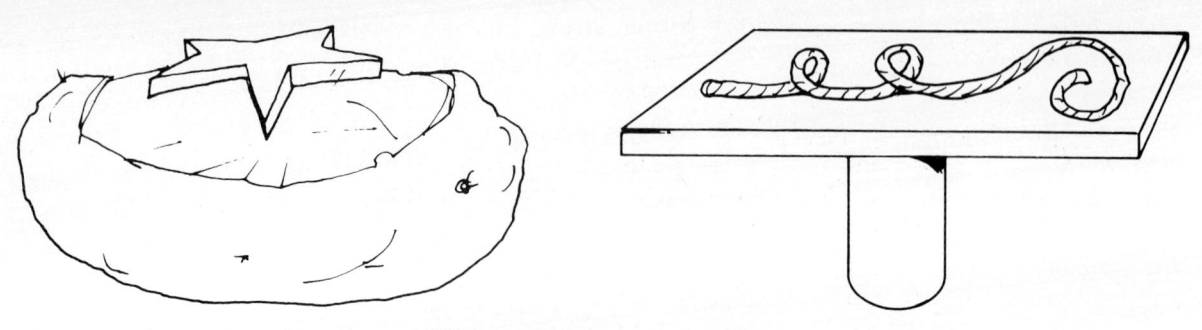

*Figure 10.1
Potato and String
Stamps*

Drawings Large crayons are easy to handle and can be used on paper, cardboard, boxes, food trays, and plastic bottles.

Rubbings Many textured surfaces (sidewalk, leaves, bricks, coins) make an excellent rubbing. The child covers the object with paper and rubs the wide length of a peeled crayon over it.

Paint and crayons A process called *crayon resist* is fun for three year olds. They draw a picture, pressing the crayon hard on the paper. The drawing is then painted with a dark-colored water paint.

Play dough or clay Clay for three year olds should be soft and easy to use. Three year olds are not interested in making objects, but enjoy pounding and patting the clay. They also like to use tools with the clay, such as cookie cutters, blunt knives, and rolling pins.

Puppets Stick, hand, and bag puppets are appropriate for three year olds. The basic form must be simple to make and simple to use.

Arts and Crafts for Four Year Olds The arts and crafts for three year olds are continued and expanded.

String painting Four year olds enjoy dipping 12-inch pieces of string in poster paint and swishing them around on a piece of paper. String painting is the first introduction to abstract design.

Mosaics Children drop gravel (for fish bowls) into shallow pans of paint, scoop them out with a slotted spoon, and place them on a screen to dry. While the gravel dries, the children draw a picture. Spread thinned white glue on the drawings; the children sprinkle each glued part with colored gravel.

Paper stencils Cut large (4-inch) circles, squares, rectangles, and triangles in sheets of poster board. Have children place these cut-out designs on newsprint and color inside the cut-out parts with broad sweeping movements of chalk. Cut-out figures of trees, cars, people, and animals may also be used.

Masks Face masks made from paper bags are great fun for four year olds. The masks can be adorned with cotton beards, yarn hair, clown face designs, or large floppy ears.

Arts and Crafts for Five Year Olds The arts and crafts for four year olds are continued and expanded.

Spatter paintings Patterns of four to eight inches in size are placed on a sheet of paper. The children dip a toothbrush in poster paint and brush it vigorously back and forth over a framed piece of screen. When the spattered paint is dry, the children remove the pattern.

Wax paper transparencies Children grate broken pieces of crayon into a bowl, then sprinkle the grated crayons on an 8 × 11 inch piece of wax paper. Over the grated crayons the children place another piece of wax

PROJECT
Recalling Your Favorite Art Activities as a Young Child

Usually the fun things of life bring pleasant memories. Art activities encourage creative expression while at the same teaching basic skills.

1. Describe your favorite art activities as a five year old.
2. Do you remember the art materials you used at home? At school? Make a list of the materials.
3. Can you remember what skills your early teachers taught you? Describe how they taught these skills.
4. How did your parents respond to your early art activities? Write a paragraph describing their reactions.
5. Did your teachers encourage you to enjoy art? If yes, in what way?
6. Compare your early art experiences in school to the present-day methods and theories of art instruction discussed in this chapter.

paper the same size as the first. A piece of newspaper is placed over all and, under your supervision, the children iron the paper with a *warm* (not hot) iron. When the crayon wax is melted, punch a hole in the top of the wax paper and have the children hang them in the sunlight.

Papier-maché birdhouses Have each child blow up a 10-inch balloon (they may require help getting it started). Cut newspaper into wide strips. Children dip these strips into paste mix (see previous recipes) and wrap around balloon, covering entire balloon in equal layers. Hang the balloons by a string until dry. Cut a hole in the side for a bird entry and paint.

Ceramic objects Make salt dough from recipe provided earlier. Have children model any object they wish. Let dry and paint. Salt dough does not need to be baked to harden.

CHILDREN'S BOOKS ABOUT ART

Books are always a valuable asset in any curricular area. In art most of the books for young children are about color or shapes. Colors come in many shapes and therefore may cause children to hesitate when trying to identify them orally. True red, blue, green, and yellow, as well as other colors should be used as examples for teaching names of colors in the beginning stages.

Borton, Helen. *Do You See What I See?* New York: Abelard-Shuman, 1966.
Bright, Robert. *I Like Red*. New York: Doubleday, 1959.
Brown, Margaret Wise. *The Color Kittens*. New York: Golden Press, 1958.
Carle, Eric. *My Very First Book of Colors*. New York: Thomas Y. Crowell, 1974.
———. *My Very First Book of Shapes*. New York: Thomas Y. Crowell, 1974.
———. *My Very First Book of Words*. New York: Thomas Y. Crowell, 1974.
Creton, Gladys Yessayan. *Me, Myself and I*. New York: William Morrow, 1969.
Hoban, Tana. *Circles, Triangles and Squares*. New York: Macmillan, 1974.
Johnson, Crocket. *Harold and the Purple Crayon*. New York: Scholastic Book Services, 1955.
Kalusky, Rebecca. *Is It Blue as a Butterfly?* New York: Prentice-Hall, 1965.
Lionni, Leo. *The Greentail Mouse*. New York: Pantheon, 1973.
———. *Little Blue and Little Yellow*. New York: Astor-Honor, Inc., 1959.
Maestro, Giulio. *One More and One Less*. New York: Crown Publishers, 1974.
Reiss, John J. *Colors*. Scarsdale, N.Y.: Bradbury Press, 1969.
———. *Shapes*. Scarsdale, N.Y.: Bradbury Press, 1974.
Sandberg, Inger, and Lasse Sandberg. *Nicholas's Red Dog*. New York: Delacorte, 1967.
Spilka, Arnold. *Paint All Kinds of Pictures*. New York: Henry Z. Walck, 1963.
Steiner, Charlotte. *My Slippers Are Red*. New York: Knopf, 1957.
Tison, Annette, and Taylor Talus. *The Adventures of Three Colors*. World, 1971.
Wolff, Robert J. *Seeing Red*. New York: Charles Scribner's Sons, 1968.

Summary

The four basic theories of teaching art give teachers a choice in how they are going to teach art. Because of the many opportunities and wide selection of content to be taught, teachers also have a wide variety of choices from which to select the content to be taught.

In this chapter we have tried to present materials, theories, and activities that can be used creatively. Children need to have direct instruction in how to use the art media as well as free, unstructured opportunities to use the materials. As much as possible, art activities ought to be integrated into other subject areas being taught.

DIFFERENTIATING AND INTEGRATING MINI UNITS

The following mini units are examples of activities that will give children art experiences for skill development. At the same time they expand, in the context of art, children's knowledge of other subject areas. These mini units are *not* evaluative procedures for skill or knowledge in the subject areas; they do measure maturity in ability as the school year continues.

Mini Units Differentiating and Integrating for **Three Year Olds**

	September	*January*	*May*
Topic	Animals I know.	Drawing to music.	Dabbing designs.
Objectives	To provide children with an opportunity to cut and paste.	To provide children with an opportunity to identify color with music.	To provide children with an opportunity to create varying abstract designs.
Materials	Pages torn from magazines that have pictures of animals on them, 8 × 11 inch newsprint, scissors, paste.	Paper, crayons, record (or tape) of Hawaiian music, record player.	Paper, poster paint, paper towels.
Procedures	Children find animal pictures. They cut around the picture and then paste it on paper.	Give children paper and crayons. Explain that they are to listen to music and color the way the music makes them feel.	Place a small amount of red, yellow, and green poster paint on a paper towel. Crumble three paper towels in wads. Have children dip wads into one color at a time and press them on the paper.
Evaluation	Discussion of the animal names, where they live, and what they eat.	Children's ability to listen and draw.	Children's ability to do the activity.
Integrating skills	Oral language development. Science content. Social studies content. Eye-hand coordination.	Music. Listening. Eye-hand coordination. Small-muscle development.	Eye-hand coordination. Following directions. Small-muscle development.

Mini Units Differentiating and Integrating for **Four Year Olds**

	September	January	May
Topic	Puppet faces.	Hand prints.	Nutshell fun.
Objectives	To provide children with an opportunity to work with paper, paint, and crayons.	To provide children with an opportunity to work with plaster.	To provide children with an opportunity to make toys.
Materials	Paper plate, popsicle stick, poster paint, crayons.	Plaster mix, paint, hook eyes.	Walnut shell halves, clay, paper, toothpicks, scissors, glue.
Procedures	Have child paint a face on plate. Staple plate to stick.	Mix plaster in small batches. Form a 2-inch ball of plaster; flatten the ball into a free form. Have child press hand into plaster. Push hook eye into one edge. When dry let each child paint own handprint.	Animals can be made by adding clay feet and heads to shell. Boats can be made by sticking a toothpick sail in a piece of clay stuck in a shell.
Evaluation	Observation of children using puppets.	Finished product.	Finished product.
Integrating skills	Language arts.	Listening. Following directions.	Physical activity. Oral language.

Mini Units Differentiating and Integrating for **Five Year Olds**

	September	January	May
Topic	A molded mask.	Sock beanbags.	Tie dyeing.
Objectives	To provide children with an opportunity to work with aluminum foil, yarn, and paint.	To provide children with an opportunity to sew and to play with made object.	To provide children with an opportunity to work with cloth and dye.
Materials	Aluminum foil, poster paint, yarn, scissors, elastic tape.	Dried beans, an old sock, embroidery thread, plastic needle, scissors.	Large white cotton handkerchief, rubber bands, stones, dye (hot water, not boiling water brand).

Mini Units Differentiating and Integrating for **Five Year Olds** (*cont.*)

	September	*January*	*May*
Procedures	Cut aluminum foil in 30-inch lengths. Fold the lengths three times. Press the fold over child's face, making facial characteristics in foil. Then make slits for eyes, nose, mouth, and hair. With scissors, child can enlarge slits to shape desired. Help child tie yarn for hair. Tie elastic tape to hold on mask. Have child paint mask.	Have child fill one old sock with beans just over the heel. Have child sew the sock closed at top of heel. The leg part of the sock is used to grab and throw the beanbag.	Place two small stones in various places on the handkerchief and tie off each group of stones with a rubber band. Dip tied-off section into dye. Rinse in cold water.
Evaluation	Observation of ability to mold aluminum and use paint.	Observation of ability to sew.	Ability to accomplish the task.
Integrating skills	Following directions. Facial expressions (social studies). Small-muscle development.	Physical activity (beanbag games). Eye-hand coordination.	Gift giving (social studies). Small-muscle development. Eye-hand coordination.

EVALUATION OF INDIVIDUAL DIFFERENCES

Children of the same chronological age differ in attainment of performances and skills that are expected in young children. The following mastery lists shows the differences that can exist in one class in level of attainment of a few of these skills. A study of these lists will help you ascertain how the children should be grouped for instruction and for participation in the various centers. For example: In October, thirteen of the three year olds could not manipulate clay. In January seven children were still having difficulty: by May only one child was still unable to manipulate clay.

Mastery of Molding Clay (Pounds, rolls in thin ropes, and shapes balls) (Age range 3.1 to 3.3 by October 1)

Name	October	January	May
Barry	no	yes	yes
Costos	no	no	yes
Cheryl	yes	yes	yes
Vicki	no	yes	yes
Glenna	no	no	yes
Nelliana	yes	yes	yes
Bob	no	no	yes
Martha	no	yes	yes
Gerardo	yes	yes	yes
Kim	no	yes	yes
Bruce	no	no	yes
Jack	no	no	no
Alice	yes	yes	yes
Lane	no	yes	yes
Erick	no	no	yes
Tommy	yes	yes	yes
David	no	yes	yes
Orie	no	no	yes

Mastery of Drawing Basic Forms (Circle, oval, square, rectangle, lines) (Age range 4.2 to 4.4 by October 1)

Name	October	January	May
Joanne	no	no	yes
Ranjit	no	no	yes
Betty	no	yes	yes
David	no	yes	yes
Renee	no	no	yes
Millie	no	no	yes
Walter	no	yes	yes

Mastery of Drawing Basic Forms (cont.)

Name	October	January	May
Joel	no	no	no
Christina	yes	yes	yes
Charlotte	no	yes	yes
Philippas	no	yes	yes
Donald	no	no	no
Bela	no	yes	yes
Edith	no	no	yes
Shirley	yes	yes	yes
Mary Louise	no	no	yes
Casey	no	no	no
Basdeo	no	no	yes

Mastery of Spatter Painting with Stencil (Age range 5.3 to 5.4 by October 1)

Name	October	January	May
Gwen	no	no	no
Les	no	yes	yes
Alonzo	no	no	yes
Marilyn	no	yes	yes
Anne	no	no	yes
Wilma	no	no	yes
Taito	no	no	yes
Lois	no	yes	yes
Michael	no	no	no
Judy	yes	yes	yes
Sally	no	yes	yes
Morris	no	no	yes
Donna	no	yes	yes
William	no	no	yes

Mastery of Spatter Painting with Stencil (cont.)

Name	October	January	May
Toyozo	no	no	no
Jack	no	no	no
Fred	no	no	yes
Theos	no	yes	yes
Jane	no	yes	yes
Toney	no	no	yes
Leveriano	no	yes	yes
Blair	no	yes	yes

LEARNING GOALS FOR CHILDREN

Consider the skills expected of children in most schools before they leave kindergarten. This will give you perspective on your contribution to their learning experiences.

- The child can identify and name the eight basic colors: red, blue, yellow, orange, green, purple, brown, and black.
- The child can sort objects according to shades of color.
- The child can reproduce a made pattern of cube blocks or symbols on cards.
- The child can manipulate scissors well enough to cut paper.
- The child can copy a square, circle, oval, rectangle, and lines.
- The child can pat, pound, roll, pinch, and shape clay.
- The child can embroider with a large plastic needle.
- The child can weave yarn or jersey strips.
- The child can paint at an easel without spilling or dropping paint.
- The child can make collages out of various materials.
- The child can spatter paint.
- The child can draw a picture, using crayons of different colors.
- The child shows interest in using crayons in different ways.
- The child can use his or her hands in several ways to make designs in finger-paint.
- The child shows interest in the crafts.
- The child shows interest and asks questions about painting, prints, sculpture, pottery, and weaving done by others.

BASIC SKILLS SEQUENCE CHART

See page 189 for an explanation of how to use skills sequence charts.

Art Skills

Key symbols: (✔) Introduction   (✔✔) Extension and Reinforcement

Skill	Level 1	Level 2	Level 3
Drawing			
Drawing from memory	✔	✔✔	✔✔
Develop a visual concept of the basic human form	✔	✔✔	✔✔
Develop size and spatial relationships	✔	✔✔	✔✔
Develop size relationships, such as height, weight, and body build		✔	✔✔
Draw from observation: size, shape, overlapping, overall design, or composition on page		✔	✔✔
Practice drawing from large to small		✔	✔✔
Develop concepts of basic shapes and proportions of the human face			✔
Develop powers of observation and awareness of detail			✔
Develop accuracy of memory, thinking in terms of proportion, perspective, detail			✔
Create a unified drawing that is original yet uses ideas from other pictures			✔
Painting			
Work with large pieces of paper, choose suitable colors, mix colors, use a variety of patterns	✔	✔✔	✔✔
Draw and paint from observation of the child's world with emphasis on shape, color, size, texture, detail		✔	✔✔
Create a painting that conveys a mood of excitement			✔
Extend awareness of detail			✔
Use watercolor as a medium for expression and learn its characteristics and ways of handling it			✔
Sculpture			
Observe for specific purposes	✔	✔✔	✔✔
Make a clay sculpture	✔	✔✔	✔✔

Art Skills *(cont.)*

Key symbols: (✔) Introduction   (✔✔) Extension and reinforcement

Skill	Level 1	Level 2	Level 3
Learn the concept of variety within a limited subject matter	✔	✔✔	✔✔
Make a paper sculpture, using cylinder formation, pasting, cutting on fold, curling, color combinations		✔	✔✔
Create a three-dimensional form by utilizing a natural form as a base			✔
Use materials imaginatively and appropriately			✔

Crafts

Skill	Level 1	Level 2	Level 3
Make a bowl or pot by hand using a simple method	✔	✔✔	✔✔
Use the incised line as a simple type of decoration	✔	✔✔	✔✔
Weave a simple form		✔	✔✔
Develop logical sequence of thinking		✔	✔✔
Develop ability to cut straight and curved lines		✔	✔✔
Develop sensitivity in color selection		✔	✔✔
Make a useful object that is also attractive		✔	✔✔
Make a simple strip papier-maché object		✔	✔✔

Graphics

Skill	Level 1	Level 2	Level 3
Learn the concept of graphic arts as a printing process	✔	✔✔	✔✔
Learn the concept of a repeat pattern	✔	✔✔	✔✔
Think logically	✔	✔✔	✔✔
Fold paper accurately	✔	✔✔	✔✔
Use a simple graphic arts process of object printing		✔	✔✔
Create more complex forms out of combinations of simple shapes		✔	✔✔
Use a monoprint graphic process			✔
Experience the spontaneous look of the medium and the reversed image			✔

Appreciation

Skill	Level 1	Level 2	Level 3
Learn the work of a master artist	✔	✔✔	✔✔
Relate a creative activity to the work of a famous artist		✔	✔✔
Expand creativity through the use of an unusual theme			✔
Develop appreciation for an artist's use of color, line, and form to create feeling			✔

ADDITIONAL READINGS

Bos, Beverly J. *Don't Move the Muffin Tins: A Hands-Off Guide to Art for the Young Child*. Carmichael, Calif.: Burton Gallery, 1978.

Brittain, W. Lambert. *Creativity, Art, and the Young Child*. New York: Macmillan, 1979.

Carico, Nita Cox, and Jane Calvert Guynn. *The Dried Flower Book*. New York: Doubleday, 1962.

Cherry, Claire. *Creative Art for the Developing Child: A Teacher's Handbook for Early Childhood Education*. Belmont, Calif.: Feaman Teacher Aids, 1972.

Croft, J. Doreen, and Robert D. Hess. *Activities Handbook for Teachers of Young Children*. 2nd ed. Boston: Houghton Mifflin, 1980.

Franks, Olive R. "Scribbles? Yes, They Are Art!" *Young Children*, 34 (July 1979), 15–22.

Haskell, Lendall L. *Art in the Early Childhood Years*. Columbus, Ohio: Charles E. Merrill, 1979.

Keimo, Jean Fincher. *What Can I Do Today?* New York: Pantheon, 1971.

Lasky, Lila, and Rose Mukerji. *Art: Basic for Young Children*. Washington, D.C.: National Association for the Education of Young Children, 1980.

Pile, Naomi F. *Art Experiences for Young Children*. New York: Macmillan, 1973.

CHAPTER 11
Music

Exploration Tasks

After studying this chapter, you should be able to complete these tasks:
- Discuss and describe several theories of music instruction.
- List motor-rhythmic activities and select appropriate music to accompany the activities.
- Plan music appreciation lessons for several classes.
- Choose songs to integrate other subject areas with the teaching of music.
- Describe the techniques of teaching a song.
- List rhythm band instruments and explain how to use them.
- Select music records, tapes, filmstrips, and books suitable for young children.
- Plan lessons for teaching rhythm, melody, and tone.

The legitimate goal of education is to assist each learner to become all that he is capable of being. The goal is not to force him to become something he is not. For too long we have defined equal education as the equal opportunity to become carbon copies of ourselves.

Kenneth S. Goodman

OVERVIEW

Music in its many forms provides an emotional extension of feelings and contributes to the general social and emotional stability of children. During the early years, music provides pleasure through freedom of physical movement, freedom of oral expression, and freedom to be creative with sound.

Children differ in their choices of which phase of music is most enjoyable. Some like the melody of music and therefore prefer singing or participating in clapping, walking, stamping feet, and in other body movements. A few will enjoy merely listening to music and wish little or no additional physical involvement.

The teacher should provide opportunities for participation in all phases of creative music, for exposure to many musical forms, and for integration of music activities into the other subject areas. Sometimes musical activities are devoted purely to an extension of music appreciation. At other times musical activities are an enrichment of the total program.

THEORETICAL CONTEXT

Theories are usually based on research. Valid research in music is very difficult to accomplish with three- and four-year-old children because they are generally unable to understand the tasks in the testing procedures. Observational methods, therefore, are the most common techniques used for developing innovative methods of instruction.

Petzold reported, in a six-year study ending in 1969, that if a child does not acquire an aural (listening) understanding of the elements of music while young, musical development will be severely limited.[1] Pflederer designed musical tasks based on Piaget's principal of conservation.[2] Five year olds exposed to problems of meter, rhythm, and time gave answers characteristic of Piaget's preoperational thought. They solved these problems by clapping, tapping, or singing to themselves. Moorhead and Pond discovered that children like to repeat the same sounds over and over in a melodic phrase.[3] Jersild and Beinstock, in a 1935 study of three year olds, found that the children usually preferred higher notes, had no preference for tonality, preferred singing within the range of middle C to A, and are more capable of responding accurately to rhythmic patterns if the tempo is fast. From

---

[1] R. Petzold, "Auditory Perception by Children," *Journal of Research in Music Education* 17 (1969): 82–87.

[2] M. Pflederer, "The Responses of Children to Musical Tasks of Conservation," *Journal of Music Education* 12 (1964): 251–68.

[3] G. E. Moorhead and D. Pond. *Music of Young Children I: Chant* (Santa Barbara: Pillsbury Foundation Studies, 1941).

the results of their study, Jersild and Beinstock recommend that teachers should not try to teach children to keep perfect time to specific musical patterns.[4]

Current methods of teaching music to young children have been influenced by several teachers of music in other countries. Dalcroze, a Swiss, developed a method of three components: eurhythmics or rhythmic movement; solfege, singing a melody with syllables; and improvisation on the piano. Kodaly, a Hungarian composer, believed that all children, even the very young, should learn to read and write music. Orff, a German composer, believed that young children should be taught music through dance, movement, and speech.[5] Suzuki, a Japanese violinist, founded the Talent Education Institute in 1948 to teach the very young (three year olds) to play the violin by the rote method.[6]

In the United States the Pillsbury Foundation School, founded in California in 1937, emphasized each child's individual interests and skills in music.[7] In 1964, the Ford Foundation and Music Educators' National Conference developed a program to familiarize music teachers with modern music and with creative music activities, and to help children obtain improvisational skills. Since 1970 several American music educators have compiled and written material to help children create, improvise, compare, and rearrange music to satisfy their own needs and skills. These helpful resources for teaching music are listed among the additional readings at the end of this chapter.

MOTOR-RHYTHMIC ACTIVITIES

Often teachers plan music motor-rhythmic activities for whole groups of children, even though at various stages of development children do not perform as well in a large group as they do individually or in small groups. When teaching the very young it is best to let those children participate who wish to.

[4] A. T. Jersild and S. F. Beinstock, *Development of Rhythm in Young Children*, Child Development Monographs No. 22 (New York: Teachers College Press, 1935).

[5] B. Landis and P. Carder, eds., *The Eclectic Curriculum in American Music Education: Contributions of Dalcroze, Kodaly and Orff* (Washington, D.C.: Music Educators' National Conference, 1972).

[6] J. D. Kendall, *The Suzuki Violin Method in American Music Education: What the American Music Educator Should Know about Shinichi Suzuki* (Washington, D.C.: Music Educators' National Conference, 1973).

[7] See G. E. Moorhead and D. Pond, *Music of Young Children I: Chant* (Santa Barbara: Pillsbury Foundation Studies, 1941).

Certain types of music are conducive to different types of motor responses such as clapping, rocking or swaying, tiptoeing, walking, jumping, sliding, skipping, bouncing or bobbing, galloping, running, dancing, hopping, and marching. Music selection, therefore, limits or expands physical expression according to the musical selection. Another limiting factor in movement to music may be the room arrangement. Expressive responses to music require floor space that is clear of big rugs, furniture, and other children.

Part of music involvement in motor-rhythmic activities is recognizing which type of rhythmic notation is appropriate for the selected activity. The fundamental beats of $\frac{3}{4}$, $\frac{4}{4}$, and $\frac{2}{4}$ are usually used for clapping, rocking, swaying, dancing, walking, tiptoeing, swinging, running, trotting, jumping, and bouncing, while $\frac{6}{8}$ time is good for galloping, hopping, and marching. Marching can also be done to $\frac{2}{4}$ and $\frac{4}{4}$ time. Skipping requires either $\frac{6}{8}$ or $\frac{2}{4}$ time. Music appropriate for various motor-rhythmic activities include the following songs:

Rocking, swaying, and swinging

"Swinging"
"Rock-a-bye Baby"
"The Farmer"
"Oh, Where Has My Little Dog Gone?"
"Autumn Leaves"
"I'm a Little Teapot"

Clapping

"Baa, Baa, Black Sheep"
"Are You Sleeping?"
"Who Will Come with Me?"
"Jack and Jill"
"Intry Mintry"
"Johnny Works with One Hammer"
"Miss Mary Jane"
"Bingo"
"Hush, Little Baby"
"This Old Man"

Walking, tiptoeing

"Walk Along, John"
"Let's Go Walking"
"Gavotte and Variation"
"The Elephant"
"Hey, Betty Martin"

Running

"Children's Ballet"
"The Elephant"
"Dappled Pony"

Skipping

"Lazy Mary"
"Skip to My Lou"
"Jack and Jill"
"Intry Mintry"

Marching

"Yankee Doodle"
"The Love for Three Oranges March"
"Marching Song"
"Marching Around the Alphabet"
"The Number March"

LISTENING

Listening to music provides many opportunities for children to respond rhythmically, to relax emotionally, and release tensions through appropriate behavior. Many children enjoy music best when they are listening and are not physically involved in any action connected with the music. Listening for relaxation should include some of the classics such as: "Lullaby" by Brahms, "March of the Toys" by Herbert, "In the Hall of the Mountain King" by Grieg, "A Midsummer Night's Dream" by Mendelssohn, "Nutcracker Suite" by Tschaikovsky, "Air on the G String" by Bach, "Moment Musicale" by Schubert, "Waltz in A-flat" by Brahms, "On the Wings of Song" by Mendelssohn, "Waltz of the Flowers" by Tschaikovsky, and "The Swan" by Saint-Saens.

Children can also listen to music to learn the content of other subject areas. Listening is a major component of any lesson. Therefore a variety of listening activities that include music will provide enjoyable experiences in learning. The following music is appropriate for young children.

Right-left hand concept

"Jimmy Crack Corn," *Exploring Music*, 1
"Bow Belinda," *Exploring Music*, Kindergarten
"Looby Loo," *Exploring Music*, 1

"Put Your Hands Up In the Air," by Hap Palmer, *Learning Basic Skills Through Music*, Volume 1
"Hokey Pokey," *Music for Early Childhood*

Songs and activities that involve counting

"The Number March," by Hap Palmer, *Learning Basic Skills Through Music*, Volume 1
"Five Little Chickadees," *Exploring Music*, Kindergarten
"The Elephant," *Exploring Music*, 1
"Johnny Works with One Hammer," *Exploring Music*, 1
"Take Away," by Hap Palmer, *Learning Basic Skills Through Music*, Volume 2
"Seven Steps," *Exploring Music*, 1
"Count with Me," *Music for Early Childhood*
"Twosies," *Music for Early Childhood*

Songs that aid in teaching color

"Colors," by Hap Palmer, *Learning Basic Skills Through Music*, Volume 1
"Little Red Caboose," *Exploring Music*, 1
"Choosing Shoes," *Exploring Music*, Kindergarten
"Jennie Jenkins," *Exploring Music*, Kindergarten
"Autumn Leaves," *Exploring Music*, 1
"Parade of Colors," *Learning Basic Skills Through Music*, Volume 2
"Color Song," *Music for Early Childhood*

Science

"Ballads for the Age of Science" (Recordings), Experimental Songs, Space Songs, Weather Songs. Order from: Lyons, Inc., 430 Wrightwood Avenue, Elmhurst, IL 60126
"First Snow," *Exploring Music*, Kindergarten
"Winter Wind," *Exploring Music*, Kindergarten
"It Rained a Mist," *Exploring Music*, Kindergarten
"May Snow," *Exploring Music*, Kindergarten
"Snowballs," *Making Music Your Own*, Kindergarten
"Weather Song," *Making Music Your Own*, Kindergarten
"Snow," *Beginning Music*
"Rainbow Song," *Music for Early Childhood*
"Autumn Leaves Now Are Falling," *Exploring Music*, 1
"Spring Is Coming," *Making Music Your Own*, Kindergarten
"May Baskets," *Making Music Your Own*, 1
"A Gust of Fall Wind," *Making Music Your Own*, 2

"Summer, Goodby!" *Making Music Your Own*, 2
"Winter, Goodby!" *Making Music Your Own*, 2

Social studies

Home and family

"Helping Mother," *Music for Early Childhood*
"My Family," *Music for Early Childhood*
"My Son John," *Music for Early Childhood*
"Quiet, Quiet," *Music for Early Childhood*
"Rocking with Grandfather," *Music for Early Childhood*
"With Daddy," *Music for Early Childhood*
"Mothers Make a Home," *Making Music Your Own*, Kindergarten
"After School," *Beginning Music*
"Mind Your Mother," *Beginning Music*
"Grandmere's Song," *Exploring Music*, 1
"Hush, Little Baby," *Exploring Music*, 1
"Shoheen, Sho," *Exploring Music*, 1
"O Mama, Hurry," *Exploring Music*, 1
"Sleep, Baby, Sleep," *Exploring Music*, 1
"My Family and Pets," *This is Music*, Kindergarten
"I Love My Family," *This is Music*, 1
"Little Family," *This is Music*, 1
"Beautiful Home, Sweet Home," *This is Music*, 1
"Miss Polly Had a Dolly," *This is Music*, 1
"Mother's Knives and Forks," *This is Music*, 1
"Dance to Your Daddy," *This is Music*, 1

Community helpers

"I Like the Policeman," *Music for Early Childhood*
"It's Fun to Go to the Grocery Store," *Music for Early Childhood*
"The Mailman," *Music for Early Childhood*
"Old MacDonald," *Music for Early Childhood*
"Fire Song," *Music for Early Childhood*
"Mister Policeman," *Making Music Your Own*, Kindergarten

Transportation

"Allee, Allee O," *Exploring Music*, Kindergarten
"Clickety-clack," *Exploring Music*, Kindergarten
"I Rode in a Jet," *Exploring Music*, Kindergarten
"The Wheels of the Bus," *Exploring Music*, Kindergarten
"Boats," *Exploring Music*, Kindergarten (poem)

"Riding in My Car," *Making Music Your Own*, Kindergarten
"Riding in the Bus," *Making Music Your Own*, Kindergarten
"The Train," *Making Music Your Own*, Kindergarten
"Let's Take a Little Trip," *Making Music Your Own*, Kindergarten

Holidays

"Holiday Songs and Rhythms," Hap Palmer Record

Halloween

"Five Little Chickadees," *Exploring Music*, Kindergarten (change words to "five little goblins")
"It's a Pumpkin," *Exploring Music*, Kindergarten
"Halloween Night," *Exploring Music*, Kindergarten
"Jack-o-Lantern," *Making Music Your Own*, Kindergarten
"The Witch Rides," *Making Music Your Own*, Kindergarten
"Halloween" by Ives, *Exploring Music*, 1 — Instrumental
"Five Little Pumpkins," *Exploring Music*, 1

Thanksgiving

"Five Fat Turkeys," *Exploring Music*, Kindergarten
"A Child's Thanksgiving," *Exploring Music*, Kindergarten
"I'm a Very Fine Turkey," *Making Music Your Own*, Kindergarten
"Over the River and Through the Wood," *Exploring Music*, 2
"Thanksgiving," *Making Music Your Own*, Kindergarten
"Grandpa's Turkey," *Exploring Music*, 1
"I'm Thankful," *Exploring Music*, 1

Christmas

Since there are so many Christmas songs, look up your favorites in the index of any books you have available.

Hanukah

"Little Candle Fires," *Exploring Music*, Kindergarten
"My Dreydl," *Exploring Music*, Kindergarten
"Joyous Chanukah," *Making Music Your Own*, Kindergarten
"In the Window," *Exploring Music*, 1

Easter

"My Easter Basket," *Making Music Your Own*, Kindergarten
"Parade Song," *Making Music Your Own*, Kindergarten
"Easter Time," *Exploring Music*, Kindergarten
"Funny Bunny," *Exploring Music*, 1

Valentine's Day

"Valentine's Day," *Making Music Your Own*, Kindergarten
"Valentine Dance," *Making Music Your Own*, Kindergarten
"My Valentine," *Exploring Music*, Kindergarten
"The Ribbon Dance," *Exploring Music*, 1
"A Tisket a Tasket," *Exploring Music*, 1

Listening to and singing music are closely related. The preceding music can also be sung.

SINGING

Children often express themselves in spontaneous song. Singing is a natural, happy occurrence and therefore should be part of every day's program. Any group of children will demonstrate a wide range of differences in voice quality and ability to sing. In selecting songs teachers should remember to select songs with the vocal range suggested by Jersild and Beinstock.[8]

Songs can be sung during sharing time, play time, on field trips, or with rhythmic activities during dramatizations and with instruments and records.

The following terms and definitions will help you understand terms used in the discussion of the teaching of music.

AB   A musical form consisting of two contrasting sections (example: Verse-Refrain)
ABA   A musical form consisting of three sections: the first and last sections are the same, the middle part is different
Bar lines   The vertical lines on the staff used to mark off groupings of beats, thereby dividing the music into measures
Body instruments   Different parts of the body, used in rhythmic fashion to accompany speech or song; that is, stamping feet, patting ("knee slapping"), clapping hands, snapping fingers
Chord   A combination of three or more different tones sounded simultaneously
Dynamics   Degrees of loudness or softness; may be indicated by the musical symbols *f, ff, mf, p, mp, pp,* and so on
Form   The "design" of music
Harmony   The combination of tones sounded simultaneously; a related succession of chords
Introduction   A preliminary part of a musical composition
Measure   The space on a staff between two bar lines

"Teacher, you forgot something."

"What did I forget, Barry?"

"You forgot a little song before we went home."

---

[8] *Development of Rhythm in Young Children*, Child Development Monographs No. 22 (New York: Teachers College Press, 1935).

PROJECT
Remembering Your Early Singing Experiences

Learning simple songs is usually a common experience of young children. Young children often have favorite songs that they sing or hum as they do other things.

1. Do you remember the first song you sang? What was it? How did you learn it?
2. List all the songs you can remember learning as a young child.
3. Describe your first music class. What techniques did your teacher use to teach you songs?
4. Observe a classroom teacher teaching young children a song. Make a list of the techniques used. How do these differ from the way you were taught songs as a child?

Melody   A rhythmically organized succession of single tones; that is, the "tune"

Ostinato   A short pattern repeated over and over again

Patting   Slapping the thighs lightly, just above the knees; a basic rhythmic body instrument used to accompany speech and song

Phrase   A natural division of the melodic line, usually ending with a longer note; comparable to a sentence in speech

Pitch   The highness or lowness of a musical sound

Pulse   The underlying beat present in most music

Rest   A sign indicating silence in music

Rondo   A form in music with which a recurring section, the first section, alternates with a number of different contrasting sections (ABACA)

Staff   The five lines and four spaces on which musical notes are written

Tempo   Time; rate of speed

Theme   A musical idea

Tone color   The quality of sound; timbre

Singing should be a "happening" many times during a day. You can greet children with a song, children can sing their favorite songs as they get their wraps for going outside, they can hum or sing a song as they work (as long as it doesn't disturb others), a lullaby is great for nap time, and a record playing in the quiet corner can be fun to sing along with as a child paints.

MATERIALS AND EQUIPMENT

A variety of instruments, records, song books, and tapes will provide many opportunities for creative activities by both the teacher and the children. As with other material and equipment, be selective in usage and do not have all of it available at one time. Children should participate in music activities until they are comfortable in the activity.

Musical Literature

The earliest literature for children is often musical lullabies, songs, and nursery rhymes. These are sung, chanted, or read to children as they wake up, dress, or do their daily activities. Examples are "Good Morning to You," "Row, Row, Row Your Boat," and "Hickory Dickory Dock." There are several Mother Goose and song collections that will aid you as a teacher and are good suggestions for parent resources. Some suggested titles are:

Battaglia, Aurelius. *Mother Goose*. New York: Random House Picturebook, 1973.

Fujikawa, G. *Mother Goose*. New York: Grossett & Dunlap, 1975.

Opie, Iona, and Peter Opie. *The Oxford Dictionary of Nursery Rhymes*. Fair Lawn, N.J.: Oxford University Press, 1951.

Porter, Elizabeth. *Baby's Song Book*. New York: Thomas Y. Crowell Co., 1972.

Tudor, T. *Mother Goose*. New York: Henry Z. Walck, 1944, 1976.

Wright, B. F. *The Real Mother Goose*. Chicago: Rand McNally, 1978.

Records

Records that build music skills

Hap Palmer Record Library. Order titles below from Educational Activities, Inc., Freeport, NY 11520.

    AR 514 *Learning Basic Skills Through Music, Volume 1*
    AR 522 *Learning Basic Skills Through Music, Volume 2*
    AR 521 *Learning Basic Skills Through Music: Building Vocabulary*
    AR 526 *Learning Basic Skills Through Music: Health and Safety*
    AR 523 *Modern Tunes for Rhythms and Instruments*
    AR 527 *Mod Marches*
    AR 533 *Creative Movement and Rhythmic Exploration*
    AR 519 *Patriotic and Morning Time Songs, Grades 1–4*
    AR 538 *Holiday Songs and Rhythms*
    AR 545 *Homemade Band*
    AR 524 *Folk Song Carnival*

AR 518 *Simplified Folk Songs*
AR 540 *Math Readiness: Vocabulary and Concepts*
AR 541 *Math Readiness: Addition and Subtraction*
AR 543 *Getting to Know Myself*

Adventures in Rhythm with Ella Jenkins. Order titles below from Adventures in Rhythm, 1844 North Mohawk Street, Chicago, IL 60614.

7664 *You'll Sing a Song and I'll Sing a Song*
7665 *Play Your Instruments and Make a Pretty Sound*
7638 *Call and Response Rhythmic Group Singing*
7631 *Little Johnny Brown*

Fundamental Rhythms for the Young Set LP 3090; *Alley Cat* (45 rpm) No. 503. Order from: Kimbo Educational, Box 246, Deal, NJ 07723.

Sounds of New Music FX 6160. Order from Folkways Records, 906 Sylvan Avenue, Englewood Cliffs, NJ 07632.

Movement and Dance Records. Order titles below from Lyons, Inc., 430 Wrightwood Avenue, Elmhurst, IL 60126.

In Sounds from Way Out (Vanguard Label)
Listen, Move and Dance Volume 1
Listen, Move and Dance Volume 2

Movement and Dance Records. Order titles below from Educational Activities, Inc., Freeport, NY 11520.

Dances Without Partners, Album No. 32
Pre-Square Dance
Basic Mixer Music

Dance-A-Story Albums. Order titles below from RCA Records, Educational Sales, P.O. Box RCA 1000, Indianapolis, 46291.

LE-101 *Little Duck* (for ages 3–7)
LE-102 *Noah's Ark* (for ages 3–9)
LE-103 *The Magic Mountain* — Set A (for ages   –12)
LE-104 *Balloons* (for ages 4–12) — LE-101-104
LE-105 *The Brave Hunter* (for ages 5–8)
LE-106 *Flappy and Floggy* — Set B (for ages 3–7)
LE-107 *The Toy Tree* (for ages 3–7) — LE-105-108
LE-108 *At the Beach* (for ages 5–12)
Complete set, LE-101 through LE-108

"Meet the Instruments" Series, Bowmar #124. Order from Bowmar Records, Inc., 622 Rodier Drive, Glendale, CA 91201.

Happy Time Records. Order from Eye Gate House, 146-01 Archer Avenue, Jamaica, NY 11435.

Packet #GHT-1000A
Packet #GHT-1000B
Total package (A&B) GHT-1000X

Records that coordinate music with other subjects

Ablyoyo and Other Story Songs for Children, Folkways FTS 3100 (1968)
Animals (Best in Children's Series), Bowmar CL 19
American Folk Songs for Children, Folkways FTS 31501 (1968)
Animal Folk Songs for Children, Folkways FTS 31503 (1968)
Birds, Beasts, Bugs and Little Fishes, Folkways FTS 31504 (1968)
Fables (Best in Children's Series), Bowmar CL 22
A Gathering of Great Poetry for Children, Caedmon TC 1235-1238 (1968)
Music for Children (Carl Orff and Gunhild Keetman), Angel Records 3582 B (1959)
Poems and Songs for Young Children, Spoken Arts 1060 (1971)
The Red Balloon, Nonesuch Records H 72001
So Early in the Morning: Irish Children's Traditional Songs, Rhymes, and Games, Tradition TLP 1134
Songs for Singing Children (John Langstaff and Children's Chorus), Odeon CSD 1470
Songs to Grow On (Woody Guthrie), Folkways Records, FTS 31502
A Treasury of Folk Songs for Children, Elektra EKL 223 (1963)
The Unicorn in the Garden (James Thurber), Caedmon TC 1398 (1972)

Record companies

Order catalogs from:
    Bowmar Records, 622 Rodler Drive, Glendale, CA 91201
    Educational Activities Inc., Freeport, NY 11520
    Folkways, 701 Seventh Avenue, New York, NY 10036
    Columbia Children's Record Library, CBS Inc., 15 W. 52nd Street, New York, NY 10019
    Weston Woods Studios, Weston, CN 06883

Instruments

Rhythm band instruments

Rhythm sticks
Tone blocks with mallets
Sleigh bells
Ankle bells
Wrist bells

Cymbals
Triangles and beaters
Jingle clogs
Castanets
Tambourines

Latin American rhythm instruments

Maracas
Claves
Guira with scratcher

Wood blocks
Sand blocks
Castanets

Each child has an opportunity to play an instrument in rhythm band activities.

Drums

Tub drums
Tom-toms
Bongo drums

Congo drums
Mano drums
Hand drums

Other instruments

Melody bells
Recorder
Tone bars

Jingle bells
Kazoo

Instruments for the teacher

Zither
Pitch pipe

Autoharp
Xylophone

SUMMARY

Selecting a theory and content for teaching music to young children is difficult because of the lack of thorough research in the area but we have tried to present some basic information on teaching music that should aid your planning of music lessons. Some of the materials that this chapter describes are basic items for each room while others may be shared among several teachers. The many musical activities for integrating music into the other subject areas should help you provide many musical experiences for your children.

DIFFERENTIATING AND INTEGRATING MINI UNITS

These mini units for music, as those for other subject areas, are developmental in design. They provide reinforcement of previously learned skills as well as a setting for teaching new skills as children mature. Music fits into your teaching plans for mathematics, language arts, and social studies.

Mini Units Differentiating and Integrating for **Three Year Olds**

	September	*January*	*May*
Topic	An outdoor concert.	A march around the block.	Tiptoeing to "Swan Lake."
Objectives	To provide children with an opportunity for free movement to music.	To provide children with an opportunity to march to music.	To provide children with an opportunity to participate in a ballet.
Materials	Record (or tape), record player.	Portable tape recorder, tape of marching music.	Record player, record of "Swan Lake" ballet.
Procedures	Play record as children move to music.	Line children up by pairs. Play tape as children march on sidewalk.	Take off shoes and dance on tiptoes to music.
Evaluation	Observe performance.	Observe performance.	Observe performance.
Integrating skills	Physical activity. Listening. Following directions.	Physical activity. Listening.	Physical activity. Listening.

Mini Units Differentiating and Integrating for Four Year Olds

	September	January	May
Topic	Galloping on the farm.	High and low.	Beating the drum.
Objectives	To teach children rhythm.	To teach children to identify high and low sounds.	To teach children rhythm.
Materials	Film of horses galloping, record, "Little Gray Ponies."	Song, "I'm Tall, I am Small"; "Ring a Ring O' Roses."	Drum and beaters, records.
Procedures	Practice galloping to music.	Sing songs. Have children reach high or low.	Let children take turns beating the drum to the tempo.
Evaluation	Observe rhythm of galloping.	Observation of response.	Recognition of tempo.
Integrating skills	Observation skills. Listening. Social studies.	Following directions. Oral vocabulary. Physical activity.	Listening. Physical activity. Following directions. Taking turns.

Mini Units Differentiating and Integrating for Five Year Olds

	September	January	May
Topic	Skip around the rug.	Rhythm band march.	Sing refrains.
Objectives	To teach children how to skip to music and rhythm.	To teach children to play rhythm band instruments.	To teach children to be aware of repeated sections of music.
Materials	Record: "Skip to My Lou," record player.	Rhythm band instruments, records.	Songs: "Up on the Housetop," "Jennie Jenkins."
Procedures	Demonstrate how to skip. Have children practice. Play music and skip.	Demonstrate how to use instruments. Let children practice to music.	Have children listen to songs. Have children stand up on the verse and sit down on the refrain. Have children sing songs.
Evaluation	Performance.	Performance.	Performance.
Integrating skills	Physical activity. Following directions. Listening.	Listening. Physical activity. Following directions.	Language development. Listening. Physical activity.

Individuals differ in musical performance just as they do in other areas. Even though music is often taught to a whole group, do not expect each individual to react in the same way. The following evaluative progress lists of children show how each group differs even at the same chronological age in their individual mastery of a designated skill or performance. Each list also acts as a criterion for grouping the children for instruction of certain activities.

EVALUATION OF INDIVIDUAL DIFFERENCES

Mastery of Responding to Music by Marching on Tiptoes (Age range 3.2 to 3.4 by October 1)

Name	October	January	May
Charlie	no	no	yes
Pauline	no	yes	yes
Bonnie	no	no	yes
Flavio	no	yes	yes
Robert	no	yes	yes
Signie	yes	yes	yes
Karl	no	no	no
Robin	yes	yes	yes
Wesley	no	no	yes
Karen	no	no	no
Juan	no	yes	yes
Imbert	no	yes	yes
Lee	no	no	yes
Doug	no	yes	yes
Garry	no	no	yes
Albert	no	yes	yes
Joyce	no	yes	yes
Nikolai	yes	yes	yes

Mastery of Identification of High and Low Sounds (Age Range 4.1 to 4.3 by October 1)

Name	October	January	May
Marie	yes	yes	yes
Nelliana	no	yes	yes
June	no	no	yes
Barbara	no	yes	yes
Ann	no	no	no
Reuben	no	no	yes
George	yes	yes	yes
Robert	yes	yes	yes
Sarah	no	yes	yes
Nan	yes	yes	yes
Louis	no	yes	yes
Milton	no	yes	yes
Brenda	yes	no	yes
Nancy	no	yes	yes
Jesse	no	no	no
James	no	no	yes
Paula	no	no	no
Hollie	no	no	no
William	no	yes	yes
Dominic	yes	yes	yes
Nolan	no	no	yes

Mastery of Identification of Fast and Slow Tempos (Age Range 5.3 to 5.5 by October 1)

Name	October	January	May
Toney	no	no	yes
David	no	yes	yes
Yaraslav	no	yes	yes
Janice	no	yes	yes
Pat	no	no	yes
Leigh	no	no	no

Mastery of Identification of Fast and Slow Tempos (cont.)

Name	October	January	May
Roger	no	no	yes
Hyman	no	no	yes
Eugenia	no	yes	yes
Tom	no	no	yes
Joe	no	no	yes
Donna	no	yes	yes
Maria	no	no	yes
Peggy	no	yes	yes
Val	no	no	yes
Emory	no	no	no
Nico	no	yes	yes
Joann	yes	yes	yes
Harris	no	yes	yes
Ronnie	no	no	yes
Joy	yes	yes	yes
Nada	no	yes	yes

LEARNING GOALS FOR CHILDREN

The list of exit skills for kindergarten children — the performances expected of them before they progress to first grade — will help you organize your musical teaching activities to provide the best possible environment for children to achieve these goals.

- The child can imitate the teacher in clapping out a simple pattern.
- Given two sounds, the child can state which is louder, which softer.
- Given two notes, the child can state which is the high note and which the low.
- The child can respond to fast music by running on tiptoe and to slow music by walking slowly.
- On hearing a familiar story with various character voices ("The Three Bears"), the child can identify characters by the tones of their voices.
- The child can respond appropriately to the direction "Walk when you hear music. Stop when the music stops."

87
88
89
90
91

✔ The child can identify five common sounds in the immediate environment or from a tape recording (water running, door closing, and so on).

✔ With eyes closed, the child can identify the instrument the teacher plays (cymbals, triangle, tambourine, or other).

BASIC SKILLS SEQUENCE CHART

See page 189 for an explanation of how to use skills sequence charts.

Music Skills

Key symbols: (✔) Introduction   (✔✔) Extension and Reinforcement

Skill	Level 1	Level 2	Level 3
Rhythm			
Respond to the basic pulse of music with the appropriate body movement or rhythm instrument	✔	✔✔	✔✔
Distinguish between the beat (the basic pulse of the music) and the rhythmic pattern of words	✔	✔✔	✔✔
Begin to recognize simple rhythm patterns within a song	✔	✔✔	✔✔
Become aware of long and short tones and relate to line notation	✔	✔✔	✔✔
Distinguish between the basic beat and the rhythmic pattern of the melody or words		✔	✔✔
Become aware of whether a song moves in two or threes		✔	✔✔
Begin to read simple rhythm patterns from notation			✔
Melody			
Recognize sounds as being "high" or "low"	✔	✔✔	✔✔
Begin to discriminate between smaller pitch differences	✔	✔✔	✔✔
Become aware that a melody may move up, down, or stay the same	✔	✔✔	✔✔
Sing short melodies on pitch	✔	✔✔	✔✔
Recognize and sing previously learned melodies	✔	✔✔	✔✔
Associate number or letter notation with pitch		✔	✔✔
Become aware of musical symbols as music books are used			✔
Become aware of major and minor melodies and chords			✔

Music Skills (cont.)

Key symbols: (✔) Introduction   (✔✔) Extension and reinforcement

Skill	Level 1	Level 2	Level 3
Form			
Recognize that most music is divided into phrases	✔	✔✔	✔✔
Recognize that songs may have like and unlike phrases	✔	✔✔	✔✔
Recognize that some music contains repeated sections	✔	✔✔	✔✔
Recognize and demonstrate phrase length through imitative echo clapping	✔	✔✔	✔✔
Become aware of "like" and "unlike" phrases in music		✔	✔✔
Recognize simple two- and three-part form		✔	✔✔
Become more accurate in echo work, using longer phrases and incorporating pats, claps, snaps, stamps, and rests		✔	✔✔
Recognize by sight and sound the length of a phrase			✔
Harmony			
Recognize when harmony is or is not present	✔	✔✔	✔✔
Recognize that harmony is a combination of two or more tones		✔	✔✔
Become aware of the need for a change of harmony within a song		✔	✔✔
Play and sing songs that use different types of harmony			✔
Tempo			
Recognize that music has tempo	✔	✔✔	✔✔
Distinguish between fast and slow tempos	✔	✔✔	✔✔
Distinguish between obvious tempo differences between compositions		✔	✔✔
Recognize that the tempo may change within a piece of music		✔	✔✔
Recognize that tempo affects the expressive purpose of music			✔
Tone Color			
Distinguish between broad categories of instruments	✔	✔✔	✔✔
Distinguish between broad categories of singing voices		✔	✔✔
Dynamics			
Identify obvious changes in dynamics and relate them to musical expressiveness	✔	✔✔	✔✔
Recognize the appropriateness of certain dynamics in music	✔	✔✔	✔✔
Recognize that every sound has some degree of loudness or softness		✔	✔✔
Demonstrate an awareness of the expressive qualities of dynamics in singing, playing, or listening			✔

ADDITIONAL READINGS

Adkins, D.C., and M. Greenburg. *Music for Preschool Accompanied by Songbook*. OEO Final Report No. 9929. ERIC Document No. ED060948. Washington, D.C.: U.S. Government Printing Office, 1971.

Andress, B.L., et al. *Music in Early Childhood*. Washington, D.C.: Music Educators' National Conference, 1973.

Aronoff, Frances Webber. *Music and Young Chidlren, Expanded Edition*. New York: Turning Wheel Press, 1979.

Bayless, Kathleen M., and Marjorie E. Ramsey. *Music: A Way of Life for the Young Child*. St. Louis, Mo.: C. V. Mosby Co., 1978.

Beckwith, Mary. *So You Have To Teach Your Own Music*. Englewood Cliffs, N.J.: Prentice-Hall, 1970.

Bergethon, Bjornar, and Eunice Boardman. *Musical Growth in the Elementary School*. New York: Holt, Rinehart & Winston, 1979.

Findlay, Elsa. *Rhythm and Movement: Applications of Dalcroze Eurhythmics*. Princeton, N.J.: Summy-Birchard, Inc., 1971.

Greenberg, Marvin. *Your Children Need Music*. Englewood Cliffs, N.J.: Prentice-Hall, 1979.

Haines, B. Joan, and Linda L. Gerber. *Leading Young Children to Music: A Resource Book for Teachers*. Columbus, Ohio: Charles E. Merrill, 1980.

Landis, Beth, and Polly Carter. *The Eclectic Curriculum in American Music Education: Contributions of Dalcroze, Kodaly, and Orff*. Washington, D.C.: Music Educators' National Conference, 1972.

McDonald, D.T. *Music in Our Lives: The Early Years*. Washington, D.C.: National Association for the Education of Young Children, 1979.

Raebeck, Lois, and Lawrence Wheeler. *New Approaches to Music in the Elementary School*. Dubuque, Iowa: William C. Brown, 1980.

———. *Orff and Kodaly Adapted for the Elementary School*. Dubuque, Iowa: William C. Brown, 1977.

Reynolds, Jane L. *Music Lessons You Can Teach*. Englewood Cliffs, N.J.: Prentice-Hall, 1970.

Zimmerman, M. P. *Musical Characteristics of Children*. Washington, D.C.: Music Educators' National Conference, 1971.

CHAPTER 12
Play and Movement

Exploration Tasks

After studying this chapter, you should be able to complete these tasks:
- Define play and movement education.
- Describe the functions of play.
- List the differences in the play of three, four, and five year olds.
- Discuss the research findings on cultural influences on play.
- Select games appropriate for young children.
- Design indoor and outdoor play areas.
- Select equipment and materials appropriate for young children.
- Plan and execute movement activities.

Our conscience and our commitment have to be our prods. . . . Not pressure, not tension, not competition, treating a day as if it were a race, a life as if it were a war, people as if they were an army, children as if they were cattle to be paraded and judged and always found wanting. These sicken the human spirit.

James L. Hymes, Jr.

OVERVIEW

What is play? Play has many definitions. Probably because of these diverse definitions children's play is one of the least understood functions in an early childhood program. For most adults play is a leisure-time activity, indulged in only after they have completed their responsibilities of making a living, keeping house, and providing other essential services for their families and themselves. Therefore, to many adults play is relaxation.

For young children, however, play is not a leisure-time or relaxation activity. Play involves actual physical movement, mental concentration, emotional stability, and social growth. Young children are happiest and learn more quickly when they are touching, moving, talking, and sharing while they are involved in an activity.

The act of playing with the basic materials and equipment found in an early childhood classroom or playyard provides stimulating and productive learning opportunities. A child's physical development implements and encourages further mental, social, and emotional growth; it is as important as learning to read. *Play* as we discuss it in this chapter refers to the physical actions of the individual through the use of equipment, materials, activities, and games.

Movement education is a part of physical play. The components of movement involve *what* the body can do — locomotion; elevation; and such movements as turn, open, and close; *how* the body moves — heavily, lightly, suddenly, slowly, controlled, or free; and *where* the body moves — far, near, high, low, right, left, straight, angular, and so on. Movement also involves *relationships;* the parts of the body to other parts of the body, individuals to other individuals, and groups of individuals to other groups of individuals. Through knowledge of how a body moves the child develops a sense of self, learns social movement skills, develops an aesthetic pleasure for movement that leads to symbolic body representation (dance), and learns to use the body to control and express emotional feelings.

THEORETICAL CONTEXT: PLAY

Is the ability to play taught? Is play physical imagination? Is release of excess energy the goal of play? Does a child go through all the developmental stages of the human race through play actions? Is play a preparation for work in later life? Is play an escape from unpleasant events? Is play an interpretation of a familiar event? Do play activities occur in definite stages of sequence?

At some time during the last two centuries, one or several of these theories were advocated by leading theorists of the time. Among the theorists were Schiller, Spencer, Hall, Groos, Buhler, Piaget, Erikson, Frank, and Kagan.

No one theory seems to provide an answer to what play is or should be. The more recent theorists suggest that play is necessary and important for a child's spontaneous, undirected pleasure and socialization. Generally these

Play and movement are essential aspects of early childhood education.

theorists — including Sutton-Smith, Murphy, Des Lauriers, Skeels, Rheingold, Mahler, and Millar — recognize several factors as extensions, stimulants, and enrichments to play activities.[1] Play is as individualized as any other experience a child has. A 1978 publication on research on children's play, *Activity and Play of Children*, is an excellent guide for establishing scientific evidence about play.[2]

In the foreword of *Group Games in Early Education: Implications of Piaget's Theory*, Piaget has written, "Play is a particularly powerful form of activity that fosters the social life and constructive activity of the child."[3]

---

[1] Sources are K. Buhler, *The Mental Development of the Child* (London: Routledge & Kegan Paul, 1973); Eric Erikson, *Childhood and Society* (New York: Norton, 1950); Lawrence Frank, "Play Is Valid," *Childhood Education*, 45 (1968), 443–40; K. Groos, *The Play of Man* (New York: Appleton, 1901); George Stanley Hall, *Youth: Its Education, Regimen and Hygiene* (New York: Appleton-Century-Crofts, 1907); Jerome Kagan, "Inadequate Evidence and Illogical Conclusions," *Harvard Educational Review*, 39 (1969): 247–77; and Jean Piaget, *Play Dreams and Imitation in Childhood* (New York: Norton, 1962).

[2] M. J. Ellis and G. J. L. Shotz, *Activity and Play of Children* (Englewood Cliffs, N.J.: Prentice-Hall, 1978).

[3] Constance Komii and Rheta DeVries, *Group Games in Early Education: Implications of Piaget's Theory* (Washington, D.C.: NAEYC, 1980).

If you are interested in using Piaget's cognitive theory in your classroom, you will find this book helpful in extending his theory. Another helpful source for establishing a Piaget-based play program is *Constructive Play: Applying Piaget in the Classroom*.[4]

Play at Different Ages

The function of play differs at varying chronological ages. Three year olds like to pretend, act out, and play roles; they have difficulty separating real people and animals from pretend characters and animals. Three year olds are also great collectors of playthings that are attractive to them, such as books, dolls, cars, puzzles, airplanes, colorful small boxes, buttons, and other odds and ends. Three year olds also like repetition. They enjoy playing the same games over and over, as well as playing with the same toy or doing the same activity many times. At this age the child changes roles and activities often, usually going from one extreme to the other — the quick shift from a mother rocking her baby to a horse galloping in the fields is not unusual in play activities of three year olds.

Four year olds are more imaginative and aggressive in their play. Ghosts, monsters, and dinosaurs are some of their favorite characters. Television cartoon characters also appear in their role playing. Four year olds differ from three year olds in that they are starting to know the difference between real and imaginary characters. Because four year olds' coordination is more developed than three year olds', they enjoy toys and equipment that have movable parts or removable parts. Hide-and-seek games, whether hiding something in the room or hiding themselves on the playground or school-yard, bring great delight to four year olds.

Five year olds begin to play games that have rules and objectives. They often play out their fears in the housekeeping or truck centers by role playing their feelings in a situation they control. Aggressive behavior is sometimes released by pretending to be a monster and scaring adversaries. Muscle development and coordination have improved and the children are able to handle smaller, more complicated toys and tools. A few five year olds are able to ride two-wheeled vehicles. Tall block towers seem to fascinate some of them while others are greatly interested in building intricate buildings.

Cultural Influences on Play

Studies of cross-cultural and social level differences in play activities suggest and describe definite divergence in play responses. Smilansky studied underprivileged children from the Middle East and North Africa who had

The kite the five year olds were flying became hopelessly entangled in a tree. As they jiggled and wiggled the string, Diane looked up to the sky and said, "Well, God, you are up there, you can knock it down if you want to." At that moment the string broke and the kite remained in the tree. Diane summed it up with, "Well, he didn't want to."

---

[4] G. E. Forman and F. Hill, *Constructive Play: Applying Piaget in the Classroom* (Belmont, Calif.: Brooks/Cole, 1980).

immigrated to Israel and who were failing school subjects.[5] Her experimental kindergarten program included a group of advantaged children as well as the immigrants and was designed to provide sociodramatic play situations that included role-playing — housekeeping center; truck and block center; and firefighters, nurses, doctors, police, and other adult roles. Smilansky discovered that the immigrant children did not engage in any imaginative play. All of their play was realistic. The advantaged children engaged in both imaginative and realistic play activities.

In another cross-cultural study, Butler studied the Eskimo adults' relationship to their children and found the adults completely indulged their children.[6] Their permissiveness allowed them to laugh at behaviors that would be punished in our culture: sassiness, hitting, and refusal to obey, for example.

Whiting collected data of descriptions of activities and toys used by children in six cultures.[7] Her findings indicated a wide variation in fantasy and imaginative play — from none in a few societies to complex and symbolic play in several other societies.

In a 1962 comparison study of advantaged and extremely disadvantaged children of Asia and North America, Murphy found that all the children in both cultures role played familiar activities. But disadvantaged children in both cultures had limited curiosity, were not creative with oral language, and couldn't play act a preplanned activity such as "You be sick and I'll be the doctor."[8]

In *The Drifters*, several researchers analyzed the physical manifestations of children and parents from lower-class families.[9] The three general conclusions reached by these researchers were: Children portrayed or imitated the observable physical traits of adults and other children; children imitated situations literally; and adults in these families exhibited aggressive verbal behavior to their children and in turn when the children were role playing adults they yelled, cursed, and used severe physical punishment with dolls and other objects in the activity.

In another study, Kniveton and Pike compared middle-class and lower-class boys in early childhood classrooms.[10] They found that middle-class

---

[5] S. Smilansky, *The Effects of Sociodramatic Play on Disadvantaged Children* (New York: Appleton-Century-Crofts, 1973).

[6] B. Butler, "Eneprit: A Hot Idea from the Eskimos," *Day Care and Early Education* (1973): 16–18.

[7] B. Whiting, ed., *Six Cultures: Studies of Child Rearing* (New York: Wiley, 1973).

[8] L. Murphy et al., *The Widening World of Childhood* (New York: Basic Books, 1962).

[9] E. Pavenstedt, ed., *The Drifters* (Boston: Little, Brown, 1967).

[10] B. Kniveton and C. Pike, "Social Class, Intelligence, and the Development of Children's Play Interests," *Journal of Child Psychology and Psychiatry*, 13 (1972): 167–81.

boys played with a greater variety of toys than did lower-class boys in the same setting.

In a study limited to black families, Baughman and Dahlstrom related home surroundings to children's behavior.[11] They found that parents who played with their children and who had pleasant daily lives enhanced their children's sociability. Children whose parents did not play with them and whose daily life was unpleasant were less sociable in their play activities.

In a 1978 study on parent play with two year olds, the findings indicated that the majority of the two year olds in an orphanage who were well cared for but who lacked someone to play with were mentally deficient, while a similar group of children whose mothers were incarcerated in a penitentiary nearby but who had regular time for playing with them had learned all the skills normal for a two year old.[12]

PHYSICAL ACTIVITIES

Constant physical movement is normal for young children. Usually the "sitting still" activity is so fleeting that observers of young children wonder if they ever stop. Running, hopping, swinging, swaying, dancing, and climbing do not have to be introduced in most cases. What does have to be taught is control of the action and when, where, and how to do the activity safely. Three, four, and five year olds play alongside other children or with one or two children. They do not naturally seem to play in large groups. Since participation in group activity is a learned skill, children need many opportunities to play in small and informal groups before whole group games or exercises are introduced.

In carefully chosen games and movement activities, children will learn to cooperate within common general requirements without losing the opportunity to perform as individuals at their own ability level. These games and movement activities should provide action for all participants. Young children do not stand, sit, or wait for very long — sometimes not at all. Therefore, as a teacher you must analyze each piece of equipment and each activity for potential physical involvement in addition to determining the number of children who can actively engage in play.

Young three year olds are ecstatic daredevils when balancing on a low wall, a balance beam, or a log. A very bouncy rocking horse also brings great pleasure. The balancing activity can include several children; the

---

[11] E. Baughman and W. Dahlstrom, *Negro and White Children: A Psychological Study in the Rural South* (New York: Academic Press, 1968).

[12] D. Reiss and H. A. Hoffman, *The American Family*. New York: Plenum, 1979.

rocking horse is for one child at a time. Older three year olds enjoy rolling hoops; tossing bean bags; kicking, rolling, and bouncing balls (not catching); walking; climbing; and running. All these activities can involve several children at the same time.

Four year olds usually have mastered the tricycle and have had a brief fling with scooters. Slides, swings, rope ladders, something soft to jump on (bean bag chairs, rubber rafts, foam rubber mattresses), and something to punch such as punching bags, balloons, or pillows provide the individual active play four year olds like.

Children at this age are not steady walkers. They can walk at an adult's average pace, but not for long. Walking activities cannot be hurried and need to allow for resting. Otherwise you'll arrive at a busy street corner with fifteen to twenty children who wish to sit down!

Five year olds enjoy jumping distances, either from a high bench or box or just on the ground. They also enjoy climbing to the "top" of things. Vocabulary includes "Watch how fast I can run." "I can skip all the way to the fence," and "I can run farther than you can!" Hide-and-seek and tag games are great group involvement activities. These experiences help the teacher introduce the concepts of rules and responsibilities of group games.

EQUIPMENT SELECTION

Many indoor and outdoor activities of children are determined by the equipment, space, and surfaces available for their play.

Criteria

Equipment can improve the quality of the learning experience if selected with the following specifications:

Simplicity Too many details or parts hinder creative uses of the equipment. Cardboard boxes and unmarked blocks of varying sizes are examples of simplicity in design. Equipment should have no sharp points.

Versatility Much of the equipment should be usable in many different situations. Balls, bean bags, dolls, blocks, wagons, and so forth should be as easily used outside as inside the classroom.

Usability Children should be able to use the equipment without fear of breaking it or hurting themselves and without constant adult supervision.

Durability Wooden equipment should be made of hardwoods that are less likely to splinter. Rubber tires on wheeled toys are more durable than wood or plastic.

Availability Store equipment in a place accessible to children. Too many toys and too much equipment are confusing. All children should have an opportunity to play actively at all times. Several things should be available so that children have a choice. Some equipment should involve more than one child, such as housekeeping furniture, kitchen appliances, grocery store goods, swings, balls, and slides. Climbing bar equipment will always provide an available alternative.

Space (indoor) Adequate floor space requires thirty-five to sixty square feet for each child, depending on the number of children in the room. The larger the group of children, the less square footage each has. Equipment takes up space whether it is in use or not. Wheeled vehicles need space for movement.

Space (outdoor) Safety is an important consideration in planning any area, especially for outdoor play. Allow two hundred square feet per child, adjacent to easily opened school building doors and with easy access to toilets and water. It must be fenced and any exits in fencing should have latches beyond the reach of children.

The U.S. Consumer Product Safety Commission suggests the following precautions concerning the choice and placement of permanent equipment on a playground.

- All equipment should be stable; legs should be set in concrete below ground level.
- Any exposed screws or bolts should have covered caps.
- Don't buy equipment with open-ended hooks. (Chains or ropes can easily come unhooked.)
- Be sure all hanging rings are between five and ten inches in diameter so that children cannot get their heads or limbs caught in them.
- Don't put the equipment on concrete or asphalt; use sand or grass.
- Put swings at least six feet from fences or other objects.
- Choose lightweight flexible seats for swings instead of metal or wooden seats.

Surfaces (indoor) Since children often play and sit on the floor, its surface should be easily cleaned, warm, and noise resistant. Carpet is desirable in two places: the housekeeping area where quiet play takes place and the block building area. Areas for water play, sandbox, painting, and wheeled vehicles should have an easily cleaned, smooth surface.

Surface (outdoor) Outdoor play includes climbing, jumping, running, swinging, gardening, using wheeled vehicles and toys, water play, sand play, and sometimes small animals in cages. Therefore, the surface of an outdoor playground must include grass for running, sitting, and tumbling; sand under swings, slides, and climbing bars to cushion falls; soil for gardening; sandy areas for sandboxes; paved areas for wheeled toys; and brick, concrete, or other patio-type surfaces for water play. Some spaces should be in the shade and some in direct sun. All surfaces should drain well after rain or snow. The need for sun, shade, drainage, and wind vary according to the sections of the country in which you are teaching.

Storage (indoor) Every classroom needs adequate storage space in cupboards, cubicles, bins, shelves, cabinets, and boxes. Movable storage units are more flexible than built-in storage units. Mobile units can be used as room dividers or to change the size of areas. The backs of these units may be used for bulletin boards that are at the eye level of the children. Balls store better in a bin or box as they cannot roll out.

Storage (outdoors) Some outdoor equipment must be protected from the elements. The most practical way to protect them is a storage shed built on the side of the school building. A shed twelve feet long, five feet deep, and five feet high will store water play tools, carts, gardening tools, sandbox toys, wagons, slides, and tricycles.

Basic Indoor Equipment
Three and four year olds

Play structures

Crawling tunnel
Steps
Climbing fence
Seesaw
Rocking horse

Vehicles

Stick horse
28-inch wagon
13-inch tricycle
Double wheel wheelbarrow
Rocking boat

Ladders and bridges

8-inch walking board
6-inch bouncing board
Balance board
18-inch sawhorse

Balls

13-inch ball
10-inch ball
7-inch ball

Dramatic play equipment: review the social studies chapter.
Sand and water play equipment: review the science chapter.
Replica toy equipment: review the social studies chapter.
Block building equipment: study equipment for five year olds in this chapter.

Five year olds

Play structures
Tumbling mat
Crawling tunnel
Jumping steps
Rock and row boat
Play house
Tent
Truck inner tube
Rocking horse

Ladders and bridges
Wood bridge ladder
24-inch wooden sawhorse
18-inch wooden sawhorse
Bouncing board
Walking board
Balance beam

Vehicles
28-inch wagon
36-inch wagon
Scooter
16-inch tricycle

Balls and ropes
24-inch ball
16-inch ball
10-inch ball
8-inch ball
Skipping rope
Jumping rope

Wooden unit building blocks and boards

80 half units 1¼" × 2½" × 2¾"
360 units 1⅜" × 2¾" × 5½"
240 double units 1⅜" × 2¾" × 11"
80 quadruple units 1⅜" × 2¾" × 22"
60 pillars 1⅜" × 1⅜" × 5½"
30 cylinders 2¾" diameter × 5½"
15 cylinders 1⅜" diameter × 5½"
30 circular curves 1⅜" × 2¾" × 90"
15 elliptical curves 1⅜" × 2¾" × 90"
40 large triangles 1⅜" × 2¾" × 5½"

Hardwood boards — sanded
5 1" × 6" × 24"
5 1" × 6" × 36"
5 1" × 6" × 48"
5 1" × 6" × 60"
3 1" × 12" × 24"
3 1" × 12" × 36"
3 1" × 12" × 48"
Roof and floor boards
2 1" × 24" × 24" (exterior plywood)
2 1" × 24" × 36" (exterior plywood)
2 1" × 36" × 36" (exterior plywood)

15 small triangles 1⅜" × 2¾" × 2¾"
200 1-inch color cubes
4 large arches 1⅜" × 5½" × 11"
4 large switches 1⅜" × 11" × 11"
4 small switches 1⅜" × 6" × 11"

Accessory materials for block play such as replica animals, trucks, cars, boats, airplanes, people, dolls, and buildings are listed in the social studies chapter.

Basic outdoor equipment

Three and four year olds

7-foot-high bucket swings
42-inch-high triangular ladder
Crawl-through tunnels
4-foot-high slide
24-inch wagon
16-inch rubber-wheeled tricycle
Balance board
Wooden barrels and kegs
Stick horses
Covered sandbox
Steps
Ramp
Stationary spring riding animals

Rope ladder
2-foot-high seesaw
7-inch ball
10-inch ball
18-inch ball
Wading pool
Jumping board
Pedal cars
Slide
Merry-go-round
Rowboat
Sawhorses

Five year olds

Swings, canvas bucket, or tire casing seats
Rubber-wheeled wagon, 36-inch body
Horizontal ladder
Rope ladder or knotted rope ladder
Crawl-throughs, tire casing, or sewer tile
Truck-tire-casing fort, three casings high
Earth-mover (tractor)-tire-casing for balancing edge
Climbing treehouse
Jungle gym
Steering wheels attached to wooden frame (mobile)
Horse riding saddle

Large wooden packing boxes
Wooden or plastic barrels
Playhouse
Hanging bars
Seesaw
Merry-go-round
Tubs, buckets, pitcher pump
Tire inner tubes
Punching bag
Climbing frames
Balls
Jump ropes
Pedal cars
Pond for fish and sailing boats
Gardening, water, and sand play material: review the science chapter.

Two-person rubber raft
Pup tent
20-inch, rubber-wheeled tricycles
Steps for climbing and jumping
3-foot ramp for sliding and jumping
Sandbox

Wheelbarrow
Scooter
Indoor building blocks may also be used outdoors.
Replica toys; review the social studies chapter.

Basic Equipment for Handicapped Children

A-frame exerciser, portable
Sway bridge
Safety slide with rails on steps and slide, portable
Sand and water play trough accessible to wheelchair's use
Walking trainer with hand rails and foot guide

Regardless of the type and amount of facilities and equipment, the teacher's resourcefulness, initiative, and creativity are the most valuable assets in any active play situation. Through the teacher's ingenuity, the space and equipment stimulate the children to acquire new goals, understandings, and experiences.

GAMES FOR YOUNG CHILDREN

Musical Chairs   Without removing chairs; all children continue to play throughout game.

Fruit Basket Upset   Children sit in chairs in a circle. Each child is given either the name of a fruit or the actual fruit. One child or teacher who is "it" does not have a chair. When "it" calls the name of one fruit all children who have that fruit change seats and "it" tries to steal a seat. The person left out is then "it" and the game continues. "It" may also say "Fruit basket upset" and all players change seats. If actual fruit is used, children may be allowed to eat the fruit afterwards.

Bean Bags   Throw the bean bags into a box as a target. Or, have children throw bean bags to each other, first calling out the name of the child the bean bag is being thrown to.

Sling the Statue   "It" takes each player by the hand, one at a time, and slings the player around. Children must remain like statues in the position in which they fall. "It" chooses one "statue" who most closely resembles an object or position "it" imagined before he or she started the game.

Examples of objects are chair, building, Statue of Liberty, and doll. Examples of activities are cooking, sewing, shoveling, hammering, and sleeping.

Name and Touch   Teacher names parts of the body and the children must touch the correct part — for example: elbow, arm, hand, fingers, feet. When children can do this correctly, the game may be made more delightful by the teacher's touching some part of her or his own body other than what she or he calls out. Children have to remember to touch what is said rather than what the teacher touches.

Simon Says   Players do exactly what "it" tells them to do, as long as the request is preceded by "Simon Says." (Example: "Simon Says kick your feet.") The person who forgets and does the action when "it" does not precede the request with "Simon Says" becomes "it" and the game continues.

I Spy   Child who is "it" thinks about some object in the room. Other children ask yes-or-no questions about the object until they can identify the object.

Red Rover   Players make two lines facing each other, holding hands. Taking turns, each team calls "Red Rover, Red Rover, send (name) right over." The child who is called runs and tries to break through the handhold of two people on other team. If successful the child chooses a player and returns to the original side; if not the child remains on the other side.

Duck, Duck, Goose   Child who is "it" goes around the outside of a circle of seated players, touching each child on the back and saying "duck" or "goose." If called "goose," the touched child chases "it" around the outside of the circle. Object is to tag "it" before "it" gets into the seat of the person called "goose."

Police Officer and Lost Child   Teacher takes the role of a mother whose child is lost. One player is chosen to be the police officer. Officer asks what the lost child was wearing. "Mother" describes the clothing of one of the players. Officer tries to find the lost child from the description.

What Is Missing?   Place five or six objects on a table. Children identify each object. Children close their eyes while the teacher removes one or two objects. Children open their eyes and decide what is missing. A variation of this game is to cover the objects after they have been named and have children tell what objects are under the cloth.

Suggestions for other games

Drop the Handkerchief
Dodge Ball
Throwing Ball
Here We Go Loop-t-Loo
Farmer in the Dell
London Bridge

For other games, read *A Guide to Fun and Learning in the Romper Room Years: The Wonderful World of Play*.[13]

THEORETICAL CONTEXT: MOVEMENT EDUCATION

In 1970 two associations concerned with the physical education of young children joined to sponsor an annual conference devoted entirely to that topic. The two associations were the National Association for the Education of Young Children (NAEYC) and the American Association for Health, Physical Education, and Recreation (AAHPER). The four main purposes of the conferences were to develop an understanding of the significance of physical activity; to examine research on motor development; to study the relationships of motor development to social, emotional, and intellectual development; and to suggest environmental facilities to encourage motor development.

Movement education is not new. Scholars in ancient Greece stressed harmony between body and mind. Until the twentieth century, however, physical education was stressed for developing the body, not as a part of the total development of the whole being. In the 1930s emphasis was given to the parts of the human being. But this approach didn't seem to work, and from 1940 to the 1950s the concept of the "whole child" was developed. In the 1960s educators again returned to emphasis on intellectual subjects — probably because of the space race. Now, in the 1980s, movement education reflects the past and new research — body and mind, aesthetic awareness, the whole child, individual differences and complexity of the interaction of all those factors affected by the individual's environment.[14]

Because of the thoroughness of the present approach in research and study of movement, three general trends or theories have developed. These

---

[13] Maria W. Piers and Genevieve Millet Landon, *A Guide to Fun and Learning in the Romper Room Years: The Wonderful World of Play* (Pawtucket, R.I.: Hasbro Industries, 1978).

[14] National Association for the Education of Young Children, *The Significance of the Young Child's Motor Development* (Washington, D.C.: NAEYC 1971).

Demonstrating how a movement is to be done can be helpful.

theories are the *developmental* approach, emphasizing emotions, social relationships, and physical development; the *cultural representation* approach, emphasizing external measurable and observable skills; and the *cognitive-affective* approach, emphasizing the environmental interactions of sequencing, reasoning, problem solving, and differentiating in a developmental setting.

Developmental

The child growth and development theorists, represented by Bailey, Herkowitz, and others, believe that motor skills and movement play have value because they establish mastery of large-muscle movement.[15] In this they provide an opportunity to build self-confidence. Children learn to control their abundant energy with creative movement; they develop coordination of the whole muscular framework of the body; they collaborate socially in peer groups; and, through the combination of all these factors, they can develop a self-concept of well-being and adequacy.

Cultural Representation

Theorists in favor of the cultural representation view of movement education, including Cratty, Kephart, and others, believe that the first task of

---

[15] E. Bailey, *Discovering Music with Young Children* (New York: Philosophical Library, 1958); J. Herkowitz, "A Perceptual-Motor Training Program to Improve the Gross Motor Abilities

the teacher is to impart knowledge, rules, and values obtained from the past.[16] Recommended movement activities are highly structured; emphasis is on learning to follow directions. Many of the activities require use of small muscles, rather than large. Workbooks, sewing cards, tracing cards, and chalkboards may be used. Tracing and copying geometric forms are common. Physical activities include specific directions such as "Walk slowly forward on the balancing board in baby steps and look straight ahead. Do not look at your feet." "Bounce the ball alternating hands as you bounce it." "Jump in and out of the hoop." Children repeat the activity until they can do it successfully. The theorists recommending this type of movement education do not stress social, emotional, or creative responses. They recognize individual differences in rate of performance although the sequencing of each skill is predetermined.

Cognitive-Affective

Currently the most commonly used theory of movement education, the cognitive-affective approach is both structured and unstructured.[17] The teacher's role is to design a physical environment and develop activites that will stimulate the child to be creative, physically active, and challenged to explore this environment through reasoning and problem solving on an individualized basis. Structure is an outgrowth of access to the same materials and activities. The unstructured feature of the theory occurs because the children are allowed to react without direction as long as the play is not destructive. Teachers must have a thorough knowledge of child growth and the development stages, identified by Piaget, Bloom, and Erikson, and knowledge of John Dewey's progressive education-by-doing theory.

The cognitive-affective approach includes some aspects of the previous two theories: it encourages perception, sociability, sense of self, sensory perception, values, and aesthetic experiences through music and dance. This theory probably is more conducive to movement education per se than are the other two theories.

---

of Preschoolers," *Journal of Health, Physical Education and Recreation* 41 (1970): 449–96; L. Kohlberg and R. Moyer, "Development as the Aim of Education," *Harvard Educational Review* 42 (1972): 449–96; P. Smith, "Perceptual-Motor Skills and Reading Readiness of Kindergarten Children," *Journal of Health, Physical Education and Recreation* 41 (1970): 47.

[16] B. J. Cratty, *Intelligence in Action/Physical Activities for Enhancing Intellectual Abilities* (Englewood Cliffs, N.J.: Prentice-Hall, 1973); B. Godfrey and N. C. Kephart, *Movement Patterns and Motor Education* (New York: Appleton-Century-Crofts, 1969); N. C. Kephart, *The Slow Learner in the Classroom* (Columbus, Ohio: Charles E. Merrill, 1960).

[17] For information about methods, see Anne G. Gilbert, *Teaching the Three R's Through Movement Experiences* (Minneapolis, Minn.: Burgess Publishing Co., 1977); Donald Gingrich, *Relating the Arts* (New York: Center for Applied Research in Education, 1978); Bette J. Logsdon et al., *Physical Education for Children: A Focus on the Teaching Process* (Philadelphia: Lea and Febiger, 1977).

PROJECT
Providing for Play and Movement Activities

As you study activities for young children you will need to balance your subject area activities with play and movement activities.

1. Choose a theory of play and develop a unit using activities and materials to reinforce the theory you have selected.
2. Select two or three of the games in this chapter and teach them to three, four, and five year olds.
3. Read one of the books on cultural play and write a short essay on the cultural play in your own neighborhood.
4. Select one of the theories of movement education and interview a physical education supervisor on how that theory is used in the school system.
5. Observe a movement education class of young children and write a description of the activities taught.

Children and Their Bodies

Not only are young children small, but they are usually fast and full of energy. They are also highly dependent on their bodies for information. They acquire most of their knowledge by constant movement. Being fast and small is probably essential for their information-gathering processes. By age six they are highly conversant in one form of communication: movement. For years each child has moved in response to visual, auditory, and kinesthetic data.

Jean Piaget's studies of child development show that children learn through movement activity and that intuitive and verbal levels of ability have a base in motor experience. Children cannot move to the verbal level without a strong foundation in concrete manipulation of their bodies and of objects around them. Only over a period of time do sensorimotor experiences (experiences combining movement activity with information gleaned from the five senses) become internalized as thought. At any given time in the children's development, one level of understanding may predominate but will not exclude the rest. According to Piaget, the teacher can impart little knowledge but can provide situations that allow the children to learn on physical and mental levels.

During the last fifteen years, extensive research indicates that the ability to comprehend and use language often depends on the acquisition of several motor experiences. According to Ebersole et al. there are six stages of learning based on movement and perception.[18] These stages are discussed on pages 52–53.

MOVEMENT ACTIVITIES

Curriculum Integration Through Pantomime

Nonverbal actions are an ideal source for the quiet-time activities essential in a well-balanced program for the very young. Pantomiming can be used individually or with small or large groups. Nonverbal actions include any physical activity that can be done without the use of oral language. What can a young child pantomime?

Role playing   A familiar person or activity is a natural place to begin. Sweeping, mopping, shoveling, washing dishes, brushing teeth, drinking a liquid, eating with a fork or spoon, and combing hair are a few activities children have fun doing.

Work activities   What does a bus driver do? What does a typist do? How does a police officer direct traffic? How does a soldier march? What does a telephone worker do? What does a carpenter do?

Machine activities   These activities provide an opportunity for the teacher to observe a child's understanding of the concept and use of simple machines. In the family center children have an opportunity to use many simple machines such as an egg beater. At a quiet time one child can act out an event in the family center while others guess what is being pantomimed. Children can imitate the movements of machines. They can be trains, airplanes, typewriters, or the pendulum of a clock.

Imitating animals   This pantomiming is great fun for the young. Waddling like a duck, hopping like a rabbit, moving quickly like a mouse, flying like a butterfly (slow flaps) or a bumble bee (fast flaps), or walking like a turtle are a few examples.

Physical movement   Have a child pantomime a physical movement such as take a giant step, yawn, touch your toes, scratch your head, jump up, chew gum, sweep the floor, bat a ball, skip, jump rope, wink, rub your

---

[18] Marylou Ebersole et al., *Steps to Achievement for the Slow Learner* (Columbus, Ohio: Charles E. Merrill, 1968).

arm, pat your face, or slap your leg, while others copy the action. During these activities the teacher observes the children as they participate. Which children have poor or adequate physical coordination? Which have poor or adequate concepts of the materials, objects, and events in their environment? Play an oral game with them such as "What am I doing?" "Show me how to use this," or "Tell me the name of this." Other oral activities are described in the language arts chapter.

Activities and Equipment for Movement in Space

Movement activities should be planned in relationship to how the body develops. Physicians tell us that the body parts develop from the large to the small.

Head		
Trunk		
Neck		
Arms		
Legs	*to*	Fingers
		Hand
		Wrist
		Eyes

The eyes are the very last to develop in this sequence — an important fact to remember when evaluating the child's ability to begin decoding printed letter symbols.

Awareness of how these parts of the body can move in space is important to teachers in understanding the significance of children's physical actions or lack of action and is especially important in planning a movement education program for an individual child.

The following outline of body activities (the influences of weight, strength, reaction time, and flow of movement; where the body moves in space; and how it moves) will aid you in analyzing your instructional plans and your classroom and play area space as well as help you diagnose your children's strengths and weaknesses in total body usage.[19]

Body movements in space

Dancing	Marching	Sprawling
Hopping	Jumping	Rolling
Crawling	Twisting	Stretching
Squatting	Sitting	Skipping

---

[19] For more information on movement development, read Louise Skinner, *Motor Development in the Preschool Years* (Springfield, Ill.: Charles C. Thomas, 1979).

Running	Bending	Throwing
Swinging	Sliding	Stepping
Walking	Pulling	Pushing
Lifting	Creeping	Rocking
Balancing	Galloping	Climbing
Spinning	Falling	Twirling
Catching	Hanging	Tumbling
Wiggling	Leaping	Toddling

Influences of body characteristics

Overweight for body build and height limits the freeness of movement of the extremities, slows pace of activity, and shortens the length of time of the activity.

Underweight for body build and height limits usage of equipment and shortens time of the activity.

Strength determines the exactness with which the activity is accomplished.

Reaction time influences the precision of each movement.

Flow of movement extends the continuity of the sequence of the actions.

Where the body moves in space

Up	Down	In
Over	Under	Through
Between	Outside	Inside
Around	Near	On
Low	High	Middle
Front	Back	Bottom
Top	Left	Right
Angular	Sideways	Past
Forward	Backward	

How the body moves in space

Bent	Curved	Twisted
Straight	Extended	Closed

Movements of the body in space are expanded, limited, controlled, and enriched by the equipment and surfaces available during the activity. For instance, sand is great for jumping and walking; satisfactory for marching, running, or leaping; but no good for sprawling, crawling, and tumbling. Those activities are best left to grassy or rug areas. Tiled or smooth floors encourage spinning, sliding, creeping, and pushing. Mounds of grassy dirt and paved walks encourage some activities, while flat lawns and bare ground extend others. Permanent equipment in the outside play area should be placed so that each item implements a creative pattern of obstacles for moving around, through, and between and at the same time leaves wide-open spaces. Mobile equipment for the outside play area should be lightweight or wheeled. Indoor play space should have both smooth and carpeted areas. Indoor equipment should be easily shelved and moved or placed in the space so that it encourages physical responses.

Although almost all equipment and material provide physical activity, some are more conducive to movement education than others. The following items used in conjunction with the previously discussed activities will stimulate creative responses in the environmental setting.

Bean bags	3-foot plywood circles
Yarn balls	8-foot × 2-foot plywood rectangle
Hula hoops	
Balance beams	4-foot plywood squares
Rotating ball (hung by cord)	Tumbling mats
Riding-horse sticks	Step-on shapes
2-inch plastic tape	Rope
Beach balls	Yarn
Clutch balls	Red rubber, all-purpose balls
Parachute	Large medicine ball

SUMMARY

Play in early childhood classrooms is the least understood activity of all the activities that go on in these classrooms. We have tried to provide information in this chapter to aid you in helping parents and others understand play so they will recognize the importance of play and the different types of play. Movement education does not cause such concern because of the visual structure apparent in the activities.

The theories of instruction, materials, and activities provided in this chapter are examples of what can be done in these areas but they are not conclusive lists. You'll want to be creative and provide opportunities in both areas that will take account of the individual differences of each child.

DIFFERENTIATING AND INTEGRATING MINI UNITS

Individualized opportunities for physical movement are very important for young children. These activities should reinforce skills and knowledge the children have already mastered and teach new skills as well. Play activities are easily integrated with music, dramatic play, and regular indoor and outdoor activities. The following mini units for play and movement education provide a quick and easy way to involve many children simultaneously in a physically active project. Before you begin your teaching career, copy these mini units, and others in this book, on file cards and file them in an appropriate box. You will find them useful in the future to add variety to children's physical activities.

Mini Units   Differentiating and Integrating for **Three Year Olds**

	September	*January*	*May*
Topic	Walking a rope.	An obstacle course.	Spring flowers.
Objectives	To develop control of walking coordination.	To develop a sense of self in space.	To develop freedom of movement with limited directions.
Materials	30 feet of half-inch rope.	Two tables, two cardboard boxes, two large pillows.	Record (or tape), record player, space to move.
Procedures	Place the rope on a smooth surface in a zigzag pattern. Have children walk on one side of rope in baby steps.	Children crawl under the tables, through the cardboard boxes, and over the pillows.	Discuss with children how flowers move — they sprout, bloom, sway, and follow the sun. Demonstrate the movements for each. Play record and let children be "flowers."
Evaluation	Ability to walk near rope without crossing over it.	Ability to go under, through, and over.	Performance.
Integrating skills	Visual perception. Physical balance. Following oral directions.	Listening to directions. Object identification. Taking turns. Making a line.	Science. Listening.

Mini Units   Differentiating and Integrating for **Four Year Olds**

	September	*January*	*May*
Topic	Walking the dragon.	Bobbing balloons.	Bean baggery.
Objectives	To improve body balance.	To improve eye-hand and body coordination.	To improve strength in hands and arms.

Mini Units Differentiating and Integrating for **Four Year Olds** (cont.)

	September	*January*	*May*
Materials	Approximately 50 bricks, a papier-maché dragon's head patterned after the Chinese festival dragons.	Cord, four balloons, and a support (tree limb, parallel bars, or similar).	Beanbags, box with low sides, tire casing, or chalk circle.
Procedures	Place bricks on floor or on play surface in a wavy line. Use a few bricks for "spines." Put dragon's head at one end. Children walk and balance on bricks.	Tie each balloon to a cord. Tie each cord to a main cord so balloons are positioned at different heights. Hang balloons over support and pull them up and down slowly while two or three children try to jump up and touch them.	Draw a line about eight feet from each object. Children stand behind line and toss bean bags into target (box, tire casing, or chalk circle).
Evaluation	Ability to walk on bricks.	Ability to jump, reach, and aim hand.	Control of beanbag when thrown.
Integrating skills	Whole body coordination. Visual coordination.	Visual focusing. Eye-hand coordination.	Following directions. Identification of objects.

Mini Units Differentiating and Integrating for **Five Year Olds**

	September	*January*	*May*
Topic	Riding a paintbrush.	Snowflake waltz.	A trike-hike.
Objectives	To develop lateral movement.	To develop individual creative movement.	To develop leg muscles and alternate foot movement.
Materials	A 2-inch, corner paint roller with 5-foot extension handle, poster paint in several colors, 12-foot strips of 36-inch wide paper.	A day when light, fluffy snow is falling. Select a snow song from the music chapter.	A tricycle, school play yard, a prize (piece of candy, balloon, or similar) for each child.

Mini Units Differentiating and Integrating for **Five Year Olds** (*cont.*)

	September	*January*	*May*
Procedures	Have child dip roller in paint. Place roller on edge of paper and have child ride the stick, making sharp lateral movements while moving forward.	Play music and let children interpret falling snow through body movements.	Hide prizes behind objects in the play yard. Take three children out at a time; have them ride tricycles to where prizes are hidden then return.
Evaluation	Ability of child to move laterally.	Observation of children's movement.	Ability to pedal and control tricycle.
Integrating skills	Following directions. Whole-body control. Concept of space. Art.	Listening.	Following directions. Object identification.

Play and movement provide opportunities for creative and individualized performances just as other curriculum areas do. Performances in play and movement are always visible and easily observed for collecting data. Data collection is valuable when it is used to improve instruction. Therefore data such as these lists reveal should be used for grouping children according to need and as a basis for individualizing instruction.

EVALUATION OF INDIVIDUAL DIFFERENCES

Mastery of Climbing Stairs Using Alternate Feet (Age range 3.1 to 3.2 by October 1)

Name	October	January	May
Tibor	no	no	yes
Jewell	no	no	no
Eduardo	no	yes	yes
Bettye	no	no	yes
Mary	no	yes	yes
Fred	no	no	yes
José	no	yes	yes
Carson	no	no	no
Jo Anne	no	no	yes

Mastery of Climbing Stairs Using Alternate Feet (cont.)

Name	October	January	May
Lee	no	no	no
Corine	no	no	no
Bennie	no	yes	yes
Emanuel	no	yes	yes
Jessal	no	yes	yes
Dana	yes	yes	yes
Taisto	no	yes	yes
Amy	yes	yes	yes

Mastery of Riding a Tricycle (Age Range 4.3 to 4.5 by October 1)

Name	October	January	May
Torsten	no	yes	yes
Jerome	yes	yes	yes
Jim	no	no	yes
Ruth	yes	yes	yes
Brenda	no	yes	yes
Randall	no	no	yes
Cleve	no	yes	yes
Haldane	no	no	no
Hazel	yes	yes	yes
Willie	no	yes	yes
Steve	yes	yes	yes
Linda	no	yes	yes
John	yes	yes	yes
Sarah	no	yes	yes
Nyung	no	yes	yes
Dan	yes	yes	yes

Mastery of Pumping a Swing (Age Range 5.0 to 5.4 by October 1)

Name	October	January	May
Beverly	no	no	yes
Ben	no	yes	yes
Arsinio	no	yes	yes
Patricia	no	yes	yes
Clifford	yes	yes	yes
Earl	no	no	no
Lelia	yes	yes	yes
Theodor	no	no	yes
Ellen	no	no	yes
Burl	no	yes	yes
Beula	no	yes	yes
Carl	no	no	no
Philip	yes	yes	yes
Leonila	no	no	yes
David	no	yes	yes
Nikolai	no	no	yes
Jerry	no	yes	yes
Huldah	yes	yes	yes
Levador	no	no	no
Peggy	no	no	yes
Lynne	yes	yes	yes
Bill	no	yes	yes

LEARNING GOALS FOR CHILDREN

Listed below are the skills expected of kindergarten children before they are ready to exit into first grade. Understanding these goals will help you recognize your role in the teaching of physical skills to young children.

- ✔ The child can catch a lightly-bounced utility ball from five feet.
- ✔ The child can throw a 2-inch ball underhand with each hand.
- ✔ The child can throw a 2-inch ball overhand with each hand.
- ✔ The child can kick a utility ball with each foot when it is rolled to him or her.

390 / *Curriculum*

171 ✔ The child can do a broadjump (both feet) from one line to another, with
172   lines twelve inches apart.
173 ✔ The child can jump off climbing stairs without fear.
174 ✔ The child attempts climbing rope ladders and climbing boxes.
175 ✔ The child uses a slide without help.
176 ✔ The child can pump a swing.
177 ✔ The child can crawl alternately in and out of the rungs of a horizontally
178   placed ladder.
179 ✔ The child can walk up and down stairs, one foot after the other, without
180   holding on.
181 ✔ The child can hit a rotating ball with palm, forearm, elbow, head, and
182   fist.
183 ✔ The child can walk a balance beam without falling off.
184 ✔ The child can do a back arch.
185 ✔ The child can do a backbend.

BASIC SKILLS SEQUENCE CHART

See page 189 for an explanation of how to use skills sequence charts.

Physical Education Skills

Key symbols: (✔) Introduction   (✔✔) Extension and reinforcement

Skill	Level 1	Level 2	Level 3
Start, stop, change speed and direction	✔	✔✔	✔✔
Do basic tumbling stunts	✔	✔✔	✔✔
Do various locomotor and nonlocomotor skills	✔	✔✔	✔✔
Toss, catch, and strike with small objects	✔	✔✔	✔✔
Respect property and its care and use	✔	✔✔	✔✔
Follow rules	✔	✔✔	✔✔
Cooperate and participate in a group	✔	✔✔	✔✔
Accept winning, defeat, and criticism	✔	✔✔	✔✔
Perform locomotor and nonlocomotor skills with a partner		✔	✔✔
Understand concepts of directionality		✔	✔✔
Demonstrate agility		✔	✔✔

Physical Education Skills *(cont.)*

Key symbols: (✔) Introduction (✔✔) Extension and reinforcement

Skill	Level 1	Level 2	Level 3
Throw, catch, and receive various size balls and objects		✔	✔✔
Demonstrate kicking skills		✔	✔✔
Demonstrate static and dynamic balance		✔	✔✔
Hit a ball with hand and bat		✔	✔✔
Demonstrate self-discipline when playing		✔	✔✔
Demonstrate trapping skills			✔
Throw two-handed for distance and accuracy			✔
Dribble a ball while changing hands, direction, and level of movement			✔
Throw a small ball with one hand			✔
Long rope jumping			✔
Jump rope individually			✔

ADDITIONAL READINGS

Bucher, Charles A., and Nolan Bucher. *Physical Education for Children: Movement Foundations and Experience*. New York: Macmillan, 1979.

Butler, Annie L., Edward Earl Gotts, and Nancy L. Quisenberry. *Play as Development*. Columbus, Ohio: Charles E. Merrill, 1978.

Croft, J. Doreen, and Robert D. Hess. *An Activities Handbook for Teachers of Young Children*. 3rd ed. Boston: Houghton Mifflin, 1980.

Frost, Joe L., and Barry L. Klein. *Children's Play and Playgrounds*. Boston: Allyn and Bacon, 1979.

Hewitt, Karen, and Louise Roomet. *Educational Toys in America: 1800 to the Present*. Burlington, Vt.: Robert Hull Fleming Museum, 1979.

Newsom, John, and Elizabeth Newsom. *Toys and Playthings: A Practical Guide for Parents and Teachers*. New York: Pantheon, 1979.

Schwartzman, Helen B. *The Anthropology of Children's Play*. New York: Plenum, 1978.

Sutton-Smith, Brian, ed. *Play and Learning*. New York: Wiley, 1980.

PART FOUR
The Child's Well-being

A synopsis of related factors associated with teaching: A child's health, a child's behavior, and a child's family.

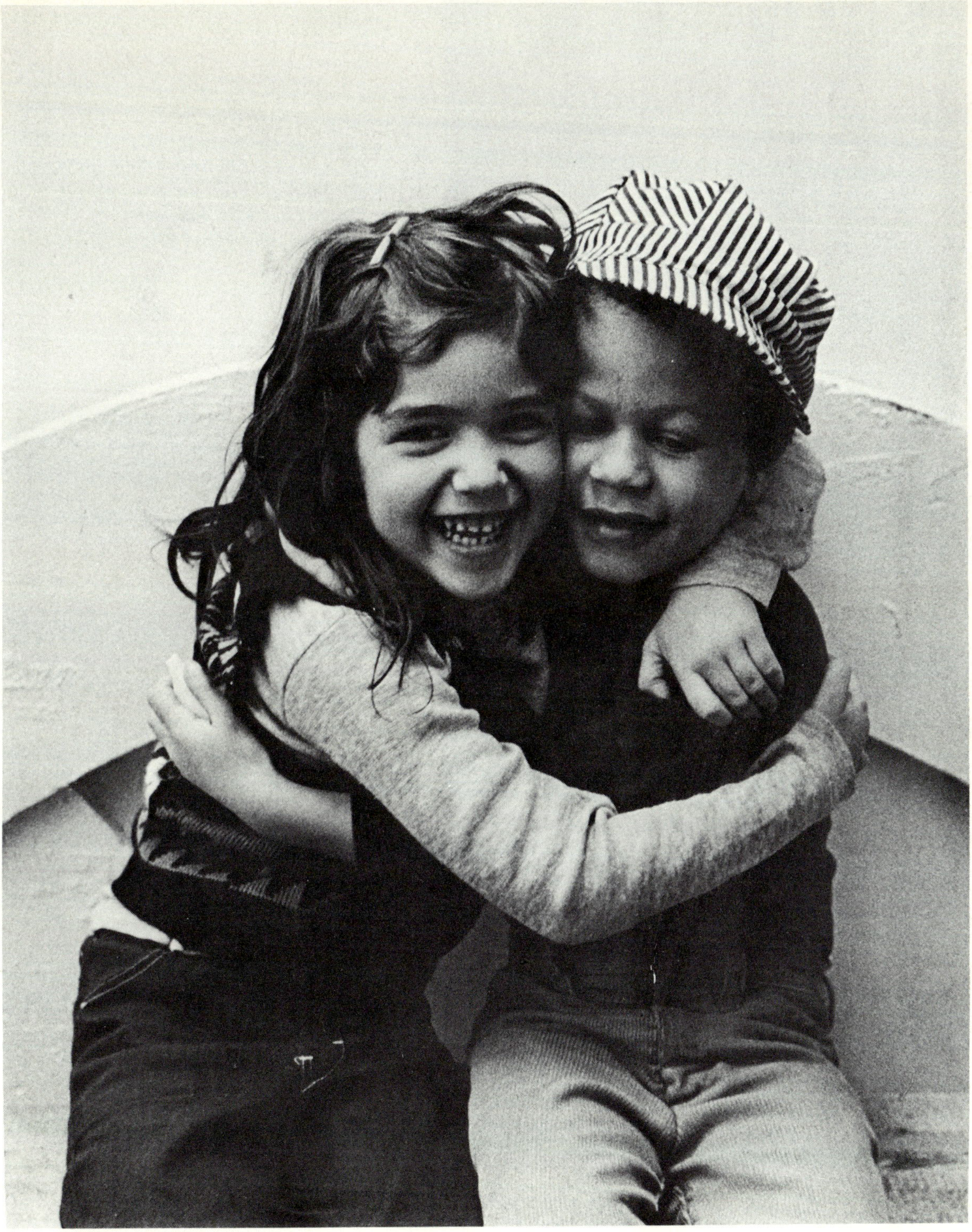

CHAPTER 13

Health, Nutrition, and Disease

In addition to continuity over time there is also continuity within the person — a connectedness of brain and heart, of body and mind, of feelings and intellect.

Ira J. Gordon

Exploration Tasks

After studying this chapter, you should be able to complete these tasks:
- Identify the habits that promote good health.
- Plan activities that will reinforce proper health habits.
- Respond to common illnesses or accidents of young children.
- Work with other concerned adults in your school setting to plan and implement a good nutritional program.
- Plan programs of family education in nutrition education.
- Explain what a balanced diet is and why it is important.
- Identify communicable diseases.

OVERVIEW

What is health? What is nutrition? What are the common diseases of childhood? *Health* refers to the general well-being of the body that is free from disease or ailments. *Nutrition* is the act or process of nourishing the body through nutrients that sustain and promote growth, replace loss, and provide energy. The term *disease* indicates a morbid condition of the body or part of the body.

HEALTH

Health is sustained by several factors other than proper food and lack of disease.[1] Rest for young children is very important. Just as there are individual differences in social, emotional, physical, and intellectual growth, there are differences in the amount of rest or sleep needed by children. Generally, ten to twelve hours of sleep are required each night. In addition, most children require a nap in the early afternoon. Other rest periods during the day may be necessary for some children. Stacking rest cots or rest mats are a must for full-day or day-care situations. Cotton sheets can be purchased, or large bath towels can serve as sheets or covers. Whatever is used must be washable and labeled with each child's name. If the sheets or towels are not washed at school, send them home regularly to be cleaned. When the children are in school for two or two and a half hours a day, a rest on a rug will be sufficient.

Cleanliness

Young children usually love water but that doesn't mean that the water reaches the "right spots." Paper towels and small bars of soap are a daily necessity. The object of the "game" is to develop in children a pleasure in being clean and a habit of washing hands as well as covering sneezes and coughs. By providing time and direct supervision of hand washing before meals, after activities that include soiling of hands, and after trips to the toilet, teachers will instill in children the habit of washing their hands often.

Regular school or institute-type paper toweling is not as easy to manipulate as the absorbent soft paper toweling purchased for homes. Since young children often need their faces (including eyes and nose) and hands cleaned,

---

[1] References for the chapter are: Martin I. Green, Producer, *A Sigh of Relief* (New York: Bantam Books, Inc., 1974); David Hend, *Save Your Child's Life* (New York: Dolphin Books, 1974); *The Concise Home Medical Guide* (New York: Grosset & Dunlap, 1972); and Virginia E. Pomeranz, M.D., and Dodi Schultz, *The Mothers' and Fathers' Medical Encyclopedia* (Boston: Little, Brown, 1975).

The school day provides many opportunities for teaching young children good personal hygiene habits.

the home toweling is more satisfactory. To save paper, tear each sheet off the roll and cut each towel in half. Small hands need only small towels.

Many of the cleanliness habits that need to be taught to children do not occur in a school setting — shampooing hair, putting on clean clothes, bathing, combing and brushing their hair, or caring for their teeth. Because these activities usually occur at home, teachers have to plan to teach cleanliness through vicarious experiences. Pictures, charts, discussions, role playing, dramatizations, and dramatic play with dolls will stimulate learnings conducive to good cleanliness habits. Sometimes, in a full-day program or in a day-care center, children do have the opportunity to perform some of these activities. Each comb and toothbrush should be labeled with the child's name and should frequently be rinsed in a disinfectant and then in extremely hot water.

Temperature and Air

Other important factors for good health include room temperature and fresh air. A room thermometer is a must. The thermometer should be placed about three feet from the floor (at child's level) and away from direct sunlight or drafts. A temperature of 70°F will encourage activity and ensure adequate warmth. Young children are near the floor; since hot air rises, the floor air is cooler than 70°F. If a thermometer is placed at the teacher's eye level and set at 70°F in the winter time, the children will be comfortable. In the summer, a temperature of 75°F is adequate.

Fresh air is also a necessity. Opening a window and leaving the classroom door ajar will provide circulation of the air. If the weather does not permit open windows or other fresh air during the regular class time, open windows during lunch, library time, or even during a "walk" in the halls or a "visit" to another classroom.

Common Happenings

Toileting needs to be planned for long before the school year begins. Young children may be toilet trained before they come to school but being toilet trained does not mean they can observe a preplanned schedule. Bathrooms should always be conveniently located for easy access by the children. Keep a supply of training pants and blue jeans on hand for the occasional wetting accident. Parents can be asked to contribute outgrown garments to meet this need.

Vomiting is another common occurence. Handy towels and water will soon help clean the child. Place towels over the vomit and spray the towel with a room deodorizer to eliminate the odor. If the other children cannot see the vomit, they will not react to it. Cool water on the child's face and a rest on a cot is usually sufficient cure. If the child appears to have a fever, however, arrange for the child to go home.

Convulsions, which can be caused by a high fever, are not common. When a convulsion occurs, the body goes rigid and begins shaking; the eyes roll, the neck arches, the tongue flips back, and thick saliva forms around the mouth. Place the child on his or her side, with top knee bent forward to keep this position so the saliva drains from the mouth. The convulsion will last only a minute and the child will become limp and appear to have fainted. A doctor should be called; the child should be taken to the doctor's office or to a hospital.

The more common "events of the day" include bumps, cuts, bites, scratches, stings, sprains, and broken bones.

A bump that swells may be very sore. A sealed plastic bag with a few ice cubes in it will relieve the pain and swelling and will keep the ice cubes contained and the child dry. If the child is hit on the head and vomits, pales, and gets sweaty or sleepy, the child should be taken to a doctor immediately. These are symptoms of a concussion.

Cuts or abrasions happen often on the playground. Use soap and water to clean the cut. Ice will stop the bleeding from a cut. Gauze and tape may be necessary for some cuts. Some deep cuts may need to be soaked in warm water so that dirt and other fine particles can be washed away.

Splinters are common if you have many woodworking activities or if some of the wooden play equipment is old. Disinfect the area of the splinter and pull the splinter out with a pair of tweezers. If the splinter is embedded, use disinfectant. Bandage the skin and notify parents about the splinter when the child is ready to go home.

Bites from mosquitoes, flies, spiders, ants, gnats, and chiggers can cause itching that can be very annoying and uncomfortable to the very young child. Severe scratching of itches may produce open sores. Full-strength vinegar, used immediately, will relieve the itching. Severe bites can be relieved with alternate hot and cold salt water solutions.

Bee and hornet stings can be relieved. Be sure the stinger is removed, then spray with an anesthetic disinfectant spray. Suck the bite and spit out whatever saliva you have in your mouth. Place an ice cube directly on the bite or make a paste of baking soda and cover the bite. Continued use of the anesthetic spray will relieve the pain.

Because children are physically active almost all the time, sprains and even broken bones occur occasionally. How do you tell the difference between a sprain and a broken bone? Signs of broken bones are a sharp pain, paleness, sweating, chills, fainting, double vision, a leg the child can't stand on, or a hand the child can't make into a fist. Sprains are painful but the area can be moved and bear weight immediately after the sprain. Sprains require ice packs for the first twenty-four hours to keep the swelling down and soaking in a hot water, salt, or epsom salt solution until the soreness is gone.

If you believe a bone is broken, keep the child warm to prevent shock, place ice on the area of the break and take the child to a doctor or hospital immediately. Once the area begins to swell the doctor has to wait for the swelling to go down before setting the bone and putting it in a cast.

The Abused Child

Recent studies have shown startling statistics about child abuse in the United States. If a child comes to school with unusual bruises or relates events that would indicate he or she is being abused, notify your principal or director. Community service organizations are prepared to help in these matters. If parents discuss child abuse with you, suggest that they contact Parents Anonymous, 2810 Artesia Boulevard, Redondo, CA 90278. This organization has local groups in many cities and may be listed in the telephone directory.

NUTRITION

Throughout the school years a child receives information and data about the foods and liquids that are important for physical growth, energy, and good health. The early years are the most important years for this instruction because it is during this period that lifetime eating habits are established.

Nutrients

The Parent's Role Since most of the meals and snacks during a day are eaten at home, teachers must plan many opportunities to help parents understand what a balanced diet means. Not all foods contain the same nutrients and when they do they are not present in the same amounts. The nutrients of foods are proteins, carbohydrates, fats, vitamins, and minerals. It is not enough to know what the nutrients are. Parents need to know what each nutrient provides for body growth and what too much of any one of these nutrients can do to the body.[2]

Proteins are found in many foods, but mostly in meat, fish, poultry, eggs, cheese, and milk. Proteins build muscles, provide energy, and help heal cuts and broken bones.

Carbohydrates are the main nutrient of sugary and starchy foods such as candy, soft drinks, cake, spaghetti, and bread. Carbohydrates provide quick energy but will turn into excess fat if not eaten in moderation.

Fats are found in meat, oils, cream in milk, and nuts. Fats also provide energy and if eaten in the extreme will cause excess body fat.

Vitamins are also important in a daily diet. Vitamin A keeps skin healthy, helps vision, and may help colds. Vitamin B_1 aids digestion and the nervous system and helps convert foods to energy. Vitamin B_2 promotes healthy gums and eyes and helps in the use of oxygen in the blood. Liver, milk, eggs, fish, and peanuts are natural sources of B_2. Vitamin C is also good for gums, skin, and muscles and aids in the development of strong bones and teeth. Citrus fruits, tomatoes, cantaloupes, and strawberries provide this vitamin; because vitamin C cannot be stored, one or more of these fruits must be eaten each day. Vitamin D helps develop teeth and bones. Lack of this vitamin will cause bowlegs in young children (rickets). Sunshine, fish liver oils, and most milk and margarine have vitamin D.

Niacin is considered a vitamin and is important for healthy skin, nerves, and in the use of other nutrients. Pork, veal, beef, liver, fish, and eggs are natural souces of niacin.

Some minerals are found in all solid and liquid foods. The minerals needed most are calcium (eggs, milk, cheese, and greens), which helps develop teeth and bones, stops bleeding, and aids in muscle development; phosphorus (seafood, bananas, tomatoes, and small amounts in other foods), which helps develop bones, teeth, the nervous system, and assists other nutrients in creating energy; iron and copper (liver, dark leafy vegetables, and egg yolk), which are needed to develop the blood; and iodine (seafood and iodized salt), which controls energy usage.

Water, fiber, and calories are not nutrients, but are important to a well-balanced diet. Water makes up two-thirds of body weight and must be replenished regularly. Fiber (roughage), the part of foods not dissolved in the digestion process, is found in fruits, vegetables, and whole (not refined) grains. Fiber is necessary for proper intestine and bowel usage. Calories

---

[2] For information about nutrition, see *Nutrition Education for Young Children* (Washington, D.C.: U.S. Government Printing Office, Superintendent of Documents [SLS]).

are the measure of the energy in the food eaten. Energy comes from two sources — food intake and body fat. Calories must be balanced for proper weight in relation to body build.

The Child's Role The children's role in good nutrition is to:

- Eat a variety of foods containing nutrients balanced for bodily needs
- Not overeat in relation to body size and energy needs
- Be the bearer of nutritional information to parents

The Teacher's Role The teacher's role in good nutrition is to:

- Provide snacks that promote good health
- Aid the school food specialists in serving foods that will please young children in taste, color, and amount of each serving
- Praise children for trying new foods
- Remember that children differ in eating patterns just as adults do (some eat a large breakfast and very little at lunch; some eat a large lunch and two other small meals; and some like their large meal to be in the evening). If you have a question concerning a child's food intake discuss the matter with the child and parents.

Dan: "Teacher, do I gotta clean my plate?"
Teacher: "Have you tried a bite of your rice?"
Dan: "Yes."
Barbara: "No, he didn't, teacher! He didn't even try a tiny bite."
Dan: "Yes, I did too."
Barbara: "No, you didn't."

You will notice that insistence on "cleaning the plate" is not included on this list of a teacher's role in establishing good eating habits. There is nothing magic about eating all of the food on a plate. If you notice that a child is not eating any of one or two items on the plate, encourage the child to taste one bite. If the food is commonly served for school lunches, arrange the seating so that children who relish a particular item are sitting near a child who is not eating the item. If the child hesitates to eat the food because of unfamiliarity, the enjoyment of peers will soon encourage at least one try.

Servings What is a child-size serving for children ages three to six? Information distributed by the National Daily Council suggests the following serving sizes:

6 oz. of milk
4 oz. of juice
1 medium sized egg
1 2½ to 3 oz. piece of meat
¼ cup of cooked cereal or ½ cup ready-to-eat cereal
1 slice of bread
½ or 1 medium-sized piece of fruit
2 to 4 tablespoons of a vegetable

Be sure that snacks help teach good nutrition.

Daily Requirements For the average-sized, active three- to six-year-old child, the daily amounts of the preceding foods are:

- 3 servings of milk or equivalents in cheese or ice cream (as well as milk in desserts, cereals, soups, and so forth)
- 1 or 2 servings of meat or fish, poultry, cheese, eggs, dried beans, peas, or peanut butter
- 1 serving of orange, grapefruit, peach, apple, plum, prune, or tomato
- 2 or 3 servings of vegetables (remember, navy beans and peas are high in protein and are found in the meat category)
- 3 slices of bread or cereal (macaroni, noodles, rice, or spaghetti may be substituted)
- 6 to 8 glasses of water (child-size glasses are 6 ounces or ¾ cup)

Snacks Snacks during the day can ruin a well-planned, balanced diet and often are the cause of tooth decay. Recommended snacks include raw vegetables, fruits, crackers, cheese, some cereals (check label for dextrose content), or pretzels. Children are attracted to bright colors in food — red, orange, green, yellow — but do not like strong flavor unless it is sweet.

Recent Research on Balanced Diets

In a July 28, 1976, statement to the Senate Select Nutrition Committee, Dr. Gio B. Gori, deputy director of the National Cancer Institute's division of cancer cause and prevention, reported that improper diets are related to 60 percent of all types of cancer in women and 41 percent of those in men. The report emphasized that an unbalanced diet is *not* the cause of cancer but is *associated* with the development of the disease. Since eating patterns are developed during an individual's early years, the importance of an early introduction to balanced meals cannot be stressed too much.

Nutrition and the Disadvantaged Child

School-setting programs for young children should be concerned about each child as a total human being. This includes adequate nutrition, rest, and activity. Young children who live in an environment limited in educational opportunities may also be fatigued, hungry, ill, parasitized, and brain damaged because of poor diet and alcohol and drug use of the mother during pregnancy. Such children should be given medical treatment to correct as many problems as possible, nutritious meals at school, and individualized programs for rest and activity. Parent education programs may help. Remember that many of these parents have limited reading ability; many of the activities and information for parents should be oral and pictorial. An interesting book on this topic is Herbert E. Birch and Joan Dye Gussow's *Disadvantaged Children: Health, Nutrition and School Failure* (New York: Harcourt Brace Jovanovich, 1970).

DISEASE

Young children normally are subject to sore throats, headaches, stomachaches, nausea, earaches, chills, and fever. Fortunately they are very communicative about their discomforts, and the symptoms of illness are generally visible — dullness of eyes, flushed skin or pallor, coughing, sneezing, running noses, stuffed-up nostrils, crying, irritability, and rashes.[3]

Allergies

A record of known allergies for each child should be separated from other medical records and listed by child on a separate report for each teacher. Allergies can make children miserable. (And the teacher also — there is nothing like a wheezing, teary eyed, flushed five year old gasping for breath to unnerve an unsuspecting teacher!) Don't expect young children to remember what they are allergic to. The teacher will have to remember for them and this handy list of allergies can calm many a teacher as well as children.

[3] See also *The Concise Home Medical Guide* (New York: Grosset and Dunlap, 1972). Virginia E. Pomeranz, M.D., and Dodi Schultz, *The Mothers' and Fathers' Medical Encyclopedia* (Boston: Little, Brown, 1975).

PROJECT
Understanding the Health, Nutrition, and Diseases of Young Children

An understanding of the related factors of health, nutrition, and disease will help you provide better care for each individual in your classroom.

1. Contact your local public health organization and collect the materials they have pertaining to the health of young children.
2. Visit a classroom and observe the hands of the children. Make a list of all the places and things the children touched between the times they washed their hands.
3. Interview teachers and principals to find out what kinds of injuries they have treated in the last month.
4. Visit an early childhood classroom during lunch time and record what the children were served and what they ate and didn't eat.
5. Prepare a handout for families on good nutrition habits for children.
6. Interview several parents to find out the illnesses their children have had and the medicine their children take.

Communicable Diseases

After a few years of teaching you will become expert at identifying communicable diseases. Pinworm, ringworm, scabies, impetigo, and conjunctivitis (pink eye) are all highly contagious. Often by the time the disease is identified several children in the room will have contracted the disease. Medication is required for each, extreme caution in disinfecting all items used is necessary, and a doctor's written statement of noncommunication of disease is recommended. The following diseases are communicated during the incubation period.

Disease and incubation period	*Symptoms*	*Isolation and control of contact period*
Chicken pox, 14 to 21 days	Fever, red spots, loss of appetite	6 days and symptom free — no control of contacts
German measles, 14 to 21 days	Cold, fever, rash, swollen glands	4 days or until all symptoms are gone — no control of contacts

A child who looks like this may not only be tired and cranky; he may also be ill.

Infectious hepatitis, 10 to 40 days	Fever, nausea, headache, fatigue, abdominal cramps	7 days or until all symptoms cease — no control of contacts
Measles, 10 to 14 days	Cough, fever, red eyes, runny nose	7 days or until symptoms cease — no control of contacts

Mumps, 18 to 21 days	Sore throat, pain and swelling around jaws, fever, nausea.	7 days or until swelling is gone — no control of contacts
Poliomyelitis, 7 to 14 days	Fever, headache, sore throat, stiff back and neck	7 days or until well — no contacts and children exposed should be under medical surveillance for two weeks
Scarlet fever, 2 to 7 days	Sore throat, fever, rash, vomiting	4 days or until symptoms cease — no control of contacts

SUMMARY

An understanding of the health, nutrition, and diseases of young children is important for two reasons. First, you need to be able to recognize symptoms of illness and malnutrition before the problems become acute or before an epidemic occurs. Second, teachers often provide information to parents about their child's health, nutrition, and diseases. As this communicator of information, you need to be accurate. This chapter contains basic information on classroom care and problems, nutrition, and identification of diseases, which can then be shared with families. There is probably no more important chapter in this book than this chapter. The physical well-being of the learning child is of utmost importance.

LEARNING GOALS FOR CHILDREN

When children are ready to leave kindergarten, they are expected to have mastered relevant skills and knowledge regarding the care of their own bodies. If you understand these requirements you will be better able to impart information at the appropriate levels.

- The child can take off and put on wraps without assistance.
- The child covers mouth and nose when coughing and sneezing.
- The child can use toilet facilities without assistance.

- The child washes hands before eating and after toileting.
- The child demonstrates the correct procedure for brushing teeth.
- The child is interested in his or her physical appearance — hair combed, cleanliness, and neatness of dress.
- The child can use a knife, fork, and spoon properly — holding them correctly and using the right utensil for the type of food to be eaten.

ADDITIONAL READINGS

Allen, K. E., V. A. Holm, and R. L. Schiefelbusch, eds. *Early Intervention — A Team Approach*. Baltimore: University Park Press, 1978.

Cronin, Godfrey E., and William M. Young. *400 Novels: The Future of School Health in America*. Bloomington, Ind.: Phi Delta Kappa, 1979.

Greene, Walter H., Frank H. Legos, and Patricia M. Legos. *Health Education in the Elementary School*. New York: Macmillan, 1978.

Rubin, Zick. *Children's Friendships*. Cambridge, Mass.: Harvard University Press, 1980.

Wanamaker, N., K. Hearn, and S. Richarz. *More than Graham Crackers: Nutrition Education and Food Preparation with Young Children*. Washington, D.C.: Association for the Education of Young Children, 1979.

CHAPTER 14
Behavior and the Family

Giving and receiving are basic human patterns and provide for expression of love, affection. . . . Thus we show courtesy and respect for others' dignity and integrity.

Lawrence K. Frank

Exploration Tasks

After studying this chapter, you should be able to complete these tasks:
- Describe positive and negative behavior.
- Explain why some types of behavior need to be limited.
- List types of negative behavior and ways of controlling and stopping it.
- Discuss the research findings on causes of differing types of behavior.
- Identify the nonverbal cues that transmit feelings and reactions.
- Plan activities that will develop good manners.
- Discuss the findings of the research on home environment influences on behavior.
- Identify problems that may arise in family education.
- Discuss the elements important in home visitation.
- List factors that aid school visits by parents.
- Plan successful parent conferences.
- Develop several ways of communicating with families.

OVERVIEW

Why include behavior and family education in one chapter? Research on the social development of young children has shown that what adults do, both as teachers and parents, makes a considerable difference in the total development of a child. Each provides a learning environment, models behavior, and gives direct instruction to children.

The old "hands off" position of educators toward families has changed to a "we need you" attitude. The realization that families influence children's feelings, attitudes, social actions, and social language has led to the establishment of many home-based projects in which educators, families, and children become a team to improve the learning environment. Young children imitate what they hear and see in both the home environment and the school environment.[1]

BEHAVIOR

Behavior comes in many forms: hugs, kisses, "thank you's," "please," sharing, giggles, smiles, quiet play, boisterous pushing and shoving, fussiness, whining, foul language, backtalk, bickering, fistfights, kicking, hair pulling, pinching, biting, tantrums, lying, jealousy, anger, and stealing.

The hugs, kisses, giggles, and smiles are very acceptable behavior and therefore present no problem as long as they are controlled. Children, however, should not be allowed to hug and kiss their way into becoming shy tyrants! The gentleness of a hug, pat, or touch, along with a smile and quiet voice, is often all that is needed to "cure" a social relations problem.

Play that is destructive, loud, and boisterous has to be stopped immediately because of the danger of possible physical harm. Channeling such play into a more acceptable form or complete withdrawal of the play equipment and separation of the participants in violent play will stop the problem for the moment. This action should be reinforced not by nagging or warnings but by an explanation of why equipment must not be broken; why yelling and screaming cannot be allowed; and why boisterous play such as pushing and hitting, even though done "in play," will soon lead to a child's being hurt. The section of this chapter on television as a behavior model and the research findings on aggression will provide additional suggestions for coping with aggressive behavior.

William had enough curiosity for the whole class. He also had to touch everything he saw, which led to many a dropped and broken object. The teacher developed the strategy of holding William's hand while "he looked." One day as the teacher was reading a story to the group, William slipped his hand under the teacher's hand holding the book and whispered in her ear, "I think you'd better help me hold my hand cause if you don't it's going to hit Gregg."

---

[1] See, for example, Alice S. Honig, "The Young Child and You — Learning Together," *Young Children*, 35 (1980): 2–10; Jerry J. Bigner, *Parent-Child Relations: An Introduction to Parenting* (New York: Macmillan, 1979); and Edward Kifer, "The Relationship Between the Home and School in Influencing the Learning of Children," *Research in the Teaching of English*, 11 (1977): 5–16.

What to Do and When

Although teachers and parents must remain "in charge," children should be encouraged to participate in discussions, express ideas, and make choices. Making a choice brings up the topic of voting. There are some things you don't vote about! For instance, the sex of the visiting kitten, whether or not Jack is bad, or whether or not you'll have an ice cream lunch are not topics that should be voted upon. Never put a choice or happening to a vote unless all the options are satisfactory outcomes. A child may advance the suggestion of taking a "vote" on something probably because an older brother or sister is learning about voting in school.

Young children need time to obey. If you use a positive technique such as "If we put our things away quickly, we'll have time for a longer story (or music, or art)." Usually children will respond because of the unknown factor in the new event. They also need an advance notice of the close of an activity. A ten-minute warning will allow a child to adjust to the idea of stopping the activity. If the child is happily building the greatest super highway ever, the time will allow the child to adjust to its destruction or time for the child to talk you into letting the highway stand for awhile (not a bad idea!).

At times during the day you will need the attention of the whole group while they are busily engaged in individual activities. Don't yell! Flick the lights off and on (slowly), play a chord on the piano, or ring a small bell when indoors. Outdoors, blow a whistle, beat a tom-tom, or ring a bell.

When do you expect instant obedience? Any time children are in a situation where they may harm themselves or others, or when they may cause serious damage to materials or equipment. As a teacher you will soon develop a tone of voice that requires instant obedience, provided you do not use that tone too often. Learn to separate emergency situations from the normal; use your voice as a deterrent only when *absolutely* necessary. A shake of the head, a stern look, or standing near the children will usually stop unwelcome behavior.

If none of these suggestions work, separate the individuals involved in the activity. A quiet corner, surrounded by partitions you can see over, which contains many small toys available for play, often helps calm an especially boisterous child. Child-size rocking chairs are good sitting spots for individuals who are a little steamed up. Let them rock for awhile. Do not put a time limit on how long they must sit or stay in a quiet corner. Children have no sense of time and the length of time really has no connection with the disruptive behavior. Children should be limited in their activities for a short time and then *not* permitted to go back to the situation where the disturbing behavior occurred.

At times you may not see or hear the beginning of a disturbance. Generally if you talk to the children involved, you will find that one child wants what

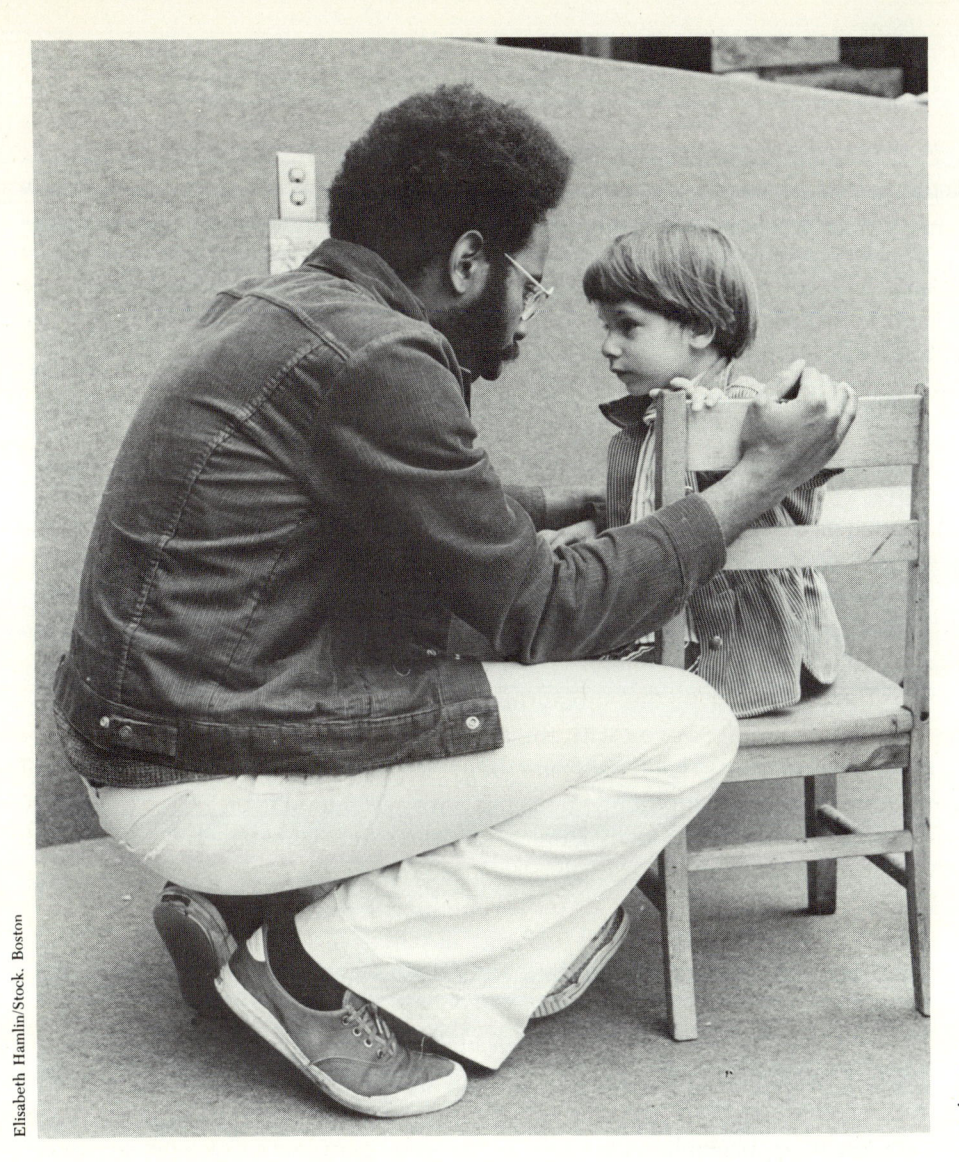

Sometimes children need time by themselves, away from other children and distractions.

another child has. Sharing is important, but you have to be careful when teaching children to share that you don't also teach them that if they yell and scream enough they get their own way. Soon you will know your children and can recognize those who want something just because some one else has it. For such children, write their names down for a later turn with the toy. Crying and tantrums are not the most pleasant aspects of life, but apparent ignorance of the behavior seems to work sometimes — as long as the "eye in the back of your head" is working full time. (The section in this chapter on research on aggressive behavior provides additional techniques on this type of behavior.)

Fussiness may be caused by tiredness, hunger, or sickness. A cracker or two may help and a rest on a cot with the child's own blanket will make a three or four year old feel better. A fussy five year old may need active movement. A run around the playground may help. Refer to Chapter 13 for illness symptoms.

Whining and foul language are learned. The whining child may not feel well and should be checked for signs of illness first. Second, listen to what the child is whining about. If the child is whining because he or she has nothing to do, no one to play with, or is bored, make little or no comment and start talking to another child. Ignoring this type of whining and talking in a normal way won't reward the whining quality of voice and will provide a conversation for the child to join.

Foul language is heard and therefore learned. Needless to say, young children hear foul language and use it. The first step is to ignore the language. The second step in such a case is to explain to the child that such language is not used at school. The third step is to notify parents of the language and try to identify the source. If the source is controlled, the language should cease. This is not easy, however, because what is considered foul language in the general social culture of the school setting may be considered normal in the subculture of the child's social setting. Parental influence is so interwoven with the school behavior of children that teachers must have parents' good will and help in planning and carrying through with behavior development. Working with parents will be discussed later in this chapter. The fourth step in stopping foul language is to help the child use acceptable words such as *gosh, darn, no, gee whiz, well now, don't* — all of which seem to be acceptable to adults.

Backtalk is normal for three, four, and five year olds, as discussed in Chapter 3. The "no's," "I won't's," "I don't have to's," "dummy's," and "stupid's," can be eased somewhat by ignoring the behavior, not answering any conversation that contains the backtalk, and, in extreme cases, isolating the child from the situation with a firm reminder that you do not accept the behavior. Do not get into an oral confrontation with the child — you may get more backtalk.

Karen: "You'd better let me have that or I'll hit you!"

Holly: "It's mine! Give it to me."

Karen: "Let go!"

Holly: "Teacher!"

Bickering seems to occur with young children when they are in the same setting with the same children for over half an hour. With adequate planning, activities should change about every twenty minutes for young children and through normal interests children should be involved with different children throughout the day.

Fistfights may occur for a variety of reasons; one child has what another wants; one child has said something another doesn't like; one child is in another's way; or one child is sitting, standing, or playing too close to another. Children like space — unless they are hugging each other! Fistfights between the young are usually spontaneous and short-lived. When fights occur, put the participants in different areas. If you leave one child in the same area, the other may soon come back to continue the fight. After about ten minutes, discuss with the children why fighting is wrong and give them alternatives — moving away from the fighter, saying "I'll let you have it in a minute," or saying "Ask the teacher if you may have it." If one individual continues to use physical action, have that child sit in the quiet corner for a few minutes and then have the child tell you why he or she fights. If the child doesn't know, have him or her stand near you and think about it while you are watching. Some teachers also try the "talking method." They keep up a continuous chatter about outcomes of fights with no questions while the child stands. Five year olds find this is so boring that fighting loses its appeal. Of course, there are those who have been taught to fight at home; even with parental help, the fighting habit is not easy to cure.

Children who are kickers, pinchers, hair pullers, and biters all have their day when playing with their peers or when being limited in their behavior by adults. This behavior is not unusual. At the first indication of such behavior, put the attacker in the quiet corner. For the remainder of the day, limit behavior by not letting the child sit or stand by friends, be first in anything, sit by you, or hold your hands (that's a reward!). Each time you limit the child's actions, repeat "No, you may not (*play ball*) because you (*kicked*) John." Do not tell the child she or he was bad. Just remind the child of the inappropriate behavior.

Frequent tantrums are a sign of a very tired, neglected, or spoiled child. The child who is very tired just can't handle any more problems. This type of tantrum generally occurs in the late afternoon or evening. A neglected child may have a tantrum at any time; usually, however, you will find that other children have been receiving a lot of attention. This problem will be helped by giving the child more attention and by including the child in group praise and responsibilities. The spoiled child who has learned that a tantrum is a sure way to get his or her way can be a serious problem. Try to ignore the behavior. Do not let the child have his or her way (unless you were wrong in the first place). Parents need to be included in solving this problem. The spoiled child is a problem anywhere. The child who rolls on the floor and kicks should be ignored, but viewed with that eye in the back of your head. One technique used successfully by some teachers is to say to the children, aide, or other adults, "Please don't step on Jack." Another technique was used by a teacher who had a child who had a tantrum in the lunch room whenever he didn't get to sit by his favorite friend of the moment. The aide and the child went to the lunchroom first. The child ate at one table and the aide ate at another table, behind the child. At the end of twenty minutes, lunchtime was over regardless of amount of food eaten. The child then stayed in the school room with the aide while the other children ate. The aide did not play with the child while he was in the room. He had to amuse himself. Another teacher had a child given to staging a tantrum several times a day. The teacher would take all the other children out of the room immediately (to the library, outdoors, for a walk in the hall) and leave the crying, kicking child in the room. The aide watched the child but did not talk to her. The desire to be part of the group soon made both these spoiled children stop their tantrums at school.

Children lie because they have done something they know they'll be punished for, they are trying to cope with a problem, or they don't remember what happened. Generally if teachers are responsible in their expectations of young children and in their type of punishment, children will not lie. One young man named David was late to school every morning for several days. He lived less than a block from school. For the first three days, his explanation was that a dog wouldn't let him come to school. The teacher asked that a parent walk the child to school, but the father insisted the child walk by himself. On the fourth day, the child explained that a lion wouldn't let him come to school. For three days the teacher walked halfway to David's house and waited for him; he was twenty-five minutes early. The next day David was ten minutes late so the teacher went to find him. There he was, sitting on top of the jungle gym with a huge dog looking up at him. David's father didn't want him to be afraid of dogs, so the dog became a lion. Children become very imaginative when they have problems. When you know the tale cannot possibly be true, look for the cause.

Four year olds love to tell big tales. Enjoy them. If you think the child is actually lying about something, ask questions such as "How did it happen?" The child may need to think about the problem for a while. If you know how something happened or can make a pretty good guess, explain how the problem happened and have the child sit in the rocking chair for a while. You do not need to accuse the child of lying. He or she usually knows it.

Jealously is not uncommon in young children. They are very sensitive to unfairness, lack of attention, or classroom favoritism. Every child, every day, needs a special smile, a greeting, or some of your time. You will start the day off right if you greet each child, help with wraps, and be available for conversations. Those children who tend to be more jealous than others can be helped by making them helpers and carers for others.

Stealing doesn't occur very often but when it does the culprit may be hard to find. A huge, glossy red marble, the very favorite of a young man named Doug, disappeared one day just before time to go home. After looking on the floor and in pockets, all of the children set about trying to find the marble in the room. No marble! The teacher gathered the children on the rug and discussed the problem of the lost marble. Donna, usually a non-squirmer, kept squirming. The teacher guessed that the huge marble was hidden rather uncomfortably underneath her. The teacher asked each child to think of their favorite toy. Then she asked several of the children (including Donna) what they would do if someone had taken the toy. The girl's answer: "I don't know." After the discussion each child lined up for the long walk down the hall — still no marble. When Donna's mother came to pick her up, the remaining children immediately told her about the disappearing marble. The mother took one look at her daughter and walked her back to the room. When the teacher returned to the room, the huge red marble was on her desk. Mother and child were both rather teary eyed. The teacher had given the child every opportunity to "find" the lost marble — looking on the floor, checking pockets, searching through all the toys, and thinking about it during the discussion. The child, now belligerent, threatened to steal it again. The teacher suggested that the mother and child take the marble to Doug's house and give it to him.

As this example shows, at times regular methods do not work. If the marble had not been so large, the mystery probably would never have been solved. Such purposeful stealing needs to be punished. In the case of Donna, her mother and father decided that she could not watch her favorite TV programs (the family watched their programs); furthermore, the usual stop at the grocery store for a candy treat and an overnight guest on Friday night were eliminated for one week. These limitations were not because she took the marble but because of her belligerent attitude. Although Donna did not take anything again (to the knowledge of parents or teacher), she continued to threaten for several months.

Some problems of behavior occur once and never again, while others occur over and over. Children differ in social and emotional development just as they do in physical and intellectual development. In discussing each problem and ways of handling the problem, spanking has not been mentioned. If unacceptable behavior continues and a quiet corner, a rocking chair, separation in play, discussion, parent involvement, and elimination of some after-school privileges do not improve behavior, the child may have to be excused from school with an explanation to the parent. Do not tell the child he or she is bad, or mean, or that you don't love him or her. Just say the child forgot how to behave. Do not threaten children with a visit to the principal's or director's office as a punishment. The principal or director should visit the children's room often, and visits to his or her office should be frequent and happy — to show an especially good picture, a new hair cut, or to share a "happening." Teachers who have used this approach consistently have found that it works even with unusually active misbehavers. One teacher developed the following chart and placed it on the side of her storage cabinet so that the aide, parent helper, student teacher, or substitute teacher would use the same approach.

> Only when there are significant alternatives and opportunities to choose from will the question, "Who controls?" give way to the more important question, "What kind of learning environment is best for my child."
>
> Roland S. Barth

Behavior Limitations

1. Have child sit in rocking chair until physical appearance is calm.
2. Have child play in quiet corner until child asks to join the group.
3. Discuss reason for child being in rocking chair or quiet corner before allowing to rejoin the group.
4. If a child is especially unruly, list what was done; have the child tell the parent about it over the phone before leaving school. Explain to parent how you have disciplined the child.
5. If a child is especially unruly in one activity (riding the tricycle, block building, playing in the sand), do not let child participate in the activity for two days.
6. Write down on paper or chalkboard how you have limited behavior. In this way you will not forget the limitation and can be consistent.
7. If all else fails, write down what the child has done and take the child to principal's or director's office for further punishment. Not all behavior requires a spanking. The child may sit in the office for awhile, but may need to be sent home if the behavior is completely uncontrollable.

Several common procedures for behavior control will be discussed in the following section on research findings on social development in young children.

Research on Behavior

A 1976 report published by the National Institute of Education summarizes the psychological research findings on aggression, motivation, achievement, praise, helping others, development of moral judgment, self-discipline, and cooperation.[2]

Some of the findings suggest that the tendency of teachers to punish the aggressor first and then console the victim may be better handled by stepping between the children involved, "ignoring the aggressor but paying attention to the victim." Nonintervention may be interpreted by the aggressor as approval, and the distress of the victim may be considered a reward. Therefore, after righting the situation and comforting the victim, you should limit the aggressor's behavior in physical movement or oral participation.

Another important finding of the research data does not support the idea that children have an innate aggressive drive that can be displaced by kicking trees or punching pillows. One study found that boys who were allowed to punch a rubber clown to release their hitting and kicking tendencies were more aggressive toward other children when playing games and in free play than were boys who were restrained from any aggressive behavior. Other studies found that games and toys with aggressive themes tended to promote aggression in other situations. Games and toys that require more than one child (seesaws and rocking boats, for example) tended to encourage cooperation among the children.

This summary of research findings provides suggestions for constructive behavior; it lists references for more detailed descriptions of the research; and it has an extensive bibliography for further reading.

Another research study, conducted by Ronald Drabman and Margaret Hanratty Thomas under the sponsorship of HEW's National Institute of Mental Health, reported findings on the influence of the conduct of TV actors on the behavior of young children.[3] Drabman and Thomas selected forty third graders (twenty males and twenty females) from a predominantly white, lower-middle class neighborhood in Orlando, Florida. One by one

---

[2] Wendy Conklin Roedell, Ronald G. Slaby, and Halbert B. Robinson, *Social Development in Young Children: A Report for Teachers*, National Institute of Education Series (Washington, D.C.: U.S. Government Printing Office, 1976).

[3] Ronald Drabman and Margaret Hanratty Thomas, "Exposure to Filmed Violence and Children's Tolerance of Real-Life Aggression," ERIC document no. 097975. (Washington, D.C.: U.S. Department of Health, Education and Welfare, 1976).

the children viewed either a taped segment of a nationally televised detective show noted for its violence or a segment of the same length from a baseball game. Twenty children saw the detective show and twenty saw the baseball game.

After a child had watched the show for fifteen minutes, the child was told that a friend scheduled to work with a group of four and five year olds in an adjacent portable classroom called and couldn't come. The researcher said the friend had to do some personal business for a few minutes and needed the child to watch the young children for a few minutes. The third grader was told that the portable classroom had a closed-circuit camera and that all the child had to do was watch the set; if any of the preschoolers got in "trouble," the researcher was to be summoned at once. Another videotape of a five-year-old boy and a four-year-old girl was then run over the closed-circuit channel. The play of the children became rougher and rougher and eventually the picture blacked out, suggesting that the TV camera had been broken. The audio portion continued for a short time, leaving the third grader without any doubt that the fight was still raging. Soon the audio stopped also. Meanwhile the researcher waited outside the room where the third grader was watching the mayhem on the TV. If the researcher had not been summoned within two minutes of the loss of the audio portion of the video tape, the researcher re-entered the room.

Of the twenty third graders who viewed the violence of the detective show, seven did not call the researcher at all; one of the twenty children who watched the baseball game did not call the researcher at all; the thirteen children who viewed the violence who did summon the researcher were slower to alert the researcher than were the nineteen children who viewed the baseball game. The conclusion of this study and a similar study conducted by the researchers supported their hypothesis that exposure to televised violence may make young viewers more tolerant of real-life aggression and less likely to intervene.[4]

Watching television has become a way of life for children. Because of their inability to separate fact from fiction, they not only become placid about violence, they often model behavior that appears to be silly or funny. This behavior can cause severe problems both in school and at home.[5] To change objectionable programming, teachers and parents can write to the Federal Trade Commission, Pennsylvania Avenue at 6th Street N.W., Washington, D.C. 20001 and can join an organization called Action for Children's Television (ACT), 46 Austin Street, Newtonville, Ma. 02160.

[4] For additional information, read Betty M. Caldwell, "Aggression and Hostility in Young Children," *Young Children*, 32, 2 (January 1977): 5–14.

[5] For research data on television and behavior, read Dr. George Comstock, Senior Author, *Television and Human Behavior* (New York: Columbia University Press, 1978).

Nonverbal Behavior

As a teacher you cannot rely on your listening skills to determine the feelings or behavior of the children in your room. Young children's verbal responses are based on limited experiences and are only part of their reactions to the environment.[6]

Facial expressions, gestures, eye contact, posture, and energy changes transmit feelings and reactions. These types of communication are identified as *nonverbal behavior cues*. Some of the more common types of nonverbal cues include:

Downcast eyes	Furrowed brow	Smile
Mouth twitch	Biting tongue or lips	Scowl
Dropped head	Gleam in eye	Frown
Drooped shoulders	Extended lower lip	Drooping mouth
Limp arms	General body slouch	Extended chest
Red face	Reflexed arm muscles	Clenched fists
Rigid body	Pale face	Body withdrawal

Young children are very attuned to nonverbal stimuli communicated by their peers and by adults. Children's physical and verbal behavior is often influenced by the nonverbal cues extended by the teacher. As a teacher you need to study your own nonverbal behavior as well as your children's. You may be causing your own problems!

Manners

What are good manners for children? Learning to share toys and take turns are probably the first manners that have to be learned by young children. These two are essential manners for a classroom of youngsters simply because of the limited toys available and the common interests of children the same age. Sharing and taking turns is a long-term goal and has to be taught by example, fairness, and many different opportunities. Sharing and taking turns should occur often to reinforce the idea that everyone gives up something and everyone gets something. An egg timer is an inexpensive item for timing the play for sharing and taking turns. The timer provides a visual clue to children that time is passing, and they can see when it is time for their turn. For older children, a clock with large numbers and hands may be used. The children can watch until the large hand reaches the number the teacher has designated. A wind-up timer with a buzzer is perhaps the best device for this purpose. The buzzer emphasizes the end of the time and also alerts the teacher to the passage of time. It is expecially helpful

---

[6] For more information, refer to B. Rowen, *The Children We See: An Observational Approach to Child Study* (New York: Holt, Rinehart and Winston, 1963).

when four or five activities are going on at the same time and you haven't an aide.

Table manners are second to sharing and taking turns only because eating doesn't occur as often as human contact in an early childhood classroom. Nevertheless, table manners are begun the first day of school. Table manners should be observed on each occasion of eating something at snack time. Hands are washed, the children are seated, napkins are used; children can serve the crackers, juice, milk, or fruit. Everyone waits until the last person is served and until the servers are also seated. As everyone eats, including the teacher, the teacher begins a conversation with the children. The children's need for conversations and for help in remembering to keep elbows off the table, to keep napkins in laps, and to chew with mouths closed are all good reasons for the teacher to join children at their snack time.

Besides the daily snack time, there are many other opportunities to reinforce mealtime manners. Parties are always a great joy for children. Besides the usual birthday and holiday parties, you can always celebrate the first signs of spring, Mary's new brother, a visit by the principal, and the arrival of the new pet hamsters!

One classroom teacher of four year olds bought a plastic tablecloth for snack time and always placed some type of arrangement in the middle of her three tables: sometimes beautiful fall leaves, sometimes interesting weeds or wild flowers, at other times potted ivy, and occasional artificial flowers. The four year olds enjoyed their pretty tables so much that they had a near riot when a substitute teacher neglected to "set the table" two days in a row!

Mealtime manners are taught and caught! Only through practice and observation of good table manners can children learn the manners you wish them to have.

Company manners are also learned from example and are easier to teach when the children are younger. Greeting classroom guests by shaking their hands, taking their coats, seating them, and talking to them should be done early. Children can take turns being the official greeter. Invite parents to visit and let children do all of the greeting, seating, and serving. Only through practice will children be comfortable with these social skills.

One school secretary greeted a visiting consultant with the news that the principal had taken a sweater to a child in the kindergarten ten minutes earlier and would be back in another fifteen minutes. A little amazed at a twenty-five minute visit to deliver a sweater, the consultant asked why it took so long. The secretary replied, "The kindergartners are practicing greeting visitors, and no one has visited all week." Remember, if you are teaching greeting manners, plan for visitors!

The itching nose and the tissue box! Teachers of young children will not survive without a box or two of tissues. Noses itch and noses run — constantly. Tissues have many other uses including wiping faces, drying tears, and cleaning bruises; but taking care of sneezes and coughs seems to be the most constant and continuing use. Many teachers of three year olds will have to teach the children to blow their noses. In fact, some five year olds don't know how to blow their noses. Tell them to close their mouths and breathe hard through their noses. The financial crunch of buying tissue can be eased by cutting the tissue in half; small noses — small tissues.

Manners must be identified, planned for, taught, and demonstrated. Good manners should be shown daily by both the child and the teacher.

Praise

Catch the child being good! Praise is the oral language used to recognize appropriate and positive behavior. Oral encouragement can be given to children before they begin a task, as they are doing the task, or after they have accomplished the task. Praise words include:

Good	Beautiful	Excellent
Fine	Terrific	Very good
Great	That's right	Thank you
Much better	Good thinking	Marvelous
Congratulations	That's really nice	Keep it up

Try to use variety and expression in your comments. Spread your praise and attention to everyone in the room but don't praise every one for every activity (unless they deserve it). Over-used praise is not effective. Give the praise quietly and at the appropriate time. Children should know which behavior is being praised.

Conclusions

Behavior comes in many forms and is constant. It is good and bad and (sometimes) natural. Cultural differences will influence children's behavior as will a teacher's acceptance or nonacceptance of certain behaviors. Teachers who have extremely different behavioral codes of conduct from those exhibited by the children and parents in the school setting probably should teach in a different setting. This would be true at either end of the spectrum of behavior. Young children are greatly influenced by their teachers, as they are by their parents and peers. A teacher, therefore, must be an agent of change in some instances, a conveyor of behavior at other times, and at some times a model of consistent behavior. The realization of how behavior is acquired and knowledge of appropriate behavior will make a good teacher better.

FAMILY EDUCATION

There is no single model for successful parenthood. Teachers who believe family education will provide a simple plan for parenthood will be very frustrated. The most concerned, educated, and active parents will have moments of being thwarted, defeated, baffled, outwitted, and foiled. Teacher-parent involvement will not prevent these moments but may help parents understand that this too shall pass. At the same time, teachers must not mislead parents into thinking that growth and aging will be an improvement. The normative data characteristics, Piaget's stages of development, and Erikson's basic needs — discussed in Chapter 2 — will help you as a teacher in educating families to the fact that each individual has his or her own unique growth pattern; all will have their own difficulties and their own pleasures at each stage of development.

A worse fate for parents would be to let them rigidly follow the advice of experts or your interpretation of "the experts," The materials you share and discussions you have with parents should serve as aids rather than as answers in thinking through their decisions regarding their own children. Stress on "following the book" may make parents feel insecure in their own feelings toward the child. General knowledge of certain patterns of growth should help parents accept differences in performances of the children within their own family as well as differences within the group of like-aged children.

As these ideas and concepts are discussed with parents, teachers must recognize that they will be implemented according to home environments, values, and morals.

Home Environment Research

The effects of parental behavior, the needs of children, and the relationships of these two factors to the child's learning have been studied by several researchers covering a diversity of environmental settings. A 1975 study of homes in Arkansas disclosed two main factors pertaining to the learning performance of three year olds; opportunities for a variety of stimulation and the organization, arrangement, and order of the home environment.[7] A 1971 study of homes in Illinois by Wachs, Uzgiris, and Hunt found two factors related to a child's learning performance.[8] A positive factor was the availability of magazines to touch, see, and play with. The negative factor

---

[7] R. Elardo, R. Bradley, and B. Caldwell, "The Relation of Infants' Home Environments to Mental Test Performance from Six to Thirty-six Months: A Longitudinal Analysis." *Child Development* 46, 11 (1975): 71–76.

[8] T. Wachs, J. Uzgiris, and J. McV. Hunt, "Cognitive Development in Infants of Different Age Levels and from Different Environmental Backgrounds: An Explanatory Investigation." *Merrill-Palmer Quarterly* 17 (1971): 283–318.

was a high level of noise in the home. A 1974 study of low-income families in Florida by Gordon and Guinagh reported a difference in the performance of three year olds who had a variety of out-of-the-home experiences such as car trips, visits to a zoo, library, or supermarket.[9] The six year old boys in the study who had reading material at home had higher scores on the Stanford-Binet test; girls had higher scores if the parents stressed reading. These findings are similar to a 1973 study by Landsberger.[10] Other research studies indicate that parent modeling of reading at home during the early years is a crucial element in children's desire to read.[11] In a 1972 study of parent reading skills in rural and urban Appalachia, Guinagh and Jester discovered that just reading to children was not enough.[12] Some parents made reading so unpleasant the children never wanted to read; other parents read in such a way that children never got tired of being read to. One factor that seemed to be related to the pleasure was the conversation between parents and child related to the story. The classic studies of Burlington and Freud in 1944, Erikson in 1963, and Bowlby in 1969 provide basic research in the importance of building basic trust, attachment, affection, a stimulating environment, and consistent care.[13]

Problems in Family Education

Success in family education requires skill, patience, knowledge, understanding, and a pleasant personality. Teachers should not "tell" families what to do. Discussing, listening, and helping are the beginning steps in developing a relationship that will benefit children.

Many problems arise in the process of involving parents in the schooling of their children. These include: parents' inability to understand their role in their children's learning process; parents' fear of the unknown vocabulary of educators; parents' feelings that the teacher has some ulterior motive when asking them to visit the school; and the magnitude of the parents' personal problems.

---

[9] Ira J. Gordon and B. Guinagh, "A Home Learning Center Approach to Early Stimulation." Final Report on Project No. 1201 MH 16037-04 (Gainesville, Florida: Institute for Development of Human Resources, November, 1974).

[10] B. Landsberger, "Home Environment and School Performance: The North Carolina Experience," *Children Today* 2 (1973): 10–14.

[11] R. H. Dane, "The Identification and Measurement of Environmental Process Variables That Are Related to Education Achievement," doctoral dissertation, University of Chicago, 1963; Wachs et al., "Cognitive Development in Infants"; and Elardo et al., "Relation of Infants' Home Environments."

[12] B. Guinagh and R. E. Jester, "How Parents Read to Children," *Theory Into Practice* 11, 3 (June 1972).

[13] J. Bowlby, *Attachment and Loss, Vol. I: Attachment* (London: Hogarth Press, 1969); D. Burlingham and A. Freud, *Infants Without Families* (London: George Allen and Unwin, 1944); and Erik Erikson, *Childhood and Society*, 2nd ed. (New York: Norton, 1963).

Some programs for young children include family educators on their staffs. Their responsibilities vary greatly; you should certainly establish your own role in the family education program early in the year. Several teachers have found written notes with carbon copies a valuable means of providing family educators with information to share with parents. The written form also helps the family educator remember more exact details of the child's successes and needs.

Home Visits

Home visits can be a pleasure for parents and teachers or they can be a miserable failure. For years teachers did not communicate with parents unless their children were having problems or needed to be punished. In some situations this is still true. Home visits may be instances when the shortest distance between two points is not a straight line!

A knowledge of community resources is very important to teachers when they visit homes. The availability of glasses, dental work, and physical exams is especially important to parents with limited income. Sometimes during a home visit the visitor will notice unsanitary conditions — sewage problems, lack of water, or other health hazards. Such conditions often exist in rental property. The teacher can discuss the problems with the proper school authority, who can then act as the agent of change with the right community agency.

Flexibility in planning, implementing plans, and home-visit timing and schedules are a must. All home visits include unknown factors: How long will it take you to get there? What will the mood of the parents be? What problems have occurred since the last visit? What is the current neighborhood gossip? All of these factors will influence how long you will visit and whether or not you will discuss the children and their successes and needs.

Be sensitive to the expression or nonexpression of emotions of the family group (and be aware that the family will be sensitive to your expression or nonexpression of emotion during your visit). Sensitivity to the family's value system, current needs, ways the family is meeting these needs, independence of the family, and cultural influences provide means by which to interpret children's responses to their school environment.

Another factor that will influence your home visits is the aspect of a negative environment. Coping with parent's hopelessness concerning food, work, and housing may discourage some home visitors. The home visit that ends with a "no show" parent or involves a potentially violent reaction can intimidate teachers.

Home visits are developed on such factors as the positive attributes of children; knowledge of helping agencies; flexibility in planning, timing, and schedules; and sensitivity to emotions. Recognition of the negative factors will aid teachers in meeting parents' and children's needs.

School Visits

Before a child enters an early childhood program, the child and one or both parents should visit the classroom, the playground, the bathrooms, the principal's office, and the cafeteria. Through this visit, the child and the parents become aware of the physical environment the child will confront. This initial introduction to the school setting should be a social meeting whose main purpose is to get acquainted.

When the child is about to enter the program full time, the child should be a special visitor for a day if possible. Some schools accomplish this by having their tour of the environmental facilities in March of the year the child will enroll and on special visitors' days during April and May.

Child: "Are you somebody's mother?"

Visitor: "No. I came to talk to your teacher."

Child: "Are you my teacher's mother?"

Visitor: "No, I am her friend."

Child: "Hain't you anybody's mother?"

Most parents are impressed with a well-organized, controlled classroom with little confusion. A few parents are impressed with a program of formal lessons — number drills, workbooks, and worksheets. Others think a good program is one with a pretty room in which the children do clever things. Still others believe that unlimited freedom and complete permissiveness are necessary elements of a good program. Teachers need to explain to parents the goals of their school and their programs. Parents need to be reassured that activities selected will contribute to the child's total development. They need to know that their children are involved in a satisfying program that will build a foundation for later school experiences. If parents understand the school program, their interest and cooperation will increase.

Differences in educational, social, and economic levels may cause some parents to feel insecure with the teacher or in the school situation. If this is true, the teacher must take the initiative in establishing a warm friendship. When parents are not familiar with the purpose and plan for the school activities they may be suspicious of the total program.

Parents can also block communication between home and school activities. Sometimes parents carry over childhood feelings about teachers. A few believe that "the teacher knows best." Others stand in awe of teachers, while some feel resentful toward them. Some think that they are failing as parents and need reassurance that, basically, they are doing a good job. Most parents of young children are young adults and may have financial worries. Others are working out relationships with their own parents and in-laws, and others are trying to adjust to the early years of marriage.

Teachers of young children have much to learn from parents. Parents can help the teacher understand their children, their behavior, and feelings. What happens to a child at school must be related to what happens at home. Most parents want to understand their children better. Parents can be partners with teachers, learning about their children and working out plans for helping them.

Even when teachers want to work cooperatively with parents, their own feelings toward parents may hinder their success. Some teachers resent parents and want to blame them for the children's difficulties. Such feelings can establish barriers that are difficult to cross. Other teachers regard parents as a means of fulfilling their educational goals. Unfortunately, a few fear that parents will threaten their authority in the schools.

Teachers and parents need to recognize that all these problems exist. Efforts should be made to not only recognize such problems, but to recognize each other's abilities and concern for what is best for the child.

Parent-Teacher Conferences

Parent-teacher conferences involve many hours of work; they should be well planned and should start as early in the school year as possible.

In the initial conference, the parent should be encouraged to share information on the child's interests, health, or any other pertinent area. If a printed form is used to gather data about the child, read the questions to the parent and fill in the answers, as some parents cannot read. If you read the forms and discuss the information as you write it down, you will put all parents at ease and will not treat one parent differently from the others. (Do not ask a parent if he or she can read. If you write the information yourself you ought to be able to read your handwriting!)

In this initial conference the parent should be encouraged to discuss the child and the family in general terms. The teacher should be the listener, the guide for the discussion with pertinent questions, and the one who expresses pleasure for having the child in the room.

There are basically two types of conferences — whole group and individual. Whole group conferences usually occur at night so that both parents may attend. This type of conference can be an overview of the year's program; an examination of materials and children's work; an explanation of certain phases of instruction; or can feature a guest speaker on general topics of interest: behavior, health problems, or the teaching of reading.

The individual conference is based on personal need, interest, and accomplishment. The conference may be held in the classroom, over the phone, in the home, or in the teachers' lounge. The following guide for parent-teacher conferences will help you establish a warm bond of friendship with parents.

Suggestions for individual conferences

Place Choose a place that is convenient for both parent and teacher.

Time Do not try to have too many conferences on any one day. Try to schedule them before or after school hours, at lunch, or when it is convenient for both the parent and teacher. Have parent come when he or she will not have to wait long before talking with you.

Before the conference Help the child understand that the conference is in his or her best interest. Have materials (child's folder) available for reference if needed during conference. Know the materials recorded in the folder and know which items you plan to discuss.

Opening the conference Greet the parent warmly. Do not sit behind a desk. Keep the setting as informal as possible. Talk of neutral topics or comment on some activity that is displayed in the room. This will help put the parent at ease. Remember the parent wants an honest report but also has some fear that the child is not doing well.

During the conference Make your first remarks about the child complimentary and positive. If there is a problem, be tactful: "I need help in understanding why Tommie is always hitting other children. Can you think of anything that might be causing this?" *Listen* closely and sympathetically — you will learn much that will help you deal with the child. Accept *all* that is said without resentment or shock. Concentrate on one or two things on which both you and the parent can work together to help the child.

Closing the conference Keep the conference short. Since you cannot dismiss the parent, suggest another meeting soon or say "Next time we meet let's talk about (another problem)," and stand up. Each conference should end on a note of optimism.

After the conference Record in the child's folder the date of the conference and a few pertinent comments.

Suggestions for recording child's development for individual conferences
September Evaluate individualized skills and performances on rating form.

October through December Make anecdotal records on each child.

January Re-evaluate individualized skills and performances.
   Summarize anecdotal records.
   Hold individual conferences with parents.

February through April Add more anecdotal records to child's folder.

May Re-evaluate individualized skills and performances.
   Summarize anecdotal records.
   Write a report of progress.
   Hold individual conferences with parents.

A wise teacher keeps parents informed with accurate, to-the-point information concerning the behavior and abilities of their children. The joint efforts of the teacher and parents will strengthen the children's ability to adjust to the school environment and provide satisfying accomplishments.

Suggestions for Parents

Being a good parent is a strenuous activity! Who is better prepared to help than you? No one! How can you help? One way is to give the parents of your children materials, ideas, and suggestions to help them provide a good environment for the children.

A Form for Reviewing Child's Strengths and Weaknesses with Parent

Child's name _____
Parent's name _____
Date ___/___/___   Phone call _____ Home visit _____ School visit _____
Review of curriculum _____
_____

Review of child's performance _____
_____

Review of special needs _____
_____

Review of teacher's plans for meeting child's needs _____
_____

Suggestions for parent involvement _____
_____
_____

One way to help parents help their children is in the selection of purchased materials. The following lists of play materials and their brand names will help parents buy quality learning playthings.

Development of early motor skills and sensory perception

Parquetry Blocks: Playskool
Lacing Boot: Playskool
Jumbo Beads: Playskool
Inside U.S. Map Puzzle: Playskool
Postal Station: Playskool
Col-o-Rol Wagon: Playskool
Lincoln Logs: Playskool
Match Picture — Match Word Games: Playskool
Puzzles by Sifo and Simplex: Creative Playthings
Go-Together Cards: Creative Playthings
Color Cone: Creative Playthings
Learning Tower: Child Guidance
Tinker Toys: The Toy Tinkers
Play Tiles: Halsam
Fit-a-Shape: Lauri Enterprises
Alph-a-Space: Lauri Enterprises
Etch-a-Sketch: Ohio Art
Stick-on-Games: Colorforms
Play with Felt: Milton Bradley
Puzzles: Whitman
Easy Sticker Fun: Whitman
Color Books: Whitman
Stencil and Snip: Whitman
Follow the Dot Books: Whitman
Perception Plaques: Creative Playthings
Kitten in Kegs: Child Guidance

Arithmetic items

Clock Face with Movable Gears: Creative Playthings
Giant-Grooved Domino Blocks: Creative Playthings
Number Sorter: Creative Playthings
Teach a Time Clock: Child Guidance
Learning Numbers: Child Guidance
Add a Count Scale: Child Guidance
Roundup: Industrial Plastics
Follow the Number Books: Whitman
Cardboard Numbers: Milton Bradley
Bingo: Milton Bradley
Day-by-Day Calendar: Milton Bradley

Miscellaneous items

Sewing cards
Magic slates
Paper dolls
Lotto games
Cutting games
Perception and discrimination games
Blackboard
Rhyming games
Magnetic board
Tracing shapes
Records

The second way to help parents is to give them constructive ways to involve their children in family activities. Be sure to tell parents to demonstrate the activity to be accomplished by the children. Activities that children can do and the ages at which they are capable of imitating the activity include: Dusting, 2½ to 5 years; sweeping the floor, 3 to 5 years; setting a table, 2½ to 5 years; folding a napkin, 2½ to 5 years; carrying a chair, 2½ to 5 years; washing dishes, 2½ to 5 years; washing a table, 3 to 4 years; bringing in the newspaper, 3 to 5 years; and raking leaves, 3 to 5 years. Be sure to emphasize to the family that these activities are not mastered at these ages but are imitated or role played.

A third way to help parents is to make a list of various events, places, or things to do in the community. You might also make a list of appropriate books at the public library.

A fourth way is to be creative and think up special ideas for your special children.

Other Ways of Communicating with Parents

Several times during the year you will need to communicate with parents to tell them about their children's progress, to give them information on how to be better parents, and to pass along general information about school happenings.

Activities that include parents as well as children can be rewarding — and fun.

Obviously, you cannot use the same method of communicating with all parents. Programs designed for parents who are college graduates will include printed materials such as pamphlets or reprints of articles. Programs designed for parents from poverty areas, such as public housing projects, will include many visual cues and oral materials that are simplistic in form. Parents for whom English is a second language will benefit from materials in their native language. A 1976 report of the U.S. Census Bureau states that 4 million Americans regularly speak Spanish; 400,000 use Italian; 300,000, Chinese; 300,000, French; 100,000, German; 100,000, Greek; 100,000, Japanese; 100,000, Filipino; 100,000, Portugese; and 100,000, Korean. In all, about 8 million Americans usually speak a language other than English.

Some other ways of communicating to parents include slides with taped comments set up in the school library for parent viewing; a monthly newsletter on classroom activities; bulletin board displays near the school entrance where parents pick up children; round table discussions or skits; films; excursions; weekly folders of children's work; or specially written newspaper articles.

PROJECT

Learning More About Children's Families

The involvement of a child's family in the educational process and a teacher's knowledge of a student's family life are important for successful learning.

1. Record a "show and tell" activity for three, four, and five year olds in which they describe what their families do for fun.
2. Visit a classroom and make a list of all of the places the children's families work. Visit some of these places and write a short essay on the working conditions.
3. Interview a few parents of young children and ask them what they think their children should be learning in school.
4. Develop a unit for young children designed to portray different kinds of family life (for example, typical nuclear family, single-parent family, multi-generational family, family with stepparents, family in which both parents work).

A special booklet may be available on general policies and school information. If not, develop a booklet of your own and include:

School address and phone number	Teacher's name and telephone number
Daily school hours	Daily schedules
School calendar for year	Goals of programs
Field trip policies	Suggestions about clothing
Snow day policies	Items parents can donate (empty plastic bottles, boxes, wall-paper, tile, and so on).
General health requirements	

Classroom life must not be isolated from the general cultural environment of the child. Only through a close working relationship between school and home can the child truly perform at his or her creative best.

SUMMARY

Behavior and family education are two of the most important aspects of an early childhood program. Creativity, physical and oral responsiveness, pleasure, and success are all dependent on the child's behavior patterns and on the understanding, loving, and accepting family.

Behavior of children is probably the number one concern of teachers. In this chapter we have discussed types of behavior and what to do about misbehavior. We have also discussed research on behavior and factors associated with the findings of the research that should help you understand why some children behave the way they do. In addition, we have included ways of improving behavior.

Family education is closely related to a child's behavior because usually (1) the behavior observed in the classroom is learned at home and (2) inappropriate classroom behavior is rarely improved without the assistance of the family. This chapter has provided information on research on home environments, problems in family education, and suggestions for school visits, parent conferences, and other ways of communicating with families.

ADDITIONAL READINGS

Berger, Eugenia H. *Parents as Partners in Education*. St. Louis, Mo.: The C. V. Mosby Co., 1981.

Caplan, Frank, ed. *The Parenting Advisor. Princeton Center for Infancy*. Garden City, N.Y.: Anchor Press/Doubleday, 1977.

Howard, A. Eugene. *The American Family Myth and Reality*. Washington, D.C.: National Association for the Education of Young Children, 1978.

Needler, Shari E., and Oralie D. McAfee. *Working with Parents*. Belmont, Calif.: Wadsworth, 1979.

Ohmsted, Patricia, et al., ed. *Parent Education: The Contributions of Ira J. Gordon*. Washington, D.C.: Association for Childhood Education International, 1980.

Poster, M. *Critical Theory of the Family*. New York: Seaburg, 1978.

Rubin, Zick. *Children's Friendships*. Cambridge, Mass.: Harvard University Press, 1980.

Acknowledgments

The quotations found on the following pages of the text are reprinted from *Childhood Education Journal*. Copyrighted by the Association for Childhood Education International, 3615 Wisconsin Avenue, N.W., Washington, D.C. 20016. Reprinted courtesy of the Association for Childhood Education International, Washington, D.C. The author appreciates the privilege of using these quotations in the text.

(48) Agnes Snyder   Vol. 50, No. 1, October 1973, front cover. Copyright 1973.
(86) David Hawkins   Vol. 50, No. 4, February 1974, front cover. Copyright 1974.
(96) Karl W. Deutsch   Vol. 48, No. 5, February 1972, front cover. Copyright 1972.
(105) Shirley D. McCune and Martha Matthews   Vol. 52, No. 4, February 1976, front cover. Copyright 1972.
(136) Elizabeth Prescott   Vol. 50, No. 1, January 1974, front cover. Copyright 1974.
(202) Alice Miel   Vol. 52, No. 5, March 1976, front cover. Copyright 1976.
(251) Dorothy A. Cohen   Vol. 52, No. 6, April/May 1976, front cover. Copyright 1976.
(285) Ira J. Gordon   Vol. 52, No. 3, January 1976, front cover. Copyright 1976.
(312) Nik Krevitsky   Vol. 49, No. 6, March 1973, front cover. Copyright 1973.
(341) Kenneth S. Goodman   Vol. 46, No. 3, December 1969, front cover. Copyright 1969.
(363) James L. Hymes, Jr.   Vol. 47, No. 3, December 1970, front cover. Copyright 1970.
(394) Ira J. Gordon   Vol. 48, No. 7, April 1972, front cover. Copyright 1972.
(408) Lawrence K. Frank   Vol. 45, No. 3, November 1968, front cover. Copyright 1968.
(416) Roland S. Barth   Vol. 49, No. 4, January 1973, front cover. Copyright 1973.

The part-opening photographs found in the text are reprinted from the following sources: (*Part One*) Michael Schulman/The Picture Cube; (*Part Two*) Pat Coffrey/The Picture Cube; (*Part Three*) Michael Goss; (*Part Four*) Dani Carpenter/The Picture Cube.

Index

Ability to conserve (Piaget), 293
Absorbent mind (Montessori), 36
Abused child, 399
Academically oriented preschool model, 9
Acceptance and obedience in preoperational children (Piaget), 56
Acquisition of knowledge and skills concept, 50–51
Activity and Play of Children (Ellis and Shotz), 365
Activity centers, 118–125
Adaptation (Piaget), 53
Administration for Children, Youth, and Families, 45
Administrators, in early education, 18–21
Advances in Early Education and Day Care: A Research Annual (Kilmer), 10
Affective education, 205–206
  activities for, 212–215
  books, pamphlets, and journals on, 206–209
  books for children, 209–212
Aides, in early education, 21
  typical day with three year olds, 110–111
  typical day with four year olds, 111–112
Air, fresh, and health, 397
All Alone with Daddy (Fassler), 208
Allergies, 403
Alphabet, teaching the, 159–160
Alphabet books, 170–171
American Association for Health, Physical Education, and Recreation (AAHPER), 377
American Association of Elementary-Kindergarten-Nursery Educators, 22

American Froebel Association, 26
American Home Economics Association, 22
Analyzing Classroom Activities form, 102
Anglin, Jeremy M., 63
Animals
  as classroom pets, 255, 256–259
  pantomiming, 381
  stories about, 169–170
  zoo at school, 230
Anno, Mitsumasa, 158
Anno's Alphabet Book (Anno), 158
Anthologies for children, 172–173
Ants, as classroom pets, 258
Approaches to Beginning Reading (Aukerman), 152
April Rabbits, The (Karlin), 159
Aristotle, 25
Arnstein, Helene S., 208
Art
  basic skills sequence chart, 338–339
  books for children, 330–331
  cognitive approach to, 314
  cognitive-developmental approach to, 316
  crafts for the preschool classroom, 321–322
  creative activities, 327–330
  developmental approach to, 313–314
  differentiating and integrating mini units, 332–334
  evaluation of individual differences, 334–337
  for five year olds, 329–330
  forms of, 317
  for four year olds, 328–329
  instruction in, 324–327
  learning goals for children, 337
  materials, 322–323
  media, 317–323

437

Art (*cont.*)
    observation of five year olds, 61–62
    overview of, 313
    psychoanalytic approach to, 314–316
    songs in teaching color, 346
    theories of teaching, 313–317
    for three year olds, 327–328
Art Education Association, 313
Aruego, Jose, 158
Aspects of Early Childhood Education: Theory to Research to Practice (Ronge, Layton, and Roubinek), 10
Association for Childhood Education (ACE), 22, 28
Audio-visual equipment, 131–132
Auditory and hearing disabilities, 73, 75–76
Auditory discrimination, reading readiness and, 156
Aukerman, Robert C., 152
Autonomy, sense of, 69

Backtalk, 412. See also Behavior
Bailey, E., 378
Baldwin, Bird, 41
Bandura, A., 63
Bank Street school, 9, 27
Barker, Linda A., 6n
Basic Skills in Kindergarten: Foundation for Formal Learning (Barbe), 287
Basic skills sequence charts
    for art, 338–339
    for language arts, 189–200
    for mathematics, 306–310
    for music, 360–361
    for play and movement, 390–391
    for science, 280–283
    for social studies, 247–249
Basques, 91
Baughman, E., 368
"Bean bags," 375
Behavior, 409. See also Family education
    manners, 419–421
    nonverbal, 419
    praise and, 421
    research on, 417–418
    television and, 417–418
    what to do and when, to affect, 410–417

Behavior and analysis model of early education, 9
Behavior disorders, 74–75, 77
Behaviorism, 50, 51
Beinstock, S. F., 342–343, 349
Berger, Terry, 208
Bernstein, B., 63
Bessel, H., 207
Bickering, 412
Bilingual and bicultural needs and programs, 29, 93, 142, 431
Billy and Our New Baby (Arnstein), 208
Biological science center, 123. See also Science
Birch, Herbert E., 403
Bites, insect, 398–399
Blacks, 65, 91–92, 368
Block center, 123. See also Play
Bloom, Benjamin, 6, 9, 29, 63, 379
Blow, Susan, 27, 32
Blue-backed Speller (Webster), 26
Bodies, children and their, 380–381. See also Movement education
Body movements in space, 382–384
Bones, broken, 399
Bookcases, 131
Books. See also Language arts
    on affective education, 206–209
    affective education, for children, 209–212
    alphabet, 170–171
    art, for children, 330–331
    on fingerplays, 146
    on flannelboards, 149
    mathematics, for children, 296–297
    musical literature, 351
    picture books for beginning readers, 162
    science, for children, 271–274
    on spelling, 180
    in teaching social studies, 234–238
    in teaching visual discrimination, 158–159
    touch and smell, 274
Bowlby, J., 423
Box turtles, as classroom pets, 258
Boykin, A. W., 65
Boylers, K. M., 10
Boy with a Problem, The (Fassler), 208
Brain functioning research, 65
Brick laying, 231

British Infant School, 9
Broken bones, 399
Bruner, Jerome, 6, 63
Buhler, K., 364
Bulletin boards, 131
Bumps, 398
Burlingham, D., 423
Butler, B., 367

Calories, 400–401
Carbohydrates, 400
Cardinal numbers, 292
Career opportunities in early
  education, 13–14
 in administration, 18–21
 as aides, 21
 centers for three and four year olds,
  14–17
 elementary schools, 17–18
 kindergarten programs, 17
 professional organizations, 21–22
 in teaching, 13–18
Careers, hat rack of, 229–230
Cause-and-effect organization, reading
  readiness and, 157
Centers for three and four year olds,
  14–17. *See also* Activity centers
Ceramics, 330
Chairs, classroom, 131
Chalkboard, 131
Chalk drawing, 324–325
Charles, Elizabeth, 259
Charlie Needs a Cloak (dePaola), 159
Charlip, Remy, 158
Chicken pox, 404
Child-centered approach to social
  studies, 203, 204
Child Development Associate (CDA),
  21
Childhood and Poverty (Erikson), 69
Childhood Education, 22, 28
Childhood Education Foundation,
  N.Y.C., 27
Child-inspired activities, defined, 219
Child's Conception of Numbers, The
  (Piaget), 286
Child study movement, 41–42
Christmas music, 348
Chronic physical illness, 74, 77. *See
  also* Health
Clapping, music for, 344

Class cultural differences, 92–93
Classification and relationship skills
  (Piaget), 56
Classroom organization
 activity centers, 118–125
 equipment and materials, 125–133
 factors influencing, 106–107
 individualization and grouping,
  114–117
 the room, 117–125
 schedules and plans, 107–114
Clay, 319–320, 328
Clay center, 122
Clay modeling, 326, 328
Cleanliness, children's physical,
  395–397
Climbing, 369
Closed theory of learning, 49, 50, 51
Clothing, teachers', 11–12
Cognitive-affective approach to
  movement education, 378, 379
Cognitive approach to art education,
  314
Cognitive-developmental approach to
  art education, 316
Cognitive learning observation form,
  103
Cognitive model in early education, 9
Cognitive process approach to
  teaching social sciences, 203–204
Cohen, Dorothy H., 251
Collage, 327
Color, songs that aid in teaching, 346.
  See also Art
Columbia University Nursery School,
  27
Comenius, John, 25
Committee of Nineteen, 27
Communicable diseases, 404–406
Communicative speech (Piaget), 55
Company manners, 420
Comparison, vocabulary of, 287–289
Competition (Piaget), 56–57
Conceptual stage, 53
Concrete operational stage, 54
Conjunctivitis, 404
Conservation (Piaget), 54
Conservation of quantity, 293
Construction center, 123
*Constructive Play: Applying Piaget in
  the Classroom* (Forman and Hill),
  366

Content areas, integration of, in social studies, 215–224
Content areas of instruction, defined, 203
Control of error (Montessori), 36
Convulsions, 397
Cooking, in teaching science, 266–271
Cooking center, 124
Cooperative nursery schools, 27
Corsini, D., 64
Craft center, 122–123
Crafts, 317, 321–322, 326. *See also* Art
  for three year olds, 327–328
  for four year olds, 328–329
  for five year olds, 329–330
Cratty, B. J., 378
Crayon drawing, 326
Crayon resist, 328
Creative and Mental Growth (Lowenfeld), 314
Creative dramatics center, 122. *See also* Dramatization
Creative writing center, 121–122
Cuisenaire® rods, 40
Cultural anthropology, 45
Cultural representation approach to movement education, 378–379
Culture
  categories of, 87
  defined, 87
  differences in, 89–94
  family, role of, in, 87–88
  and play, 366–368
  school, role of, in, 88–89
Culture of poverty, 93
Culture of the family, 88
Current events center, 125
Curriculum, *see* Art; Language arts; Mathematics; Movement education; Music; Physical setting for curriculum; Play; Science; Social setting for curriculum; Social studies
Curriculum integration through pantomime, 381–382
Customs, in culture, 87
Cuts and abrasions, 398
Cutting, 317, 326–327. *See also* Art
Cycles of activity (Montessori), 36

Dahlstrom, W., 368
Daily schedules, 107–113
Dalcroze, Émile, 343
Davis, Allison, 63, 87–88
Day care, 6–7
Day Care and Child Development Council of America, 22
Day-care centers, 8
  typical day for director of, 19–21
  typical day for teacher in, 16–17
dePaola, Tomie, 159
Deutsch, Martin, 63
Development
  and growth, 65–70
  normative data, 65–68
  overview of, 49
  of speech, 138–139
  stages of mental (Piaget), 54
Developmental approach
  to art instruction, 313–314
  to movement education, 378
Deviated child (Montessori), 36
Dewey, John, 26, 35, 36, 41, 324, 329
  key concepts of "My Pedagogic Creed," 37–38
Dialect, reading and, 161. *See also* English
Didactic materials (Montessori), 38
Diet, balanced, *see* Nutrition
Dietary daily requirements, 402
Differentiating and integrating mini units
  art, 332–334
  language arts, 182–184
  mathematics, 300–303
  music, 355–356
  play and movement, 384–387
  science, 274–277
  social studies, 238–243
Dinkmeyer, D., 206
Disabilities, learning, 71, 75
Disadvantaged children, 6, 63
  nutrition and, 403
Disadvantaged Children: Health, Nutrition and School Failure (Birch and Gussow), 403
Discovery approach to teaching science, 252
Discovery of the child (Montessori), 38
Discrimination, reading readiness and, 156
Disease. *See also* Health; Nutrition
  allergies, 403
  chronic physical illness, 76, 77

Disease (*cont.*)
  communicable, 404–406
  defined, 395
Display space, 131. *See also*
    Classroom organization
Dollard, John, 52
Don't Worry, Dear (Fassler), 208
Drabman, Ronald, 417
Dramatization
  and oral language development,
    146–147
  in teaching social studies, 215–219
Draw-A-Man Test, 314
Drawing, 317, 324–326, 328. *See also*
    Art
Drifters, The (Pavenstedt), 367
"Duck, duck, goose," 376
DUSO (*Developing Understanding of
    Self and Others*) (Dinkmeyer),
    206
Duty and accomplishment, sense of,
    69–70
Dying, 317, 321. *See also* Art

Early childhood education
  career opportunities in, 13–22
  early intervention concept, 5–6
  experimental models in, 9–10
  history of, 24–32
  overview of, 5
  programs in, 7–10
  purposes of, 5–7
  settings in, 7–9
  teachers of, 10–13
  today, 5–10
  traditional goals of, 5
Early childhood supervisor, typical
    day of, 19
Early intervention, concept of, 5–6
Easel painting, 327. *See also* Art
Easter music, 348–349
Ebersole, Marylou, 52, 381
Educating Children, 22
Education
  early American, 30–32
  history of, 24–32
  philosophies of, 32–46
Education for All Handicapped
    Children Act (1975), 29, 70
"Effect of Preschool Attendance upon
    the IQ, The" (Wellman), 28
Egocentric speech (Piaget), 55

Eichenwald, H., 59
Elementary-Kindergarten-Nursery
    Education (E/K/N/E), 27
Elementary school, teaching in, 17–18
Elementary-Secondary Education Act
    (1965), 29
Eliot, Abigail, 28, 41, 42–44
Embroidery, 317. *See also* Art
Émile (Rousseau), 25
Emotional normative data
  on three year olds, 66
  on four year olds, 66
  on five year olds, 67–68
  on six year olds, 68
Enabler model of early education, 9
English. *See also* Language arts
  nonstandard, 141, 161
  as second language of children, 29,
    93, 142, 431
English standard measure, 289–292.
    See also Mathematics
Enrichment, 72
Environment, *see* Social setting for
    curriculum
Equilibration (Piaget), 53
Equipment
  audio-visual, 131–132
  classroom, 125–133
  for individualizing activities, 115
  for learning at home, 429–430
  play, 229–234, 370–375, 429–430
  play, for handicapped children, 375
  resting, 131
  role-playing, 230
  sound, 132, 139
  for spontaneous play, 229–234
  for teaching mathematics, 297–299
  for teaching music, 351–354
  for teaching science, 255–256
  for teaching social studies, 225–234
Erasmus, 25
ERIC Clearinghouse on Elementary
    and Early Childhood Education,
    29, 205
Erikson, Erik H., 69, 364, 379, 422,
    423
Ethnic cultural differences, 90–92
Evaluation of individual differences,
    99
  in art, 334–337
  in language arts, 184–188
  in mathematics, 303–305

Evaluation of individual differences (*cont.*)
  in music, 357–359
  in play and movement, 387–389
  in science, 277–279
  in social studies, 243–246
Exceptional child, 70–71
  characteristics and needs of, 71–75
  support systems for, 77–79
  teaching approaches with, 75–77

Fables for children, 171
Family, role of, in socialization, 87–88, 205. *See also* Parents
Family education, 422. *See also* Behavior
  communicating with parents, 424–430, 431–432
  home environment research, 422–423
  home visits, 424–425
  parent-teacher conferences, 426–428
  problems in, 423–424
  school visits, 425–426
  suggestions for parents, 428–430
Farnham-Diggory, Sylvia, 62, 63
Fassler, Joan, 208
Father of the Man (Davis and Havighurst), 88
Fats, 400
Federal Panel on Early Childhood, 29
Federal Trade Commission, 418
Feelings, games for expressing, 214–215. *See also* Emotional normative data
Feldman, C. F., 64
Fiber, 400
Field trips, 223–224
Fights, 412–414
Find the Cat (Livermore), 159
Finger-painting, 318, 324, 327. *See also* Art
Fingerplays, oral language development and, 143–146
Fish, as classroom pets, 256–257
Fistfights, 412–413
Five year olds
  differentiating and integrating for, *see* Differentiating and integrating mini units
  full-day schedule with, 111–112
  normative data for, 67–68
  observation of: art, 61–62
  play for, 366, 369, 373–374, 374–375
Flannelboards
  and oral language development, 147–149
  replicas made of, 227–228
  in teaching social studies, 212–213
Flavell, John H., 64
Florida parent-educator model of early education, 9
Flower preservation, 317, 322. *See also* Art
Folk tales for children, 171
Food, *see* Nutrition
Food activities, teaching science and, 266–271
Ford Foundation, 343
Formal operational stage, 54
Foul language, 412. *See also* Behavior
Four year olds
  centers for, 14–17
  differentiating and integrating for, *see* Differentiating and integrating mini units
  full-day schedules with, 14–17
  normative data for, 66–67
  observation of: science, 61
  play for, 366, 369, 370, 374
Frank, Lawrence K., 42, 44, 364, 408
Freed, Alvyn M., 207–208
Freedom (Montessori), 38
Freud, A., 423
Froebel, Friedrich Wilhelm, 26, 32–35
"Fruit basket upset," 375
Fry, P., 59
Full-day schedule, 107–109
  with three year olds, 110–111
  with four year olds, 14–17
  with five year olds, 111–112
  with six year olds, 112–113
Fussiness, 412. *See also* Behavior

Games and puzzles center, 123
Games for children, 375–377. *See also* Play
  appropriate for expressing feelings, 214–215
Garden center, 123

Gardening, 265–266
"General Guidelines for Selecting Television Programming for Children," 152
Geometry, plane, 293
Gerbils, as classroom pets, 258
German measles, 404
Gesell, Arnold, 28, 41, 65
Giftedness, intellectual, 71–72, 75
Glue, making, 319
Goals. *See also* Learning goals for children
 defined, 96
 guide for observational ratings of, 100–101
 observation and, 98–103
 of teachers and children, 96–98
Goetz, E. M., 64
Goldfish, as classroom pets, 256
Goodenough, Florence, 314
Goodman, Kenneth S., 341
Gordon, Ira J., 35, 394, 423
Gori, Gio B., 402–403
Grammar, 142–143. *See also* Language arts
Greisman, Joan, 208
Groos, K., 364
Gross motor stage, 52
Group Games in Early Education: Implications of Piaget's Theory (Komii and DeVries), 365
Grouping, in the classroom, 116–117
Growth, development and, 65–70
Guilt and punishment (Piaget), 56
Guinagh, B., 423
Guinea pigs, as classroom pets, 258–259
Guppies, as classroom pets, 257
Gussow, Joan Dye, 403
Guttentag, M., 65

Half-day schedule, 109–110
Hall, George Stanley, 41, 364
Halliday, M. A. K., 64
Halloween music, 348
Handicapped children
 auditory and hearing disabilities, 73, 75–76
 chronic physical illness, 74, 77
 mental retardation, 72–73, 75
 orthopedic impairments, 74, 77
 play equipment for, 375
 speech and language disorders, 73, 76
 visual impairments, 73–74, 76–77
Hansen, L., 64
Hanukah music, 348
Harris, Dale, 314
Harris, William T., 26, 32
Havighurst, Robert J., 87–88
Hawkins, David, 86
Head Start, Project, 6, 8, 9, 18, 29, 42
Health. *See also* Disease; Nutrition
 the abused child, 399
 accidents, 398–399
 cleanliness, 395–397
 convulsions, 397
 defined, 395
 learning goals for children, 406–407
 rest and sleep, 395
 sustaining, 395
 temperature and fresh air, 397
 toileting needs, 397
 vomiting, 397
Hearing disabilities, 73, 75–76
Heglon, A., 64
Hepatitis, infectious, 405
Herkowitz, J., 378
Hess, R., 63
Hilgard, Ernest R., 52
Hill, Patty Smith, 27, 44
Hispanic Americans, 90–91
History of early childhood education, 24–32
 early American education, 30–32
Home environment, research on, 422–423
Home visits, 424–425
Honesty (Piaget), 56
Hornbook, 25
Hospital Is Where, The (Smith), 208
How to Keep Your Pet Healthy (Charles), 259
Huff, Phyllis E., 270
Humanistic psychology, 50, 51–52
Humorous books for children, 172
Hunt, J. McV., 6, 63, 422
Hymes, James L., Jr., 363

Ideational orientation, 64
 in teaching reading, 137

Identity, sense of, 70
Ideology, in culture, 87
I Have Feelings (Berger), 208
Ilg, Frances L., 65
Illness, chronic physical, 74, 77. *See also* Disease; Health
Imaginative stories for children, 168–169
Immigration trends, 90, 91
Impetigo, 404
Individual differences, as learning factor, 58. *See also* Evaluation of individual differences
Individualization, in the classroom, 114–115, 116–117
Initiative, sense of, 69
Insect bites and stings, 398–399
Institute for Developmental Studies model of early education, 9
Institute for Early Childhood Education, 98
Institute for the Development of Educational Activities (I/D/E/A), 9
Institutionalization of children, 62–63, 368
Institutions, in culture, 87
Instruments, musical, 353–354. *See also* Music
Integrating, *see* Differentiating and integrating mini units
Intellectual giftedness, 71–72, 75
Intellectual normative data
  on three year olds, 66
  on four year olds, 66–67
  on five year olds, 68
  on six year olds, 68
Intellectual realism (Piaget), 316
Interactionism, 50, 51
International Journal of Early Childhood, 22
International Kindergarten Union (IKU), 27
Interpersonal normative data
  on three year olds, 66
  on four year olds, 67
  on five year olds, 68
  on six year olds, 68
"I spy," 376

Jealousy, 415. *See also* Behavior
Jersild, A. T., 52, 342–343, 349

Jester, R. E., 423
Journal of Home Economics, 22
Journals
  affective education, 206
  early childhood professional, 22
Joyner, Jerry, 158
Jumping, 369

Kagan, Jerome, 364
Karlin, Nurit, 159
Kephart, N. C., 378
Kilmer, S., 10
Kindergarten, teaching in, 17
Kindergarten: Programs and Practices (Ramsey and Boylers), 10
Kniveton, B., 367–368
Kodály, Zoltán, 343
Krevitsky, Nik, 312

LaBelle Courier®, 167
Labor Force Report No. 130 (1980), 7
Lancaster mass education system, 31
Language
  as cultural difference, 93–94
  in culture, 87
  dialect, 161
  foul, 412
  nonstandard English, 141, 161
  oral, *see* Oral language
  primary, 141
Language and Thought of the Child, The (Piaget), 28
Language arts
  basic skills sequence chart, 189–200
  differentiating and integrating mini units, 182–184
  evaluation of individual differences, 184–188
  ideational orientation, 137
  language experience charts, 180–182
  learning goals for children, 188
  literature, 162–175
  oral language, 138–152
  overview of, 137
  reading, 152–162
  skill orientation, 137
  spelling, 179–180
  theories of teaching, 137–138
  written language, 175–179
Language disorders, 73, 76

Language experience approach to English, 161
Language experience charts, 180–181
Lanham Act (1940), 28, 42
Lanham Act War Nurseries, 28
Lansberger, B., 423
Lau v. *Nichols*, 29
Laura Spelman Rockefeller Memorial, 44
Layton, J. R., 10
Learning
  factors influencing, 57–65
  motivation and, 58
  overview of, 49
  process of, 49–57
  reinforcement and, 59
  research on, 59–65
  retention and, 58
  stages of, 52–53
  transfer and, 59
  understanding and, 59
Learning disabilities, 71, 75
Learning disabled (LD) children, 71
Learning goals for children
  in art, 337
  in health, 406–407
  in mathematics, 305–306
  in music, 359–360
  in play and movement education, 389–390
  in science, 280
  in social studies, 246–247
Learning theories, 49–53
  Piaget's theory of intellectual development, 53–57
Lesson plans, 113–114
Let's Be Together Today (Mr. Rogers), 212
Levine, Edna S., 208
Lewis, Stephen, 159
Lisa and Her Soundless World (Levine), 208
Listening, 139–140. *See also* Music; Records
Listening center, 122
Literature, teaching, 162–163
  child's part, 167–168
  storybooks for young children, 168–175
  teacher's role, 163–167
Livermore, Elaine, 159

Loban, W., 64
Locke, John, 25
Logical thinking and reasoning (Piaget), 55–56
Lost and Found (Livermore), 159
Lowenfeld, Viktor, 314
Luther, Martin, 25
Lying, 414–415. *See also* Behavior

McCune, Shirley D., 105
McFee, June King, 316
Machine activities, pantomiming, 381
McMillan, Margaret, 27, 41
Mainstreaming, 70
Malnutrition, 59. *See also* Nutrition
Manners, 419–421. *See also* Behavior
Man of the House, The (Fassler), 208
Marching, music for, 345
Masks, 329. *See also* Art
Materials
  art, 318–323
  classroom, 126–127, 132–133
  for individualizing activities, 115
  Montessori, 39–40, 115
  for play learning at home, 429–430
  for spontaneous play, 229–234
  for teaching mathematics, 297–299
  for teaching music, 351–354
  for teaching science, 255–256
  for teaching social studies, 225–234
Mathematics
  basic concepts, 287–293
  basic skills sequence chart, 306–310
  books for children, 296–297
  conservation of quantity, 293
  differentiating and integrating mini units, 300–303
  equipment and materials, 297–299
  evaluation of individual differences, 303–305
  identification in, 286
  learning goals for children, 305–306
  matching in, 286
  measurement activities, 290–292
  mental readiness for, 293–296
  metric and English standard measure, 289–292
  number concepts, 292
  numeration, 292
  overview of, 286
  plane geometry, 293

Mathematics (*cont.*)
  sequencing in, 286
  sets, 292–293
  songs and, 346
  theories of teaching, 286–287
  vocabulary of comparison, 287–289
Mathematics center, 122
Matthews, Martha, 105
Measles, 405
Measure, standards of, 289–292
Mechanism, 50–51
Media, *see* Art
"Melting-pot" concept of America, 89–90
Mental development, stages of (Piaget), 54
Mental readiness for mathematics, 293–296
Mental retardation, 72–73, 75
Merrill-Palmer Institute, 28
Methods in Human Development (Bessel and Palomares), 207
Metric measure, 289–292
Mexican Americans, 90–91
Mild retardation, 72
Miller, Neal, 52
Minerals, 400
Mini units, *see* Differentiating and integrating mini units
Mirror, in classroom, 213
Moderate retardation, 72
Mollys, as classroom pets, 257
Montessori, Maria, 27, 36, 39–40
Montessori materials, 39–40, 115
Montessori method, 9, 36–40
Montessori terms, 36, 38
Moorhead, G. E., 342
Moral teaching, 94–96. See also Socialization, teaching
Mosaics, 328
Mother Goose Tales (Perrault), 25
Mother Plays (Froebel), 34
Motivation, as learning factor, 58
Motor-perceptual stage, 52
Motor-rhythmic activities, 343–345. *See also* Music
Movement education. *See also* Play
  activities, 381–384
  basic skills sequence chart, 390–391
  children and their bodies, 380–381
  cognitive-affective approach to, 379
  cultural representation approach to, 378–379
  developmental approach to, 378
  differentiating and integrating mini units, 384–387
  equipment, 382–384
  evaluation of individual differences, 387–389
  learning goals for children, 389–390
  overview of, 364
  theories of, 377–381
Mumps, 406
Murphy, Lois Barclay, 63, 314, 365, 367
Music
  basic skills sequence chart, 360–361
  differentiating and integrating mini units, 355–356
  evaluation of individual differences, 357–359
  holiday, 348–349
  instruments, 353–354
  learning goals for children, 359–360
  listening, 345–349
  literature, musical, 351
  materials and equipment, 351–354
  motor-rhythmic activities, 343–345
  overview of, 342
  records, 351–353
  singing, 349–350
  songs and counting, 346
  songs that aid in teaching color, 346
  teaching science with, 346–347
  teaching social studies with, 347–348
  terminology, 349–350
  theories of instruction, 342–343
"Musical chairs," 375
Music Educators' National Conference, 343
My Grandpa Died Today (Fassler), 208

"Name and touch," 376
NANE Bulletin, 29
National Association for Nursery Education (NANE), 28, 29
National Association for the Education of Young Children (NAEYC), 22, 29, 377
National Committee on Nursery Schools, 28

National Laboratory on Early
  Childhood Education, 29
National School Public Relations
  Association, 10
New England Primer, The, 25
Non-English-speaking children and
  families, needs of and programs
  for, 29, 93, 142, 431
Nonstandard English, 141, 161
Nonverbal behavior, 419
Normalized child (Montessori), 38
Normative data, 41, 65
  on three year olds, 65–66
  on four year olds, 66–67
  on five year olds, 67–68
  on six year olds, 68
Number concepts, 292
Number conceptualization (Piaget), 56
Numeration, 292
Nursery school
  teaching in, 14–17
  typical day for teacher and aide,
    14–16
Nurss, J. R., 64
Nutrition. *See also* Disease; Health
  child's role, 401
  daily requirements, 402
  defined, 395
  and the disadvantaged child, 403
  parent's role, 399–401
  recent research on balanced diet,
    402–403
  serving sizes for children, 401
  snacks, 402
  teacher's role, 401

Obedience, 410–417. *See also*
  Behavior
Objectivity (Montessori), 39
Observation, 98–103
Observation forms, 99–102, 103
One Little Girl (Fassler), 208
Open-air nursery school, 27
Open theory of learning, 49, 50, 51
Operations (Piaget), 54
Oral language. *See also* Language arts
  activities for developing, 143–152
  dramatization and, 146–147
  factors affecting differences in,
    140–142
  fingerplays and, 143–146

flannelboards and, 147–149
grammar, 142–143
listening, 139–140
pictures and, 151
puppetry and, 147
speech, development of, 138–139
tapes and records, 149–151
television and, 152
Ordinal numbers, 292
Orff, Carl, 343
Organisation Mondiale Pour
  l'Éducation Prescolaire and the
  United States Committee for
  Early Childhood Education, 22
Organization (Piaget), 53
Organization, classroom, *see*
  Classroom organization
Orphanages, 368
Orthopedic impairments, 74, 77
Oshkosh Normal School, 27
Otto, W., 64

Paint, recipes for, 318–319
Painting, 317, 319, 324, 327, 328,
  329. *See also* Art
Painting center, 122
Palomares, V., 207
Pamphlets, on affective education, 206
Pantomime, curriculum integration
  through, 381–382
Paperback books for children, 173
Paper stencils, 328–329. *See also* Art
Papier-maché, 321, 330
Parents
  communicating with, 13, 430–432
  home and school visits, 424–426
  nutrition of child, role in, 399–401
  parent-teacher conferences, 426–428
  reading and, 160–161
  reviewing child's strengths and
    weaknesses, forms for, 429
  socialization, role in, 87–88, 205
  suggestions for good parenting,
    428–430
Parents Anonymous, 399
Parent-teacher conferences, 426–428
Paste, nontoxic, 319. *See also* Art
Pasting, 317, 326–327
Pavenstedt, E., 367
Peabody, Elizabeth Palmer, 26, 32
Perceptual-conceptual stage, 53

Perceptual-motor stage, 52
Perceptual stage, 52
Perrault, Charles, 25
Pestalozzi, Johann, 25–26, 32
Pets, classroom, 255, 256–259
Petzold, R., 342
Pflederer, M., 342
Philadelphia Exposition of 1876, 26
Philosophies of education, 32–46
Phonograph records, *see* Records
Photographs
  in affective education, 213–214
  for oral language development, 151
Physical activities, 368–369. *See also*
  Movement education; Play
Physical handicaps, *see* Handicapped
  children
Physical movement, pantomime,
  381–382
Physical normative data
  on three year olds, 65–66
  on four year olds, 66
  on five year olds, 67
  on six year olds, 68
Physical science center, 123. *See also*
  Science
Physical setting for curriculum
  equipment and materials, 125–133
  individualization and grouping,
    114–117
  organization, factors influencing,
    106–107
  overview of, 106
  room organization, 117–125
  schedules and plans, 107–114
Piaget, Jean, 28, 34, 65, 342, 364,
  365, 366, 379, 380, 422
  cognitive-developmental approach to
    art, 316
  on mental readiness for
    mathematics, 286–287, 293–296,
    297
  theory of intellectual development,
    53–57
Pick, A., 64
Picture files, 131
Pictures
  in affective education, 213–214
  for oral language development, 151
Pike, C., 367–368
Pillsbury Foundation School, 343

Pinworm, 404
PL 94-142, 29, 70
Plane geometry, 293
Plants, for the classroom, 255, 259
Plaster for molds, 321
Platies, as classroom pets, 257
Plato, 25
Play. *See also* Behavior; Movement
    education
  basic skills sequence chart, 390–391
  cultural influences on, 366–368
  at different ages, 366
  differentiating and integrating mini
    units, 384–387
  equipment selection, 370–375
  evaluation of individual differences,
    387–389
  of five year olds, 366, 369,
    373–374, 374–375
  of four year olds, 366, 369, 372,
    374
  games for young children, 375–377
  learning goals for children, 389–390
  overview of, 364
  physical activities, 368–369
  sand and water, 264–266
  spontaneous, 219, 229–234
  in teaching science, 264–271
  theories of teaching, 364–366
  of three year olds, 366, 368–369,
    372, 374
Playgrounds, 371–372
Plumber's box, 230–231
Poetry, for children, 173–175
"Police officer and lost child," 376
Poliomyelitis, 406
Pond, D., 342
Poster painting, 319, 324. *See also*
    Art
Pottery, 317
Poverty, culture of, 93
Practical life exercises (Montessori), 38
Praise, behavior and, 421
Prekindergarten, teaching in, 14–17
Preoperational stage, 54
  learning in, 54–57, 63–64
Prepared environment (Montessori),
    38
*Preschool Breakthrough: What Works
  in Early Childhood Education,* 6
Preschool Child, The (Gesell), 28

Preschools, teaching in, 14–17
Primary language, 141
Printing, 327. *See also* Art
Process approach to teaching science, 252–253
Professional organizations, early childhood, 21–22
Profound retardation, 72
Project Head Start, 6, 8, 9, 18, 29, 42
Projection equipment, 131
Proteins, 400
Psychoanalytic approach to art, 314–316
Psychological Care of Infant and Child (Watson), 28
Psychological needs, basic, 69–70
Public education, evolution of, 31
Public Law, 94–142, 29, 70
Punishment, 56, 59, 91. *See also* Behavior
Puppets, 328
  in oral language development, 147
Puzzles, 227
Puzzles (Wildsmith), 159

Quantity, conservation of, 293

Ramo (Hiller), 212
Ramsey, M. E., 10
Raths, Louis E., 4, 95
Rationalism, 50, 51
Read, Katherine Baker, 314
Reading, teaching, 137–138. *See also* Language arts
  alphabet, teaching the, 159–160
  auditory discrimination and, 156
  books for teaching visual discrimination, 158–159
  cause-and-effect organization, 157
  dialect and, 161
  discrimination, finer differences in, 156
  gross difference discrimination, 156
  ideas in sequence, 158
  meanings and ideas related to written symbols, 158
  parents and, 160–161
  picture books for beginning readers, 162
  picture recognition and interpretation, 156–157
  process of reading, 153–155
  readiness skills, 153, 155–158
  reading, defined, 152–153
  similarities among objects, persons, and events, recognition of, 157
  storytelling and reading to children, 164–166
  vision development and, 155–156
Reading center, 121
Reading content spiral, in two preprimers, 154–155
Reading skills, research on, 64
Records
  in affective education, 212
  that build music skills, 351–352
  that coordinate music with other subjects, 353
  for oral language development, 149–151
  ordering, 151
"Red Rover," 376
Reinforcement, as learning factor, 59
Replica toys, 225–226
Research on learning, 59–65
Resources, in social studies, 224. *See also* Equipment; Materials
Responsible model of early education, 9
Responsive Environment Corporation model of early education, 9
Rest, adequate, 395
Resting equipment, 131
Retardation, mental, 72–73, 75
Retention, as learning factor, 58–59
Reversibility (Piaget), 54
Rice, Joseph Mayer, 35
Right-left hand concept, music for, 345–346
Ringworm, 404
Rocking, music for, 344
Rohwer, W., 64
Role playing, 381
  equipment for, 230
Ronge, D. G., 10
Room organization, *see* Classroom organization
Rothman, Joel, 159
Roubinek, D. L., 10
Rousseau, Jean Jacques, 25
Rubbings, 328

Ruggles Street Nursery School, 28, 42–44
Rules and games (Piaget), 56
Running, music for, 345
Ryan, S., 64

Sand play, in the teaching of science, 264–265
Sand table center, 123
Scabies, 404
Scarlet fever, 406
Schedules, daily, 107–113
School, role of, in socialization, 88–89
School of Infancy (Comenius), 25
School visits, 425–426
Schurz, Margorethe, 26
Science
    animals as classroom pets, 256–259
    basic skills sequence chart, 280–283
    books for children, 271–274
    child's participation, 259–264
    collecting and ordering supplies, 254–256
    cooking and other food activities, 266–271
    differentiating and integrating mini units, 274–277
    evaluation of individual differences, 277–279
    experiments for children, 260–263
    gardening, 265–266
    incidental, 263–264
    individualized, 263
    learning goals for children, 280
    materials and equipment, 255–256
    music on, 346–347
    observation of four year olds, 61
    overview of, 252
    planning in teaching, 253–254
    plants for the classroom, 259
    play opportunities, 264–271
    sand and water play, 264–266
    sequential seasonal topics, 253–254
    and social studies, common topics, 221
    teacher's role, 253–259
    theories of teaching, 252–253
Science of Education and the Psychology of the Child (Piaget), 287
Sculpting, 317, 326. See also Art

Seasonal topics, in teaching science, 253–254
Self-realization approach to social studies, 203, 204
Sense of autonomy, 69
Sense of duty and accomplishment, 69–70
Sense of identity, 70
Sense of initiative, 69
Sense of trust, 69
Sensitive periods (Montessori), 38
Sensorial exercises (Montessori), 38
Sensorial materials (Montessori), 38
Sensorimotor approach to mathematics, 286–287
Sensorimotor stage, 54
"Sesame Street," 137
Sets, in mathematics, 292–293
Setting, see Physical setting for curriculum; Social setting for curriculum
Severe retardation, 72
Sewing, 317, 327. See also Art
Sewing center, 124
Share, learning to, 411–412, 419–420. See also Behavior
Siamese fighting fish, as classroom pets, 257
Similarities among objects, persons, and events, recognition of, 157
"Simon says," 376
Singing, 212, 349–350. See also Music
Six year olds
    full-day schedule with, 112–113
    normative data on, 68
Skeels, H., 62, 365
Skill orientation, 64
    in teaching reading, 137
Skill subject, defined, 203
Skipping, music for, 345
Sleep, adequate, 395
"Sling the statue," 375–376
Smilansky, S., 366–367
Smith, Grace, 208
Smith, R. J., 64
Snacks, 402, 420
Snyder, Agnes, 48
Social behavior (Piaget), 57
Socialization, teaching, 204–205. See also Behavior; Family education
    affective education and, 205–215

Socialization, teaching (*cont.*)
  process of, 87–89
  teacher's role, 205
Social setting for curriculum
  cultures, 87–94
  goals and observation, 96–103
  overview of, 87
  values, 94–96
Social studies
  basic skills sequence chart, 247–249
  cognitive process approach to, 203–204
  differentiating and integrating mini units, 238–243
  evaluation of individual differences, 243–246
  integration of content areas, 215–224
  learning goals for children, 246–247
  materials, equipment, and books, 225–238
  music in teaching, 347–348
  overview of, 203
  and science, common topics, 221
  self-concept unit, 221
  self-realization (child-centered) approach to, 203, 204
  socialization, 204–215
  theories of teaching, 203–204
  topics of work, 220–221
Socrates, 25
Some Thoughts Concerning Education (Locke), 25
Sound equipment, 132, 139
Spatter painting, 329. *See also* Art
Special education, 70
Speech
  development of, 138–139. *See also* Oral language
  language disorders, 73, 76
Spelling, 179–180
Spiral continuity, 59
Spitz, R., 62
Splinters, 398
Spodek, B., 64
Spoiled child, 414. *See also* Behavior
Spontaneous play
  defined, 219
  materials and equipment for, 229–234
Sprains, 399

Stability and Changes in Human Characteristics (Bloom), 29
Stages of learning, 52–53
Stages of mental development (Piaget), 54
Stealing, 415. *See also* Behavior
Stevenson, H., 64
Stings, insect, 399
Storage space, 131
Stories for children, *see* Books
Storytelling, 164–166. *See also* Literature
String painting, 328
Study trips, 223–224
Subset, in mathematics, 292–293
Sutton-Smith, Brian, 365
Suzuki, Shinichi, 343
Swaying, music for, 344
Swinging, music for, 344
Swordtails, as classroom pets, 257
Synthetic incapacity (Piaget), 316
Systems 80®, 167
Systems of learning, 49–57

Table manners, 420. *See also* Behavior
Tables, classroom, 125
T.A. for Tots (and other Prinzes) (Freed), 207–208
Tamer, J. M., 62
Tantrums, 414. *See also* Behavior
Tapes, 149–151. *See also* Records
Teacher(s), 10–11
  appearance of, 11–12
  attitude of, 11
  career opportunities for, 13–18
  daily schedules of, 14–17, 98–113
  as learning factor, 57–58
  relations with parents, 424–426, 426–428, 428–430, 430–432
  role of, 12–13
  training of, 11
Teacher-planned units of work, defined, 219
Teacher's materials, *see* Equipment; Materials
Technology, in culture, 87
Television
  influence on behavior, 417–418
  for oral language development, 152

Tempera painting, 324. *See also* Art
Temperature, regulation of, 397
Tennessee Department of Education, *1980 Achievement Test Results*, 6
Thanksgiving music, 348
Theories of learning, 49–57
Theory, defined, 49
Things I Hate (Wittles and Greisman), 208
Thirteen (Charlip and Joyner), 158
Thomas, Margaret Hanratty, 417
Three year olds
 center for, 14–17
 differentiating and integrating for, *see* Differentiating and integrating mini units
 full-day schedule with, 110–111
 normative data on, 65–66
 observation of: science, 60–61
 play for, 366, 368–369, 372, 374
Tilton, J. W., 52
Tiptoeing, music for, 344
Toileting needs in school, 397
Tot-Pac, 207–208
Touch and smell books, 274
Toy center, 124. *See also* Play
Toys for learning, 429–430
 replica, 275–276
Transfer, as learning factor, 59
Transitional theory of learning, 49–50, 51
Trips, field or study, in social studies, 223–224
Tropical fish, as classroom pets, 257
Trust, sense of, 69
Tucson early education model, 9
Turtles, as classroom pets, 258

Understanding, as learning factor, 59
Unit centers, 125
Units of work, in social studies, 219–223
University of Chicago cooperative nursery school, 27
U.S. Consumer Product Safety Commission, on playground equipment, 371
U.S. Department of Health and Human Services, 6n, 93
U.S. Report of the Commerce Bureau of the Census (1979), 7
Uzgiris, J., 422

Valentine's Day music, 349
Values, in socialization, 94–96
Values and Teaching (Raths et al.), 95
Verbal language (Piaget), 55
Vietnamese, 92
Viewing centers, 122
Visible World (Comenius), 25
Vision development, reading readiness and, 155–156
Visual discrimination, books for teaching, 158–159
Visual impairment, 73–74, 76–77
Visual realism (Piaget), 316
Vitamins, 400
Voice for Children, 22
Vomiting, 397

Wachs, T., 422
Walking, 369
 music for, 344
Water
 drinking, 400
 washing, 395–397
Water play, in teaching science, 264–266
Watson, John B., 28
Wax paper transparencies, 329–330
Weaving, 317, 326. *See also* Art
Weaving center, 125
Webster, Noah, 26
We Hide, You Seek (Aruego), 158
Wellman, Beth, 28
"What is missing," 376
Which One Is Different (Rothman), 159
Whining, 412. *See also* Behavior
White, Edna Noble, 28
Whitting, B., 367
Wiggin, Kate Douglas, 26
Wildsmith, Brian, 159
Wittles, Harriet, 208
Woodworking, 231–234
Work activities, pantomime, 381
Work Projects Administration (WPA), 28, 44–45

World Organization for Preschool
    Children, 29
Written language, teaching, 175–176.
    See also Language arts
    child's part, 178–179
    teacher's role, 176–178

You Are Special (Mr. Rogers), 212
Young Children, 22, 29

Zoo at school, 230. *See also* Animals
Zoo City (Lewis), 159

An Invitation to Respond

Many of the changes made in this edition of *The Early Years in Childhood Education* were based on feedback and evaluations of the first edition. Please help us respond to the interests and needs of future readers by completing the questionnaire below and returning it to: College Marketing, Houghton Mifflin Company, One Beacon Street, Boston, MA 02108.

1. Please tell us your overall impressions of the text.

	Excellent	*Good*	*Adequate*	*Poor*
a. Was it written in a clear and understandable style?	___	___	___	___
b. Were difficult concepts well explained?	___	___	___	___
c. How would you rate the illustrations and physical appearance of the book?	___	___	___	___
d. How comprehensive was the coverage of major issues and topics?	___	___	___	___
e. How does this book compare to other texts you have used?	___	___	___	___
f. How would you rate the projects?	___	___	___	___
g. How would you rate the basic skills sequence charts?	___	___	___	___

2. Please comment on or cite examples that illustrate any of your above ratings.

   _____

   _____

   _____

3. Were there any topics that should have been included or covered more fully?
   _____
   _____
   _____

4. Which chapters or features did you particularly like? _____
   _____
   _____

5. Which chapters or features did you dislike? _____
   _____
   _____

6. Which chapters taught you the most? _____
   _____
   _____

7. What changes would you like to see in the next edition of this book? _____
   _____
   _____

8. Is this a book you would like to keep for your classroom teaching experience?
   _____ Why or why not? _____
   _____
   _____